Additional Praise for *Inside the Battle of Algiers*

Viewers of "The Battle of Algiers" have always had the option of closing their eyes during the disturbing scenes of torture and other violence portrayed in the classic film focused on Algeria's War of Independence. Drif's compelling memoir, however, forces the reader to confront the daily, grinding brutality of France's settler colonial project, and the price paid by the men, women and children who participated in myriad ways in the struggle to defeat it . . .

Filled with rich detail of the socioeconomic, religious and political context of the period, Drif's account can serve as an engaging and accessible introduction to Algeria, settler colonialism, and national liberation wars for students, just as its amazing first-hand account of the role of one of the FLN's most important female fighters provides new insights and historical material for specialists.

—Laurie Brand
Wright Professor of International Relations, Univ. of Southern California

The English translation of Zohra Drif's memoirs is a publishing event. It makes available to a wider audience the life and times of an Algerian woman who was both actor in, and witness to, one of the 20th century's most dramatic independence struggles. As importantly, her autobiography reveals the lived daily realities of what she calls the Algerian "awakening." That political as well as social and cultural *prise de conscience* took place not only in colonial schools, military service, or the press but also in unexplored places, such as weekly female *hammam* sessions. There, in the "only domain where women enjoyed unquestioned, inviolable sovereignty," Algerian resistance and identity were nurtured by heroic tales from distant times—and after November 1954 by the latest news about the *moudjahidine* (anti-colonial combatants.)

—Julia Clancy-Smith
Dept. of History, Univ. of Arizona

Who is Zohra Drif? An Algerian heroine who fought the French, then spent five years in their prisons, she has not been recognized like her two co-fighters Djamila Bouhired and Djamila Boupacha. Until now. With the publication of her autobiography, *Inside the Battle of Algiers*, we have a narrative that is engrossing and also provides a new, fresh look at a critical moment in Algerian history. One of the critical but occluded players in the Battle of Algiers, she will now be known to the world through her own eloquent words. Essential reading.

—miriam cooke
author, *Dancing in Damascus: Creativity,*
Resilience and the Syrian Revolution

Zohra Drif's book of memoirs is a precious contribution to the knowledge of the Algerian War of Independence. . . . It shows the decisive role of women in the war. . . . [It] also sheds light on the miracle of culture in the resistance and the unique, historic ascent of a people that was able to escape from annihilation by finding deep within itself the resources of its values of justice and human dignity, values that have structured its faith and ethics throughout the terrible ordeal of colonial oppression, as well as on the path to political and moral victory.

The Zohra Drif's legacy is two-fold: not only was she an authentic freedom fighter during the war, but she now completes her work by leaving her testimony for her young compatriots, thirsty for truth, and eager to find the trail of the struggle to liberate themselves from the scourges of today.

—Amin Khan
author, *Nous autres, Eléments pour un manifeste de l'Algérie heureuse*

Charting the Battle of Algiers, a critical chapter in the history of the Algerian War in which she came to play a key role as an urban guerrilla, Zohra Drif has written a fascinating, detailed memoir that grants her readers an awareness of the oppression that weighed upon the colonized during the French colonial era and an understanding of the difficult struggle that led to Algerian independence. As she relates historical events through her interpretive lens, Drif insists upon the collective dimension of the war experience and women's role in it.

—Mildred Mortimer
Univ. of Colorado

Zohra Drif has given us a powerful, firsthand account of the amazingly courageous role played by women in Algeria's eight-year struggle for independence from France. A major player, Zohra hid out in the Casbah's labyrinth during the 1957 Battle of Algiers. There, she served as a courier between myriad safe houses, organizer of other partisans and even executor of a

European café bombing. Zohra unveils her raw emotions when faced with fears of capture and torture and finally betrayal from within nationalist ranks.

From start to finish, it reads like a thriller.
—**David Ottaway,**
formerly of *The Washington Post*:

Zohra Drif, a living legend of the Algerian freedom movement, was a *moujahida* for a country then held in vicious bondage by French colonialism. Here she tells the story of her journey to help free her country, a story which becomes of course the story of the Algerian war of independence. This is one of the most engaging memoirs to come out of the period of decolonization.
—**Vijay Prashad**
author, *The Darker Nations: A People's History of the Third World*

When the French edition of this book appeared in 2013, I rushed to get it and read it. Although I knew the broad outlines of the story from my early research in Algiers, my interest was especially piqued because of the author, Zohra Drif. . . . [She] has written a remarkable memoir, filled with fascinating detail about her personal story, the nature of Algerian society on the eve of independence, and the tight-knit group of militants, including herself, who organized the armed wing of the nationalist movement in the Casbah of Algiers in 1956-57. She writes with chilling honesty about her belief that it became necessary to carry the armed conflict to the French civilians in Algiers, and her own role, at age 22, in planting the bomb that exploded at the Milk Bar. . . .

Thanks to Andrew Farrand's excellent translation, English speakers can now also benefit from this vivid memoir and history.
—**William B. Quandt**
Professor Emeritus of Political Science, Univ. of Virginia

Of the many hundreds of books written about the Algerian war of independence, none matches Zohra Drif's *Inside the Battle of Algiers* for capturing the white-hot fervor of a very young Muslim woman student of impeccable family background caught up in her countrymen's savage war of national liberation from France . . .

Hers is a gripping tale, at times feminist as much as nationalist, of a conflict pitting militant anti-colonialist Muslims against a major Western power in which (refreshingly) radical Islam played no appreciable role.

—Jonathan Randal

formerly of *The Washington Post*; author, *The Tragedy of Lebanon*

This marvelous book is several important things in one. It is the story, recounted with great candor and superbly written, of a remarkable Algerian woman's journey . . . It is an extremely detailed account of the famous Battle of Algiers and of her own role in it, and one which greatly enriches specialist historians' understanding of this dramatic event. It is, in addition, a very moving tribute to the women of Algeria, which not only describes the indispensable role they performed in preserving Muslim Algerians' identity, traditions and collective self-respect throughout the period of colonial domination but equally the vital role they played, and the extraordinary courage, tenacity and resourcefulness they brought to this, in the war of liberation itself. . . .

—Hugh Roberts,
Edward Keller Professor of North African and
Middle Eastern History, Tufts Univ.

INSIDE THE BATTLE OF ALGIERS

MEMOIR OF A WOMAN FREEDOM FIGHTER

INSIDE THE BATTLE OF ALGIERS

ZOHRA DRIF

TRANSLATED FROM THE FRENCH BY
ANDREW FARRAND

FOREWORD BY LAKHDAR BRAHIMI

Just World Books
Charlottesville, Virginia

Translated and adapted from the French-language original, *Mémoires d'une combattante de l'ALN: Zone Autonome d'Alger*, by Zohra Drif (Algiers: Chihab Éditions, 2013.)

Development editing: Grey Editing
Project management and proofreading: Marissa Wold Uhrina
Typesetting: PerfecType, Nashville, TN
Cartography: MTW Design
Cover design: theBookDesigners

Publisher's Cataloging-In-Publication Data
(Prepared by The Donohue Group, Inc.)

Names: Drif-Bitat, Zohra. | Farrand, Andrew, translator. | Brahimi, Lakhdar, writer of supplementary textual content.
Title: Inside the Battle of Algiers : memoir of a woman freedom fighter / Zohra Drif ; translated from the French by Andrew Farrand ; foreword by Lakhdar Brahimi.
Other Titles: Memoires d'une combattante de l'ALN. English
Description: Charlottesville, Virginia : Just World Books, an imprint of Just World Publishing, LLC, [2017] | Translation of: Memoires d'une combattante de l'ALN. Broché, 2014.
Identifiers: LCCN 2017934399 | ISBN 978-1-68257-075-3 | ISBN 978-1-68257-076-0 (ePub) | ISBN 978-1-68257-077-7 (mobi) | ISBN 978-1-68257-078-4 (PDF)
Subjects: LCSH: Drif-Bitat, Zohra. | Revolutionaries—Algeria—Biography. | Women revolutionaries—Algeria—Biography. | National liberation movements—Algeria—History—20th century. | Algeria—History—Revolution, 1954-1962. | Algiers (Algeria)—History—20th century. | LCGFT: Autobiographies.
Classification: LCC DT295.3.D75 A313 2017 (print) | LCC DT295.3.D75 (ebook) | DDC 965/.04642092—dc23

In memory of all our martyred sisters,
In memory of all our martyred brothers,
In memory of my departed husband, the *moudjahid* Rabah Bitat, who
always encouraged me to share these memories,
To my sister Leïla, who suffered greatly as a result of my combat,
To my other sisters and brothers,
To my children and grandchildren,
To our youth.

Just World Books

Timely Books for Changing Times

Just World Books exists to expand the discourse in the United States and worldwide on issues of vital international concern. We are committed to building a more just, equitable, and peaceable world. We uphold the equality of all human persons. We aim for our books to contribute to increasing understanding across national, religious, ethnic, and racial lines; to share more broadly the reflections, analyses, and policy prescriptions of pathbreaking activists for peace; and to help to prevent war.

To learn about our existing and upcoming titles or to buy our books, visit our website:

www.JustWorldBooks.com

Also, follow us on Facebook and Twitter!

Our recent titles include:

- *Wrestling in the Daylight: A Rabbi's Path to Palestinian Solidarity*, by Brant Rosen
- *White And Black: Political Cartoons from Palestine*, by Mohammad Sabaaneh
- *No Country for Jewish Liberals*, by Larry Derfner
- *Condition Critical: Life and Death in Israel/Palestine*, by Alice Rothchild
- *The Gaza Kitchen: A Palestinian Culinary Journey*, by Laila El-Haddad and Maggie Schmitt
- *Lens on Syria: A Photographic Tour of its Ancient and Modern Culture*, by Daniel Demeter
- *Never Can I Write of Damascus: When Syria Became Our Home*, by Theresa Kubasak and Gabe Huck
- *America's Continuing Misadventures in the Middle East*, by Chas W. Freeman, Jr.
- *Arabia Incognita: Dispatches from Yemen and the Gulf*, edited by Sheila Carapico

"Free and independent to what end, if not to express oneself?
But the first task, upon obtaining one's freedom—a prize more often
seized than given—is to embark on a long quest into the past, because the
past weighs with all its gravity upon the present, and it is upon the past
that the future will be grafted."

—Mouloud Mammeri,
The Dawn of the Damned

CONTENTS

FOREWORD

Inside the Battle of Algiers is a detailed and totally honest account of some of the extraordinary events that Algeria experienced during its war for independence. When Zohra Drif was born in 1934, the large country of Algeria, located on the Mediterranean coast of Africa, had been under the control of France for more than a century. In 1848, the French government had even decreed that Algeria was a part of France; over the decades that followed, France sent hundreds of thousands of colonists to Algeria, where they were given lands confiscated from the local population and considerable help in developing and marketing the products of those lands. Hence the reference in this book to Algeria as a distinctive form of colonization—a "settlement colony." Colonialism has never been a benign undertaking, but nowhere was it harsher and more disruptive to the lives of the indigenous inhabitants than Algeria.

France maintained its rule over Algeria through the continuous use of force. Though France's own revolution in 1789 had proclaimed *La Déclaration Universelle des Droits de l'Homme et du Citoyen* and the values of "liberty, equality, and brotherhood," Paris never accorded any civic or political rights to the vast majority of the indigenous Algerians. Even the opportunity to get an education in French (the language of the state) was given to very few Algerians. Zohra Drif was one of those few. She was raised in a traditional, provincial Muslim family. Her father and many forebears had been distinguished jurists in the indigenous Islamic courts, but her parents both supported the idea that, for her high school and university education, she should enroll in French institutions in the capital, Algiers. At both levels, she was one of only a handful of Algerian students. She notes in *Inside the Battle of Algiers* that when she started her student life at the undergraduate Law Faculty, there were only six Algerian students in her class: four men and two women. The women were Zohra Drif and Samia Lakhdari. I was one of the four men. The female Algerian students were under great pressure not only to excel at their studies but also to behave with the strictest propriety.

That was in the fall of 1954. On November 1, 1954, the Algerian nationalists of the National Liberation Front (FLN) launched a sustained anticolonial uprising, to which the French government and media referred only opaquely, as *les événements d'Algérie* (the Algerian situation). François Mitterrand, who, as Interior Minister in France, was responsible for security matters in Algeria, was quick to declare that these *événements* had erupted unexpectedly, "like a thunderclap in a blue sky." The skies then grew darker by the day, as Zohra eloquently recounts in her memoir. But back in our first days at the university, neither Zohra nor I could imagine that, just eighteen months later, she would be a prominent member of the National Liberation Army (ALN) in the capital and I the representative of the FLN in Jakarta.

In this memoir, Zohra Drif paints a warm, detailed portrait of her childhood before she turns to the momentous political events that took place when she was a law student. Soon enough, she and her friend Samia both became enthralled by reports of the activities of the nationalist movement that was starting to emerge. They were both eager to reach out and connect with the nationalists and to volunteer their services to the cause. Finally, they were able to do this. For some time their main tasks were to carry messages and money for the FLN, but slowly they won the confidence of the local FLN commanders and started begging to be allowed to take part in the activities of the its military wing, the ALN.

Zohra writes that she found it unacceptable that our people were being bombed, killed, and tortured throughout the country while the European settlers lived in their part of Algiers in total peace, many of them taking an active part in the repression of the indigenous Algerians—particularly in the Casbah, the labyrinthine heart of traditional Muslim Algiers. After a bomb placed by one of those French settler groups in the Casbah killed scores of Algerians, the head of the ALN/FLN's administration in the city, Yacef Saâdi, decided to counter by placing bombs in public places in the European parts of the city.

Zohra and Samia had no hesitation in agreeing to do these bombings. Indeed, they did not just passively accept this role, they actively begged for it, arguing that they could pass undetected in the European sector of the city more easily than their male colleagues. They had even been among the first to suggest to their chief that the ALN should "take the war to the other side." These events, and Zohra Drif's role in them, were later memorialized in Gillo Pontecorvo's classic film *The Battle of Algiers*.

This book, which reads like a thriller, is the account of how two extremely shy young women from conservative Algerian families became drawn into the Algerian Revolution and were completely transformed in the process. Zohra writes about the things she, Samia, and several other female militants saw and did during our revolution. She confidently presents the perspective of a female activist in our movement, thereby adding a rare flavor to the historiography of that highly important moment in Algeria's history. The book contains some very interesting sociological touches about life in a well-to-do conservative family in a small town (Zohra's) or in the capital (Samia's). It was notable that while Zohra's mother was strongly opposed to the revolutionary engagement of her daughter, Samia's mother, the formidable Mama Zhor, became the committed accomplice of the two young women.

Zohra Drif's memoir has continuing relevance in our present era. In many Western countries, the film of *The Battle of Algiers* is still regularly shown to young special forces officers in military academies—more to give them operational pointers, I am afraid, than as an object lesson in the limited utility of military force. And some of the questions the film raises about the use of force by both colonizer and colonized are still of great importance today. In this book, Zohra Drif writes that she thought in the 1950s, and still thinks today, that "taking the war to the European community and its areas" was the right thing to do—every time the French executed one of our people, it was right to retaliate in kind. We were convinced that ours was a just war, like all the anticolonial struggles in the Third World. In that era, progressive thinkers and political activists in the West, France included, shared our view.

It was about the same time we were fighting that Nelson Mandela became the leader of the military wing of the African National Congress (ANC) in South Africa, Umkhonto we Sizwe. During his trial by the apartheid regime in 1964, he concluded his own defense of his actions with the following words:

> During my lifetime, I have dedicated myself to this struggle of the
> African people. I have fought against white domination and I have

fought against black domination. I have cherished the ideal of a democratic and free society in which all persons live together in harmony and with equal opportunities. It is an ideal which I hope to live for and to achieve. But if needs be, it is an ideal for which I am prepared to die.

In the late 1950s, it was thanks to strong pressure from international opinion that Zohra Drif and other Algerian women freedom fighters (including Djamila Bouhired) were not executed, and it was thanks to similar international action that Mandela was not sentenced to death in 1964.

Common wisdom in Western countries is quite different these days. The theory of "just war" still has currency in most Western countries (though the strict, rules-based constraints it places on "justifiable" use are, sadly, understood and supported only by a few.) Most Westerners these days think it is perfectly normal for their governments to bomb their enemies all around the world—and too bad for the "collateral" damage inflicted on civilians—but that the West's enemies have no right to respond in kind.

Like Zohra Drif, we should note, though, that there is a fundamental difference between the actions the FLN/ALN took in the 1950s and early 1960s and the horrific violence used by intolerant, radical jihadist groups like Daesh or Al-Qaeda today. In our case, our struggle was aimed first at defeating French colonialism and second at alerting and mobilizing the international community and world public opinion to lend support to our effort, as we struggled to achieve the self-determination and liberation from colonialism that the United Nations had promised us. Once we achieved our goal of national independence, we turned our attention to building our country within its own legitimate and recognized borders. It is worth noting, too, that in the 1990s Algeria was nearly torn apart by a decade-long civil war in which radical jihadists (supported by foreign circles, including quite a few in the West) tried to destroy our essentially secular political system and impose their own intolerant and deeply misogynistic views on the whole of Algerian society. So we have zero sympathy with the goals of today's violent jihadists, let alone their methods.

In 1957, just sixty years ago this year, Zohra Drif was arrested by the French and condemned to death. In 1962, when Algeria finally won its independence, she was released from prison and went on to pursue a distinguished career in law and politics. She was elected to our first National Assembly (parliament) and was later appointed to our Conseil de la Nation

(Senate), in which she served as vice president. She also married Rabah Bitat, one of the historical leaders of the Algerian revolution, whom she met in prison. *Inside the Battle of Algiers* is a crucial part of the story of modern Algeria and a unique contribution to the history of the worldwide movement to end colonial empires and win self-determination for all the peoples of the world.

LAKHDAR BRAHIMI

Former Foreign Minister of Algeria, Special Representative of the UN Secretary General to Afghanistan, Iraq, and Syria

April 2017

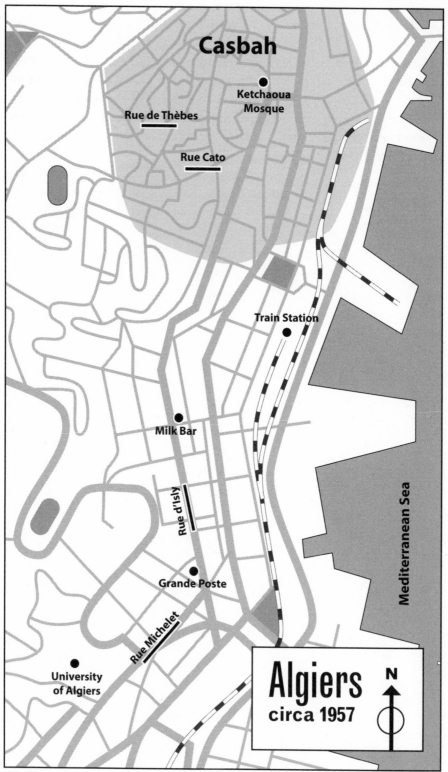

Casbah

Ketchaoua Mosque

Rue de Thèbes

Rue Cato

Train Station

Milk Bar

Rue d'Isly

Grande Poste

Rue Michelet

University of Algiers

Mediterranean Sea

Algiers
circa 1957

N

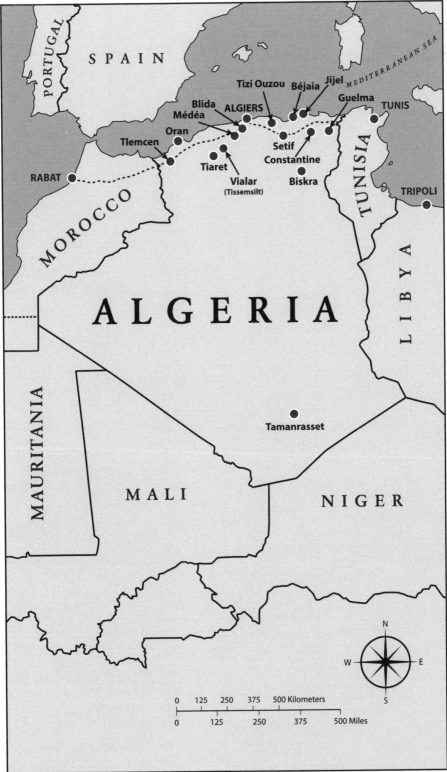

PORTUGAL

SPAIN

MEDITERRANEAN SEA

Tizi Ouzou   Béjaia   Jijel

Blida   ALGIERS   Guelma   TUNIS

Médéa

Oran   Setif

Tlemcen   Constantine

RABAT   Tiaret   Biskra

Vialar
(Tissemsilt)

MOROCCO

TUNISIA

TRIPOLI

LIBYA

ALGERIA

MAURITANIA

Tamanrasset

MALI   NIGER

N
W   E
S

0   125   250   375   500 Kilometers

0   125   250   375   500 Miles

1

IN THE FAMILIAL EMBRACE

My Lineage

I was born in Tiaret, on the Sersou plain, on December 28, 1934. In the Islamic calendar, that day fell during the holy month of Ramadan. The farm where I was born belonged to my grandfather, Hadj Abdessalem Drif.[1]

My paternal great-grandfather, Hadj Moulay Tayeb, had married in his home region and waited in vain for years to have children. Sometime in his forties, he grew desperate and decided to divorce his wife, who was evidently infertile. After dividing up his lands and belongings among his brothers and sisters, he secluded himself in the *zawiya*[2] of his ancestors—the *zawiya* of

---

1. In the Muslim world, the Arabic word *Hadj* literally denotes someone who has completed the pilgrimage to Mecca, but in daily practice in Algeria it is a term of respect for elders.
2. A *zawiya* is a mausoleum named for a particular saint (denoted by the titles Sidi or Moulay) that serves as a center of religious scholarship, pilgrimage, and worship in the North African Sufi tradition.

embedded religious beliefs

Moulay Idriss, in Volubilis, Morocco[3]—and dedicated himself to contemplation and seclusion. This radical decision was not an act of reprisal against his wife, with whom he had been very fair when dividing his wealth. Rather, it was a decision rooted in his religious beliefs, which were deeply Sufi.[4] He believed that God, by not granting him any descendants, was sending him a message instructing him to cut ties with his earthly possessions and to dedicate himself to contemplation and seclusion in the hermitage. So that was what he did.

At the mausoleum, whose *moqaddem*, or caretaker, was named Hadj Abdessalem, he devoted himself body and soul to total contemplation. It is said that during his seclusion, one evening he dreamed a particularly disturbing dream. He recounted it to the *moqaddem*, asking him to reveal its hidden meaning. The *moqaddem* replied, "I can assure you that what you have witnessed last night was no dream. It was a *ro'ya*—a vision. God has measured your piety and sincerity and decided to reward you. You must return to your homeland and to your local *zawiya*. You will ask for the hand of a young woman named Halima. Marry her and she will give you a son, whom you will name Abdessalem, and he will bring you many descendants."

He set out immediately. Back on the Sersou plain, he married my great-grandmother, who gave birth to my grandfather. But my great-grandfather was already an old man, and he died when my grandfather was just two years old. My grandfather was raised and educated by his mother's family at the *zawiya* of Sidi M'hamed Ben Amar, where he later married my grandmother Zohra, who gave him thirteen children, including my father, Ahmed. It is important to note that until the nineteenth century the *zawiyas* were the center of our education system; it was there that languages, law and *fiqh* (jurisprudence), history, geography, mathematics, and medicine were taught.

That was where my father got his start, completing his primary education in the Sersou before moving to Tlemcen for the equivalent of his secondary schooling at the Sidi Boumediene *zawiya*. He would study there for seven years before joining the Sidi Abderrahmane *medersa* in Algiers, where he would complete a third phase of his studies and earn the diploma that

---

3. Historically, the Morocco-Algeria border was something of a continuum rather than the firmly defined line it is today, with strong connections maintained between the two countries for centuries.

4. Sufism, a diverse Islamic sect known for mystical practice, is widely practiced in North Africa among other regions of the Islamic world.

allowed him to reach the prestigious—but ever-so-difficult—rank of *qadi*, or judge. To ensure that he wouldn't be blocked by the colonial administration, in parallel to his training in Islamic law he also studied at the Faculty of Arts at the University of Algiers, earning a diploma there as well. All this is to say that my father was a true scholar who had mastered two intellectual cultures. After his considerable academic training he climbed the ranks, from *aoun* (assistant clerk) to *adel* (clerk) to *bach adel* (deputy judge) before finally reaching the post of *qadi*.

Like my father's family, who derived their power and social authority from the importance of the *zawiya*, my mother's family enjoyed a similarly important religious and economic influence. My maternal grandfather, Hadj Djelloul Ben Ziane, was a descendant of the Zianid dynasty, affiliated with the Sidi M'hammed Ben Choaïb *zawiya* in Sidi El Hosni, near Tiaret. He reigned over an immense fortune, derived mostly from hundreds of hectares of fertile land and thousands of head of cattle and horses. My maternal grandfather was an incorrigible polygamist, and my grandmother Arbia, renowned for her great beauty, was his last wife. She had a single daughter— my mother, Saadia—with her husband before divorcing him when she could no longer stand his polygamy or his tyranny. Coming from a wealthy family herself, she felt she had everything to gain by reclaiming her freedom. My mother grew up pampered by her two families, who instilled in her their culture and traditions and raised her to protect and champion them, which she did until her very last breath. Before we even reached school age, for example, she forced us to learn to recite our lineage by heart.

From her origins in a family of wealthy landowners, my mother also gained a keen business sense. She oversaw the affairs of the household, where she reigned supreme over all, including land holdings, livestock, and various commercial ventures. From the age of ten, my brother Abdelkader was her intermediary with any outside associates. She taught him the secrets of the trade and saw to it that he exercised them with the utmost rigor and professionalism. My father, busy with law and literature and naturally scornful of the trivialities of material existence, would have found it hard to believe that many of the notables who sought his notarial services or legal counsel were also conducting business with his wife, who never even left the house.

My parents had eight children: five boys and three girls. I am the second, having come into the world a century and four years after the colonization of my country. In material terms I led a pampered childhood, and I was emotionally and culturally nourished by the saga of my maternal and

paternal ancestral lines, taught to me by the best teacher in the subject—
my mother. I knew from a young age who and where I was: an Algerian in
her own country. I also knew early on that my land was occupied, seized
for no purpose other than rape and theft, and that the *roumi*—the Roman,
that foreigner from the north—was both the rapist and the thief. I lived
every moment with such an acute awareness of this fact that it became like
my skin, my blood, or the beating of my heart, and was frequently revived
by events around me. As a child, when I accompanied my mother and my
aunts, traipsing together across vast fields to visit the tomb of a *wali salah*—
a local patron saint—the women explained to me that in truth these lands
belonged to such-and-such tribe, which had been dispossessed in favor of
such-and-such colonist. In doing so, they transmitted to us the history, soci-
ology, and true map of our country.

Similarly, when the European doctor was summoned to tend to my
father's fever, my mother explained to me why she was allowed to show herself before him, even though she hid herself from Muslim men. It was entirely
unthinkable, she explained, that the doctor, as a *roumi*, could constitute a

*Zohra Drif, right, with her Uncle
Abdelkader and two siblings*

potential spouse or engage in any other type of relationship. Through this "cultural sentencing," my mother condemned him to the status of a eunuch.

By now it is clear to me that my mother—along with all the women of my family—played a decisive role in shaping who I would become. I am eternally grateful to them.

About My Mother

As an orphan, my grandfather Hadj Abdessalem was raised by his maternal uncle, Hadj Tahar, head of the Sidi Abbas Ben Ammar *zawiya* and of the Ouled Qoraïch tribe. One day, when he was visiting his friend Hadj Djelloul Ben Ziane, my grandfather's uncle saw a young girl playing in the courtyard. Hadj Djelloul's young daughter Saadia, then only seven years old, was beautiful and already lively and sociable. She ably managed the traditional greetings to welcome her father's friend for the first time. Pleasantly surprised and moved, Hadj Tahar put his hand on the girl's head and, addressing his friend, asked him to promise her to his thirteen-year-old nephew Ahmed, then just a student. Saadia's father could not refuse his friend Hadj Tahar a thing, so he gave him his word.

From an economic perspective, this union was perhaps a poor choice for Hadj Djelloul. Saadia's father was a religious notable and major landowner with sizable herds of livestock, while Hadj Tahar and his family were well regarded only for the nobility of their ancestry.

Five years later, Ahmed, then eighteen, was studying at Sidi Boumediene, the renowned *medersa* in Tlemcen, when my paternal grandfather brought the promised child into his family to allow her time to adjust to her future husband's home. Having not yet reached puberty, she still played with dolls, and at first did not realize that she was changing homes in order to marry and assume responsibilities far too weighty for her young age. She passed those final years before reaching maturity playing with the little Drif girls her age, all the while being prepared by the women of the house to assume her future role. Once she reached puberty, in 1930, they were married and a joyous party commemorated the union; the young couple then only saw one another during my father's school holidays. My parents lived this way for six years: my father studying first in Tlemcen, then in Algiers, and my mother living among her in-laws. During those six years, two girls were born but did not live, followed by my brother Mohamed and then me.

Saadia Drif, Zohra's mother

One event deserves mention because it shows my mother's strong character and determination. Since her marriage, every Monday—market day—my maternal grandfather, Hadj Djelloul, had visited his daughter and brought her a small piece of jewelry. Her sisters-in-law (my paternal aunts), jealous to see her with so many rich gifts, mocked her as well as my grandfather for bad taste. So on the day after each of her father's visits, my mother began to return the gifts to the local jeweler. After several months of this, Hadj Djelloul pieced it together.

One Monday, he arrived unannounced at the Drif home and surprised his beloved daughter, who was bowed under the weight of the family's laundry. He flew into a fit of rage at the sight of his daughter subjected to the labor typically reserved for her servants—in sharp contrast to her rightful social standing—and announced his immediate decision to bring her and her two children home, all the while screaming at the Drif family, "I entrusted you with my favorite daughter, not with a servant girl!"

My brother Mohamed and I followed our mother and spent the ensuing months frolicking in what appeared to us a paradise—a spacious house on a huge property full of horses, sheep, and all manner of pets. Our living conditions had changed dramatically. We wanted for nothing until the day my father, having finished his studies, arrived from Algiers to demand his wife and children back.

Saadia, then a young mother barely twenty years old, was as attached to her own father and family as she was to her husband and children. Yet she found herself obliged to make an impossible choice: to follow her husband and definitively cut ties with her roots, or to go the other way. She did not hesitate, despite all the pressures from her own family, in choosing to join her husband. At the time this was an act of considerable courage, and of modernity. Her choice empowered my father to free himself from his own clan's oversight as well. In this way, my parents, Saadia and Ahmed Drif, settled in Tissemsilt and founded a home independent of their two families. It was a revolution against our country's traditions of social organization. We had left the extended family, centered closely around the patriarch, and become a nuclear family, all the while trying not to break from traditional society completely.

In Tissemsilt (which was called Vialar during the colonial times), they sent me to kindergarten, where I was made to memorize songs praising the glory of some marshal. I knew nothing of all this—not even the language. I was the only "native" in the class. Every morning I copied what my classmates did, standing in front of a flag I didn't know with no idea what it stood for, intoning, "Maréchal-nous-voici-nous-voilà-devant-toi."

When I returned home, I told my mother everything I had been taught. She proceeded to give me a full cultural debriefing: The flag was that of a foreign country, France, and the marshal was their leader. As for us, we were Algerians and our country was Algeria. She explained to me that the French were unwelcome occupiers, strangers to our land, our people, our religion, our language, our culture, our history. She launched into a wonderful description—worthy of the finest tales of sultans and princesses—of our ancestors, from the most distant to the very recent.

Thanks to these lessons, when I entered the Vialar elementary school at six years old, I knew that every day I was traveling between two completely different and opposing worlds—the world of my mother and the world of the French school. *mirrors that between the colonized vs. colonizer*

At home, where my mother reigned, it was completely Algerian, with our customs, our traditions, our Arabic language, our religion of Islam, our lifestyle, our history, our ancestors, and even our mythology. At school, in the outside world, France ruled, with its language, its flag, its religion, its history, and its mythology.

For nearly five years, I was the only little "native" girl at school, with my big long braids and long skirts reaching to my ankles, among the crowd (which to me seemed huge) of little European girls with their short hair and their little dresses above the knee—so short, in fact, that when they knelt they often revealed little behinds sheathed in white underwear—along with white socks and black ballet flats. The difference between me and this crowd even extended to the foods we ate at ten o'clock in the playground: they pulled out a brioche here, a croissant there, sometimes a chocolate croissant or, for the more modest, a hunk of Parisian baguette with jam or some similar European garnish.

As for me, I had my Algerian treats—*maqrouta, mbardja, msemna*, and, when my mother was short on time, a large slab of *matloue* bread with our family's honey. For a long time I didn't understand why or even how my classmates could prefer my foods over their own. It took me a long time to discover for myself just how right they were to prefer our *msemen*, kneaded by expert hands and impossible to buy outside the home. But it was hard for a child to live, alone and peculiar, in a foreign world.

Nonetheless, I completed my primary-school years as an excellent student, finishing tied for first place in my class with my classmate Roselyne Garcia. I considered Roselyne a dear friend until we reached the sixth-grade entrance exam, a major test that marked the passage from one phase of schooling to another, from childhood to adolescence, and—more so for the girls than the boys, who reached it later—from puberty into adulthood. We were in school the day the results were announced. While I, Zohra Drif, daughter of the *qadi*, managed to rank among the leading students in the region, my best friend Roselyne, the daughter of Vialar's town baker and an excellent student, had failed! My results would allow me access to the best secondary school, the Lycée Fromentin in the capital, Algiers, but at that moment I completely forgot to be happy. Overwhelmed with sincere sadness, I busied myself consoling my best friend. I was as shocked as the rest of the school at Roselyne's results—which would oblige her to repeat the year—and she herself was inconsolable. When we parted to go home that afternoon, I told her, still crying, "You know, Roselyne, everybody knows you're an excellent student. It was an accident that could have happened to even the best of us. Next year you'll see, you will get it and even be at the top of the class."

Roselyne replied, "But Zohra, it's not that. You don't understand a thing. How do I explain to my mother that you passed and I didn't? She will never understand that Zohra the Arab succeeded and I failed."

I was paralyzed with fear, unsure whether I had misunderstood or understood all too well. Soon my tears dried up. I looked her in the eye and spat back, "Well, you'll just have to explain to your mother that it was the Arabs like Zohra who invented mathematics."

Never had the distance between the school and my home seemed so long. In a few short seconds, I had just lost both my best friend and my innocence. I suddenly realized that neither my excellent grades throughout my schooling—the result of all my efforts and my ability to assimilate French language and culture—nor my more comfortable social standing compared to Roselyne, nor even my sincere feelings of friendship for her, could ever make me the equal of Roselyne, the European. With one simple sentence, she had put me in my place as the "native." *distinction of the Other*

I ran desperately to my mother, my compass in the desert, my refuge in moments of anguish. By the time I reached home, I had completely forgotten that I was supposed to be happy and had earned the right to celebrate. My mother, as master of the household, remedied that immediately. She called all the women of the staff to come wail out *you-you-you's* in my honor, and set the date for a celebration of my success. True to her ways, my mother took care of everything, including explaining to me the significance of my success: it was a well-deserved victory crowning her daughter's unceasing efforts, but it was, especially, the success of a Muslim girl. Through me, she wanted to prove to her fellow believers that the Drifs' approach was best—that educating girls was essential. She also took the opportunity to explain the reasoning behind the rigorous schedule she had always imposed on me. For her, I had to be perfect in every respect to deserve to be the example that other Algerian families dreamed of reaching, particularly our family friends with young daughters. "Zohra," she told me, "you must be the key that will open the doors for all our other girls." That night, I was both happy and scared. Happy, of course, for my success, but mostly happy just to see my mother—who was usually so severe and demanding—feeling proud of me and to hear her proclaim it aloud. And I was terrified because at eleven years old, my mother had overburdened my frail shoulders with a mission so vague in form and so daunting in the responsibility it entailed. Much later, adolescence, secondary school, and discussions with my father, Qadi Drif, would one day allow me to understand what my mother had meant.

About My Father

My father, as I have said, was a great scholar in both Arabic and French. He had completed all stages of his training in Islamic law, including seven years at the Medersa[5] Sidi Boumediene in Tlemcen, then two years at Medersa Bencheneb in Algiers.

I was always very close to him, and proud to have as my father this handsome man whom everyone respected as a *qadi*, particularly because he was so well known for his competency, his integrity, and his ability—like any great *qadi*—to listen well to others. My father was a just man and recognized as such, even by the colonists. Steeped in Algeria, its land, its people, its history and culture, he was deeply knowledgeable about all our *âarouch*, or tribes—including their ancestries, their places of origin, and the extent of their property holdings or of their deprivation.

My father was as just and rigorous in handling the affairs of his children and family inside the house as he was in judging offenders outside of it. He delegated the task of educating all eight children to my mother. I never saw my father treat his girls any differently than his boys. Even better, as I would learn much later, he actually discriminated in *favor* of his daughters. Was it because he was so aware that society wouldn't make anything easy for his girls? Certainly. My father, who so hated injustice, wanted to at least do justice to his daughters. My mother, too, regularly repeated, "I do not want my daughters to endure the same fate as me." My father was my coach, my initiator into the world of reading and critical thinking, and above all my guide when it came time to make difficult choices.

One evening my father came home and found me in tears, my history books unfolded before me. I explained that I was crying for Roland, the French knight mortally wounded by the treacherous Saracens.[6] Sprawled upon a rock, his sword in hand, he had blown his horn to alert Emperor Charlemagne, despite his fatal injury. I wept for Roland, hating every one of the cruel Saracens and hoping that Charlemagne would slice them to pieces.

---

5. A primary-secondary school common in Algeria and elsewhere in the Muslim world. Typically affiliated with a mosque or *zawiya*, during the colonial period the *medersa* would have taught young boys the Quran as well as various other subjects.
6. *The Song of Roland* is an early French epic poem in which Roland, a leader in Emperor Charlemagne's army, and his troops are killed in battle at the hands of Spanish Muslim forces—called Saracens in the common terminology of the Middle Ages.

Qadi Ahmed Drif, Zohra's father

When, through my sobs, I finally finished explaining to my father why I was crying, he burst into laughter. Then he spent the rest of the evening explaining to me who the Saracens were and how I should read and interpret the history lessons they taught me in school. Thanks to him, I learned that the Saracens were my ancestors, who fought against Charlemagne to defend their rights and their property. He showed me several examples of how the same historical facts could be recounted in different ways, depending on the interests of the storyteller. I think it was because of this episode that my father always wanted to act as my personal tutor. He knew that in the colonial education system I would only hear France's imperialist version of history. So until I finished high school, every history lesson I learned at school was retaught, dissected, and analyzed at home with my father. As a result, I learned early on that we Algerians had our truth while the French had their own.

My father always told me, "Whoever learns a people's language will be safe from their plots." I can never thank him enough for having instilled critical thinking in me, along with all its benefits.

Looking back, I realize that, if my father was not the man he was or if he had been absent from my childhood, in the best case I would have been totally assimilated by France and pressed into her service, since the entire education system trained students only for service to France. In the worst case, I would have gone mad. My father saved me from both these fates. I consider him to have been my first instructor in politics.

When it came to deciding which secondary school to attend to prepare for university, it was my father who guided me toward choosing the Lycée Fromentin in Algiers, renowned as the best. My mother and I would have gladly settled for the Lycée Miliana, which was much closer to Vialar and would have allowed me to spend my weekends at home. But my father convinced us by explaining that he wanted to give his daughter, Vialar's best student, every possible chance by studying at Algeria's greatest school. "If Fromentin in Algiers is far, so be it. I will accompany my daughter back to school each fall, and home for each vacation. You will board there and have a good friend close by, Mr. Hadj Hamou, an interpreter at the court of Algiers, who comes from Miliana, in our own region." My mother, who knew Hadj Hamou's family to be honorable and respectable in every way, was reassured, as was I.

Everything about this event—and that's what it was for me, a grand event—would be new. It would be the first time I left our home region, Vialar-Tiaret, the first time I rode a train, and the first time I discovered my country's capital, Algiers.

2

AWAKENING

Secondary School

My story at the Lycée Fromentin began with an application submitted by my father and a favorable response from the school, accompanied by certain conditions. These included the infamous list of required linens and clothes, each of which was to be marked with my student number. My mother and I spent all summer shopping, sewing, and embroidering my number on each piece of my wardrobe: two blankets, two pairs of sheets, six white underwear, three long-sleeved nightshirts, three long-sleeved aprons, and so on. On the eve of my departure, after packing my wardrobe into the large trunk my father had bought, my mother solemnly recited her final guidance and instructions: Never forget who I was, an Algerian, a Muslim, a descendant of great tribes on my father's side and my mother's, and a daughter of the Honorable Qadi Drif. I was to defend the honor of them all, come what may. And especially since I was a girl, I was absolutely required to conduct myself impeccably, because I was responsible for not only my own future but those of all the other girls from my family and my region. Utterly overwhelmed by this mission—the weight of which I thought might crush my frail shoulders—and frightened by the complete unknown into which I was headed, I couldn't close my eyes all night.

At daybreak, we left home by car for Affreville (today's Khemis Miliana), where we would catch the Oran-Algiers train. It was the first time that I had crossed this part of the region. I discovered large expanses, towns and villages like Bourbaki (now Khemisti) and Théniet El Had, with its famous cedar forest. At ten o'clock, we boarded the train and my true voyage of discovery began. Descending from the highlands, with their ochre-red soil, we arrived at the foot of Mount Zaccar and crossed a beautiful green landscape that rolled toward Hammam Righa. From there we continued to the Mitidja plain, with its fields and its orange and mandarin orchards protected by tight rows of beech trees. The trip from my red highlands to a symphony of green was an initiation for me. It was also my first opportunity to attach an image—even a blurred one, captured in passing—to places I had previously known only by name. I saw all these beautiful landscapes from the train's hallway, where I stood with my forehead pressed to the window, transfixed with wonder, feeling myself being rocked by the train's rhythm. Gradually, as we approached Algiers, we saw greener terrain, more frequent villages, and more imposing buildings.

I was still mesmerized by all this when a vast expanse of blue appeared—not above my head, but at the level of my little-girl eyes: the sea. I don't know how long I remained frozen, breathless and wide-eyed, before this glittering blue array of water, which shimmered in the September sunlight and frothed to the ebb and flow of the unceasing waves. Then we plunged into a huge train station that bustled with noise: the Algiers central station.

My father nudged me and announced our arrival in Algiers. Algiers! El-Djazaïr! Suddenly sad, I asked my father, "But where is the sea?"

"It's disappeared."

"Will we see it again?"

Anxious to disembark and collect our luggage, my father reassured me that a very nice surprise awaited me outside the station. Aided by a porter, we took the elevator up to the waterfront and Bresson Square (today's Port Saïd Square), where my father kept his word by pausing for an unforgettable sight. The trees in the square were overrun by a drove of birds whose twittering concert nearly drowned out the noise of the main boulevard's traffic. The sea was at my feet, perfuming the air. It was complete and utter enchantment. Ever since that moment, for the rest of my life, whenever I have returned to Algiers from anywhere else, I have felt that same ecstasy and that same spell.

Next came my discovery of the grand European buildings, the immense boulevard and the trolley crisscrossing it, and the distant minarets and domes of Djamaâ El Djedid (the New Mosque) and Djamaâ El Kebir (the Great Mosque), the only immediately visible signs that Algiers was a Muslim city.

Then I entered a hotel for the first time and saw my first European-style bedroom and bed. My father helped me settle in, explaining that after a short rest, we would dine in a restaurant. I didn't even know what a restaurant was! Soon we headed out, walking back up the waterfront to an immense, imposing building with a curious entryway: the Hotel Aletti, with its revolving door. I had arrived in another world, one of which I knew nothing.

We were directed toward the restaurant, where the table my father had reserved awaited us. Accustomed to our traditional *meïda* tables, arranged low on a stack of carpets surrounded by cushions, I found myself sitting on a chair at a table set with a tablecloth, plates, and silverware. My father explained to me how to use a knife and fork, then suggested that I just imitate him. I discovered that the differences between us and the Europeans did not stop at food and recipes—it extended to our very way of eating. I worked as best I could to imitate my father, who explained that it would probably be like this at school, too.

The next morning, my father helped me redo my long, thick braids. Since we didn't need to be at school until two o'clock, we decided to spend the morning in a sacred local rite—visiting the shrine of the capital's patron saint, Sidi Abderrahmane, to say our prayers.

I was excited to visit the shrine because since our arrival, with the exception of the two mosques and a few passersby who looked to be "natives" like me, I had found myself in a totally European environment filled with foreign faces. Only my father at my side, with his *burnous* robe and elegant *chèche* scarf wrapped around his head, reassured me that I was home, in my own land, in defiance of the stares that passersby shot at us as if to say that we were the strange ones here. From the hotel, we headed to the Place du Gouvernement, passed the Bugeaud School, and climbed a staircase to Rue Marengo and the shrine of Sidi Abderrahmane.

Here I discovered another city that had been hidden from view before by a high wall of European buildings. From its architecture, its streets, its inhabitants, its noises, its perfumes, from the look and demeanor of its people, I knew it was an Arab city. I was home! These were my people! A population who spoke with their eyes and whose manner was warm and reserved all at once. For the first time since arriving in Algiers, I heard my own language spoken in the streets. I was in the Casbah of Algiers!

After we said our prayers in the beautiful mausoleum, my father took me to see the famous *medersa* where he completed his Islamic law studies: the Medersa Bencheneb, with its commanding studded doors, towering marble columns, and mosaics. Without exaggerating, I think it was the most beautiful morning of my life.

We took a taxi through the city, passing along Rue d'Isly, past the Central Post Office, then Rue Michelet, the Governor-General's Palace, the Saint George Hotel, the hillside neighborhood known as La Redoute, and finally my new school: the Lycée Fromentin. After passing through the large entry gates, the taxi followed a long, wide driveway and pulled to a stop before the dormitory administration, where a dense crowd of European women clustered, accompanied by their daughters.

Our arrival had a predictable effect—deafening silence and dumbstruck stares. My father's commanding presence made us particularly remarkable. Oh my, an Arab and his daughter in this seat of French culture and knowledge! We were greeted by an elegant woman, Madame Guenassia, the chief supervisor of the dormitories. My father completed all the required paperwork, including forms noting from which religious denomination the student came and whether she could eat pork or not. We were then shown to the sixth-grade students' section, which included two classrooms, an assembly room, locker rooms on the ground floor, and two dormitories. We left my wardrobe and linens at the laundry, where they issued us what we would need for the week, as well as sheets and blankets. In the dormitory, a beehive of mothers, each more elegant than the last, busied themselves helping their daughters arrange their belongings and make their beds.

I was the only girl accompanied by her father, but he was absolutely perfect. While I stood paralyzed by fear at this world I didn't know, my father calmly and confidently helped me stow my things and make the bed, tucking the sheets tight in the European style. Seeing my distress, he shook me gently and told me that the most important thing was to work hard and always do well in my studies, which he assured me I was perfectly capable of doing, as I had already shown. As for arranging one's things and making a bed with neatly tucked sheets and blankets, it wasn't magic: just watch the others closely and imitate them.

After the challenge of the bed, we walked to my classroom to claim my desk and store my notepads and books. Careful not to leave me suddenly alone in a world that I found utterly foreign or to let me be caught off guard, my father accompanied me everywhere, explaining the why and how of everything—until the fateful moment of separation arrived. Terrified, I stood silent for fear of bursting into tears like the other girls around me, who clung to their departing mothers. My father, who rarely showed his emotions, took me in his arms and told me to be patient, reassuring me: "Soon you'll get used to your new life, and make plenty of friends. Plus, your teachers are excellent, and you will learn so many new things. The most important thing is to work hard to succeed and go on to university. I am counting on you, and I have total confidence in you." Unable to make even a sound, I didn't manage to cry out to him that I didn't want to stay there and that I wanted just one thing: to return home with him. When I finally emerged from my stupor, I saw my father from behind, departing the school and leaving me to my new life: the sole "native" girl in a French dormitory where all the others, students and supervisors alike, were French, and where the lifestyle was entirely French, down to the way they made the bed and bathed themselves. Even that we did differently.

The next day, I began classes in the sixth grade's second section. (Our grade had three sections, each with thirty students.) I was the only "native" in my grade. Gradually, I discovered that there was a "native" girl in seventh grade, another in eleventh, and one in twelfth. In other words, when I entered the Lycée Fromentin in 1947, there were just four "native" girls among the 2,000 students there! I would spend seven years at this school and throughout my time there, our number never exceeded eight. I remember that because, at our peak, we managed to fill a whole table in the dining room, making our own pork-free table—not even 1 percent of the student body!

After several weeks of feeling lonely and homesick, I spent sixth grade enjoying my studies and persevering. A lot of adaptation—and regular correspondence with my father—finally helped me to integrate and to make new discoveries each day. After washing, making our beds perfectly, and dressing, we collected our school materials and reported to the dining room, lined up two by two, for breakfast. Our classes ran from eight until eleven-thirty each morning, followed by lunch at noon, then afternoon classes from two until five. Then, back in our study hall, we worked on homework until seven. Dinner was half an hour later, followed by thirty minutes of free time. The dormitory doors closed at nine o'clock, and then we had a half-hour for washing before lights out.

I followed this schedule over seven long years, during which I learned a tremendous amount both from my books and the people around me. My favorite moments were undoubtedly the hours studying in the library and playing at the beach; the first of these gave me the chance to voyage in my mind, and the second to actually join my classmates off campus in chatting and having fun. The other girls were very nice, though I was rather shy and reserved. We often talked about our readings, or of our experiences outside school during the weekends.

I should mention that I was a special case, since except for times like All Saints' Day or May 1 (Labor Day), when the dormitories were officially closed, I preferred to spend my weekends at school. I did all my homework and read a lot. Then, on Monday, I made a good audience for my friends returning to school from home.

Those years at school, and all those discussions, taught me much about the life, culture, and lifestyle of Europeans, including their ways of thinking and of seeing us. One day my friend Olympe, back from the weekend with her parents in the town of Birtouta, recounted to us the first football match she had attended, pitting a European team against a "native" one. When asked where she was sitting and whether the crowd was mixed, she answered spontaneously: "Oh, but in Birtouta, we're always on one side and the rats on the other!" I looked at her, taken aback at the brutal realization that, in her eyes and those of the other friends participating in the discussion, I too was a "rat."

Realizing immediately that I had understood her meaning, she added, "But Zohra, you, you're not like the others!" My mother's words came back to me, reminding me of the reality: that my friendships with Europeans, however sincere they may be, would all be smashed against the wall that separated our two existences. This did not prevent me from continuing to spend time with and even befriend my classmates, but I never again lost sight of that infamous wall. To be the only "native" among three whole sections of European girls was a terrible situation. Only my abilities as an excellent student helped me, and I finished sixth grade among the leading students, to the delight and pride of my parents.

In seventh grade, the arrival of another "native" girl would forever change my life and hers.

Samia, My Friend, My Sister

One day midway through the first quarter, just after the gym class that I loved so much, I noticed a girl I had never seen leaning against the fence beside the field. Her features, facial expression, posture, and especially her gaze all said that she was Algerian like me. I immediately walked toward her and blurted out in Arabic, "You're Arab!" She responded just as spontaneously, "Yes! And you too!"

It was Samia Lakhdari, a new arrival, who from that moment would become my best friend, my alter ego, my eternal accomplice. I was no longer alone. Samia, who had just arrived at the school that day and was completely distraught and terrified in this foreign environment, now found herself coming back to life. As the "veteran" there, I took her under my wing and immediately began to reveal the place's secrets and explain its many codes and conventions to her. We soon became inseparable.

Samia was my age and lived in the seaside neighborhood of Saint-Eugène. Her father was a *qadi* in Algiers who hailed from Biskra, while her mother, Mama Zhor, was from Constantine, also in the east. On her first weekend home, when she told her parents that she had already made a friend, an

Samia Lakhdari, Zohra's close friend in school

Algerian named Zohra Drif, and described my family, her father replied that he knew Qadi Drif of Vialar very well. And so Samia's father proposed to be my host in Algiers. My father agreed right away and from then on, Samia and I spent all our weekends at her home in Saint-Eugène, where we would steep ourselves in our own culture after a week spent among the French. The moment we came home, we swapped out the Western uniforms that we found so stifling for our cute, airy *gandoura* robes. Our language, our cuisine, and our speech all changed. Everything was different from at school, even the scents in the street: jasmine, *mesk ellil*, orange blossoms, mint, coriander, cinnamon, cloves.

Our weekends began on Saturday at two o'clock and ended on Monday at seven-thirty in the morning, and were centered around our Sunday ritual: a visit to the Saint-Eugène *hammam*, or public bath, after careful preparations. Nothing was missing from our *sappa* wicker basket lined with pink satin: *fouta* towels to wrap our bodies before the steam room, *bchaker* towels to dry ourselves, a change of clean clothes, and our various oils and clays, mixed at home. Then there were the copper bucket and cups and our clogs. We threw ourselves with unparalleled happiness into all the *hammam*'s rituals and emerged scoured clean as newly minted pennies. In this way I discovered the traditions and customs of Algiers, as well as of Mama Zhor's hometown of Constantine. Her sophistication fascinated me. But soon I understood that while the details might be different, the overall logic of these traditions was exactly the same as back home in the highlands. This filled me with happiness and reassured me.

During the holidays, I rejoined my family in Vialar, spending time with my brothers and sisters, especially my brother Kader, who was also in high school in Algiers. My father would drive to pick us up there, and from the age of twelve I had to wear a veil for the ride home, a custom that continued through university. (I would not enter my town with my hair uncovered and flying in the wind until after independence.) Life in Vialar, a small colonial village surrounded by huge farms, was totally different from how I lived in Algiers. The town consisted of little more than a few government offices that the colonists found necessary and offered no social and cultural life, nor mingling of any kind. Apart from a few elites who mingled only with the Europeans, we "natives" were relegated to one edge of the town, in a separate quarter they called the "*village nègre*"! This meant that my holidays, especially the summers, were interminable periods of total isolation from the outside world—but for my brother Kader's steady supply of information and newspapers.

The summer of 1954 marked my graduation from high school, after I passed the *baccalauréat* exam.[1] This time the wait was even more interminable, since the university wasn't scheduled to open until November 12. My brothers Kader and Boumediene, still in high school in Algiers, returned home in late October for the All Saints' Day break. Each morning at ten, Kader would wait for the Algiers-Tiaret bus that brought the papers. I will never forget the morning of November 2, 1954, when Kader burst through the door and into the house's long entry hall, brandishing the newspapers like banners and jumping and shouting, "It's begun! It's begun! They set it off!" Busy in the kitchen, my mother and I looked at each other and instantly understood the reason for Kader's burst of joy: our war of liberation had begun.

I dropped everything, rushed to my brother and snatched the papers. The front page of every one was topped in bold black letters: "Series of Attacks Across the Country on the Night of October 31 to November 1." I read them from back to front at a stretch without stopping. My mother, to whom we had explained nothing and who could neither read nor understand French, had grasped it all the same. Better still, she, who often could not stand when I shirked my household chores for reading, didn't try to stop me this time. After tearing through the newspapers, we let our joy explode, and our mother tried only halfheartedly to calm us. It was as if everyone saw this war's outbreak as an explosion that had been building, unavoidably, for some time. Since the massacres of May 8, 1945,[2] in Sétif, Guelma, and Kherrata, we knew that a river of blood now separated us from the French. But since their occupation by the Germans and their defeat at Diên Biên Phu in Indochina, we also knew that they were not invincible.

My brother Kader and I deduced that if the attacks happened simultaneously throughout the country, they could only be the product of a genuine organized movement committed to confronting the colonial system with one clear objective: to liberate the country by force.

---

1. In the French education system, the *baccalauréat* exam is a standardized, multi-subject test that students take before graduation. Performance on the test determines a student's ability to access university studies or other post-secondary training.
2. In the spring of 1945, tensions between French colonists and Algerians in several eastern towns escalated into attacks and riots. On May 8, French police called in to quell the disturbances fired on unarmed Algerians, killing thousands, with some estimates ranging into the tens of thousands.

The other youth of Vialar had reached the same conclusion. The few high school students from our region had returned that summer of 1954, along with two university students: Moulay Driss Ferhat, who was studying mathematics in Algiers, and my older brother Mohamed, who was studying medicine in Nancy, France. Besides its excessive heat on the Sersou highlands, that summer had been marked by an unusual buzz of excitement that spread among the local population, fueled by news, bits of information, and extraordinary stories passed by word of mouth, all of which pointed toward an imminent upheaval across the country. Our collective imagination and our entire corpus of legends and fables were mobilized to feed these stories. The women contributed by recounting that in Orléansville (today's Chlef), a venerable old man had recently appeared, his beard pure white like his pious spirit, to announce the coming changes and call upon the *umma*—the community of believers of the Prophet Mohammed (peace be upon him)—to prepare themselves. Obviously, this character was as ephemeral as his omen, but our women relayed his message with such conviction that they managed to give him true form. All this they shared with one another during their weekly visit to the tomb of the local patron saint, Sidi Bentamra.

The Muslim Scouts

As for the town's young people, we had only two choices for socializing: either the Café Zerouali, a popular local spot that attracted "natives" from all rungs of the social ladder, or Mohand Said Café, which was considered more upscale and was frequented by those we called respectfully "the intellectuals"—who were, in fact, the Young Muslim Scouts. In truth, each of the cafés was as modest as the other; young people gathered there over a cup of tea or coffee for their interminable games of dominoes or *ronda*, a popular local card game. They dissected the various events reported by the press or circulated by word of mouth. Most of the town's boys were in the Muslim Scouts, and even a few young girls, though such mixing was still new for our society. Unfortunately, the families of many girls still withdrew them from such activities, and even from school, when they reached puberty.

Muslim scouting was a true school of patriotism and an excellent incubator for future nationalists and liberation fighters. I owe a debt of gratitude to the founder of the Vialar scout troop, Arezki Aït Hamadouche and its tireless leader Mohamed Drizi, our mentor, who facilitated our nationalist awakening. He taught us all the patriotic songs, classic and new, and helped us dissect their lyrics and meanings. As the head of the Routier-level scouts,[3] he explained to the boys how to pitch camp outdoors, survive in the forest and the mountains, and offer first aid. They also brought me news of their vigils around the campfires they learned how to start and maintain.

At these gatherings, Mohamed Drizi recounted Algeria's history, reaching back to the Berber kings Jugurtha and Massinissa, then up to the leaders of earlier insurrections against the French colonizers: the epic *cheikhs* El Haddad, El Mokrani, and Bouamama, the Berber revolt leaders like Fatma N'Soumeur and Boubaghla, and especially our hero the Emir Abdelkader. He explained to them that our people had always resisted all invaders and that we should be proud of this dignified history. He recounted the epic tale of our national movement, explaining the mission and objectives of each of its branches and subsidiaries. My brothers, faithful messengers that they were, repeated to us what they learned, allowing the whole household to take advantage of these valuable lessons and even to sing the patriotic songs.

At the beginning of that summer of 1954, the village Scouts decided to break the monotony of the long, hot days by putting on plays, which they adapted from texts by the great Algerian writer Réda Houhou and from local tales and legends. They raised funds from the village notables to cover the expenses for assembling their mobile stage, which they would set up in all the villages and towns across the region. My mother and I contributed by fashioning costumes. Unsurprisingly, the colonists and their police, thrown off guard by this sudden widespread interest in theater, followed these activities closely. Through the shows, a few local boys between fifteen and seventeen managed to unite men, women, and children, briefly transporting them from the drudgery of their "*nègre*" farm villages and the vast fields of wheat, barley, chickpeas, and lentils that they plowed, sowed, and reaped year-round for the exclusive benefit of their colonial masters. Here on the Sersou plain, renowned for the legendary riches that came from thousands of hectares of land tilled by their ancestors, these families were enduring unsustainable misery. Like their ancestors, they toiled under the broiling sun each day in their *m'dhal* straw hats, suffering not just from deprivation and hard labor but from the terrible knowledge that these vast lands that had belonged to their ancestors had been stolen from them. Now, from the edge of each town, it was the colonizers' lands that stretched as far as the eye

---

3. "Routiers" are a senior level roughly equivalent to the Eagle Scouts in the US Boy Scouts.

could see, surrounding the rose-hued tile roofs and beech trees that marked each farmstead.

These were huge farms where the colonists and their families lived apart, away from the town where the government administrations, workers, and various businesses were. In this rich Sersou, with its huge tracts of loamy, fertile land, the colonists thrived while a flock of men, women, and children, their starved faces tanned by the sun, survived off the few grains they gleaned from each harvest they completed for their European masters. As humiliating as it was difficult, this collection constituted their meager provisions for the winter. They bent over the earth, gathering handfuls of the straw left over after the harvest and sifting it through their fingers to extract the few grains of wheat, barley, chickpeas, or lentils missed in the harvest.

This image endures in my mind, vivid even today. So does that of the feet of a man who descended one day from the Ouarsenis Mountains to our town's weekly market. It was December 1944, I was ten, and it was a harsh winter. It was snowing that day and frost and ice coated the ground, leaving it hard and slippery under my shoes. My mother had sent my brother Kader and me with our coupons to buy tea and sugar from Mr. Aïssa, the Mozabite[4] trader in the market. My child's eyes were drawn to the huge man, who shivered with cold under his ragged woolen *qachabia* cloak. I stood petrified, staring at his feet, which appeared oddly shod to me. They seemed to rest on a thick brown sole. I pointed the man out to my brother who, curious as ever, suggested we touch his feet to see for sure. We circled the giant carefully, crouched, and snuck up close to touch his soles. They were tough, so we probed harder, even pinching the leathery base, but the giant above us didn't notice. Through our examination, we realized that it was in fact his own foot, so weathered that it formed a real sole: the man was barefoot and had probably never worn shoes.

And so at a very young age I came across the terrible misery to which our people were reduced. It was all around—when I went outside to play, shopped at the market, or accompanied my brothers to tell my aunts Bakhta and Aicha that my mother needed them. They lived together with their extended family in a single cramped room with a sole opening, the door,

---

4. The Mozabites are a Berber-speaking ethnic and religious minority, originally from several oasis towns in the Algerian Sahara, long reputed for their industriousness as traders.

deprived the natives physically and mentally through dignity

that led to a small courtyard partly shaded by corrugated metal sheets and burlap sacks and served as the kitchen. The rest of the courtyard was covered by a trellis that sagged in late August with heavy bunches of grapes. I loved going to my aunts' because they spoiled me with affection. But looking back much later, I can recognize the deprivation in which they lived, as well as their dignity. Despite their poverty, they had something to offer us each time we visited, and they made it a point of pride to keep their modest home neat and clean, even accenting it with basil, mint, and other fragrant herbs.

During World War II, the "natives" lived in abject poverty because the colonists—most of whom supported the Vichy government that collaborated with the Nazis—requisitioned everything of value in Algeria to sustain the German army that had been occupying metropolitan France since 1940.

Even worse than the requisitions and rationing, however, was the forced mobilization of young "native" men for the war. The street where we lived led to the local town hall. How many times as I returned home from school during those years did I witness the shocking sight of women in rags, crying and screaming in pain while lacerating their own faces? They clung to the bars surrounding the town hall and begged for their sons to be returned to them. When we ran home and told my mother what we had just witnessed, she explained that the *caïd,* the local administrator who answered to the French government, had gone into their homes and dragged their boys to war, far from home in the land of the *koffar*—the unbelievers. Of course, I didn't understand everything my mother said. But I grasped and retained one thing that I could imagine clearly: the *caïd*, an Arab like us, had forcibly taken away the sons of those women, whose pain I had seen and whose screaming and wailing I had heard. From an early age, I hated the *caïds.*

As I was saying, during that summer of 1954, the young Scouts and students performed their plays throughout the nearby villages. Their shows earned the acclaim of large audiences, composed mostly of poor farmhands and young people deprived of everything, including education and work. The shows began with an introductory speech from Mohamed Drizi, then actors performed their roles, and finally the choir closed the performance with "Alaïki Mini Essalem," the hymn to the martyrs of the Sétif massacre, and "Min Djibalina," the anthem that really galvanized the crowds. When Kader (who was very involved in these activities) came home, he told us everything in minute detail and always ended his story by saying, "Police Commissioner Garcia and Officer Abderrahmane didn't miss a thing, and were never far away. But for now, there is no problem and everything seems calm, since they still haven't arrested Mohamed Drizi." But, in fact, the moment anything happened related to the country's political life, poor Drizi was immediately arrested and thrown into prison. November 1, 1954, was no exception: Drizi was arrested and locked up, along with Zemiti, the owner of the local restaurant, and a few others.

All in all, it was a particularly eventful summer, full of activities for Vialar's youth. As for me, apart from domestic chores I contributed as a "good little girl," I helped my brother where I could, read a lot of books, newspapers, and leaflets, and talked with my father, uncles, and brothers about the situation in the country and the responses proposed by our national parties, as well as the Organisation Spéciale (OS).[5] We knew that young activists were working to free the country. We did not know where or how.

On November 2, 1954, the newspapers brought us the answer: The war had begun.

From that moment I could think of only one thing: November 12, the first day of the academic year, when I could return to Algiers to get more information and try by any means necessary to make contact with those activists, about whom I knew nothing but who were realizing my dream: to free the country. Leading up to this historic period, in seven years at boarding school in Algiers I had transitioned from innocent childhood to a more informed adolescence. Those readings and discussions with Samia and her father had helped me to forge my solid philosophical and political convictions. The deep sense of injustice stirred in me by the teachers who treated me differently simply because I was a "native" girl, and the ludicrous attacks from my peers, helped to make me a rebel earlier than my time. In fact, those seven years at the Lycée Fromentin served as a period of maturation and awakening for me. All the readings, my interactions with the administration, teachers, and our European peers, and especially the weekends in Saint-Eugène among Samia's family, had lifted the wool from my eyes about the plight of my people and our status as "French Muslims" with neither nationality nor citizenship.

---

5. A precursor to the National Liberation Front, the Organisation Spéciale was founded in the late 1940s as a clandestine Algerian movement to combat French occupation.

I finally understood that I was forbidden to be "Algerian" and expected to be "French"—yes, "French Muslim," but French nonetheless. For my teenage brain, it was too much to bear. Samia shared this almost violent tension, of course, as did another friend, Mimi Bensmaïn. While Samia and I were boarders, Mimi was a day student. So it was thanks to her that we were informed each day of all the national and international news. In memory of Mimi, I must note that, at seventeen years old, this dear friend already had an unusually strong, assertive personality. She came from a well-to-do Algiers family that had chosen to assimilate, voluntarily abandoning their identity, culture, and personal status. On her official papers, Mimi's name was Denise-Mimi. But as soon as our friend learned the significance of what her parents had imposed upon her, she had decided to renounce the first half of her name. So everyone knew her as Mimi, a perfectly normal Algerian first name. Remarkable for her tall and lanky physique, animated manner of speaking, and independent spirit that resisted all attempts at outside control, she had the confidence we lacked and an ability to forge a point of view on any subject. All three of us were very good students. Samia and I succeeded because we were unapologetic hard workers. As for Mimi, she always succeeded while seeming more at ease than us. This changed nothing in our friendship, which depended more on Mimi's willingness to suffer with us out of solidarity whenever some unfair treatment—which could only be explained by our status as "natives"—befell us.

Such was the case in the traumatic affair with Madame Levaillant, our French, Latin, and Greek teacher—and our headmistress. Since the start of my eleventh-grade year, Madame Levaillant had shown Samia, Mimi, and me nothing but unconcealed animosity and aggression. This treatment lasted all year, though it failed to dull our commitment to success or our ability to work, even if our grades suffered blatantly. We were well aware of her prejudice, which today would be considered flagrant racial discrimination, but at that time we had no choice but to make the best of our lot. Despite her unrestrained racism, Madame Levaillant was an otherwise excellent teacher to whom the French Ministry of National Education entrusted numerous trainees. When her trainees corrected our homework, we received the same marks as our European peers, which reassured us and encouraged us to work harder. For us Madame Levaillant's classes were true tests, during which we had to overcome her constant harassment while taking care not to fall into her traps. We managed until one day, a month before we were to sit for the first part of the *baccalauréat* exam, Madame Levaillant accused Mimi and me of having copied each other's work and received the school administration's approval to bring us before the Disciplinary Board!

She had, of course, instructed us to complete this assignment in teams, based on group research outside of class. Then, after we submitted the fruit of our week's labor, she accused us of having copied. For a teenager of eighteen who was in Algiers only for her studies and had always worked hard to uphold her commitment to herself and her family to succeed and lead by example, I viewed my impending appearance before the Disciplinary Board as a dreadful, slanderous affair. I had submitted my work on a Saturday and been accused the following Wednesday. I was to appear before the board that next Saturday. I spent the intervening three days crying tears of rage, helplessness, and injustice. I couldn't fall asleep. My friends did all they could to comfort me, but in vain—I remained inconsolable. How could I wash away the shame that dirtied me even though I had done nothing wrong? How would I explain to my parents what was happening to me and, above all, that I didn't deserve it? How would I get my parents to believe me? How, one month before the *baccalauréat* exam, could I avoid failing? So, with my eyes blurred by tears, I wrote my father to tell him of the tragedy that had befallen me.

On that fateful Saturday morning, Mimi and I waited alone in a dim downstairs room, dreading our impending appearance before the Disciplinary Board in the headmistress's office. Around ten o'clock, they brought Mimi in, and a half-hour later it was my turn. Shy as I was, I had vowed not to cry before the judges, to defend myself to the last, and not to let myself get upset. I entered the cold, silent room where the director sat at her desk, facing five seated professors. Without waiting, she read out the charges, explaining that this case was the culmination of years of bad attitudes and poor behavior from my whole group. Certain that our conduct had always been above reproach, I suddenly realized that the charges we faced concerned not the facts of the case but, rather, who we were. Moreover, I realized that ours was a case of collective and not individual responsibility. I especially understood that this committee before me was reproaching us three little "native" girls who had the audacity to climb our way up to the top of the class, excelled in our studies, and, instead of spending our lives being grateful to the French and all they had given us, had conspired to assert ourselves. I knew then that we were all condemned in advance and that it was useless to try to convince them of my innocence. The sentence was handed down: the maximum penalty. Our guilt would be noted on our permanent school records. Their goal was clear: to diminish our chances of passing the *baccalauréat* exam. While I had walked into the Disciplinary Board hearing crushed by rage and injustice, I left serene and filled with calm, ten years more mature!

I returned to my friends placid, determined, with my head held high. We vowed to one another to redouble our efforts to pass the *baccalauréat* at the head of the class as a means of spitting in the faces of the headmistress, Madame Levaillant, and every racist in the school. Soon after, a comforting letter arrived from my father, in which he reiterated his complete confidence in me and my abilities, calling the Disciplinary Board event a simple setback that should in no way discourage me. These words brought me absolute peace. He added that he was convinced of my intellectual honesty and certain of my upcoming brilliant success because, he wrote, "*Bon sang ne saurait mentir*"—The apple never falls far from the tree. We spent the next month working tirelessly, practically like slaves, despite the fact that we were fasting in observance of the holy month of Ramadan. We completed the exams with ease, and the results were a collective slap in the face of every member of the Disciplinary Board—and especially to its ringleader, Madame Levaillant. We scored excellent grades, including in French, Latin, and Greek. In my track, Philosophy and Letters, I was proclaimed valedictorian with distinction. At the end of the year, after the awards ceremony (where I had received quite a lot of awards), Madame Levaillant came to congratulate us. Disgusted, I spun on my heel and headed for the exit, where my father was waiting to take me home to Vialar for that long summer of 1953.

That September, I entered my final year at the Lycée Fromentin, at the end of which I earned my *baccalauréat* in June 1954. I hold great memories from my senior year. I loved the philosophy courses, taught by Madame Czarnecki, who diverged from most of the other teachers and reminded us of Madame Tomas, our geography and history teacher from the year before. Both were competent, fair, and showed no discrimination against us. (Later, I would learn that both were Marxists.) Philosophy gave me the means to analyze and understand; history was just as applicable for us, since it focused on the contemporary period.

The different disciplines, each as interesting and exciting as the last, enriched our already sizable stacks of reading, the endless debates that followed, the daily bits of news that Mimi fed us, and the newspapers we devoured every weekend at Samia's. So aware were we of current events that when, in March 1954, one fateful piece of news arrived, it instantly set us apart. Having completed the first two hours of classes, we were enjoying our ten o'clock break on the school's esplanade, which swarmed with students and their usual noise. But suddenly, a silence crept across the crowd as the news was relayed from one group to the next: France had been defeated at Diên Biên Phu in Indochina!

Though it was beautiful that morning under the blue sky of Algiers, overlooking the sparkling bay, a mournful silence enveloped the esplanade. Some students fell into tears, others were silent. It was a moment of mourning. But when Mimi, Samia, and I glanced at one another, smiles crept into our eyes as we silently rejoiced with Indochina, each of us shouting a great "Hurray!" with our eyes. And as soon as we managed to find ourselves alone, we all began asking the same question at once: Why not us? France was not invincible—the Indochinese had just proven it. Our questioning was not purely abstract of course, since we knew the reality of our own nation and were closely following the struggles led by our various parties and associations. Messali Hadj was obviously our hero, just like we admired activists like Ferhat Abbas, Ahmed Francis, Ali Boumendjel, Sadek Hadjeres, and the rest.

We also followed the debates and squabbles within the various parties. In truth, our hearts always leaned toward the free thinkers of the Parti du Peuple Algérien (PPA) and its successor party, the Mouvement pour le Triomphe des Libertés Démocratiques, or Movement for the Triumph of Democratic Liberties (MTLD). But Mimi, Samia, and I were not activists in any organization; we were mere schoolgirls in 1952. Our choices and positions were purely intellectual, and we owed them to our readings and the passionate discussions that followed. We read the literature of the Enlightenment, the history of the French Revolution, and the 1793 "Declaration of the Rights of Man and of the Citizen," which we recopied by hand and which Samia even learned by heart for the fun of it. Mimi took sometimes to Danton, sometimes to Saint Just. As for me, after tackling Montesquieu, I received an article by Clémenceau from Madame Tomas. I found it upsetting, because it was one thing to be a "native" and to live it every day, and quite another to see one's condition so described on the page.

The French defeat at Diên Biên Phu, and the independence struggles in Tunisia, Morocco, and Madagascar provided us with two key ideas. First, France was not invincible. Not only had she not resisted the German occupation but, even worse, over 80 percent of the French parliament had voted for the armistice—France's abdication to Germany—and what's more, the majority of the French elite had even collaborated with the occupiers, supporting the Vichy regime and its Marshal Philippe Pétain. We were well aware that without Britain and the United States, France would never have been liberated. Today I can understand that France was seeking to build a new national narrative by attributing its liberation to Charles de Gaulle and his band of resisters, but at that time, we were not fooled.

We knew that in France, in the face of Nazi Germany, the De Gaulles and Jean Moulins had been few and far between. In 1952 and 1953, along with our assiduous daily reading of the *Alger Républicain* that Mimi Bensmaïn snuck into school under her overcoat for us, our excellent teacher Madame Tomas helped us to understand that, in addition to millions of deaths, World War II had produced a new division between the two new powers, the United States of America and the USSR. A new world map had been drawn in which France, the former imperial power that had been reconstructed entirely thanks to the Americans' Marshall Plan, had become a quasi-satellite of the United States. For Samia, Mimi, and me, the question had been on which side to situate ourselves, knowing that our country was composed of three French *départements* but also that our people's interests were diametrically opposed to those of our colonizers. In the end, based on our logic and our conscience, we sided with the Soviet camp. This does not mean that we felt close to the Communists—even if we did find them more humane and respectful and admired them for their activism. (Madame Tomas was a good example.) We simply classified all the parties, movements, associations, and newspapers based on their positions vis-à-vis us "natives" and our condition as colonized noncitizens, and vis-à-vis the colonial system as a whole. We were becoming sufficiently mature and well versed in literature, history, and politics to know that the Communists had not only condemned the peaceful protests of May 8, 1945, but also endorsed the fierce repression and therefore the massacres themselves, through an analysis that they alone were capable of and that simply did not hold water. All three of us sympathized with the Amis du Manifeste et de la Liberté (Friends of the Manifesto and Liberty, or AML) and "leaned MTLD." We respected the *ouléma* clerics' association, even if we found them somewhat lukewarm in their positions; our favorite face was Sheikh Larbi Tebessi. Ferhat Abbas also impressed us. We were very proud of him and followed and dissected all his statements and his speeches, even though we thought that his Union Démocratique du Manifeste Algérien (Democratic Union of the Algerian Manifesto, or UDMA) was wasting its time by participating in elections where the die had been cast in advance.[6] We were skeptical that our people could be emancipated by the ballot box while still under the colonial system; in fact, we didn't believe it at all.

Our favorite was undoubtedly Messali Hadj, and the party we felt closest to was the MTLD. We shared its reading of our people's situation and the reasons for their extreme misery, deprivation, and illiteracy, which Hadj ascribed to one factor: settler colonialism and its unjust system of economic, social, cultural, and political domination. We were in complete agreement with the MTLD when it characterized the colonial system as a racist one based on the prejudice of European superiority over the "natives," who were reduced to the status of subhuman foreigners in their own land. We shared and admired the accuracy of his diagnoses and the courage of his positions. Most of all, we admired and respected his commitment to defending the popular masses and the poor (that is to say, the overwhelming majority of our people) and our right to independence, whatever the price. These were the forefathers of our independence movement. They spoke for us all. In them we perceived truth and legitimacy. There were even cases where activists from different factions within the nationalist movement lived under the same roof. For example, my uncle was for the UDMA and my brother Kader for MTLD. Mama Zhor, even if she wasn't a card-carrying member, was a model PPA-MTLD independence activist. Samia's father and brother Malek were committed nationalists. Both were comfortable in their own culture and capable of navigating that of the French. They were more measured, more cautious, and less radical than Mama Zhor, and both had participated decisively in our intellectual development and awakening.

It was Malek who introduced us as schoolgirls to the cinema and theater and their power. He also taught us the use of statistics, especially those that were carefully distorted by the colonial administration in order to serve as "scientifically substantiated" knowledge of the social, political, and cultural life of our people. He repeated that our own well-to-do families were just a tiny drop in the ocean of unbearable misery in which our people tried to survive by begging on their own lands, in their own homes. "Nearly 50

---

6. In the aftermath of World War II, Ferhat Abbas's UDMA was one of several pro-independence, nationalist Algerian parties that decided to compete in elections for the Algerian Assembly. More hardline forces spurned these contests, which French authorities were rumored to have rigged in favor of compliant candidates.

percent of us are unemployed and the average European's income is ten times that of a 'native'!" he proclaimed repeatedly. Then he would add, "Don't think that you—that we—are representative of our masses of totally illiterate youth: less than nine out of every hundred 'native' children attend school, and an even tinier fraction of those reach university." He spat that phrase out with <u>dull anger, contained but very much visible.</u> In moments like those, Samia and I withdrew into embarrassed silence, feeling almost guilty to be so privileged.

Twenty years our senior, Malek regained his composure and his jovial and conciliatory nature, excused himself, and explained to us that on the contrary, we should take advantage of the resources and opportunities before us in order to help our people later. "It's young girls like you who will change things for the greater good. Someone who can't read, write, or even manufacture a needle can do nothing for his people, and certainly can't liberate them."

Bolder now, Samia retorted, "No assembly chosen by such an electoral masquerade will change things!"

Malek burst out laughing before confiding in us, mysteriously: "I agree with you, but the time has not yet come to upset everything, because the people aren't ready yet."

In my young head, I wondered what the people weren't ready for and sank into sad thoughts, full of bitterness. The overwhelming images came back to me of each time I entered an Arab neighborhood in Algiers, far from the sanitized streets, gleaming villas, and imposing European buildings: a crowd of men, women, and children, all of them destitute, starving, their gazes dignified and sometimes even proud, bent under the deprivation that makes the stomach of anyone who sees it ache like the hunger of those suffering from it. Tears of rage came to my eyes, but before they could begin to flow, Malek was shaking me and demanding in Arabic, "What's the matter, Zohra? *Gharqou bouabrek*?" (Did all your ships just sink?)

I collected myself and found the courage to tell him what evil I saw in the elections and in a constituent assembly where a European voter had the same political weight as nine Muslim ones. I explained that nine hundred thousand Europeans dominated and crushed nine million Muslims through their laws, their brute strength, and their system of privileges. That the poverty and illiteracy of our people were the consequences and not the cause. At this, Malek laughed even harder and predicted that I would have a long and illustrious legal career.

To this was added the crushing defeat of France at Diên Biên Phu and the victory of the Indochinese, which we followed as if it were our own victory and that of everyone in our situation. The Malagasies, followed by our brothers in the Maghreb, finally convinced us that we were facing a new historical era marked by uprisings and movements of peoples claiming their rights to self-determination and independence.

During our many discussions and debates, Mimi, Samia, and I arrived without fail at the same conclusion: Why not us? It had to happen, it was inevitable.

Once I had my *baccalauréat*, I decided to attend law school in order to defend our future fighters, never doubting that one day or another the explosion would take place. But I did not know that it would be the same year as my *baccalauréat* exam and entry into university.

The University

After my childhood in Vialar, then seven years at boarding school in Algiers, when I arrived at university I was again confronted with a completely new life. I had to manage autonomy and freedom, two situations that were totally unknown to me until that point and for which I had never been prepared. During high school, even when I left the school each weekend, it was to go to a family home—Samia's. Suffice it to say that we left that dormitory to go to another, just one that was more humane and in line with our culture. Even when we went to the *hammam* or the movies, we were always chaperoned by Samia's mother or her older sister Leïla.

The academic year began on November 12, 1954. A few days earlier, my father had accompanied me from Vialar to help me settle into the residential campus in Ben Aknoun, a suburb of Algiers. As he prepared to leave, my father, knowing my crippling shyness, took a moment to explain to me that I was beginning a new stage of my life. With his legendary composure and sensitivity, he reminded me of the advice my mother had spent the eve of my departure repeating directly and without adornment: "My daughter, you are going to live alone in a big city, a place of many dangers. You will be in college with a lot of boys. You must never forget that we are sending you there for your studies, and that your reputation as a young lady must remain intact and absolutely flawless.

"You will be far away, but remember that your father has many friends in Algiers and they will always have an eye on you. If, God forbid, you were to commit an irreparable mistake, the shame would be upon you, upon your father, and upon us all. And you must never forget that we are not French: they have their culture and their traditions, and we have ours. Keep in mind that you are responsible for your honor and all your people's, and that by your conduct, you will either be the key that will open the door of all possibilities to our other girls, or you will close it forever."

Suffice it to say that these words did not make for a peaceful night, nor did they alleviate the anxiety that already gripped me at the idea of going to live alone in Algiers. Despite that, I was still grateful to my parents for having insisted to our whole region that my right to education was equal to their sons'. With every diploma I received or exam I passed, the local notables came to see my father to ask my hand for one of their sons, saying that it was high time I was married. The day after I passed my *baccalauréat* exam with distinction, a large delegation of men from my father's tribe came to his office to congratulate him and express their pride in his daughter, the

Zohra Drif at University of Algiers

only Muslim girl to have spent so long away from home studying among Europeans, while preserving intact her honor and that of the whole tribe. Nonetheless, they felt that it was time for me to marry, as I had reached, if not surpassed, the age for doing so. Clearly, no one among this delegation could conceive of one of their girls studying until the age of twenty, much less going even further.

My father listened to them, thanked them, and explained that he had other plans for his daughter than marriage, including sending her to university. At these words, the head of the delegation, stunned and outraged, retorted: "Zohra is a woman and even if she studies all her life, she will always be one. She will never become a man." Seeing the futility of negotiating for his daughter's future, my father cut him short: "Zohra is my daughter and not the tribe's. I am responsible for her, and I make my choices and will accept the consequences." That evening, when my mother recounted the incident to me, I understood the true struggle that my parents were waging. It was a struggle against the racist and discriminatory colonial system that offered nothing to their daughter and made nothing easy for her, but it was also a struggle against their own people to recognize girls' rights to education and thus to autonomy.

Thus, at twenty, I came to appreciate the scope and importance of this battle that my parents waged within a system that gave all women one mission: to be a wife and mother. Nothing else. Naturally, for this reason I have always felt a strong sense of loyalty and a great debt to them, because the worst thing I could do would be to betray their struggle and their hopes for me. For that reason, with all of my heart and will, I have made it a point of honor never to violate or upset our rules and our codes. My duty felt almost like a military mission. I was carrying the immense hopes that came along with this combat in service of all our girls.

Another reason pushed me to take on this mission: settler colonialism, which brought with it a massive presence of Europeans whose looks toward us were at best condescending and at worst downright contemptuous. Through my hard work and success, every day I refuted their prejudices. At the same time, I felt the duty to bear my culture and identity like a standard to constantly show our difference: I am not—and will never be—you; you are not—and will never be—me. But my community's codes and rules were a fundamental marker of my identity. To betray them would amount to surrender, which was out of the question. All this is to explain our actions, mine and Samia's, after our arrival downtown for our first year of law at the central academic campus of the University of Algiers.

In the law college, there were some 200 students from across Algeria, as well as Tunisia and Morocco. From the very first day, when a professor conducted the opening roll call, we counted. Of those 200, there were just six "natives": two girls (Samia and me) and four boys (one of whom was a certain Lakhdar Brahimi, who would go on to a celebrated career in international diplomacy). Since we all had the same education and culture, we maintained an unspoken agreement to apply our social codes from day one. This meant that, while Samia and I had no problem conversing with our French peers, whom our culture considered mere asexual beings, it was quite different with our four coreligionists. We watched each other surreptitiously and, if our eyes ever met, the absolute rule was to stare straight through them, unrecognizing. When forced by our professors to join the same library research team, we addressed each other exclusively through a European go-between. That was the rule, and we respected it: *el horma*, strict separation of the sexes.

Samia and I decided to take up another challenge: to outperform even our Algerian comrades. Through our success and our impeccable behavior, we hoped they might come to see us as models for all the sisters and daughters in their families. We threw ourselves into this challenge as one would into a new religion. Looking back, I can now see that we were very unpleasant—even unbearable. So much so that one day in the study hall, when a fellow "native" student approached me to ask for some information about one of our classes, my instinctive reaction to reject him was so brutal that the poor boy took to his heels without even asking for explanation. I still feel embarrassed—even ashamed—when I recall that episode. At the same time, he must have understood my reaction, since he certainly never would have allowed his own sister to speak to one of our men to whom she was not married—not out of contempt, but rather out of respect for our rules. (Fortunately, that student and I met again after independence and had a good laugh about the incident.)

Our codes and rules did not prevent Samia and me from sampling our new life and discovering the many beautiful and mysterious sights of Algiers. Unlike Samia, who lived with her parents in Saint-Eugène, I had a room in a girls' dormitory. To reach the university campus each morning, I took the bus across the leafy paradise of Ben Aknoun, the buzzing main street of El Biar with its countless shops, then the hillside of Tagarins with its mosque, balconies, terraces, and in the gaps between the buildings, its glimpses over the sea. From there we followed the Boulevard de Lattre

de Tassigny (today the Boulevard Frantz Fanon), the view over the sparkling blue sea marking my memory each day as we flew along the sweeping descent. In spring, this morning descent was accompanied by the scent
of jasmine mixed with honeysuckle and wisteria, and on the afternoon
return, the inimitable scent of *mesk ellil.* When I arrived each morning at
the law school, I found Samia waiting for me, and we would duck into a
small café for the daily celebration of our freedom. We would each order
a coffee and croissant and quickly scan the newspapers that Samia had
already bought. Together we would decide on our plans for the day, then
head off to class.

I spent my weekends and holidays at Samia's. On those occasions, especially in spring and fall, we preferred to make our way from campus to Saint-
Eugène on foot, beside the seafront. The enchantment of that view never
failed to rouse a swell of emotion within me. As soon as we passed the
Central Post Office, then the Hotel Aletti, we already felt at home. We suddenly felt bolder and dared to speak at full volume in Arabic for the final
stretch toward home, where we arrived happy to be alive and eager to share
our joy with those around us.

Algiers was, and still is, boundless—not in size, but in the emotions it
evokes and the surprises it has always held: its ability to offer a pedestrian an
unexpected street, a life-saving staircase for a shortcut, an oasis of dappled
green shade with lovely scents and jubilant birds. Moments of rest in the
public squares and parks were the rewards we earned for our efforts to discover them.

Despite its imposing martial look and its intention to symbolize the
eternal French presence, for us the statue of Général de Bourmont perched
on his prancing horse in the Place du Gouvernement actually marked the
start of "home." That's because the square was surrounded by the Djamaâ
El Kebir, the Djamaâ El Djedid, and the Djamaâ Ketchaoua, not to mention
the numerous passages leading toward our Algerian city, the Casbah. The
French had an uphill battle in this regard, as their Place du Gouvernment
was located solidly in the lower Casbah.

We were fascinated by the Casbah, its history and its stories, but the
only points within it that our parents had authorized us to visit were the
shrine of Sidi Abderrahmane and the National Library. Those limits only
served to encourage our fascination; our dream was to one day discover
the Casbah and its labyrinthine passages in detail. So many things pushed

us toward it: our readings, the stories told in our families, and the nights of *bouqalate*[7] poetry and fortune-telling sessions with the women of Saint-Eugène. Every time we asked a neighbor where she had bought some beautiful fabric, intoxicating perfume, or cute object, the answer was always the same: the Casbah.

Samia and I, on the other hand, did our personal shopping on Rue Michelet and Rue d'Isly, the two main commercial streets of Algiers, where we found all the major brands, plus department stores like Le Bon Marché and Les Galeries de France. We shopped there with unconcealed happiness because everything we could want was available, and we could discover the joys of choosing our outfits and accessories and the pride of paying for them ourselves. With time, we developed our taste and conquered all the secrets of European elegance, an asset that would prove useful down the road.

From the start of our first year, we had a very busy schedule divided between lectures, tutorial sessions, practicums, and library research. We managed to organize ourselves in record time in order to take full advantage of our favorite classes and to enjoy our free hours discovering Algiers alone as adults, without a chaperone. We took in countless postwar Russian and Italian films that opened our horizons, and we never missed a lecture by Professor André Mandouze, a champion in the fight against colonialism and its misdeeds. In his lectures we heard a completely new discourse—and discovered Europeans who shared our ideas and views. Followed each time without fail by heated (sometimes even violent) debates between his followers and his detractors, Professor Mandouze's lectures were held in the Faculty of Arts. We discovered the lectures and discussion sessions of Jean Sénac, whose articles in *Alger Républicain* we discovered only then. Sénac's lectures, too, usually ended in fights. Though our codes and rules of conduct dictated that we shouldn't attend these debates, we did, and our lives were totally turned upside down by them—and by daily access to magazines

---

7. The *bouqala* (plural, *bouqalate*) sessions are an iconic historical tradition of Algeria's women. The practice centers on oral recitation, composition, and improvisation of short poems as a means of both transmitting traditional stories and foretelling future love, betrayal, marriage, or other fortunes. Usually performed in private among the women present at family gatherings, the ritual is led by an elderly woman respected for her recitation skills.

and newspapers, including the local press (like *L'Écho d'Alger*, *La Dépêche Quotidienne*, and *Alger Républicain*), the metropolitan press (including *France-Observateur*, *L'Express*, *Le Monde*, and *L'Humanité*), and magazines (such as *Esprit* and *Les Temps Modernes*). Thus, within that first academic year of 1954 and 1955, we did our best to fill in the information gap left by all the preceding years.

Above all, we finally had access to the publications of the many parties and associations comprising our national movement: the UDMA's *La République Algérienne*, the PPA-MTLD's *L'Algérie Libre*; and *El Bassaïr*, published by the *ouléma*. The press brought us information, opinion pieces, and analyses from various perspectives, while lectures by the very individuals engaged in the early struggle gave us the means to separate the wheat from the chaff. Most importantly, we discovered the Algerian writers Mohammed Dib, Mouloud Feraoun, Mouloud Mammeri, and a bright and punchy columnist in *Alger Républicain* who was far younger than we ever imagined: Kateb Yacine. All this information nonetheless failed to lead us to an answer to the question that became our obsession: How could we get in contact with the organizers of the November 1, 1954, attacks? Who were they? We knew that neither the local nor the French press would bring us answers.

From the beginning, that same press had condemned the liberation war. Even the very sympathetic *Alger Républicain* had announced a "suicide attack" in its headline the next day, earning our profound disappointment. Then, throughout that academic year, the media regularly announced—with supporting photographs—the arrests or deaths of individuals we all knew to be activists, even if the press labeled them common criminals. The more the French press downplayed the November 1 movement's activism and distorted its nature, the less we believed the media and the stronger our conviction grew that this movement was the single best way to respond to French colonialism. Several other factors reinforced our profound certainty. First was the wholly unjust nature and utter violence—exercised throughout all aspects of daily life for over a century—of the French policy of colonization by mass settlement. We had no need of the press nor of lectures and debates to understand this truth, not amidst our people, deprived of their territory, their history, their identity, and even their name. We did not have the right to be "Algerians," we were the "Muslim French." The land that we tilled with our own hands was robbed and raped on a daily basis, while our people were reduced to "native" status; the Native Code[8] denied us not only the rights of citizenship but even basic recognition as a people. Samia and I knew this reality intimately. We never let our membership in the very small privileged class lull us into believing otherwise, staying grounded thanks to our families—both of which were very vigilant in educating us on our historical context and identity—and our personal experiences in the French education system. Besides the press, there were other, more precise and credible reports passed secretly by word of mouth, reaching us via Samia's family, in the *hammam*, or even at the university. This information so sharply contradicted the reports in the colonial press that it revealed the latter to be nothing more than a crude propaganda tool.

The only domain where women enjoyed unquestioned, inviolable sovereignty was the *hammam*, where women of all backgrounds, social standings, and ages gathered in solidarity, momentarily free from the twin powers that imposed themselves upon us—men and the French. The *hammam*'s magical steam could sweep away all of their economic, social, and political barriers. This was where the details of great exploits and achievements reached us, narrated as only Algerian women could do. They wove tales like they wove carpets or embroidery, with meticulously recounted places, dates, names, and other minutiae. As if anticipating our imaginations' wanderings, they also added links to our own history and legends, our illustrious ancestors, our mythical heroes, and even to the *souhaba*—the companions of our Prophet Mohammed (peace be upon him). In the *hammam*, the women told us that henceforth our heroes were called *moudjahidine*, or combatants, and that those who were killed by the French army would be known as *chouhada*, or martyrs. In their accounts, the *moudjahidine*, cloaked in a divine aura, were all tall, strong, handsome, and virtually invincible because, even when dead, they had the ability to reappear in another form. We lapped up the words, not missing a single detail of their stories, which could be divulged only in this haven of trust and secrecy.

---

8. France's Native Code, or Code de l'Indigénat, was a series of laws that defined the status of indigenous peoples living under French colonial rule, granting them rights inferior to those of French citizens and subjecting them to a special legal regime. Largely developed in Algeria in the nineteenth century, the code came to be applied across France's global empire.

After every visit to the *hammam* we emerged galvanized, mobilized for the cause, and more convinced than ever that the movement led by the November 1 attackers was alive and well and firmly rooted in the popular will—in strong contrast to the colonial propaganda. It was a real revolutionary movement. But our enthusiasm inevitably collided with the fact that Samia and I still couldn't get in touch with these revolutionaries. We rushed home from the *hammam* each time, hurrying to share the wealth of information we had gleaned with Samia's mother. Mama Zhor was a direct descendant (on her mother's side) of the Emir Abdelkader, our country's early revolutionary hero, and she seemed to have an almost instinctive national consciousness. She was always fully committed and would later even go so far as to clash with her husband to cover for us. From the start she had shown herself to be a willing accomplice, and we considered her our closest ally.

It was during a heated debate in Samia's family in November 1954 that we saw just how far each person's devotion to independence might go. One weekend, Samia's father came home carrying the declaration from the *ouléma* clerics' association that unequivocally condemned the outbreak of the liberation war as well as its instigators. He read us the statement and tried to sell us on the *ouléma*'s "more realistic" and less dangerous alternative. Knowing that we had been in favor of the liberation war from the start, this was no doubt his attempt to head off any desire we might have to support the *Novembriste* camp and stamp out our enthusiasm once and for all. While we dared not push back hard against Monsieur Lakhdari, who was a learned *qadi*, after all, his wife Mama Zhor came to our rescue, opposing his arguments firmly and presenting her opinions with unwavering conviction. She concluded with an appeal that caused her husband to change the subject and stalk out, slamming the door behind him: "On one side are France and its allies, and on the other there are the young revolutionaries who want to liberate the country. We must decide who we are and choose sides. For or against our country's independence, whatever the cost. Your *ouléma* don't have the right to draft such a declaration about our fighters."

From that day forward, our view of sweet Mama Zhor was never the same, even though we already loved and respected her greatly before this incident. Where before she had been content merely to guide us from a distance in between her household chores, her actions on that day aged us by ten years by showing us the importance of experiences lived, contemplated, communicated, and ripened into true wisdom. She had given us the argument that would forever stay with us and that would guide us toward the liberation movement. In fact, Mama Zhor had expressed loud and clear just how we felt inside, in our own confused way that we could not yet name and so dared not speak aloud to anyone. In doing so, she not only stated the equation in clear terms, but went beyond that and forced us—her husband, her daughter, and me—to choose sides. From that instant, our choice was made: our camp was that of the Novembristes and the war of national liberation. All this with Mama Zhor's complicity, cover, and reassurance.

Our debates with Malek every weekend throughout 1954 pushed us to ask him for more information and publications. We suspected he was close to the UDMA and Ferhat Abbas, but he practiced absolute discretion regarding his outside activities and would never confirm it for us.

The final reason for our choice to join the leaders of November 1, 1954, was our country's situation beginning in May 1945. I was ten and a half years old then, and what I remember is an atmosphere of fear, repression, and arrests, with frightened whispers between the adults at home. Sometimes groups of men came to meet with my parents at night. It was an atmosphere of total secrecy and danger. As soon as they locked me in the kitchen with the other women and children, I knew there were strangers in the house, and even without seeing them I knew they were our people. I knew never to ask questions or talk of it with anyone, for fear of endangering my father and the whole family. Nobody had told me so; I simply knew it without explanation, instinctively. Especially since, some time ago, my paternal uncle had had to disappear to escape the wave of arrests targeting young people in our area. When I asked where he was and why he had disappeared, the older women took on a grave tone, lecturing me and making me promise not to ask questions or to speak of the family's affairs outside the home. They managed to inculcate all of us children with a culture of secrecy and distrust of others.

At the same time, they taught us songs which, they explained, we could only hum among ourselves at home, in a whisper, and never outside. I understood much later, in high school, that these were the nationalist PPA anthem and a tribute sung to our martyrs killed by the colonial forces in Sétif on May 8, 1945. That day, which Mimi, Samia, and I revisited less than a decade later, would constitute for us—without any doubt—an irreparable and definitive break with the colonial system. Samia and Mama Zhor, who hailed from Constantine, not far from Sétif, carried the massacres with them as a precise, vivid, and painful memory. Every weekend Mama Zhor reserved a few hours, almost like a ritual, first to recount to us the courage of our people, who had come out unarmed and empty-handed to demonstrate for their right to freedom on the very day of Europe's liberation—to which they had contributed by the thousands as members of the French army. Then she recounted the savagery, cruelty, and barbarism of the French in the face of the demonstrators. Tens of thousands of families were bereaved, especially in Sétif, Guelma, and Kherrata. Some of Mama Zhor's own relatives and friends had been massacred, while others were imprisoned and subjected to the most inhumane of tortures. She would repeat their names and describe how they had been eliminated or tortured. Many of them had ended up in a mass grave. Mama Zhor always came back to the Scouts—children massacred in spite of their total innocence—in Sétif, the evils of the colonial officials in Guelma, and the gaping wound of the humiliations heaped upon the women, old men, and children of Bejaia and the nearby Babor Mountains by the thugs De Gaulle had sent to quell the demonstrators. It was a Tuesday, the market day in Sétif and many of our people, including dirt-poor farmers and mountain villagers, had come into town.

They had joined the demonstration called by the PPA, falling in behind the Muslim Scouts and young students—one of whom was from Mama Zhor's family. One of the youth was wearing our red, white, and green flag, flown for the first time in public. At the sight of the flag, the Europeans flew into a rage and began shooting indiscriminately. With our brothers unarmed and defenseless, it was carnage. A two-week manhunt followed, with the French raiding everywhere from Sétif to Constantine, Bordj Bou Arréridj to Kherrata and Guelma.

In Guelma, the deputy governor, a sinister man named Achiary, headed a militia of Europeans that conducted a hunt of unprecedented brutality against the Arabs. They even invented a new extermination method: they threw adults and children into ditches and poured quicklime on top of them. De Gaulle sent the air force to bomb the poor survivors, women and girls fleeing devastated farmsteads around Kherrata and Sétif. After two weeks of carnage and tens of thousands killed without even a proper burial, the French tapped Général Raymond Duval, a friend of De Gaulle's, to organize a mock surrender ceremony on our behalf, heaping further humiliation and cruelty onto our suffering. As Mama Zhor recounted to us, in the narrow plain of Melbou, near Bejaia, this general and his army gathered the Babor Mountain peoples—women, children, and the elderly included—and required them to kneel and ask for forgiveness, declare their submission, and proclaim, "We are dogs, and long live France." On May 11, the French also organized a show of force by marching the infantry, navy, and air force before the transfixed "natives."

Less than ten years later, it was 1954 and our struggle had begun. At this point in her story, Mama Zhor would inevitably burst into tears, crying, "*Wach yaqdar el meyyet fi yed el ghassal?*" (What can a corpse do in the hands of its embalmer?) Then, almost begging, she would exhort us to "never forget our dead and never trust France—our enemy and the enemy of our Prophet." We gave our word, vowing to avenge our martyrs one day.

Each May 8 was a holiday; while for our European comrades it was V-E Day, a day of celebration and joy, it was quite different for us: a day of mourning and commemoration. From eleventh grade in 1953, when we were nineteen, we shifted from an emotional commemoration to a celebration of political conviction to a voluntary remembrance.

The same atmosphere of restlessness and excitement I had left in Vialar also reigned at the University of Algiers. Samia and I had found Mimi, who, true to form, fit in with bewildering ease in this world that seemed totally new to us. Mimi had enrolled at the Faculty of Arts. Unlike us, she had friends among both the Muslim and European students. Naturally, our stuffy attitude amused her no end; she called us "the two little nuns" and tried to loosen us up, laughing all the while. Mimi, whose family hailed from Algiers, knew absolutely everything about the city's chic side, the university and its student clubs, and all the ideas circulating there. When we arrived there as novices, it was she who helped us get our bearings, pointing out the leaders, activists, and supporters of each current: the Communists, the Christian left, the local chapter of the Association of North African Muslim Students (AEMAN), and the *ultras*—the infamous gang of *pied-noirs*[9] thugs, who by then were already led by the sinister Pierre Lagaillarde. Mimi was an active member of the AEMAN and its women's section. Like any good activist, she did everything she could to recruit us. Her timing was good, as the university's AEMAN chapter was due to hold its general assembly to review its activity report for the past year and elect its new leadership.

Mimi deployed magnificent arguments, explaining that the campaign for the election of officers was in full swing and was very heated because it included student activists of various national parties—the MTLD, the

---

9. *Pieds-noirs*, which translates literally to "black feet," was the term used to denote European settlers in French Algeria who, over 132 years of settlement in Algeria, had developed a culture partly distinct from that of metropolitan France.

UDMA, the *oulémas*, and the Communists. She invited us to join the AEMAN in order to vote and influence the selection of its leaders. Despite her considerable powers of persuasion, we consistently met her advances with polite, cold, stubborn refusal. Our choice was already made. We knew exactly what we wanted: to join the ranks of those who had launched the events of November 1, 1954. Our only problem was how to get in touch with them. Also, we knew from our readings, from films on the anti-Nazi resistance, and from our discussions with Malek that the most critical quality of clandestine militants was their absolute discretion and ability to avoid detection by the enemy. We dared not explain all that to Mimi, who at best would have laughed in our faces for our pretention and, at worst, might have dissuaded us by recalling the dangers of the terrible repression that the French press did not hesitate to hint at. In the face of our silence, Mimi unveiled her best argument: "Listen, girls, everyone knows who you are and what you're made of. But all the same, you can't possibly think that you'll spend your university years as solitary little girls, unaffected by the AEMAN except for being looked at by its members as sympathizers of the colonial administration."

Mimi managed to rattle us with that argument, even though, in substance, we continued to think that its meetings, general assemblies, and journal articles were not at all the response that the country's situation demanded. Nonetheless, Samia, more stubborn than a mule, stood firm and announced that it was impossible for her to attend the general assembly anyway, since its proceedings began at six o'clock, after the end of classes, and her family's rules required her home no later than six-thirty. As for me, always a good sport, I reluctantly agreed to accompany Mimi, but not without a heavy heart and anger at having to violate a rule that Samia and I had sworn to and had never before transgressed: to remain completely anonymous and unknown to the French intelligence services, which of course followed everyone's activities. Mimi was happy, no doubt because she could now announce that she had a new recruit; as for me, I was furious at myself.

The next day I went with Mimi to an AEMAN assembly for the first time. When we arrived, the lobby was already swarming with a noisy crowd of young people (including a few young women) who slowly made their way into the dining hall, where a podium had been erected on a makeshift stage. I filed in behind Mimi, who greeted some, called out to others, shot a remark at one group, and laughed at the jokes that abounded along her route. My friend was so popular that she eclipsed everyone around—to my great satisfaction, because it allowed me to pass totally unnoticed. I huddled in a chair in a dark back corner, more interested in watching the faces of the participants than in following the debates, of which I heard little. Yet this general assembly elevated the student activists from the separatist MTLD to the leadership of the University of Algiers's AEMAN chapter.

Mimi gave us the news the next day. She still had not given up hope of recruiting us and continued to pester us, proposing that we present newly published books, like Malek Bennabi's *Vocation of Islam,* or write articles for the magazine, particularly on the issue of "Algerian women and the veil." Finally fed up, Samia and I explained to her firmly and plainly what we thought: that however noble their objectives might be, the AEMAN's activities nonetheless remained astonishingly futile and completely out of proportion to the daily sacrifices of those who had taken up arms to free the country. In our youthful radicalism, we barked at our poor Mimi, "This is a moment for neither meetings nor articles. It is a call to arms."

But Mimi, every bit as intelligent and convinced of her cause as we were of ours, retorted: "Of course! But weapons need meetings and words to carry them."

"We have the same objective," we replied, "but perhaps not the same paths for reaching it."

These tough exchanges did nothing to harm our strong friendship, and we continued to view each other's choices with respect. Our goal was the same: to liberate the country. *from settler colonialism*

In Search of the November 1 Organizers

Every day, Samia and I reminded ourselves of the soundness of our decision to remain discreet, avoid attracting attention with public declarations, and preserve our anonymity, despite the rumors that labeled us as supporters of the administration. Our approach was clear, planned, and decided. We wanted to be recruited by the fighters' "secret organization" to mobilize in Algiers and, little by little, to convince them to dispatch us to the armed groups, since we were convinced that it was essential to bring the war into the French neighborhoods and the European city.

In 1955, Algiers, like every other Algerian city, was divided in two: on one side, the Arab quarters, and on the other, the European quarters, separated by an intangible yet impassable wall that imposed a *de facto* apartheid. As Mouloud Mammeri once wrote, "Standing before the wall, one saw the ferocity of those guarding its gates." The war unfolded in the Arab towns and quarters, in the countryside, and in the mountains. The European quarters bathed in a revolting tranquility compared to the terrible repression that the indigenous civilian population suffered.

Samia and I thought we had huge advantages: we were two women with a European air and allure and perfect mastery of the French language and culture. We were from well-to-do families and totally unknown to the French security services. We were certain that we could be of great assistance to our fighters because we could easily sneak everywhere without raising the Europeans' suspicions the way an average "Mohamed" or "Fatima" would. But our problem remained unchanged: how to get in touch with "the organization." Through whom? We decided to scrutinize and listen carefully to everyone in our environment in hopes of detecting clues or someone who would lead us to those we sought. We started at the university, with Mimi's AEMAN friends, but it seemed that in this spring of 1955, the new chapter leaders were focusing their efforts and discussions on creating an organization strictly reserved for Algerian Muslim students—the future General Union of Muslim Algerian Students, or UGEMA. And what links did they have with the fighters? We detected none. Among our friends and family we found no clues either. Everywhere we turned, we hit a wall. And yet, somewhere, we knew the Novembristes existed.

All the while, we assiduously attended our courses, practicums, and tutorials, determined to succeed in the year-end exam in June 1955. For me, failure was simply unthinkable—it would have meant my definitive return to Vialar and my confinement, dashing any hopes of making contact with the fighters. We also spent many hours in the law library, where we often crossed paths with the second- and third-year Muslim students.

One day in the spring of 1955, I arrived and ran right into my old philosophy professor, Madame Czarnecki, whom I remembered so fondly. We fell into each other's arms like old friends, then went for a coffee and fell to chatting about what the press had euphemistically dubbed "the events." I could tell that Madame Czarnecki was as humanistic and progressive as ever, she who had suffered so much from Nazism and had seen so many parents and relatives perish in the concentration camps. Naturally we discussed the notion of resistance, its limits, the forms it could take, and the radical choice of armed struggle. I discovered that I shared more than friendship with Madame Czarnecki; we also shared a solidarity and a thirst for justice, just like two starving people could share a piece of bread. She engaged with me not from upon the pedestal that she deserved as an excellent philosophy teacher, but from her own memories of suffering, unbearable injustice, and absolute evil.

She recounted the armed resistance by the Jews of the Warsaw Ghetto, and the massacres that followed. With that example, she tried to convince me that, while she understood the causes that had pushed the Novembristes to take up arms, she feared for the future of this armed movement. It risked being crushed, she said, by a disproportionate imbalance of force. She tried to explain the odds facing a poorly armed movement battling a strong, established state with a professional army and seasoned police force. At one point, I countered that if I had been in the Warsaw Ghetto, I would have been on the side of those who had decided to die with weapons in hand, especially since they were condemned to perish anyway. Madame Czarnecki's eyes filled with tears. She took me in her arms and begged me to understand that not all Europeans were the same: that many sympathized with us, and that the issue was not a matter of ethnicity but of justice and freedom. She invited me to attend one of the meetings she organized in her home each Thursday to bring together Europeans and Muslims. While my timid, reserved nature would normally have pushed me to decline her invitation, I decided to accept. The following Thursday, after my classes, as promised, I came to Madame Czarnecki's large apartment in the modernist Aéro-Habitat building.

I was so paralyzed by the thought of having to enter a *salon* full of strangers alone that I struggled to convince myself to go. But what ultimately pushed me was my hope of perhaps meeting someone who could finally put me in touch with "the organization." I did my best to be among the last to arrive, and Madame Czarnecki greeted me with her usual kindness. She pulled me into the salon, which already burbled with conversations and laughter, and introduced me to all present as "one of the most brilliant and engaging students I taught in philosophy class at the Lycée Fromentin." I found a seat in a corner and began following the discussion, which of course centered on the situation in the country, as well as how it was covered by the local and metropolitan press, notably the leftist *France-Observateur* and *L'Express* but also *L'Humanité*, *Le Canard Enchaîné*, *La Croix*, and *Alger Républicain*. I immediately noticed that I was the only Muslim woman, though several of my male co-religionists were immediately recognizable thanks to the roll of their "r"—an identifying marker that they cultivated knowingly.

Needless to say, I didn't utter a single word, but my attention was particularly attracted by a young Algerian who was recounting facts that no newspaper had previously reported. I was sure because I devoured the press daily, from cover to cover. I concluded that his information was too specific not to have come straight from the source—the "secret organization." When we took leave of Madame Czarnecki, he approached me and introduced himself: Mahmoud Bouayad, an assistant librarian at the National Library. I introduced myself in turn: Zohra Drif, first-year law student. He did not conceal his surprise and repeated in his heavy accent, "Law student?" We decided to walk a bit together since we were headed the same way, he to the National Library in the lower Casbah, and I to the bus stop and then the Ben Aknoun dorms. There again he let his astonishment show, repeating, "The Ben Aknoun dorms?"

As we walked, I trembled, imagining his thoughts: "A curious Muslim girl who studies law and lives on the Ben Aknoun campus, where the boys' and girls' dorms are side by side!" At the same time, I glanced nervously right and left, examining every passerby, searching for one with the probing eyes of one of my father's spies, who my mother had warned me would be surveilling me everywhere, at all times! My frenzied, frantic search for the Novembristes ultimately led me to break many of our sacred taboos, though for a good cause. I was walking alongside an unknown young man at nightfall! But what did I care—if he could be the one to finally put me in contact with the legendary fighters, come what may!

We walked a long way, during which Monsieur Bouayad, having clearly recognized the state of terror in which I found myself, took it upon himself to lead the conversation, which boiled down to an interrogation about my family, my region, and my plans for after graduation, punctuated from time to time by his fraternal advice. I answered his questions in monosyllables. When we finally arrived at the Place du Gouvernement, he handed me his card and assured me that he was at my disposal for any research needs or book recommendations. I thanked him and boarded the bus.

I returned triumphantly to the dorm that night. The next day, I found Samia in our little café and excitedly told her all about the meeting at Madame Czarnecki's, down to the last detail. She made me repeat what each of the attendees had said. Like me, she was particularly attracted to the words of Monsieur Bouayad, and came to the same conclusion. Here was the contact we had been seeking for months; we absolutely had to find a way to meet him again. Decisive, she announced that it was up to me alone to reestablish contact quickly. Her own presence might raise his suspicions, she explained: "Those people are real clandestine operatives who only trust those they know well." She added, "If he learned that you had told me all this, he would lose trust in you and cut off all contact. He trusts you, since he's given you his card, and you absolutely must not spoil this trust. It's our only chance!" With that question resolved, we moved on: How to bring up "the secret organization"? As usual, Samia intended to plan every step, to rehearse it all like a play—from my arrival at the National Library to raising the subject in question to the resolution. She made me memorize my lines, refusing to let me take this decisive step without having thoroughly prepared, leaving nothing to chance or improvisation.

I decided to go Thursday afternoon after class. On the way, I walked past Ketchaoua Mosque, a majestic monument with two imposing minarets that the Europeans had distorted into a cathedral, though we "natives" continued to call it Ketchaoua Mosque. I continued for a few meters, then turned into an alleyway where, on the left, I reached the National Library, housed in the beautiful palace of the former Ottoman governor, Mustapha Pacha. I found the thick wooden entry door open and passed inside to the central courtyard, which was surrounded by several rooms. I looked everywhere among the people on the ground floor—the only part open to the public—but could not find Monsieur Bouayad anywhere.

After a while, I thought of fleeing, fuming at Samia for leaving me alone to face such an unprecedented situation. But how could I retreat now, so close to our goal? I decided to ask one of the librarians where I could find his colleague Monsieur Bouayad. "Do you have an appointment?" he replied. I hesitated for an instant, then said yes, and gave him my name. I was preparing to leave empty-handed, furious at myself, at Samia, and at these mythical characters who made me act against all common sense, when the librarian returned and asked me to follow him.

Monsieur Bouayad's office was on the top floor. It looked cramped and stuffy, with books covering every surface and piled on the desk he sat behind. He rose to greet me, showing no sign of surprise, and asked me to sit before him.

My confidence was failing me, but the books came to my rescue; to revive my confidence, I asked if I could have a look at the tomes displayed on the shelves, the ones decorated in Arabic calligraphy. He accepted graciously and showed me several, explaining the spelling differences between the Maghrebi, Levantine, Persian, and Iraqi Kufic texts. After explaining this and more of the illuminated manuscripts' secrets, Monsieur Bouayad—who certainly knew that I had not made the trip to the library to see some hidden tomes I had not even known existed—kindly asked me how he could help me. For an instant, I panicked, trying in vain to remember the different scenarios that Samia and I had envisioned and even rehearsed, before deciding to dive in and recite my speech from my heart, without looking at him. I explained, stammering, how I had been struck by the precision of the unreported facts he had recounted during our first meeting at Madame Czarnecki's salon, where I had deduced that he was certainly in contact with members of the "secret organization" that I had been seeking so ardently ever since November 1, 1954, in order to fight alongside them. I didn't raise my eyes, and he sat silently while I continued my monologue, determined not to stop until I had fully outlined my request. I stayed the course, explaining how and why I wanted to participate in the armed struggle, and finished by presenting the advantages of having a recruit like me, with a European look, educated in French and thus able to "pass" anywhere around town. I insisted that "the organization" would certainly need people like me to operate in the European city. I concluded by begging him to forward my request, even if he considered it inadmissible. After what seemed to me an interminable silence, Monsieur Bouayad asked me where I had gotten this crazy idea that he would be in contact with any such secret organization. If I was lacking for hobbies, he said, he would put me in touch with some women who led a charitable association.

Only then did I look up at him. I brushed his proposal aside by stating how passé I found the idea of charitable activities when our people were being arrested, tortured, and massacred, especially when the best among us were sacrificing their lives for our country's freedom. With that, I stood up, thanked him for his hospitality and informed him that I intended to return to have an answer to my request. And with that, I left his office without even looking at him.

Much later, while I was living in hiding during the infamous "Battle of Algiers," I would recognize the folly of my approach in light of the terrible pressure to which activists and their families were subjected and the round-the-clock surveillance that Muslim intellectuals suffered. I would also come to appreciate the composure that poor Monsieur Bouayad had demonstrated. Indeed, he did not know me; I might have been a decoy or an "administrative agent," as we said in those days. I met him again much later, after independence. Since he didn't bring the episode up, neither did I.

It was March 1955 and, despite my failure at the National Library, Samia and I continued our quest, ever on the lookout for a sign of how we might join "the organization." The second semester of the academic year passed quickly, and we were soon facing our first-year law exams. We plunged into studying, working like maniacs, and both of us succeeded brilliantly that June. So I returned to my family in Vialar, where a welcome surprise awaited me: as a reward for my efforts and brilliant results at university, my father had decided that, in early August, I would accompany him to France, where he went every summer for the natural thermal spas. This particular summer, the destination was Luchon, a spa town in the Pyrenees. For the first time in my life I would discover France, this country that had colonized us and whose history and literature so fascinated me. In the final days of July, my father and I returned to Algiers to take the plane, a double-decker Breguet Deux-Ponts, to Toulouse—a new experience for me. From there we took the train to the mountains and the Luchon resort. I spent a month reading in my room and all over the sprawling hotel grounds and walking with my father in the village and the surrounding countryside. Obviously, everything was different from back home, but what struck me most was the peaceful silence in which the villagers of Luchon lived. At times, I wondered if these peaceful inhabitants knew where Algeria was, or even that there *was* a land called Algeria. In Luchon, we bought the local newspapers as well as the national ones and found a seat on a café terrace to read them and sip lemonade. Like a protective bubble, the village's ambiance and the distance that separated us from our country served to dampen the echoes of the events that the newspapers brought us.

One afternoon, my father handed me a local newspaper which indicated—with the photos to prove it—that the head of the Tunisian nationalists, Habib Bourguiba, was also in Luchon for a cure. Of course, I knew of and admired the Tunisians' and Moroccans' struggles for their independence, and the names of their leaders were familiar to me. The next afternoon, as I was reading in the hotel's grand park, I saw a young man wrapped in a cloak and wearing a scarf walking toward us, surrounded by three men of considerable heft. It was Bourguiba! I wanted to run to him, greet him, to thank him on behalf of all our peoples for the fight he led, but my father dissuaded me, explaining that his bodyguards would never let me get close. So I had to satisfy myself with watching, enthralled, and telling myself that one day we too would have a leader who would walk that way, surrounded by bodyguards to signify his importance in our eyes and the world's.

3

FIRST CONTACT WITH THE FLN

Another Massacre, Another Turning Point

During the last week of our stay in Luchon, the metropolitan press reported in its usual style on some disturbing developments in our country: "hordes" had overrun Philippeville (today's Skikda) and the entire coast of the North Constantinois and committed "abuses" against European property and persons. In response, the colonial authorities had been obliged to restore order and arrest "dangerous individuals already wanted by the police." From that point, I had one desire: to return home to get the real story from my brother Kader and his friends.

When my father and I finally returned, the atmosphere in Vialar was heavy and tense, the "native" population more anxious and insular than ever. My uncles and brothers, especially Kader, reported to us what had really happened on August 20 at Skikda, a region that had already paid so dearly. Ever since the massacres of May 8, 1945, the population of the eastern Aurès Mountains in eastern Algeria and that whole region had never felt any relief from harassment, repression, and pressure, not to mention the immense misery in which they were trying to survive—especially after November

1, 1954, since it was from there that the guerrilla army was launched. After the outbreak of the war of liberation, the colonial authorities had unleashed their troops on the farmsteads and their inhabitants. Civilians were hit with fierce repression and unheard-of massacres, especially during "Operation Violet" and "Operation Veronica" in January and February 1955. The colonial media machine worked nonstop for months, exalting its "cleansing" of "outlaws" and *fellagas*—this last word coined from the Algerian Arabic word for "explode." It was a real psychological bludgeoning intended to reassure the Europeans and terrorize the "natives" by wiping out any leanings of sympathy toward the Novembristes. After months of steamrolling, of abuses of all sorts, of collective punishment and devastating napalm fires, our civilian population of the North Constantinois was cornered, overwhelmed, and desperate. On August 20, they had risen up across all the towns and villages to put our old saying into practice: Better to die fighting than to die for nothing! Armed with sticks, pitchforks, scythes, and knives, the poor mountain people attacked everything that in their eyes represented the *roumis* and their unjust power.

They killed 120 people, including seventy Europeans and fifty assimilated Muslims whom they considered traitors. The Europeans were shocked. Fear and suspicion were everywhere, and the local and metropolitan press spread word of the "*fellagas'* atrocities." Of course, the colonial administration's reaction was not long in coming; Governor Jacques Soustelle ordered a repeat of the massacres and collective abuses of May 8, 1945. The colonial army implemented the order, assisted by European civilian militias thirsty for vengeance, with the mayor of Philippeville, one Monsieur Benquet-Crevaux, at their head. Governor Soustelle himself gave the orders to shoot the prisoners, and bomb their farms, and burn the land with napalm. Thousands of men were rounded up in the Skikda stadium and coldly gunned down. With a lump in his throat, Kader recounted how the dead lay everywhere, so numerous that they had to use a bulldozer to dig trenches to bury them. My face bathed in tears, I asked him the number. He replied, his eyes red with rage, that Soustelle himself had cited 1,200 dead, but that the *kleb ben kleb* (dogs, sons of dogs) must have massacred no less than 15,000. We had no way to verify the exact toll.

When I left for Luchon, I had left behind a playful, exuberant younger brother full of silly ideas and always ready with a joke. But I returned to find that in those few weeks Kader had aged several years, filled to the brim with a pent-up anger so strong that it darkened his gaze. My mother, aware of this worrying change in her son, wondered aloud, "Why did these poor mountain people choose to head toward certain death anyway?" At this, Kader exploded, finally giving free rein to the rage that inhabited him, "But mother, don't you know what those 'mountain people,' as you call them, have suffered every day since November 1, 1954, just like all your brothers everywhere and even here in our home? I'm sure you could never have stood even a hundredth of what the *roumis* inflicted on them. So yes, if the *roumis* want war, they will have it!" That day I felt much closer to my Kader, even if he had become more reserved, more secretive, and more mysterious than usual. I understood that my brother was completely committed to the fighters. I didn't need to ask him anything, I just understood, that was all.

When in November 1955 my brothers and I returned to our schools in Algiers, we all noticed that the atmosphere was the same everywhere. The rupture between us and the Europeans, military or civilian, was consummate and irreversible. They were on one side and we were on the other. Worse still, for us it was now "us or them." The events in the North Constantinois and the fierce repression that followed had dug a fissure, now unbridgeable, between the *roumis* and the Muslims. Distrust, fear, and insecurity were all around.

In each "Mohamed" and "Fatima," the Europeans now saw a *fellaga* in the making. Samia and I viewed any rapprochement with the Europeans and any participation—even electoral—in the colonial system as a betrayal, pure and simple. Far from intimidating us or tempering our enthusiasm, the climate of insecurity and widespread suspicion reaffirmed our conviction that a struggle to the death had been launched against the colonial system, and pushed us more than ever to participate actively however we could.

Back at the university, I found the same excitement and the same impatience for battle, which was already leading us toward the inevitable confrontation with the *ultras*. Indeed, in December 1955 the Algiers section of the UGEMA had barely just released the list of its officers—among them two female students, Hafsa Bisker as secretary general and Zoulikha Bekaddour as treasurer, for the first time—when they were confronted with the arrest of four of their members whom the police suspected of belonging to our country's nascent independence movement, the Front de Libération Nationale (FLN): Amara Rachid, Mohamed Lounis, Mustapha Saber, and Ahmed Taouti. The UGEMA leaders immediately organized meetings and rallies at the university and the dormitories to denounce the arrests and define the actions to be taken to ensure the release of our brothers. Even high school students were not left out. Kader, then in eleventh grade at the high school in Ben Aknoun, often came to visit me on the residential campus, accompanied by his friends (including Miloud Brahimi, who would go on to become a prominent lawyer and human rights champion) and bring me information and organizing instructions. Delegations of university and high school students were sent—some to police stations, some to the prosecutors in Algiers and Tizi Ouzou, some to the colonial administrations—to locate our arrested brothers, protest their illegal detainment, and demand their release.

To show the protest movement's strength, demonstrate its broad representation, and affirm its members' determination, the UGEMA declared a general strike for January 20, 1956. All the Muslim high school and university students participated in the strike; the mobilization and solidarity were total. Our four arrested brothers received provisional releases, and we later learned that they went immediately into hiding in the *maquis*—that is to say, in the mountains and the bush outside our major cities—to join the armed struggle and avoid the masquerade of a trial that certainly awaited them. We viewed this result as a victory, which further strengthened our fighting spirit and mobilization. At the same time, in addition to the colonial regime, we were obliged to face the university's racist *ultras*. Besides fighting us, the *ultras* struggled with perhaps even more hatred against the progressive European students' associations, among them Communists and Pierre Chaulet's leftist Catholics.

Nor did the *ultras* spare anticolonial students and teachers, like André Mandouze. One day they decided to violently block Mandouze from reaching his classroom and teaching because they considered him a *fellaga*. The UGEMA decided to break this siege. All the Muslim students mobilized, with the progressive European students alongside them. Despite the massive presence of *ultras*, with their unspeakable methods, Mandouze managed to deliver his entire lecture, surrounded by our activists for his protection.

The clashes with the *ultras* continued unabated and with increasing violence. Then, one day, the *ultras* launched a general strike to protest a measure announced by Soustelle that they felt was too favorable to Muslims. Soustelle and the entire French administration, aware of the widening gap between them and the Muslims and the dangers this could pose for the survival of the colonial system, wanted to win over some of the "natives." So they decided to open an accelerated training center for administrative staff, aimed at young Muslims who had never completed high school. Never mind that this represented just a drop in the ocean of illiteracy, unemployment, and absolute misery in which the overwhelming majority of our people lived—the *ultras* considered it too generous toward the Muslims. They called for a general strike against the plan and organized what they called a "university blockade": a human chain to wall off the campus and prevent all access.

In response, the UGEMA called on students to break the blockade, and the inevitable happened. We overtook their cordon by force, reaching the classrooms amid a confused melee of blows and insults in all directions. As usual, Samia and I used our big backpacks as shields, wrapped our heads with scarves to cushion any blows, and plowed into the fray like bulls. My brother Kader had already taught me all the best techniques for self-defense and breaking human chains, just in case. It was doubtlessly during one of these fights that some student had noticed Samia and me. Several days after the clash with the *ultras*, at the end of morning classes, a young man approached me and asked if I was Mademoiselle Drif. Of medium height, thin and well groomed, with the complexion and accent of a European, I figured him for a Spaniard. I immediately replied yes, and before I could even ask what he wanted of me, he introduced himself: "I am Boualem, the brother of your friend Saléha Oussedik."

Contact at Last

Saléha Oussedik had been a fellow student, one year behind us at the Lycée Fromentin.

We knew her well and thought highly of her, since we had shared seats at the "pork-free table" for several years. She was an excellent student. Of course, I wondered what had become of Saléha after the *baccalauréat*, which she must have passed with flying colors the year after me. I asked in what university she was enrolled. Her brother Boualem, embarrassed, explained that their father had refused to allow Saléha to attend university, since it could not guarantee gender segregation like the Lycée Fromentin could. But he had conceded to her studying at the teachers' training college in Bouzaréah, which offered girls-only boarding. Saléha had suffered greatly from her sentence, which she viewed as an enormous injustice, but it was unthinkable to oppose the *pater familia*; being a teacher, he said, was still better than being a housewife! I told him he had a lot of nerve to accept Saléha's fate and then to come and speak to me, a young woman free to pursue higher studies like he was, at the university that was so "dangerous" for his sister. I turned my back on him and asked that he not speak to me again.

I recounted the incident to Samia, proud of my reaction, which left me feeling like I had avenged our friend. But Samia reminded me that Saléha had talked often of Boualem, who was very close to her, very nationalistic, and full of ideas that their father considered dangerous for his son and his family. She reminded me of Saléha's love and admiration for her brother, more specifically his courage and total commitment. Samia proposed that I resume contact with him; neither he nor our parents would find fault if we were to befriend him, since he was Saléha's brother and she would surely have talked of us to him before. "I'm sure this time is it. He'll be the one to put us in contact with 'the organization.' Zohra, you dream too much to observe closely, but I already knew what he looked like and recognized him among the shock troops in our battles with the *ultras*."

Thus it was decided to reestablish contact with Boualem Oussedik, and it was up to me, once again, to do it. I accepted without complaint, as the desire to do battle with our colonizers burned more strongly in me than any other consideration. A few days later, sitting in the same spot as the last

Boualem Oussedik, her link to the FLN

time, I saw him climb the stairs. I rose, determined to finally broach the subject. It was disconcertingly simple. He explained that he fully shared and understood my reaction to the fate imposed on his sister, but that he had been unable to do anything to help her. Our conversation flowed from one subject to the next, and very soon we were chatting like old friends. We spoke of UGEMA and the AEMAN women's group. I explained that, without doubting the sincerity of their nationalist convictions, I found their tactics out of sync with what was required. As students, favored by chance at birth, we owed it to ourselves to engage in the armed struggle, participate fully, and invest ourselves completely. I spoke at length, with passion but with composure, and Boualem Oussedik listened with unconcealed interest. When I had finished, I expected him to challenge me by defending the validity of the circles, articles, and UGEMA meetings, but to my surprise, he asked me on whose side I hoped to fight: The Mouvement National Algérien (MNA), the FLN, or the Parti Communiste Algérien (PCA)? I turned his question back on him: "If I told you the FLN, could you put me in touch with them?" He responded, calmly and ever confident, "I'll try."

I couldn't believe it. I stared at him, incredulous, searching for something to reassure me he was serious or, if not, a sign that I should melt into the ground from shame and fear.

Boualem Oussedik did not flinch. His face, so cheerful at the beginning of our conversation, was now as stiff as marble. We parted, me mute and him repeating "I'll try" in place of goodbye. We had spoken for two hours, like brother and sister. We shared the same identity, the same painful memory of the horrors and injustices our people had suffered for so long, and, most remarkable of all, the same desire to confront our colonizers. This feeling of fraternal solidarity and tacit collusion is not something one decides on, nor is it something one proclaims aloud. You just live it. We were about to live it as fellow combatants, all throughout the Battle of Algiers and our time in prison. But we would also live it with the majority of the population, whatever their social standing.

When Samia joined me for class, she found me stunned and troubled. I fell into her arms and begged her to skip class so I could recount everything. Shocked but happy, she nodded and we skipped our classes for the first time. I recounted everything to her, down to the last detail—the discussion, questions, responses, the atmosphere, Boualem's expressions, and his attitude, alternately playful and grave. I gave special attention to the last part of our exchange: his questions, my own in response, and his enigmatic final phrase, "I'll try." I concluded my account by telling Samia: "You know, Boualem Oussedik is just like you and me, and Malek and Kader." Samia gazed at me silently for a moment, then said, "If you feel this way, then it's true! But we must not repeat our mistake at the National Library." Why had Boualem spoken so frankly, listened so patiently, and left open the door to some future collusion? Samia put it down to our long friendship with Saléha.

But we still couldn't say with certainty whether we should rejoice. We concluded that from now on we would never again miss any classes at the university and that we would be there every day, even during our free time, in hopes of hearing his answer. We spent a week waiting in torment and were finally preparing to abandon hope when destiny came knocking.

It was one of those beautifully sunny Algiers winter days. We were leaving the Morand Lecture Hall when we stumbled into Boualem Oussedik, who seemed to be holding the door an extra long time, perhaps looking for us. In a fun, playful mood, he spoke first, asking Samia, "If I'm not mistaken, you must be Samia Lakhdari!" Without hesitation and as naturally as can be, my friend extended her hand and said, "Yes, and you must be Boualem Oussedik, Saléha's brother." We exchanged some small talk before deciding to head out for a walk along Rue Michelet, which was packed with people. Without warning, the moment we had dreamed of for over a year was announced as if it were the most banal thing ever, by a grinning Boualem: "The two of you have an appointment at Laférièrre Square tomorrow afternoon at four o'clock sharp. You will go and sit on one of the benches, with the newspaper *Le Monde* resting visibly on your lap. A man will meet you."

Samia responded, "Laférièrre Square? That's just a short walk from the university, across from the Grande Poste!"

"Exactly," he replied.

Samia and I looked at each other, dumbfounded. I knew she was thinking the same thing as me: "An appointment at four o'clock, right in the heart of the European city, with an underground fighter?" Boualem wished us good luck, a smile pasted on his face, his left hand running through his tousled hair and his right outstretched to wish us farewell. Once we had reflected further on the message, we felt calm but somewhat skeptical. In fact, we were groggy, as if stunned by a punch. Before I had even expressed it, Samia responded to my wish: "Tonight, why don't you just sleep in Saint-Eugène?" We needed to stay together. It was our first mission and we wanted so desperately to live up to the confidence placed in us. From that moment on, we were inseparable. We gave no sign to anyone of our meeting the next day, of course. We passed an almost sleepless night, before attending classes the next day as if everything were as natural, normal, and usual as could be. And then the moment of the fateful appointment arrived!

Our Meeting

It was another beautiful day in Algiers. The late afternoon sun splashed across the treetops that shaded the small Laférièrre Square, where men and women with obvious European features crisscrossed incessantly. *Le Monde* in hand, we hadn't yet sat down at one of the green wooden benches when a man, not too old but older than Boualem, strode up to us. "My God! It's Georges Brassens!" I thought. The resemblance was uncanny: this man had the same bald head, the same eyes, the same broad mustache hiding his mouth and square chin as the famous poet and singer.

He addressed us simply: "Hello! You're right on time. Shall we take a walk? It would be better this way." We flanked him as we walked past the Grande Poste, then along the Rue d'Isly. It seemed as if he had known us forever. He asked us about our schedules, clearly already knowing everything about us and our studies. He asked us to tell him the days when we didn't have classes, and afterward addressed Samia: "What is the latest time by which you absolutely must be back home in Saint-Eugène?"

Our contact seemed perfectly aware of our state of total bewilderment. When he finally slowed to a stop and announced he was leaving us, he told us to call him Kamel, and to meet him three days later at the entrance to the law faculty, on the left. "Amid all the students, we won't draw any attention." And with that, Kamel left us, silent as statues. We headed for Samia's house. We didn't exchange a word the whole way. I had a heavy heart, conscious of the gravity of the decision we had made, of the decisive and significant turn our commitment—which until then was purely intellectual—had taken, and searched the depths of my soul for the strength and energy to meet the expectations of those who were placing such immense confidence in us.

It was at that moment that I remembered Madame Czarnecki speaking to me of the Warsaw Ghetto: "They did not resist with weapons, for they had so few. They fought with the strength provided by the conviction not to die for nothing, and the energy given by the hope that their certain death would save at least one, maybe two others." Then Malraux came back to me.

Samia, who was in the same state I was, shook me from my memories, pushing me to hurry up because she was impatient to see Mama Zhor and announce that the long-awaited miracle had finally occurred. In truth, we felt an irrepressible need to be reassured. And Mama Zhor, more than anyone else, had the ability to do so. We shut ourselves in her room and recounted what had happened, from yesterday's meeting to this afternoon with "Brassens," which is what Samia and I called our contact, Kamel. Before we even told her of our doubts and our need for reassurance, she let out a shrieking *you-you-you-you* in a traditional sign of celebration, and explained that we had been chosen by God to help bring justice for the *umma* of Prophet Mohammed (peace be upon him). Samia and I went rigid with fear that the neighbors would hear her *you-you-you-you*'s and come to inquire about the occasion, but she reassured us: "All the ladies nearby know that you study hard and hold your own against the French even in their own university. I will let everyone know that you just beat them in an exam."

A few ladies from the neighborhood knocked at the door as we had feared; Mama Zhor, undaunted, did exactly as she had said. Once back with us, she explained that she was not lying, because what we experienced was for her the greatest success in the hardest exam in the most difficult university: the university of our struggle against French colonization, begun way back in 1830 by her great-grandfather, the Emir Abdelkader! Mama Zhor succeeded not only in reassuring us of our strengths and abilities, but also in sweeping away all our doubts. She swore on the Quran that our secret would be forever safe with her. She assured us of her unwavering and unconditional support and urged us never to trust anyone but the brothers, Allah, and his Prophet. "Hold fast to Allah and this land that He has blessed: He will help you and protect you." She spent the evening spoiling us with sweets and reassuring us. It was a very good, very long night.

Our First Missions

Three days later, Kamel handed us a small satchel where we found thick envelopes, taped shut, each bearing the name of a recipient. The corresponding addresses, all in a single neighborhood, Belcourt, were noted in a list Kamel gave us separately. We were to destroy the list as soon as our mission was completed.

Unlike Samia, who had been to Belcourt several times to visit her aunt and cousins, I didn't know the area at all. Back in Saint-Eugène that evening, we worked out all the locations, thanks to Mama Zhor, who knew Algiers and its many secrets. She explained that all our destinations were in the Muslim quarter of the neighborhood, around Sidi M'hamed and El-Aqiba. Obsessed by the need to protect our anonymity and not draw attention with our European appearance in the heart of an Arab neighborhood, we decided to don the *haïk*, the classic veil of Algiers, well known as being difficult to wear. Ever the perfect accomplice, Mama Zhor gave us two *haïks*—broad white sheets that would cover us from our heads to our calves—and two *âadjars*—the finely stitched lace veils that completed the traditional outfit. We would drape ourselves in these once we arrived in Belcourt to begin our delivery route and nobody would suspect a thing.

The next day, a *haïk* and *âadjar* neatly folded and hidden in each of our bags, we took the trolley from the Place du Gouvernement to Belcourt. I discovered the east side of Algiers, the Place du Premier Mai, the wide boulevard with its elegant arcades that extended from the Jardin d'Essai[1] in Hamma over to Sidi M'hamed, the mausoleum of one of Algiers's patron saints. We hopped off the trolley and entered the mausoleum and its sanctuary, from which we would soon emerge veiled in our *haïks* and *âadjars* like all the ladies of Algiers.

But to my chagrin, I discovered that it was very difficult not only to wear the costume, but to do it in the particular local style. The only veil I knew how to wear was the one worn in my home region from the age of twelve: a large cream-colored rectangle we draped from head to ankles, leaving the whole body covered except for a single eye, considered a sufficient opening to judge where you were setting your feet. We held it in place by attaching it to our waist and clutching it at our chest with both hands, just below the chin. But veiling oneself in the Algiers style was different and required both real know-how and dexterity. I had neither. After several attempts, believing that I had finally gotten the hang of it, I followed behind Samia, who was perfectly draped, and we left Sidi M'hamed to embark on our tour. No sooner had we stepped outside than my *haïk* slipped every which way, sometimes leaving my head uncovered, sometimes half my body visible to all who passed. The more frustrated I grew, the more I set Samia writhing with laughter, while passersby looked on with amused glances. Many of the

---

1. Originally launched as an agricultural testing ground for crops and exotic plants from France's many colonial possessions, the Jardin d'Essai (Botanical Garden) came to serve as a central green space for the city of Algiers.

men of Algiers we passed undoubtedly recognized me as a poor novice. Just as I was about to break down in tears, a middle-aged man with a paternal air gently took me by the elbow and asked me to follow him into his shop nearby. We followed him into his tiny dressmaker's workshop, which he closed behind us. With incredible speed and skill, he hitched the veil to my dress with a few expert stitches, explaining that it wouldn't come off so long as the stitches stayed intact. He wished us good luck without asking a thing about us, not even a single question, and without us uttering a word. As we returned to our route, he bid us a simple farewell, *"Allah yahfadkoum."* (May God protect you.) "You're in luck: at this hour, only our people are out." It was eight-thirty in the morning.

That day, the fraternal solidarity and tacit collusion of our people took the form of that poor old dressmaker. Wherever he is, I implore God to bless him for eternity. He must certainly have been among our brothers in arms, or at least among their fervent supporters. We will never know. We just knew that he saved us from the many dangers that could come with a mission like ours, which proved to entail delivering the envelopes containing solidarity allowances to the families of FLN activists who had been arrested, disappeared, or executed by the colonizers. The old dressmaker near Sidi M'hamed had helped us recognize that any mission, no matter how innocuous it seemed, deserved careful preparation, sparing no detail—even training in how to wear a veil like the women of Algiers.

In Belcourt, our landmarks were the mausoleum of Sidi M'hamed, surrounded by its vast, steep cemetery, and El-Aqiba, an alley that seemed almost vertical and that hosted a daily market. A multitude of small shops opened onto the street and a dense crowd pressed through, most of them "natives," judging by the graceful silhouettes of women in their *haïks*. Several families on our list lived along the Boulevard Cervantes. The grandeur evoked by the name of Don Quixote's author could not hide the misery and deprivation of those who lived along it.

The street was lined with modest houses with red tile roofs and iron gates, painted wagon-wheel green, that opened onto tiny courtyards emitting a veritable symphony of scents, dominated by jasmine each morning and *mesk ellil* each evening. A few hours later, just before lunchtime, we were greeted not only by the flowers, but also by the enticing smell of *mqatfa* soup—instantly identifiable by the bewitching odor of coriander—or sardines like no others, stewed in fiery hot *derssa* garlic sauce and cumin. We typically made our rounds in the mornings, between eight-thirty and eleven-thirty. The street was quiet at that time, the only passersby being a few young girls playing hopscotch and boys spinning tops or kicking away at a makeshift ball of rolled newspaper wrapped tightly in yarn. Samia and I would track down the house number we were looking for and knock on the door, which was often ajar. Sometimes a woman in loose *seroual* pants would jump up from the copper pot where she had been squatting, washing clothes, and run to let us in. Then came other women, some very young, some with babies in their arms. The rooms we visited all functioned simultaneously as a bedroom, kitchen, bathroom, and living room; they were kept in a state of order and cleanliness that we found strikingly impressive.

Whenever we arrived we were greeted warmly, with humility and unshakable dignity. Never did any of the women—our sisters, bound by shared destiny—let us leave without insisting (by invoking God, his Prophet, our sacred bonds of sisterhood, and our principles of hospitality) that we taste some small treat, a cake or jam, lovingly prepared in their home. Ah those *maqrouts*, so warm and dripping with honey, and those sweet orange jams!

Some went so far as to block the exits of their abodes while swearing that as long as we had not "tasted the salt"—which could be as simple as sipping a coffee—they forbade us from leaving. The salt, oh, the salt! It symbolized one's word given and never taken back, sisterhood sealed and never undone, and especially the commitment that the secret we shared would never be betrayed. I will never stop paying homage to these women: they not only maintained the fire in the hearth of our hearts so that our flame would never be extinguished even in the worst of storms, they also served as our rear guard. We were nothing without them—without them being the first to confront the noise and fury of the French soldiers, their police, and the *harki* traitors who collaborated with them.

From one day to the next, from mother to daughter across an unbroken chain of generations, they maintained the vast, deep garden of our history—in the face of regular and methodical devastation by our enemy, going back to 1830—weaving and reweaving the fine threads of our collective memory. They taught us that we had indeed existed as a people, that we existed today as brothers, and that we would exist as a future nation of free citizens. Of course, they could neither read nor write, but they held immensely rich, diverse knowledge of life that no historian, no anthropologist, no academic could challenge, much less dispute. Algerian women from Belcourt to the Casbah, Saint-Eugène to Tiaret, Vialar to Constantine, Skikda to the

Djurdjura, the Aurès to the Sahara, from east to west and from north to south, made their mark for all eternity on our land, our history, our friends and our enemies alike.

In Belcourt, the women received us every time as if they were waiting for us. After each visit, as we searched for next family's address, we tried to guess how each of the women who had just gathered to greet us in the courtyard might be connected to the brother in arms whom the FLN had sent us to help by the letters we carried. Who was his mother? Who was his wife? Who were his sisters or daughters? We made small talk with them about the latest news, as if to avoid talking of the missing fighter. But their eyes, my God . . . their looks communicated all the sadness, all the distress, all the anxiety in the world: The brother, the son, or the husband, was he dead? Disappeared? Or simply arrested and thrown in jail? Or fled underground, to the *maquis*? Their eyes questioned us, probed us, but their gestures comforted us and gently enveloped us in the most fraternal embrace humanly possible. We were the living and palpable connection to their missing fighter, just as they were for us the magical manifestation of our unknown brother.

In these city-dwellers in Belcourt, I recognized the same dignity I saw in my aunts Bakhta and Aicha in their *"nègre"* village near Vialar. The poverty in which they lived seemed powerless against their memory and culture, a reservoir of knowledge that allowed them to remain upright and dignified even in the worst moments. Their looks, their expressions, were never those of a people defeated or surrendered. They seemed to say to the enemy, "You may have beaten us for now, but we will again become what we once were—a free people." It was this that allowed me, when I met someone, regardless of his social or intellectual level, to know immediately whether he was Algerian or not.

Samia and I always finished our tours reinvigorated, revitalized by the feeling of serving our cause and the brothers who had launched the war, to whom we were deeply grateful. Our visits reinforced—not that it was necessary—our belief that the FLN responded fully to the expectations of the vast majority of our people.

After our missions, we met Brassens, our contact, to whom we reported on our expeditions through the streets of Belcourt. He was kind and affable but somewhat reserved. By mutual agreement, we kept these appointments brief, limiting them to our quick reports and a handoff of a new batch of envelopes to distribute to Belcourt, Diar Echems, La Redoute, or Zghara.

This arrangement lasted two months, until the day Brassens came to the rendezvous point on Rue Négrier, parallel to Rue d'Isly, just behind the Galeries de France department store, accompanied by a small man, frail and thin, whose mischievous eyes kept inspecting us, leaping from one to the other as if he wanted to learn our features by heart, yet at the same time constantly sweeping all around the street. This fellow, I said to myself, sure was used to clandestine living.

The Desert Fox

Brassens introduced us to his comrade, using "Nabila" for Samia and "Farida" for me. Then he wished us luck and left us with him.

Our new chief started up Rue Négrier at a quick clip toward the *gouvernement général*, the seat of the French colonial administration. When we reached the end of a street that opened onto the main avenue, he stopped and declared: "This is the site of our next meeting, in two days at eleven o'clock. That's it for today, we just needed to meet one another." With that he spun and walked off briskly, his hands in his pockets.

We were beside ourselves with joy, since we interpreted these new arrangements as an expression of the brothers' satisfaction with our work; perhaps now they would assign us more important tasks? We had to continue to execute the tasks entrusted to us carefully and faithfully, to convince them with our unwavering commitment and sacrifice, before asking—if we would one day decide to ask—to join the armed groups. Samia and I honed our arguments as we followed the boulevard back toward the university, which we had somewhat deserted since devoting ourselves body and soul to our new activity. We decided to spend the afternoon trying to catch up, since our repeated visits to Belcourt had led us to miss many courses, practicums, and study sessions.

Sadly, the university taught us nothing about our country or our people. We learned more through our activism than through our studies—from our families and neighbors, our visits to the *hammam* and to the combatants' families, and also our chief. Thanks to them, we knew exactly what the colonial press, which took its orders from the regime, meant by "law enforcement operations" and "pacification."

Samia and I regularly encountered survivors who had escaped burned or bombed-out villages in the mountains of Blida, Medea, Palestro, or the Djurdjura. The women told us in minute detail (as if to exorcise all the horrors they had suffered) of the methods the French army used: encircling, raiding, napalm bombing, even forcing men—all of them civilians—to draw straws to see who would be coldly executed before the terrified eyes of their women and children. These horrors could culminate in wiping entire villages and their occupants from the map. They even included the use of collective rape as a weapon of mass—and enduring—destruction.

I will never forget a tall young girl, beautiful with her cascading ebony hair, translucent skin, and gazelle-like eyes, but whose hands and feet were constantly bound. She occasionally emitted a scream that chilled our blood. Her host family, that of a resistance fighter felled in battle in Kabylie, finally gagged her to avoid attracting attention. Aldjia was sixteen and had taken refuge with her mother, Djouhar, at the home of Fatima, a widow and mother of four. Their village, in the region of Tigzirt, had sustained bombardments for twenty days. On the twenty-first day, the army invaded. The soldiers killed all the men and boys and placed the girls in the rooms of the empty houses. For a whole week, the soldiers took turns raping every young girl in the village without stopping. When Djouhar was finally able to retrieve her daughter, she found her body, her soul, and her senses wrecked forever. Now her limbs were shackled because Aldjia constantly self-mutilated and tried to escape. Fatima whispered the entire tragedy to us through tears. Then the other women of the house who had gathered to receive us all recounted to us the French army's punitive attacks on the defenseless civilian populations. We communed in shared pain and grief, and oh my God, what unbreakable solidarity. Although the French colonial propaganda machine encouraged them to do so, never once did one of these women hold the FLN indirectly responsible for her misfortune. On the contrary, they all identified with "the organization," venerated its fighters, and firmly believed in its ideals.

To the lawyer in me, Aldjia will forever represent the thousands of girls—civilian victims in every sense—whose bodies and souls were used as a theater in the total war waged by the French army on behalf of its "civilized" state using gang rape—a weapon that destroyed during, after, and forever. The women's accounts, far from discouraging us, strengthened our determination to confront the Europeans and their colonial system. The night before each meeting with our chief, we rehearsed our request to be assigned a role in the armed struggle, but once face to face with him, we always dared only answer his questions. Yet there was no shortage of reasons for taking up arms, especially after the visit of Guy Mollet, president of the Council of Ministers, and Max Lejeune, Secretary of State for War, to Algiers on February 6, 1956.

In France, the center-left Front Républicain coalition had won the legislative elections, carrying to the head of the Council of Ministers Mollet, the leader of the deceitful Socialists, whose campaign slogan was "Peace in Algeria"—which he promised to achieve through a few small half-measures. In Algiers, the Europeans—their system, their newspapers, and their *ultras*—did not see it that way. At the university, in the cafés and local newspapers, we witnessed frenzied shouting matches that pitted an overwhelming majority on the *ultras'* side against a tiny minority supporting the micro-reforms. The latter group's goal was not to bring into question the colonial system of domination, but to concede a few crumbs to the starving, illiterate millions that the "natives," crushed by misery and repression, had become. In these French-on-French verbal altercations, the *ultras* saw this misery as proof of the almost genetic inferiority of the Muslims, who should "thank God for having sent the Europeans to civilize them," while the tiny center-left minority viewed it as the consequence of an error of economic and social strategy that could be corrected by creating a few jobs and opening a few literacy and vocational training classes. The real underlying causes—essentially the system of colonial domination—were never raised by either group. As for the questions of the "natives'" political status, their rights to freedom and dignity, not a chance.

For us as second-year law students, it was more than Samia and I could bear. In early 1956, we had such a harsh discussion with our friend Mimi that we almost reached the breaking point. She arrived one morning bursting with excitement and announced to us the "big news" that a group of French intellectuals, headed by the *pied-noir* writer Albert Camus, had launched a so-called "appeal for a civil truce." She explained to us that these intellectuals were very influential in France and that, since the Front Républicain had won the elections, everything would change for our people. Of course Mimi knew nothing of our membership in "the organization," of our clandestine activities, and telling her about it all was out of the question. So our discussion stayed on the purely intellectual grounds of Camus's principles and what we had read of him in *Alger Républicain*.

Samia reminded her that "Camus is fully French, while we are 'natives,' that is to say beings with inferior rights, with no access to citizenship or French nationality. And since we are colonized, we also don't have the right to be Algerian. In short, we are neither French nor Algerian; we are 'nothing' to the French government. We are a people denied even its essence and its existence, a people that has undergone a system of absolute and intolerable domination for 126 years! To top it all off, this system declares that Algeria is part of France. Which means that the Europeans and Camus are at home here and that we are strangers in our own land."

I added, "Does your 'appeal for a civil truce' pose the problems in these terms? Does it say that the colonial system is the origin and cause of our plight? Does it say that the only solution is the abolition of that system—its demise by any means necessary?"

Mimi, shaken by so much virulence, retorted, "You are extremists and your position will get us nowhere. Read Camus's coverage of the living conditions of our people in Kabylie and you will see that he is sincere. He is on our side."

Samia, with false calm, shot back, "Ask your friend Camus how his country, France, was freed from Nazi occupation. It was 'extremists,' the resistance and the Americans, who liberated France, not any calls for a civil truce. Why didn't Camus and his friends propose a civil truce to the Germans to resolve their country's occupation? And as for Camus's reports in *Alger Républicain*, we have read them. In his eyes, our problem is poverty due to unemployment and illiteracy, while for us, the misery is only a consequence of our true problem, which is called French colonization. For him, systemic reforms are sufficient, while for us, the solution lies in the death of the system that he is part of. You literature students should pick a new favorite writer. I suggest you get to know Malraux. Then you will understand that in truly historical moments, it is those who resist, the 'extremists,' as you call them, who are right."

Mimi stared at us, tears in her eyes, and left without uttering a word.

We had no time to regret our acrimony, since a few days later, on February 6, 1956, Guy Mollet arrived in Algiers, where he was welcomed with a hail of tomatoes and hysterical boos from the Europeans, who had been whipped into a white-hot frenzy by a campaign from the Committee for the Defense of French Algeria, all faithfully relayed by the press. On February 9, Robert Lacoste, a Socialist—yet "French Algeria"—activist, was appointed Resident Minister in Algeria. Less than a month later, in March 1956, the French assembly voted to give Mollet "special powers." The message was clear: Algeria must remain French. The colonial system, with its slate of domination, humiliation, oppression, misery, repression, and nullification for the "natives" alongside the outrageous political, economic, and cultural privileges of the European minority, would stand. For this it was necessary, through total war and "special powers," to crush the separatists and quash any attempt by Muslims to join them.[2] The French people's elected representatives, including the Communists, would spare no expense.

Guy Mollet and the Front Républicain weren't holding back either: they increased the length of military service, inundated Algeria with an army of nearly half a million highly equipped men, and locked down the country.

Algiers was teeming with soldiers in March 1956, just after the French National Assembly's "special powers" vote. On March 16, a general curfew from midnight to five in the morning was declared across greater Algiers in response to attacks that our activists had managed to organize. The previous day, our brothers had succeeded in torching the gas station just near the university. Samia and I were proud when we saw the destruction. It was only fair, because we could no longer stand the sight of these happy Europeans bathing in the sweetness of life, in tranquility and in peace, while our own people were being oppressed and massacred, burned and raped, across the mountains and the countryside. Despite the curfew, the attacks continued, and the Europeans in Algiers began to fear more and more. Of course, their army and police forces retaliated in the most ferocious and savage ways: like they had in the mountains, they applied collective punishments, besieged whole neighborhoods, and made mass arrests, without any proof, just to intimidate, terrorize, and eliminate "the rebellion" or any inclination to support it.

Samia and I had fallen so far behind in our second year that to fully catch up would have required a colossal effort, perfect attendance, and extensive research on doctrine and jurisprudence. I soon realized that it was hopeless and that we would never be ready for our exams in June 1956. Our public law professor was Monsieur Hassan, an Algerian adjunct who taught in Algiers and Paris. During one of our practicums, our group was hit with a pop quiz. Absorbed in our new activities, Samia and I had done little preparation, and it showed in our grades. At the end of class one day, Monsieur

---

2. As "the Algeria question" grew ever more pressing in the mid- and late 1950s, a sizable portion of the *pied-noir* community in Algeria came to see France's policies toward Algeria's indigenous peoples as overly soft, and instead embraced various separatist scenarios in which Algeria would gain independence from France—but as an effective apartheid state that would maintain the *pieds-noirs'* privileged status at the indigenous population's expense.

Hassan surprised us by asking that we see him in his office. Crushed by the shame of being publicly called out before all our fellow students, we came only once the lecture hall was completely empty. He was waiting for us. He asked us to confirm our names aloud, then said: "From the beginning of the year, I noted the presence of two Muslim students, Mesdemoiselles Zohra Drif and Samia Lakhdari, and you should know that I looked up your first-year results. There was nothing to say; they were very good, even excellent in some subjects. I was proud of you. However, the responses you submitted at the last quiz correspond neither to your results from the previous year nor to the image that I had of you both. What's happening? Does public law not interest you, or have you simply decided to no longer do your work?"

We were petrified with shame before Monsieur Hassan. Here was one of our own, an adjunct law professor, disappointed at our work—which was frankly bad, if not downright terrible—and pressing us to explain ourselves. What could we say? How could we answer? That we weren't the same Mesdemoiselles Drif and Lakhdari we had been last year? That our life was now devoted to missions that had nothing to do with law or the university? That they consisted of transporting packages and envelopes of varying sizes and thickness, taped shut, with nothing but a single name on them, and depositing them at the addresses listed on the separate paper, which we were to destroy after each mission, and never to record the addresses on the paper itself? That our meetings with our contact took place out in the streets and not on campus? That before leaving us, he always set the place, day, and time of our next meeting, which could come as soon as later the same day, at another location, after we had accomplished our mission? That he waited for us to bring him the package we had been given in one of the Belcourt homes, without knowing a thing about its contents or sender? That we fulfilled these tasks with devotion and conviction, but also with a mortal fear that twisted our guts with worry that he might not come? That we knew from the very first meeting what our handler's absence at the appointed time and place would signify? That in that event we should never, under any circumstances, return to our other meeting places but instead return immediately to Samia's home in Saint-Eugène and wait patiently to be contacted again? This was what ran through my head as I sat, my eyes fixed on the floor, unable to return Monsieur Hassan's gaze, which waited patiently for our arguments justifying our new status as "losers, and proud of it." Overwhelmed with shame, on the verge of tears because our reasons were so unspeakable, we walled ourselves up in a deafening silence that ultimately discouraged Monsieur Hassan in his attempt to lead us to salvation. He dismissed us, furious and sad.

Once outside, Samia somehow still found a shred of humor: "He has just lost his two brilliant token Muslim students forever. Poor Monsieur Hassan! Hasn't he realized that while he prattles on in the enemy's universities, our people are at war?" Samia laughed, but it was a nervous, bitter laughter. We left the campus for our new rendezvous point with our chief, in a neighborhood I had only ever crossed by bus: El Biar, with its lively shopping avenues. Our missions allowed us to discover all the neighborhoods of Algiers and its suburbs. Since we had no doubts about our victory, we promised each other that after independence we would write a guide called *Algiers by Brassens and the Desert Fox* (the nickname we had bestowed on our new handler).

Arriving in El Biar, we scouted out the street and number of our rendezvous and, since we were early, turned off and soon found ourselves facing a wide, beautiful square, revolting in its sweetness, happiness, and *joie de vivre*. Nothing but Europeans! We sat on a bench and watched them swim in their happiness, as if no "native" existed in this land that they had seized thanks to the strength of their army. As if whole regions of the country had not been swept by "the fine-toothed comb" and suffered horrific bombardments. After a moment, with the casualness of youth, I said to Samia: "When we have our independence, I'm going to live in El Biar." I would go on to keep that promise, though not the one about the Algiers guide.

During our meeting with the Desert Fox, I dared to briefly outline our theory about the need to bring the war into "enemy territory" by using people like us. He listened politely, then took his leave. Samia put the issue back on the table at the next meeting, with much more conviction. She argued that the only ones experiencing the war were our people in the mountains and the countryside. Oran, Constantine, Bône, and Algiers left nothing to be desired compared to cities in metropolitan France; the Europeans lived here in peace, security, and tranquility, far from the war and its horrors. It was essential to make this population suffer the war too, and explained how "the organization" could use young girls like us—who could circulate without difficulty and without arousing the suspicions of the French—by integrating us into the armed groups. The Desert Fox, ever tight-lipped, listened without interrupting and without comment. He gave us his instructions and left. We decided to go in search of Boualem Oussedik to make our case.

The Desert Fox's Arrest

We were focused on finding Boualem when misfortune struck us in the final week of April 1956.

One morning on the bus to campus, I glanced at the newspaper a nearby passenger was reading and was suddenly shaken by a violent tremor. In large, bold letters across the front page, the terrible news danced before my eyes: "Terrorist Chief of Algiers Arrested." Staring at me was a photo of our handler, the Desert Fox, with chained hands, looking stubbornly straight ahead. I averted my eyes with difficulty, telling myself not to let anyone notice how upset I was. I couldn't see a thing. I'll never know how I found myself at the entrance of the café where Samia and I usually met. But as soon as I arrived, our eyes met: She knew!

We needed a very strong coffee to drag us out of our despondent state. Our chief was so scrawny that more than once we had asked ourselves if he hadn't been suffering some serious illness. How would he withstand systematic mistreatment and torture? Samia laid out all the newspapers she had purchased and we devoured them, hypnotized by the determined look of the Desert Fox under arrest and by his real name: Mustapha Fettal. Fear and anguish seized us. Just how much information did our enemy now have?

The more we reflected, the less we could answer these questions. The Desert Fox would be tortured to death. Of that we were certain. All the papers had dedicated several articles to his arrest that left no doubt about the treatment he would receive, but also left us dumbfounded at something else: the Desert Fox was not just our leader but the "head of armed combat in Algiers"! We, mere novices, had been acting under the direct leadership of the senior military commander! We realized that our greatest wish had been fulfilled without our even knowing. Of course, we knew nothing about him except a pseudonym, and even then just a first name, which we had replaced between ourselves with "the Desert Fox." But besides knowing our real identities and status as our second-year law students at the University of Algiers, what other information did he have on us?

He had to be made to "spit it out" by any means necessary, and torture was the one the colonial power most favored: pliers to rip off fingernails and flesh, electricity applied to the most unexpected parts of the victim's body, the torch, the bottle, the cloth, the bathtub, etc. We dared not formalize the question that burned on our lips: "Would the Desert Fox, once under torture, speak about us?" To dare to say it aloud would have been the supreme sacrilege: the Desert Fox was the great leader of Algiers and we now accorded him superhuman powers.

After the fear and anxiety, it was rage and revolt against so much injustice, so much unfairness: the scrawny, chained Desert Fox facing off against an entire state. Then, paradoxically, pride. We were proud to belong to the FLN. We were proud to be the sisters of the Desert Fox, so slender but so dignified and so determined. Then came joy. Yes, joy, at having discovered that not only had our desire to join "the armed organization"—expressed both to Brassens and Boualem Oussedik—been granted, but our brothers had put their trust in us.

The explosive mix of conflicting feelings put us in a paradoxical, nearly euphoric state. We wanted so much to cry out *you-you-yous* in honor of the Desert Fox and all the "terrorist" leaders, as the enemy press called them—in honor of our newly discovered status as "terrorists," as the enemy called us. Alas, we were sitting in a European café, so we stowed our *you-yous* in the oppressive silence of our hearts, with tears of elation. Then Samia's question put an end to our inner turmoil: "What will we do now? What's the protocol now that our big brother is under arrest?"

We chose the only reasonable option available to us under the circumstances, which was to wait for "the organization" to reestablish contact with us. We found some small comfort in knowing that the repressive machine would surely interrogate him about people more important than us, two poor female students recruited just a few months earlier, with no armed attacks on their record. We decided that I should move in with Samia in Saint-Eugène. Samia explained in a whisper, "If they come to arrest you in the night at the dormitory in Ben Aknoun, no one will come to inform me at home. Remember that besides Mimi and Boualem Oussedik, who don't even live on campus, we know nobody." She was right, and we knew, thanks to our law classes, that the worst thing that could happen if you were arrested was for it to remain a secret. Despite our exhaustion, Samia managed to make me laugh: "Their police services wouldn't dare venture to Qadi Lakhdari's home unless they had irrefutable evidence. And what could the daughter of a *qadi* of Algiers and granddaughter of the great *mufti* of Constantine and the daughter of a *qadi* of Vialar have in common with an infamous 'outlaw'? Their foolish, evil racism will blind them again. So just come stay with us—Mama will be delighted."

We went to the dormitories to collect a few of my things while it was still daylight, then to Saint-Eugène. We fell into Mama Zhor's arms crying and recounted to her the whole affair. She cried with us, consoled us, and asked Allah, his Prophet, and all our saints to protect our chief and keep him alive. She raised both hands to heaven and prayed to God to break our enemies with his unequaled power. She repeated, "Our leaders were chosen by Allah for the power he granted them, and let us never forget that even when the *koffar* beat them, they don't die. They go to heaven, where they remain eternal and Allah replaces them with many, many others here on earth. But the *koffar* do not believe in such things, and so much the better—It is God once again who has blinded them!"

And so we settled in at Saint-Eugène to watch and wait in vain for the reappearance of Boualem Oussedik—whom we had not seen since our last meeting in December '55—to deliver us from fear and put an end to our wait.

The UGEMA Strike

For some time now, an idea had been percolating, whispered among the Muslim students, and finally it came to fruition. The UGEMA called for a general student strike to show support and solidarity with the national liberation struggle of our people under the FLN's leadership. Obviously we were in solidarity—but a boycott of our studies and exams at this moment would represent a catastrophe for us, because it would cut us off from "the organization." Not only would we not be present at the university, we would be obliged by Monsieur Lakhdari to stay home. Worse still, I was sure that my parents would demand that I return to Vialar. Farewell to the struggle, farewell to "the organization"!

It looked plausible to us that the decision had come from the FLN leadership, but we nonetheless decided to try to convince the UGEMA leaders that a general academic strike was perhaps not the best way to show our solidarity. Despite its political impact, it could endanger the development of our national liberation struggle by allowing the French security forces and *ultras* to identify all the nationalist students. We felt strongly that this would compromise their contribution to our struggle.

A few days later, we learned that a meeting of all the Muslim students would take place in late afternoon at the Robertsau campus. Samia and I spent all afternoon honing our arguments and decided that we would both speak. But when we reached Robertsau, I was seized by panic at the thought of having to speak in public, to the point that I had only one wish—to find myself far, far away. Despite my panic attack, I went to the meeting and found myself in what seemed to me a huge yard full of young women and men talking, laughing, and calling out to one another. I didn't see a single friend among them. I had decided to let Samia speak first, hoping not to have to take the floor myself. Someone climbed up to a podium facing the noisy crowd of students and asked for silence. Just then, to my right I saw a group of young men heading for the podium in single file. The crowd quieted down and one of them, very tall with thick hair thrown back, mounted the platform, asked again for silence, and, taking the microphone, began to read a declaration. It was a call for the general strike of all classes and exams in solidarity with our people's struggle for independence. The text was adopted by a voice vote and, to my relief, was not submitted for debate. The start of the strike was set for May 19, 1956. As soon as we were outside, I realized that the die was cast. I would be summoned by my parents to return immediately to Vialar, where it would be impossible for me to continue my activism. We absolutely had to find an airtight reason to convince my family to let me stay in Algiers. The next day, I asked my brother Kader to contact our father and explain that the strike only concerned the male students. By way of a response, my father arrived the following week to help me with my luggage and accompany me home.

And so I left Algiers, hopeless, at the beginning of June 1956. It had been nearly a month and a half since our chief had been arrested and the "organization" still had not reestablished contact with us. Later, during the Battle of Algiers, I would learn that Mustapha Fettal was imprisoned in the Barberousse prison. He would spend five years there on death row, to be released only after the signing of the Évian Accords, when France ceded Algeria. At independence, I would find him newly appointed to the post of police chief of Algiers. I am proud to have him as a brother and a friend, he who was a genuine Novembriste, an extraordinary activist, and a peerless leader. As luck or fate would have it, he had been alongside my future husband, Rabah Bitat, in the infamous group that triggered the war of liberation in Algiers on November 1, 1954.

Summer in Vialar

Before my father's arrival to take me back to Vialar, I spent the last two weeks of May 1956 at Samia's.

There we witnessed—with front-row seats, since Samia's house overlooked the arena—nearly five thousand of our men being packed into the

Saint-Eugène stadium. The night before, during the curfew, the French army and police had surrounded the Casbah and conducted indiscriminate arrests. They had gathered thousands of innocent men in trucks that now arrived in long convoys to dump them at the stadium. Men were in pajamas, others in their undershirts, many barefoot: they had clearly been wrenched brutally from their beds. The procession of trucks lasted at least three hours.

The colonialist press encouraged the crackdown by justifying it and calling for even harsher treatment of the "suspects," who were nothing but poor unarmed civilians. This same press did the *ultras'* dirty work, serving as their mouthpiece so that Lacoste would refuse the clemency requests filed by the lawyers of nationalist activists who had been sentenced to death. Every day, the colonialist media called for the authorities to make an example of someone, and for more repression.

Ten days after my arrival in Vialar I learned of the first two executions: Ahmed Zabana and Abdelkader Ferradj. I was bursting with rage to be stuck in Vialar, unable to go outside or to pour out my pain. I hated the entire world: the French, who were hunting us in our own country; my parents, who were depriving me of any outside contact; Samia, on whom all my hopes were resting; and Boualem Oussedik, who had vanished without a trace. How to contact him was the last topic that Samia and I had discussed. After two weeks of ruminating in Vialar without any news from Samia, I shifted all my hopes onto my brother Kader, who had promised to join me at the end of June. He told me, "You'll see. In Vialar, it will be better than in Algiers. Everybody knows us in the region—there will be no need for a test." I didn't understand what he meant about a "test" but I appreciated the "us" in "everybody knows us." It seemed my brother was not excluding me from his plans—if they existed at all. But meanwhile I was stewing in Vialar, where my mother had welcomed me in an unusual outpouring of affection. I didn't sulk or express the slightest sign of my bad mood: my mother would never have tolerated it. But my apathy and the silence in which I enveloped myself, locked away all day in my room, struggling to keep my attention on books, irritated and worried her. I was cut off from the world of the living, and the daily hubbub suffocated me. At that time, telephones were still not widespread: only the government buildings and wealthy colonists had them. I was cut off from Samia with no means other than the mail to get in touch with her. But the mail was out of the question for security reasons. The more time that passed, the more I closed inward upon myself.

In the last few days of June, Kader arrived. I pestered him with questions about the group of young people who had not returned to the village. He invariably replied that he knew nothing and advised me not to ask such questions. He left in the morning, announcing to my mother that he would be away all day, spending his time in Tiaret, Burdeau, or Victor Hugo. I asked him what he did with his days and if I couldn't be of any use to him.

Kader mocked my "preposterous suppositions," swore to me that he was telling my mother the strict truth, and explained to me that it would be suicidal to try anything in Vialar since the colonists watched everything and everyone, "even the flies!" My mother, concerned about her son's daily disappearances, insisted that my father send Kader away on vacation to Nancy, where our elder brother was a medical student. But Kader didn't want to go and swore up and down that he was perfectly happy at home. My father reassured my mother, reminding her that Vialar was a small village where nothing could escape anyone.

That was how I spent the month of July 1956 in Vialar—trying to guess what activities Kader was involved in and listening to gossip. The fighters had attained the status of legends, fascinating some and terrorizing others. People were proud of them and believed that they were invisible to the French soldiers. Everyone was grateful to them for having injected a dose of fear into the hitherto carefree lives of the colonists. It was only fair. It was clear that our movement drew its strength from its roots in our population. Kader brought me information about ambushes in the Ouarsenis Mountains and attacks in Algiers, which had grown increasingly frequent since the execution of Zabana and Ferradj. We were incensed at our imprisonment in Vialar, and Kader repeated, "The fear needs to switch sides." I agreed with him, but could do nothing.

Toward the end of July, my father came home from court and informed me that Samia had telephoned him. She had asked him to inform me that the strike had been lifted for girls, which meant I was to return as soon as possible to Algiers to prepare for the exams set for late September. I understood immediately that "the organization" had reestablished contact with her, but I let nothing show. Instead, I immediately began voicing my concerns about our ability to adequately prepare ourselves to face the written and oral exams in such a short time.

I had just barely a month to prepare for the exams. I asked my father: "We'll leave tomorrow? I need to get back to work quickly to try to be ready. I haven't opened a single book since I arrived." I was about to go to my room to begin preparing my things when my mother, unable to contain herself, burst out at me: "It is out of the question for you to go to Algiers. You can't possibly imagine that we'll swallow this tale of a strike for the boys but not the girls!"

Frightened, I tried to calm her. I explained that Samia would never have dared to invent an excuse just to get me back to Algiers and suggested that she question Kader to confirm that the strike now involved only the boys. I knew I could count on my brother's cooperation. But my suggestion had the opposite effect, since my mother ordered me to shut up and repeated that never, not ever, would she allow me to return to Algiers, and said to me angrily, "I wasn't born yesterday. If you think I don't understand why you've changed so much, you're mistaken. I brought you into this world and not the other way around, and just because you study in the university and I haven't doesn't mean you can fool me. You want to go back to Algiers to return to those people who want to hide behind women to bring down France. Well, you will not leave this house. You're no different from your girl cousins, and there will be no more question of studies in Algiers. As for those who want to confront France, let the men do it themselves!"

Terrified, I looked to my father, begging for his support. Dejected, he stayed silent, eyes downcast. So I locked myself in my room, awaiting Kader's return to ask him to confirm that the girls were exempted from the strike. I also wanted to ask him to help me, if it came to it, to flee if my father refused to accompany me. Kader returned, confirming the girls' exemption without hesitation, and even elaborating on the reasons why. My father pretended to believe him while my mother, still beside herself, decided that for the sake of her honor I should admit there in front of everyone that I wanted to return to Algiers to join those who had taken up arms against France. Kader tried to save me, explaining that if that were the case I would never have returned to Vialar in June and would instead have simply disappeared underground like Drizi. My mother didn't want to hear a word of it and kept repeating that I would never again return to Algiers. My father remained silent throughout the dispute, until he finally declared that the very next day he would verify for himself this lifting of the strike for the girls.

The next day, he returned early from work and informed my mother that he had checked with several well-informed people. He confirmed that the strike had indeed been lifted for girls and, therefore, we would set out as soon as possible for Algiers. My father was consciously serving as our accomplice. He gave me more than just his green light; he gave me his blessing to assume my duty to my country. He was consistent in his convictions. My mother, hopeless, could not stop crying out of powerlessness. I was upset at having caused such a family tragedy, torn between my duty to respect and obey my poor mother and my duty to my cause, my organization. My mother didn't make the task any easier with her tears, incantations, and reminders of the sacrifices made to impose upon our tribe the idea that one of its daughters had the same right to education as the boys.

I wanted so badly to take my mother in my arms, kiss her, reassure her, and explain to her that I was involved body and soul in the most sacred cause there was, the one to liberate our country at all costs. Oh, how I wanted to tell her my certainty that in my place she would have done the same. But I did none of this, tending instead to my bags in silence amid the heavy, unbreathable atmosphere that I had caused. The next day, very early, as we were leaving, my mother pulled me toward her, looked me straight in the eye, and said: "I know everything about you, including what you hide in the depths of your soul. A mother's heart never lies, and my heart spoke to me." These were her final words before she kissed me lightly and took care of the ritual of throwing water on our footsteps as the car started off, to ensure a safe trip and my certain return.

I left Vialar with a heavy heart, silently imploring God to pardon me. The journey was long and heavy, as my father remained as serious as he was silent. I steeled myself by remembering that the duty to liberate my country was more sacred than any other and that my life was no more precious than those of Ferradj and Zabana. When we reached the campus, my father lingered with me long after we had finished unpacking my things. It was clear that he was struggling to leave me. I began to fear that he would end up regretting his decision to support me and would oblige me to turn back around to Vialar. Finally, he announced his departure. He cast a glance at the bathroom, came back to the desk, flipped the pages of a book, put it down, and then looked me straight in the eyes: "I hope you are aware of the significance of your decision, and that you understand its gravity and all its implications. It doesn't only commit you. Sooner or later, the whole family will suffer for it, but that is the lesser evil, because we will face it head on. The question I pose to you is this: Do you believe, in your soul and in your conscience, that you are able and ready to confront every imaginable situation? Listen well—this is not novels and poetry. It is a war of liberation where the rule is 'win or die,' which implies a necessarily harsh, violent, even cruel reality at all times. These are situations that you cannot even imagine—you can only know them by living them. Tell yourself that this will be very hard, often unbearable for a young girl like you. Tell yourself that your discipline must be ironclad, that there is no room for sentiment, no qualms, because everyone is responsible for his life and that of all others, but most importantly for the victory of the cause. France will be merciless. They have a vast army and security services well versed in the most inhumane methods to break you down and destroy you. Your books and your law classes will be of no service to you, since the Rights of Man and Citizen, the declaration of 1793, are only valid for their people. Not for us. So here's what we'll do. I am going to get a room at the Hotel Aletti. You think carefully about everything I've just told you, and if you change your mind, come find me before noon tomorrow and we will return home."

He squeezed me tightly in his arms, he whose nature was usually so reserved, and whispered in my ear, "Do not judge your mother harshly. She reacted like any mother would. She loves you and she's afraid for you." In tears, I embraced him and asked him to reassure her, to beg her forgiveness and blessings. He handed me a big wad of bills and left without looking back, as if he knew that I wouldn't come to his hotel the next morning. Alone in my room, I let my tears flow freely and my grief well up. Then I repacked my suitcase and headed for Saint-Eugène.

4

INTO THE HEART
OF THE ARMED STRUGGLE

Recruited

It was four in the afternoon when I rang the Lakhdaris' doorbell using our code: two rings, a pause, then one more ring. Samia hurtled down the stairs to come open the door for me. She smothered me in her arms and whispered in my ear, "We're all set! They contacted me, that's why I called your father. I'll tell you the details, but don't say a thing, not even to Mama Zhor, because we are now part of the armed groups."

We took the stairs four at a time to join Mama Zhor in the sitting room. She had just set the *meïda* table for the afternoon coffee, with sweet *maqrouts* and orange-blossom water. I threw myself into Mama Zhor's arms and asked her to tell me all her news.

Once we were safely in her room, Samia told me that Boualem Oussedik had reestablished contact in early June. He had shown up at their front door in shorts and short sleeves like a *gaouri* (European).[1] Monsieur Lakhdari,

---

1. In that time (and to a considerable degree even today), it was strongly frowned upon for Algerian men to go outside in short clothes, in contrast to their European peers.

who had opened the door, nearly had a heart attack when this young man—who was obviously European given his indecent outfit—asked in French, "Is this Mademoiselle Samia Lakhdari's house?" Alerted by her father's shouts and threats, Samia peered out the window overlooking the street and recognized that darned Boualem Oussedik, who continued to insist on seeing her despite her father's protests. Mama Zhor, who knew the situation, hurried downstairs and, undaunted, pushed her husband aside and ushered the unexpected visitor into the vestibule, presenting him as Zohra's cousin! Monsieur Lakhdari was in a state of shock: "Now I've seen everything in this damned life—even a Muslim dressed like a *gaouri*, daring to cross the threshold of my home and ask to speak to my daughter!"

Thus our contact was reestablished. Samia spent nearly two months completing various missions assigned by "the organization." I listened with attention and envy, but admonished her for not having tried to bring me back sooner. She explained that she had acted according to her instructions: her contact had preferred, for safety reasons, to wait until the end of July, when a resumption of classes for girls and preparations for exams would appear more plausible to everyone. He added, "If her parents do not take the bait, we'll find another way to bring her."

Samia said that when she called my father to inform him that the strike would be suspended for girls and that I needed to return urgently to Algiers, he told her to stop recounting such nonsense. She tried swearing that it was the truth, but my father interrupted her by promising her that he would convey the message to his daughter, then hung up on her. I confirmed to her that my father had never believed our story, but that he had pretended to in front of my mother. I added that he was in his room at the Hotel Aletti, confident that I would never come see him the next morning; he had presented it without really believing it would happen. I told her how guilty I felt to have brought such pain on my mother and my family. Samia, my sister and my friend, consoled me.

She also told me how "the brothers" had mobilized their contacts—friends in the legal field and in that thin slice of Europeans who supported us—to try to obtain the French president's pardon for Zabana and Ferradj. She told me of the hysterical campaign by the *ultras* in Algiers, in Boufarik, and throughout the Mitidja, relayed by the pro-colonial newspapers—both local and in mainland France—to deny the pardons. She told me of the atmosphere throughout the Casbah on the evening of Zabana's execution:

"When they brought Zabana from his cell, all the imprisoned brothers sang our song "Min Djibalina." The executioner released the guillotine blade, but it jammed twice. The French government did not stop him from releasing it the third time. Ahmed Zabana cried out, *'Tahya El Djazair!* With us or without us, free Algeria will live!' Our brothers replied by chanting *'Tahya El Djazair! Tahya El Djazair!'* [Long live Algeria!] When the martyr's head finally rolled to a stop at the foot of the guillotine, the brothers were crying out, *'Tahya El Djazair! Allah Akbar! Allah Akbar!'*

"And in one uninterrupted chorus, the women of the Casbah roared out tens of thousands of *you-yous* that left the prison staff quaking in fear. The next day and the days that followed, thanks to the FLN, all of Algiers and then all of Algeria were sharing Zabana's last message, which his lawyer had transmitted to his mother: 'Tell my mother that I am not dying for nothing, and thus, I am not really dying at all.' By executing Zabana and Ferradj on June 19, 1956, the colonizers got the opposite of what they were looking for: thousands of men and women sought to join the FLN's ranks, especially youth who had vowed to avenge our martyrs. *'Tahya El Djazair!* With us or without us, free Algeria will live!' had become a solemn pledge for the brothers and a galvanizing message to our people."

Samia recounted this whole story in a single stretch.

She had decrypted and analyzed the situation with Petit Mourad after our brothers' execution. I asked her to tell me more. She explained that when Boualem Oussedik re-contacted her, she had met him at the university entrance and they had walked to Bresson Square to meet her new contact, Mourad, who was no more than seventeen. She dubbed him Petit Mourad. He had a dark complexion with jet-black hair, and spoke with an accent from Biskra that Samia immediately recognized, since her father was from the same town. After Boualem had introduced them and left, Petit Mourad said to Samia: "We'll board the trolley, each of us separately, at the Place du Gouvernement as if we don't know one another and take it in the direction of Saint-Eugène. Then we'll each get off at the Consolation stop, not far from the town hall and your home. Opposite is a small grocery store run by one of our own. You will follow me from afar, enter after me, and then pronounce the following password to the grocer." Petit Mourad impressed Samia, despite his youth. She followed his instructions to the letter.

After making sure no one was observing her, Samia entered the shop, where Petit Mourad had been waiting for five or six minutes. The grocery store, which I would get to know later, was nestled into a recess in the main street. A tiny shop with light-blue glass doors, it faced a pretty little garden square shaded by beautiful trees. At their feet were cement benches covered in elegant mosaic tiles. The square bustled with people every evening. The counter was just inside, not a yard from the doorway. Behind it stood a slender man with curly blond hair and blue eyes behind thick glasses. Over his shoulder, the shop's wooden shelves sagged under a variety of products. Having verified again that she was alone, Samia came forward and spoke the required phrase in a low voice. The grocer replied to her sentence and called out to Mourad, who scurried out from behind the counter like a cat. She couldn't suppress a gasp of astonishment that he could hide in such a small space. They laughed and introduced one another. Petit Mourad informed her that the grocery would be their new rendezvous point and sometimes their stash for packages. He warned her that, if ever he did not come to an appointment, she would find instructions and information with the grocer. Saint-Eugène being her neighborhood, Samia explained that frequent trips to the grocer might attract unwanted attention from curious neighbors. He replied that he would forward her remarks to the big brothers and fixed an appointment for her for the next afternoon.

The next day, as agreed, she found Petit Mourad there. He asked her: "First, are you completely available with respect to your time? Second, do you know Algiers well? And third, if the brothers entrusted you a job three hours before its execution, would you be ready to accomplish it?"

Samia replied, "First, yes, of course I am at the disposal of 'the organization.' But we must consider our society. My father obliges me to be back home before six-thirty each evening, and all the European neighbors and my family members know me. Second, yes, I know Algiers and its suburbs thanks to the missions entrusted to me and our sister 'Farida.' Third, yes, I can accomplish a mission assigned to me just three hours in advance. But in case of emergency or if the hours are indecent, could I be accompanied by my mother? She is a very reliable person, very engaged in our cause, and my best cover vis-à-vis my father, the rest of the family, and our neighbors. Fourth, I would like to ask if my friend might be able to return—sister Farida, whom 'the organization' knows well. She is with her parents in Vialar, but in my opinion we need her here."

Petit Mourad replied, "I will convey all that you have said and will bring you your instructions next time."

Before leaving, he handed her a small package, quite heavy and tightly sealed, and asked her to drop it in the mailbox of a certain building in the European city. Samia completed the task and two days later received answers to her questions: "The big brothers will tell you when you can ask sister Farida to return to Algiers, but not yet. Meanwhile, the older brothers have given their OK for your mother to accompany you in case of emergencies and indecent hours. She will take sister Farida's place."

Samia's meetings with Petit Mourad continued from mid-June to late July 1956. She sometimes came accompanied by Mama Zhor. Petit Mourad taught her a great deal about life and solidarity in our working-class neighborhoods. He taught her that the FLN's supporters and activists were much more numerous than the Europeans believed. He described our leaders' great personal virtues and courage. Mourad behaved as a reassuring protector to Samia, who eventually developed an almost maternal tenderness for him. He fascinated and amused her at the same time. One day, she told him how she had read some articles suggesting that our activists couldn't withstand French torture and eventually gave up information.

Mourad rejected the notion with a wave of his hand, saying, "You know, sister Nabila, I know brothers who, when they were arrested, preferred to swallow the cyanide capsule hidden in a secret pocket of their pants rather than confess under torture." He cited two names she had never heard before and appeared surprised at her ignorance.

Samia replied, "The less I know, the better, since I'm not sure I could hold out under torture if ever I'm arrested."

He looked at her strangely, this frail young boy who seemed to fear nothing and laughed at the thought of torture. "You have cyanide on you?" Samia asked.

"But I'm not one of the commanders!"

"You're my commander! But do you know the other ones?"

Laughing, he replied, "Not all, of course. But some, yes."

Sometimes Mourad could still seem like a child, like when he arrived with two ice-cream cones from Grosoli's, already licking his own and handing Samia hers with a laugh, not suspecting that she would lick her own only with great difficulty because of her bourgeois prejudices. Then again he could seem like an adult, responsible and courageous, when transmitting instructions, information, or packages to Samia. He was admirable during missions in the European city: "Sister, we'll take this trolley, but separately. We'll get off at this stop, each on our own sides. We'll walk on opposite sidewalks and you'll follow me, always leaving five minutes' distance between us to react in case of problems. In such cases, please do not stop. Continue straight ahead, even if you see the dogs kill me or block me. Is that understood? Look, I'm wearing a red sweater so you can see me from afar."

Petit Mourad

On July 16, 1956, Samia had an appointment with Mourad at four o'clock. She didn't find him at the grocer's. The grocer informed her that Mourad would be waiting for her the next day at eleven o'clock in the Sidi Abderrahmane cemetery, which she should enter veiled. She realized that something serious must have happened. The next day she donned a veil and went to the cemetery. She found Mourad sad, pale, and more enraged than ever. He told her two nights before, during the curfew, that *ultras* had killed dozens of Muslim civilians, including many housewives, and that they had almost succeeded in burning the Casbah's eighty thousand residents alive in their sleep. He told her how the *ultras* had driven fuel tankers to Bab Jdid,[2] where they planned to pour the gas out. It would have flowed through the Casbah below, following the old city's slopes all the way down to its lowest reaches. And then it would have sufficed to light a single match to send the Casbah up into an enormous blaze—and make it a crematorium for its inhabitants, all of whom were civilians. Only the vigilance of our people managed to avert the massacre. Mourad explained that, after having confirmed the allegations through their own contacts and informants, our leaders had decided to organize the residents to take turns standing watch all around the Casbah. The residents, having heard the trucks' rumble well after curfew, had stepped outside and, understanding what was afoot, started shouting, screaming, and encircling the trucks, barehanded and totally unarmed. The terrified *ultras* scampered away, leaving behind the instruments of the crime they had hoped to commit on the anniversary of the storming of the Bastille! The descendants of Robespierre and Danton were acting as worthy heirs of Hitler—with the collusion of the colonial regime's civil and military authorities!

This was why Mourad had been unable to make our appointment. He had been on watch the previous two nights in a row. Now Samia understood the reason for his pale, agitated state and begged him to go get some sleep. Realizing that he lived in the Casbah, she offered to bring him to her home in Saint-Eugène to eat and sleep a bit. He laughed, thanked her for

---

2. Literally meaning "new door" in Arabic, Bab Jdid, located at the Casbah's highest point, is one of six principal gateways leading in and out of the walled city.

her proposal, and swore to her that he was in good shape. He explained that the brothers were asking her to get in touch with sister Farida to bring her back to Algiers as soon as possible because "the organization" needed all its daughters and sons.

He concluded by saying, "Big sister, you have to convince Farida's father to bring her, otherwise the brothers will arrange for her escape to here, to Algiers. We absolutely must organize our retaliation! We can't let them burn our people like rats or shoot us like rabbits in the street or lop off our heads in Barberousse prison while their people live the good life! From now on, it will be 'an eye for an eye, a tooth for a tooth'!"

Samia took him like a mother in her arms and begged him to accept some cash to go buy ten ice-cream cones to toast all those who would avenge us. He agreed and they separated.

It felt like my two-month absence had lasted for years. I realized how much the situation, already tense in Algiers in early June 1956 when I left for Vialar, had seriously deteriorated, festered, and become explosive in both the literal and figurative senses. Indeed, on top of the curfew and the "special powers" whose real effects I had experienced firsthand, now they had increased the military presence. This meant the daily harassment of Muslims by the combined army and police forces, arrests by the thousands, imprisonments, torture, and summary executions. The repression was fierce: entire neighborhoods were regularly surrounded and searched up and down. Collective punishment became the daily routine. When the FLN retaliated by targeting the military, police, or their informants, as well as French economic interests, the local and metropolitan press, under orders from the colonial authorities, organized hysterical campaigns of misinformation and systematic denigration, smearing our activists as "outlaws," "*fellagas*," "criminals," "assassins," and "bloodthirsty hordes." This same press denied, minimized, or justified the torture and other systematic abuses, presenting them as "simple law enforcement operations" and the "legitimate duty of the army to protect property and persons"—European ones, obviously. Samia told me that "the organization" had circulated a leaflet to remind everyone that Zabana and Ferradj were not criminals, but authentic national liberation fighters.

It was July 30, 1956, and Samia had spent two hours recounting to me all that she had experienced in my absence. She had also mentioned that the colonial press had remained silent, then and now, on the *ultras'* crimes. But I noticed that, other than Petit Mourad, whom she had described to me from every angle, Samia had told me nothing of her actual missions. I neither remarked on it nor chided her for it, and I admired her for becoming a true guerrilla fighter—serious, disciplined, and professional. I was grateful to the brothers for not forgetting me, for having confidence in me; the situation was becoming increasingly difficult and trust, even before dedication, was from now on the most important criterion. I kept all this to myself and instead asked Samia, "Now that you've told me everything, or almost, can you explain to me what on earth inspired Boualem Oussedik to show up in shorts at your house, and stand there before your father? Have you asked him?" Samia let out her big laugh and explained that the only way to reestablish contact was for him to show up at her home, but in a neighborhood where three-quarters of the inhabitants were blue-blooded Europeans and the remaining quarter were upper- and middle-class bourgeois "natives." Boualem, a covert operator to his core, had dressed up like that to be taken for a European. And he had succeeded, since even Qadi Lakhdari himself mistook him. "Who would suspect a European student? No one. But a young Muslim, unknown in the neighborhood, would have been reported to the security services before he even got a chance to ring the doorbell," said Samia. After a wonderful dinner lovingly prepared by Mama Zhor, we headed to bed, where Petit Mourad's words about cyanide capsules returned to me.

I had always been fascinated by people who had the courage to choose the moment of their death. I had always asked myself whether I was capable of the same courage, without ever knowing the answer. I had no response that night either. I fell asleep telling myself that they could go ahead and try to torture me, and that I wouldn't say a thing because I didn't know a thing.

Samia shook me awake to let me know that she was going to her rendezvous. At noon, she told me that Petit Mourad would be waiting for me the next morning. The night seemed very long. The next day we finally left Samia's home after her father had left for his office. Oh! The joy of walking free, hair in the wind along Rue Salvandy, and descending toward the local council hall, beside the trolley stop. It was a hot and bright morning in those first days of August, fragrant with the scent of jasmine, honeysuckle, and citrus flowers. We strode firmly like conquerors, happy because our lives had purpose, and oh what purpose!

Just then I asked Samia, "So when will you stop fighting?"

She looked at me, bewildered, and replied, "What kind of question is that? And you, when will you stop fighting?"

I said, "When I die or when they break me from the inside, which amounts to the same thing. When my life no longer has meaning. You see, Zabana was beheaded, but he is still fighting! What gave meaning to his life now gives meaning to millions more lives, which is why he is not dead. He was so right to say to his mother, 'I am not dying for nothing, and thus, I am not really dying at all!'"

Samia laughed at my wild imagination, and we took the trolley to Consolation. We were about to enter the grocery store when a young girl emerged whose striking beauty could leave no onlooker indifferent.

"Wow! A *gaouria!*" Samia exclaimed.[3]

"Not at all!" I replied, recognizing a certain something in her eyes that gave her away as an Algerian like us. I did not know it, but she was Hassiba Ben Bouali, whom I would meet later, and with whom I would live through the darkest moments of the Battle of Algiers.

We entered the grocery store where I met the owner and Petit Mourad, whom I recognized immediately from Samia's description. I took a liking to him right away.

Samia introduced me. Mourad asked me the usual questions and added, "I'll be your contact and if I don't show, you will find the information either at Nabila's or here at the grocery store. Sometimes you will carry out the tasks entrusted to you alone and sometimes with Nabila. Goodbye, my sister, and good luck!" We left the store. Samia, to whom Mourad had already assigned a mission, took the trolley to who knows where. I returned to the house on foot with my basket and decoy groceries. Around noon, Samia found me there and informed me that I had a rendezvous with Mourad the very next morning at ten.

The next day Mourad instructed me to go to the neighborhood of Hussein Dey and report to a coffee roaster's shop, where I would be handed a package to hide under the fruit and vegetables in the basket he gave me. He handed me a piece of paper with the exact address of the store, to be memorized and destroyed; as with Samia, he explained how we would take the same trolley but each to his own side, how I had to follow him from afar, and so on. I fulfilled my mission and, at noon sharp, my contact handed me the package, small but heavy and wrapped in a piece of cloth. I buried it under the provisions and brought it back to the grocery store.

---

3. A foreign, especially European, woman.

During the first ten days of August, I carried fairly large packages or letters from somewhere to the grocery store or vice versa. I knew nothing and didn't want to, because the less I knew the better. Indeed, the FLN, at least in Algiers, was a very effective organization, deeply rooted in the people but also very compartmentalized. The only members I knew, at that point, were Samia, Mourad, and the grocer, about whom I knew nothing. Although I saw Mourad as our handler despite his young age, I didn't know what position or rank he held in "the organization," much less our own. The compartmentalized structure was such that, even though we were dying to hear the Desert Fox, we had never dared talk of him to Mourad.

We discussed a lot with Mourad, but our discussions always centered on "the organization's" attacks. The press always reported on their damage—exaggerating it, of course—and the arrests of our fighters, often with supporting photographs. Mourad talked to us of torture as a tool used by the French to get information about our organization, recounting the heroism of our arrested leaders and those who preferred to swallow a cyanide pill. He taught us that the rule in case of arrest was to hang on for forty-eight hours without speaking. In that period, "the organization" would have time to take steps to ensure that any information gathered would have no value. We harassed him to find out whether there were cases where the militants had spoken. He replied, "Never! I know brothers who preferred to die rather than talk. You must understand that a lot of fighters—as well as ordinary citizens—have died from torture, because it is not only the French police and military who practice it. So do the *ultras*, who have genuine torture chambers in *pieds-noirs'* private villas and warehouses." Mourad recounted to us in detail the attacks these *ultras* had organized with impunity against both our combatants and the Muslim civilian population. We listened, rapt, often stunned, and always full of admiration for this little fellow who feared nothing and knew so much. When we teased him, asking where he got this information, he laughed and replied: "I know everything. You just have to believe me and not ask questions."

I asked Mourad to tell me every detail of the torture cases and attacks organized by the *ultras*, in order for Samia and me to draft an in-depth exposé that we would try to publish in an anticolonial newspaper, thanks to our contacts with some liberal professors sympathetic to our cause. Mourad replied that that wasn't one of our missions, but that he would pass the message to our big brothers. Our enemy took many forms, and we were convinced that we should respond in just as many ways.

Rue de Thèbes

We were writing a note on this subject for Mourad to pass to our big brothers when Samia's father returned for lunch, very shaken up, and we learned terrible news. The night before, during the curfew, a bomb attack had killed dozens of people in the Casbah. We pressed him with questions, but poor Qadi Lakhdari, still upset, told us that the Casbah was cordoned off and contradictory information was circulating, depending on whether the source was Muslim or French.

Samia and I conferred with a single glance, deciding to go seek out the news as soon as he left. The grocer confirmed that the day before, at midnight as August 9 turned to August 10, a bomb had exploded on Rue de Thèbes in the heart of the Casbah, causing many deaths and hundreds of injuries. He added that the area was overrun with police and soldiers, and confirmed that the attack was the work of the *ultras*. We asked him for any news of Mourad. He had none, but said that, in any event, Mourad should be there the next morning, August 14, at nine. Anxious and distressed for our little brother, furious at such injustice, we didn't sleep the whole night, especially since the neighbors didn't stop ringing the doorbell all night to deliver various bits of news—much of it alarming—to Mama Zhor. They were all outraged and revolted; Mama Zhor channeled their anger by asking them to start collecting all the products they could, including money. Samia's older sister Leïla and brother Malek heard the news and came the next day with their spouses and children. Mama Zhor put them to work organizing the collection. When her son asked her where she would take the collected products and how, she calmly responded that the owner of the *hammam* she visited, whose parents were from the Casbah, would handle the delivery. Oh, that Mama Zhor! Samia and I knew perfectly well that she was counting on us to deliver her collection wherever necessary.

There was no mention of the *ultras* in the press, which claimed that the explosion was caused by novice fighters mishandling explosives, a "criminal act" committed by "outlaws," all the while minimizing the number of dead and wounded. Even Qadi Lakhdari, usually calm and measured, cursed and insulted the colonial media: "Explosives? It's the *ultras* who handle them over and over. Our people have never used explosives, everyone knows it. And what's more, it was a premeditated and organized attack against civilians while they slept! Everyone knows that too, except their journalists!" The worst disgrace was to accuse our fighters of attacking our own people.

We scoured the newspapers and followed the radio closely. Nothing. No statement from the authorities, no message of condolences. No European institution issued even a word of compassion.

On August 14, Samia went out very early to buy the papers and returned just as her father was sitting down for his morning coffee. We noticed, distressed and indignant, that the press had already moved on to other stories. Monsieur Lakhdari surprised us further still by declaring that alongside the war and oppression, we had to confront the terrorism of the *ultras*, whose organizations were guilty of many kidnappings, assassinations of Muslims, and bombings of trade unions and nationalist parties like the UDMA. One of his friends had told him that a whole family—father, mother, and children—had perished under the rubble on Rue de Thèbes. With that, he dropped a wad of bills on the *meïda* for Mama Zhor's collection and left. He was genuinely shocked and outraged by the attack, but it was the first time we had seen him express it.

At quarter past eight, we left the house and decided to walk the long way. Along our walk, we realized that in his outburst Monsieur Lakhdari had revealed the same information that Mourad had on the *ultras* and their terrorist organizations, no doubt thanks to his role as *qadi* and his membership in the *oulémas* association. When we entered the store at nine, Petit Mourad was already there, behind the counter, next to the owner. Our little brother was unrecognizable: pale, his eyes bloodshot, his features disfigured by anger. We took him in our arms. He didn't react to our maternal embrace. Anticipating our questions, he began to speak, all the while staring out the glass door at an invisible distant point:

"On the night of August 9 to 10, at midnight, during the curfew, the *ultras* detonated a huge bomb of at least thirty kilos in the heart of the Casbah, on Rue de Thèbes. People were sleeping. An entire block of homes was destroyed. We've counted seventy-three dead, three hundred injured, and at least that many homeless. Most of the victims are women, children, and the poor elderly. Carnage—blood everywhere, mangled limbs, shreds of human flesh, and many people trapped under the rubble. Among the wounded, many will die and others, if they survive, will be severely handicapped. One little girl pulled from the rubble has no eyes or arms. One little boy will no longer play football because his legs were crushed under fallen beams. I'm speaking only of the children who I myself carried in the initial rescue. It was carnage, my sisters, and the firefighters only arrived around two in the morning because the victims were just us, and us, we can die like rats! They came with the army and police, insulting the poor volunteers who were trying to rescue the victims.

"Our people were awakened by the blast, and came out into the streets and onto their terraces. They were filled with a black rage, and all wanted to head to the European city for revenge. The brothers couldn't let them do it, since everyone would have been massacred. One of the big brothers swore to them that the FLN would avenge them. I brought you this tract that you must read. My sisters, it was terrible: It was hell! A hell forged by dogs. A bomb in the heart of the Casbah! They want to kill us all! We must bring this hell to them! The brothers launched the reprisals yesterday: twenty civilians and ten police officers were killed. But they died a proper death, not blown to bits in their sleep! We need to transform their neighborhoods into hell like they've done to us!" Mourad had spoken without looking at us, in one long stretch, without pausing for breath. In tears, we hadn't interrupted him.

Samia suggested that he come rest at her house, since he was obviously exhausted. He refused, saying, "I'll only rest when I'm dead or when my country is free. Anyway, even if we do nothing, even when you are a child or an old man sleeping at home in the middle of the curfew, they blow you up in your sleep. So you'd better stay awake and do everything you can to bring the hell to them!"

Then suddenly, he recovered, apologized, and addressed Samia: "Sister, tomorrow you have a rendezvous at ten o'clock on Rue Henry Martin, at the bus stop across from the Rue de la Lyre market. A young brunette will be waiting for you there. She will be standing at the same stop, wearing a dark grey skirt, white top, and white summer shoes, with *Le Monde* in her hand. You will greet her and give her the password. She will answer you as agreed and you will go with her to another rendezvous spot that only she knows."

Samia asked if I could accompany her and he said, "No, sister Nabila, things will become much tougher and more serious! We'll fight back using their methods. Discipline and rigor must be our new religion. You will go alone—this rendezvous is for you alone. Farida will have other missions to accomplish." We insisted to our little brother that he rest, since "the organization" needed him. We also informed him of the collection that Mama Zhor was organizing and sorted out plans for its delivery, then we left.

Instead of returning home, we took the trolley to the National Library. That was all we knew of the Casbah, aside from the Ketchaoua Mosque, the shrine of Sidi Abderrahmane, and the Medersa Bencheneb. All these monuments were at the edges of the old city. As for the Casbah itself, we knew nothing of its heart or its other reaches. We were terrified at the idea of entering a city where, apart from the many shops, we had been told that there were only dangerous gambling dens and houses of ill repute. That's why we went to the National Library—to try to shake our inhibitions. Once there, we found the rendezvous spot perfectly well, thanks to some directions from our fellow Muslims. We located Rue Henry Martin, the market, and bus stop. From the immense bay window of the Boukerdouna Drugstore, just across from the bus stop, we would be able to watch as our contact arrived. Then I would follow them, in violation of Petit Mourad's instructions. We knew we had abandoned our discipline, but the urge was stronger than we were.

The next day, we reached the drugstore at quarter to ten and planted ourselves in front of its windows, which reflected the bus stop perfectly clearly. We carefully surveilled the area, and after five minutes saw a pretty young girl walk up. She was thin, fairly tall, dark with beautiful long brown hair, and she wore a charcoal grey skirt, white top and the white wedge heels so fashionable that summer. She held *Le Monde* in her right hand. She corresponded in every respect to Mourad's description, except that she was very elegant and nothing like the matron we had been expecting to find. After a few minutes of hesitation, Samia crossed toward the unknown young woman while I stood back. In the pharmacy's window, I watched them say hello and greet with a kiss, and knew that it was indeed her contact. They skirted the market and then plunged down Rue Randon, which was packed with people at this hour of the morning. I followed them with difficulty, fighting through the dense crowd for three or four minutes before they disappeared from view.

Panicked, I tried to move forward, then to turn around, desperately searching for Samia's red blouse, but in vain. I didn't dare to try one of the narrow cross streets all around for fear that I would never emerge. In desperation, I retraced my steps to the bus stop, where I waited for an hour in hopes of seeing Samia reappear.

When she did not, I decided to return to Saint-Eugène. I arrived home a few minutes before noon. Seeing me alone, Mama Zhor set to worrying about her daughter's absence. I explained to her that she had stayed at the National Library to do some more research, and that I had come home to write.

Volunteers for Death

At half past twelve, Monsieur Lakhdari arrived, and I gave him the same excuse for his daughter's absence. We sat down for lunch and he congratulated me for our seriousness in our studies, noting: "The strike will eventually be lifted, and it's best to be ready for your exams." After his departure, I excused myself and shut myself in Samia's room to begin an interminable wait.

Around five that evening, Samia finally reappeared. She climbed the stairs four at a time and we shut ourselves in together. Ecstatic, her face shone as if struck by a divine revelation or the arrival of Leilat Al Qadr.[4] I forced her to sit, calm down, and explain in detail why she was so elated. She took me in her arms, repeating that our brothers were great people, wonderful, fabulous, and many other superlatives—each one was more extraordinary than the last. Then she whispered in my ear, "That's it, we are part of the armed groups. Do you realize, Zohra? Our dream has finally come true! Our big brother told me so today."

Then she told me everything. The young woman's name was Djamila Bouhired. They had taken several turns and entered a marvelous home that Samia described as "a home straight out of the Thousand and One Nights," built on three levels in our traditional style around a central courtyard, its patio surrounded by marble columns. Djamila's family occupied the top floor and rented out the two below. When they arrived, Djamila asked Samia to wait on the first floor with a lady who would prove to be, we would later learn, the *moudjahida* Fatima Meziane, known in the household as Fettouma. Welcoming and affable, she put Samia at ease by introducing her to the people whose framed photos beamed down from a beautiful antique-style sideboard. Thus Samia learned the real name of her new contact, as Fettouma explained that Djamila's family, the Bouhireds, were the house's owners.

Moments later, Djamila returned and led Samia to the top floor, where they were received in a large room with modern furnishings. A beautiful woman, young like them, received them there. Djamila called her *oukhiti* ("little sister") and presented her as the wife of her younger paternal uncle.

4. The "Night of Power" is a holy night in the Muslim calendar that commemorates the night the Quran was first revealed to the Prophet.

Samia was struck by the warmth of their welcome. After all the welcome rituals, Oukhiti left the room and left her place to a man barely older than Djamila, with the face of an Italian actor and the charm of a leading man, smiling and affable. All three took seats around the table and the young man set about breaking the ice. He had clearly guessed that Samia was rewriting her preconceptions about the Casbah and its inhabitants. He welcomed her, making it clear that he was fully aware of the missions she had completed thus far, and shared his positive assessment of her work. Samia, grateful, introduced herself briefly. The brother listened to her with great kindness, always smiling, even though he seemed to know more about Samia than she knew herself, then got up and invited her to follow him. They walked out to the landing then into another room, where three men the same age as the first sat. One was tall and blond with blue eyes, like a Viking (Abdelghani Marsali); another tall and dark, with laughing eyes and a smile that seemed impossible to erase (Ali la Pointe); and the last was dark, of medium build, and rather taciturn (Rachid Kouache). Two machine guns leaned against the

Zohra (right) with Djamila Bouhired

Fatiha Hattali, known as Oukhiti

wall. The men rose, all smiles, and warmly shook Samia's hand in welcome. The six of them sat down at the table to eat and discuss. They all called the one who had accompanied her El Kho ("Brother"). She soon realized that he was *the* "big brother"—their leader.

This was Yacef Saâdi, the head of the armed groups in the Algiers Autonomous Zone (AAZ).[5] His simplicity, vitality, and approachable nature disconcerted Samia, who almost wept with gratitude and thanks. But the others were not to be outdone. Ali, very much the jokester of the group, kept cracking jokes and laughing at his misadventures. Abdelghani and Rachid seemed more cerebral, and their softness contrasted sharply with the machine guns propped behind them. As for Djamila, she was striking in her natural elegance, the refinement of her gestures and language, and a presence that seemed to support the whole house, like a pillar without which the world would collapse. Beautiful Djamila reigned like the only daughter in a family of boys. And it was true—Samia felt like she was in a big family who

5. The Algiers Autonomous Zone (AAZ, or in French, ZAA) was one of the administrative divisions used by the FLN to organize their campaign against the French colonial system. Further details can be found in Chapter VI.

had opened their arms to her. And from that family emerged an atmosphere of complete solidarity and unbreakable fraternity, filling the whole room and beyond and penetrating every one of Samia's pores. She realized that these people were life itself and all its promises. And it was because they embodied life itself that they fought and waged war to earn it: to free the country, whatever the price. The stakes were enormous.

They ate and talked at length with a natural and deliciously contagious refinement. Samia, amazed, was still lost in her thoughts when Abdelghani, Rachid, Ali, and Djamila got up and left the room with a polite goodbye, leaving her alone with El Kho. He explained that following the *ultras'* attacks, the FLN had decided to retaliate. He informed her that a plan was being prepared and asked, "Are you still willing to be inducted into the armed groups?"

"Sure," Samia replied. "This has always been my wish and Zohra's, and our message. May I speak about it with Zohra? You certainly know Zohra, or sister Farida if you prefer."

"Yes, you may talk with her. But understand that this will involve bombs and serving as volunteers for death."

Samia: "I understand. We agree. What do we have to do?"

"We will contact you to explain more to you in due time. Until then, discipline, rigor, and the strictest discretion are essential," he said. "I will leave you now. Goodbye and good luck."

Yacef Saâdi (El Kho), head of the Algiers Autonomous Zone

Ali la Pointe

Samia stayed there, alone, understanding now why El Kho was the leader. What a difference between the man who had put her at ease throughout lunch and the one who had spoken with her one on one! The second did not smile and did not seem to have time to waste with the undecided or the hesitant. Djamila soon returned, accompanied by the beautiful Oukhiti. They cleared off the lunch dishes, chatting idly and laughing. Then Djamila announced that it was time to leave and accompanied Samia back to the bus stop, where she caught the trolley home.

Between Our Life and Our Mother Algeria, We Choose Our Mother

I need to explain why our induction into the armed groups was, for us, more than just the result of a desperate search, but an immense honor that "the brothers" bestowed upon us. We read a lot and were very influenced by the writings of the Bolshevik Revolution, the Spanish Civil War, and the anti-Nazi resistance. We read and reread *Democracy in America* by De Tocqueville and had understood, ever since the end of high school, the fate that France hoped to relegate us to: the same as that of the Native Americans.

This is what France had wanted to do in Algeria with its policy of conquest via massacres, genocides, and smoke-out exterminations,[6] then its policy of colonization via forced dispossession against the Algerian population and their replacement by European settlers. To do all this, France mobilized its imperial army, the Warnier law, the Senatus-Consulte, and its Native Code—which, despite its repeal in 1947, was still in force in 1956. Samia and I had always been convinced that if France hadn't yet imposed the American Indians' fate on us, it wasn't because she didn't want to, but because she wasn't yet able to. This was because our people had always resisted, from Emir Abdelkader to Fatma N'Soumeur, from Boubaghla to Cheikh Al Haddad and El Mokrani, from Bouamama up to Zâatcha, and so on.[7]

Our nineteenth century was one of mass slaughter that made rivers of our ancestors' blood flow, thousands of hectares of their land burned and seized, and countless cities, towns, and villages ransacked and set alight. Our twentieth century was no better; the massacres of May 8, 1945, and August 20, 1955, ended up serving as fuel for the fire that our brave combatants lit on November 1, 1954, and that would not be extinguished until our country's liberation, and rightly so. We had always believed that our misfortune, our bondage, our negation as a people and nation went hand in hand with the system of settler colonialism.

As a result, we always believed that our liberation and our affirmation would come with the end of colonization. We had always considered it better to die with honor in the armed struggle for dignity and liberation than to survive in the disgrace of tolerating colonization—and by settlement, at that. Liberty, dignity, and honor: three supreme values, three inalienable rights defined in the Universal Declaration of Human Rights.

But France recognized none of these rights for us, a colonized people reduced to "native" status. Does this mean that for France, this so-called "Mother of Arts, of Weapons, and of Laws," we weren't human beings? It seems we were not! Never was our people's status as human beings in our own right, with the sacred rights that went with it, considered or even

---

6. Smoke-outs, or *enfumades*, were a tactic employed by the French army in their conquest of Algeria, particularly in the 1840s. The tactic consisted of lighting a fire at the mouth of a cave, filling it with smoke, and asphyxiating anyone inside. Historical accounts describe episodes where groups of up to several hundred Algerians—many of them civilians—were killed through this tactic.

7. Algerian leaders of various anticolonial resistance movements in the nineteenth century.

suggested. At best, they saw us as idle hands for whom someone needed to create a few more jobs, and empty bellies to whom someone needed to throw a few more scraps. Could the "natives" desire freedom and dignity like all peoples? Could we commit to these values, even to the point of making the supreme sacrifice? That was what we held as more than just an ideal, it's what shaped our souls and our deepest beings in 1956, as it does today.

In a free and independent country, these questions could be a harmless intellectual concern for a student thesis. For Samia and me they constituted a life-or-death issue, individually and collectively. And even when viewed with a critical eye, we considered (and still consider) that only those who had "tasted" the colonial system as we had could respond to it.

Take a young Patrice Lumumba,[8] whose body, soul, and country were subdued, enslaved, and colonized, and compare him with a Belgian or a European of the same age whose body, soul, and country were free and independent, and ask them the same questions. Or, if you prefer, summon the souls of Mahmoud Darwish and his people's Israeli colonizers, and ask them the same questions. Or, if you like, summon Federico García Lorca from Spain or Aminatou Haidar, the noble Saharawi activist whose people and country are still occupied by Morocco, and ask them the same questions. I could go on like this at length, since, sadly, there still exist peoples and countries deprived of their rights. But what I know already is that a deep sense of honor and attachment to this greatest of values—freedom—would prohibit any dignified and honorable person from engaging in such question games if he or she has never lived in the cynically abject and unfair conditions I have described above.

But those were precisely the conditions in which we Algerians lived in 1956 and in which we had lived for 126 years. That was why, knowing the stakes full well in our hearts and souls, Samia and I made the choice to become "volunteers for death"—"bombers" or *bombistes*, as they would later call us.

Perhaps the reader of today expects me to regret having placed bombs in public places frequented by European civilians. I do not. To do so would be to obscure the central problem of settler colonialism by trying to pass off the European civilians of the day for (at best) mere tourists visiting Algeria

---

8. Patrice Lumumba was a leader of Zaire's (today's Democratic Republic of the Congo) liberation movement against the Belgians and, after independence, the country's first democratically elected leader.

or (at worst) the "natural" inheritors of our land in place of its legitimate children. I will not adopt this position because I hate lies and their corollary, revisionism, whatever they are and wherever they come from. Samia and I did not regret our actions in 1956 or 1957, nor do we today, nor will we ever. I speak here in my own name and on behalf of my friend and sister Samia Lakhdari, who died in the summer of 2012. What's more, if today, God forbid, my country were to be attacked and occupied by a foreign force, I know that even at my advanced age, propped up on a cane, I would be with all those (and I know there are many of them, in Algeria and elsewhere) who would offer their lives to liberate our land and its people. In declaring this, I seek neither to boast nor to challenge anyone. I am simply trying to convey an idea, a simple conviction related to the concept of responsibility.

In August 1956, Samia and I, assuming full responsibility, chose to become "volunteers for death" to recover and free our mother, Algeria—who had been taken by force, raped, and kidnapped for 126 years—or to die. Faced with the choice between our mother and our lives, like Camus, we chose our mother. Yet in truth, we did not face the same dilemma as Camus, who, ordered to choose between justice and his mother, sacrificed justice. In fact, his mother being his country, France, as a colonial power she was antithetical to justice.

Our own mother being Algeria, her liberation was one and the same with justice.

As for the civilians who perished during the war of national liberation, if they are Algerian, I would propose that they go to the ALN fighters and ask them, "Why did we die?" I know that the ALN will reply, "You are dead because your lives were part of the price we had to pay for our country to be free and independent."

And if they are French, I would propose that they go see the French authorities and ask, "Why did we die?" I do not know what the French authorities would say, but I would propose to them the one real truth there is: "You died because you were among the hundreds of thousands of Europeans that we used to subjugate and occupy a foreign country, Algeria, so that we could make it our settler colony."

In any case, this will not make me forget all the French who chose justice and the values of freedom and dignity (of which their own homeland boasted) and joined our camp. I will be eternally grateful. I will not finish this long and necessary clarification without affirming my deep conviction: The only case where a people has the right and duty to take up arms is when its country and territory are attacked by an external force. This is called self-defense. That was our case in November 1954 and throughout our struggle.

Our Preparations

In August 1956, after the *ultras'* bombing against the inhabitants of Rue de Thèbes in the Casbah, Yacef Saâdi decided to induct Samia and me into the armed groups as volunteers for death. We were not prepared for either armed combat or placing bombs. I might also add that, at twenty-two, we had hardly ever even seen a gun (apart from in films), certainly not an explosive device of any kind. That we had never touched or handled a weapon goes without saying. What's more, the sheltered milieu we came from, so particularly protective of women, did not leave us predisposed to armed combat (on the contrary!). That was why, in addition to the happiness and honor we felt at having been chosen by El Kho, we also felt two kinds of fear. The first was the natural human fear of death. If we recognize this as the annoying but inevitable unwanted guest that it is, we can manage it, tame it with conscious mental effort, especially if we come equipped with our values, sacred principles, culture, and diverse references, the most effective of them being our slogan: "Our lives are not worth more than Zabana's and Ferradj's."

The second and more difficult fear to manage was of not being up to the task, or even failing altogether. What saved us was Samia's meticulous, almost obsessive character in the face of any mission, even the most trivial. She always insisted on dissecting everything, analyzing it, imagining and planning it in advance, then practicing every last gesture, look, word, and outfit. So we set ourselves the objective of overcoming this second fear by preparing ourselves mentally, psychologically, and politically.

The FLN's militant literature was very helpful for our political preparation, especially the tracts published before and after Zabana's and Ferradj's executions, and those denouncing the *ultras'* Rue de Thèbes bombing and promising vengeance for our people. But the text that galvanized us the most was undoubtedly the letter Zabana had sent his mother through his lawyer, which the FLN reprinted and distributed everywhere. In October 1955, during one of his trips to Switzerland, Samia's big brother Malek had procured the issue—banned by the colonial authorities—of the weekly *France-Observateur* in which Ramdane Abane had given an interview to the courageous journalist Robert Barrat. Mama Zhor lovingly hid this interview, alongside the call from November 1, 1954, in the immaculate folds of her stack of sheets, which she kept washed, starched, ironed, and stored safely in an imposing armoire whose key never left her bra. Trained in French schools, we naturally searched French texts and extracted arguments expressed in terms of rights, duties, universal values, and humanist principles.

That was why we returned to the National Library to borrow any book that might satisfy our craving: classics on the French revolution, particularly the work of Michelet and all the speeches of Danton, Robespierre, and Saint Just. As law students, we were particularly taken with Montesquieu's *The Spirit of Laws*, the Clémenceau texts that Madame Czarnecki had offered us during our senior year, and of course the 1793 *Declaration of the Rights of Man and Citizen*, of which we could recite Article 35 by heart: "When the government violates the rights of the people, insurrection is for the people and for each portion of the people the most sacred of rights and the most indispensable of duties." We also frequented the major movie theatres, on the lookout for any film on the anti-Nazi resistance. Then there were the writings of André Malraux and Victor Serge, and the poems and maxims written by René Char when he was underground in France's resistance against German occupation. This is not to forget novels by new Algerian authors, like *The Fire* by Mohamed Dib and *The Forgotten Hill* by Mouloud Mammeri, and articles by Kateb Yacine. Being almost illiterate in classical Arabic, our knowledge boiled down to patriotic songs learned by heart in the Muslim Scouts. But Mama Zhor alone could provide all the references and intellectual nourishment we needed.

Samia and I had deliberately committed a serious breach of the FLN's ironclad discipline—a discipline without which, we were fully convinced and aware, no armed struggle could succeed. But how could we not involve Mama Zhor?

It is important to note that the FLN was working through civilian activists and fighters before the massacre at Rue de Thèbes. Even when our fighters killed European civilians, it was because they were involved in the cruel atrocities against our people or because they had murdered our own, as with the *ultras* and with "native" collaborators. Before Rue de Thèbes, neither the FLN nor ALN[9] had any bombs, explosives labs, specialists in the explosives

---

9. The Armée de la Libération Nationale, or National Liberation Army (ALN), led the armed side of the independence struggle while the FLN managed the political front, though in practice the two organizations overlapped substantially.

field, or activists prepared to place bombs in public places. When Samia and I were inducted heart and soul to be "volunteers for death," our organization had no sort of "training school" or "preparation and conditioning center" like the French army and its minions did. We didn't even have special meeting sessions to prepare us, not a single brochure to guide us. I do not confess this today to heap blame on our organization. On the contrary! This shows that we were activists, combatants for the sacred cause of our country's liberation, not "criminals" or "outlaws" as the colonial authorities and their press called us. Furthermore, this means and proves (as if proof were needed) that our bombings were a response—completely necessary but not premeditated—to the bomb attacks perpetrated by European civilians against our people. That war and its carnage were felt only by our people and in our neighborhoods, while the Europeans continued to lead the sweet *belle vie* in "their city," well protected by masses of soldiers and police.

So my confession aims clearly to justify, fifty-seven years later, why Samia and I decided to include Mama Zhor, our sweet accomplice and best cover of all time, as soon as El Kho proposed our admission into the armed groups. We did so, of course, without his knowledge. Indeed, I have perhaps not shared enough about Mama Zhor's considerable role, not only in building our awareness and facilitating our maturation but also in firming up our commitment. She personified the power of our ideals and presented an impregnable bulwark against all sowers of doubt and discouragement. Unlike us, she had no need of Saint-Just or Danton or Montesquieu. She was all of them at once and more.

When Samia and I informed Mama Zhor, she began to swear upon her copy of the Quran that she would take the secret with her to the grave. Then in a trembling voice, full of concern for our lives, she explained that it was our *mektoub* (destiny) to have been chosen by El Kho. That our fate as *fiday-ate* (female freedom fighters) was desired and designed by God, and we must live it as an honor and a privilege. She offered to participate in preparing and executing our missions alongside us, and we accepted. That was our second breach of the FLN's strict rules of discipline. Fortunately, our organization was neither a crime syndicate, like the *ultras*, nor a crypto-fascist militia in the pay of the French services, like "the Red Hand," which itself had inhumane disciplinary rules and penalties for disobedience.[10] We belonged

---

10. A terrorist organization operated by a branch of the French security services, the Red Hand (*La Main Rouge*) targeted prominent advocates of the Algerian independence movement in Europe and elsewhere in the 1950s.

to an organization of activists, most of them very young, humane, full of life, and worshiping life, animated by and willing to die for our noble goal. Our organization drew its strength from the justice, nobility, and legitimacy of its ideals and from its roots in the people, who carried and protected it. The FLN, in turn, trusted the initiative and inventiveness of its fighters.

We had argued that if we were recruited into the armed groups, we could better blend into the European civilian population and conduct missions with far less risk of being arrested or killed. El Kho had heard our message clearly and accepted it; we were grateful to him. In addition, El Kho, as a leader responsible for and respectful of his activists, allowed us to participate in the selection and identification of the targets for our future attacks. That was why, while very much aware that we were committing two breaches of the disciplinary rules, we decided to persist, knowing that the only lives at risk were ours and Mama Zhor's, since we knew nothing of "the organization" or anyone in it. We threw ourselves into the concrete preparations for our mission by walking in the European neighborhoods throughout the last days of August and first weeks of September. After meticulous observation, I chose the Milk Bar on Rue d'Isly and Samia opted for the Cafétéria on Rue Michelet, across from the university. The Milk Bar symbolized colonial modernity in the service of the Europeans, their offensive carefree attitudes, their shameful indifference to our woes, and the arrogance of the colonial regime—especially since the café-bar abutted Place Bugeaud, named for the sinister exterminator of our people. As for the Cafétéria, it was the trendiest meeting spot for the European *jeunesse dorée*, especially the *ultras* students. We would later learn that Djamila had chosen the Air France agency at the prominent Maurétania building, since it stood as an official symbol of the France that all of us hated. Samia gave word of our choices and El Kho accepted them.

The next step was to study our targets, their surroundings, and their clientele in minute detail. Then came selecting our outfits, bags, shoes, hair, and makeup. Supervised by Mama Zhor, who was infallible in these subjects, we bought summer dresses and the smartest matching shoe-and-bag combinations and went to Roques, the best hairdresser, whose haircuts transformed me into a true Bretonne woman and Samia into a real Corsican.

Having never done our makeup before, we let the salon's specialist (guided, of course, by Mama Zhor) layer on all the necessary products, explaining the secrets of discreet yet effective application as she put her precious advice into practice on our faces. When we finished up and paid cash—generously—she invited us to return for a free combing and touch-up if needed.

On September 28, Samia and Djamila brought out the first three bombs from the Casbah—where they had been assembled by brother Abderrahmane Taleb (known as Dahmane), whom we would meet only later—to stash them in an apartment at 5 Rue Borely la Sapie, in Bab El Oued.

Earlier that month, the colonial army had locked down the Casbah, enclosing its eighty thousand inhabitants in what amounted to an open-air prison. High barbed-wire barriers were erected around the old city, and access limited via fixed military checkpoints installed at the various points that normally connected the old medina to the rest of Algiers. Soldiers at the checkpoints searched all "suspicious persons"—which might as well have meant everyone, since the rule was that every "native" was suspect, if not outright guilty. All this to say that the operation to transport the first three bombs was a high-risk mission that demanded courage, composure, and self-control. Escorted at a distance by brothers ready to respond to unforeseen circumstances, Djamila and Samia carried out their missions without incident. Samia told me that when they reached the final checkpoint, one of the soldiers on guard had asked them what they were carrying in their beach bags. With a smile, Djamila replied, "Why, bombs, of course!" The soldier, Djamila, and Samia laughed at her joke and the two young girls, elegant and all smiles on the outside, passed through the checkpoint smoothly, in a hurry to get to the beach. They cried out to a group of French soldiers perched on a Jeep, who responded, "You two are lucky!" to which Djamila replied, "Just come with us!" But they excused themselves, explaining that their service came first. Samia told me all of this on the evening of September 28, still impressed and full of admiration for our sister Djamila's courage, composure, self-control, and presence of mind.

The Fateful Day Arrives

We went along with Samia's favorite exercise: repeating everything in advance while mimicking the gestures, expressions, and approach to adopt that Sunday, September 30, 1956, at 6:25, 6:30, and 6:35—the date and times for which the three bombings had been set. Having received the address a week in advance, we had time to study our route options and propose the best one to El Kho for validation and possible correction, and then to practice and time the trip. We took the simulations seriously, timing our route on foot from Bab El Oued to each of our targets, carrying our handbags and a second bag loaded with at least ten pounds of provisions.

We went by the Cafétéria at different times of the day and entered once, made up and wearing wigs, to scout out precisely the right spot to hide a bomb. Leather benches ran along the walls at right angles, facing round tables and comfortable leather armchairs. By dropping the contents of one of our handbags and kneeling down to pick them up, we verified discreetly that there was empty space under the seats and the benches, and estimated the depth of the space under the benches. We noted when the crowd peaked—between five-thirty and eight, at the end of those Mediterranean summer days. Samia, ever meticulous, watched the clients, servers, and young women who frequented the Cafétéria: their clothes, how they wore them, their postures, the way they talked and behaved, their hairstyles . . . everything, absolutely everything, in order to mimic them perfectly once the day arrived. In truth, I found my friend's zeal excessive. While I was convinced of the need to leave nothing to chance, I kept thinking that we also needed to be prepared to face the unforeseeable—that single, unimaginable speck of chance. I concluded that we had a duty and obligation to develop our composure, our assuredness, and our self-control, keeping all our senses alert to be able to dominate two enemies—fear and disarray. I thought of the death of Cicero, who stayed stoic, calm, and serene at his own execution, alive, not exhaling so much as a sigh upon his own death.

The situation I faced at the Milk Bar was totally different. This newly constructed corner café, opposite the colonial army's headquarters, had been designed to give its customers the feeling of being outdoors as they enjoyed cold drinks and ice cream at moderate prices on their way back from the beach. Its lateral walls were made entirely of glass, open to the outside via a transparent door leading out to Rue d'Isly. A second, equally transparent door opened onto the side street. There, the café extended onto a sidewalk terrace filled with tables, umbrellas, and stools. After careful observation, it became clear that our biggest challenge would be to place the bomb without its being discovered immediately. The small, rectangular interior was ringed by a wall of mirrors. Along the crowded bar, three or four stools, mostly unoccupied, perched on tall metal legs.

The staff, just two servers and a busboy, responded promptly to orders. I realized very quickly that the only possibility for me to plant the bomb on the big day would be to sit on a stool at the counter, slip my beach bag between the legs of the stool and, when leaving, try to push it as close as possible to the counter. I would have to hope that the customers, drunk on sunshine, joy, and peace while our own people were being raided and massacred, would not notice a thing. I also realized that I would have to delay my departure until as close as possible to the moment of the explosion, and that I would have to leave by the door that opened onto Rue d'Isly, since the other was too blocked by the terrace tables and the crowd of customers. Samia shared my conclusions. Determined not to let her add to my stress, I refused to let her bring up what had not ceased to gnaw at her from the moment we saw my target from across the street, which was then confirmed when we entered to drink a soda: inside the Milk Bar, there was no nook or cranny where I could conceal the bomb, which Samia told me was large.

I studied the Milk Bar's atmosphere and surroundings and rehearsed the walk from Rue Borely la Sapie to my target, to choose the best route in light of the police and army checkpoints and roving patrols, to note their frequency and number, and to measure the time needed for the journey. Samia and Djamila did the same. Each of us knew exactly what to do, the precise route to walk, the places to avoid, and how to act in the face of every situation we had previously imagined. We were as ready as we could be, I repeated to myself: stoic.   _composure_

Then came the fateful day.

Samia and I had gone about our usual early-morning routine, haunted by the thought that this would either be the last day of our lives or the one that would determine all that would follow in our struggle and in our existence. We were well aware that we had as much chance of failure as we did success. Moreover, failure could take many forms, the worst one being our arrest and the torture that would surely follow.

We were to plant each bomb, ensure that it was not discovered before exploding, then make sure not to be arrested. From the day El Kho had accepted the targets we proposed, we had decided to leave nothing to chance. On the morning of September 30, 1956, Samia, her mother, and I arrived at the very chic Salon Rocques on Rue d'Isly, close to the Milk Bar, for a combing and touch-ups to our makeup, just as the employee had offered two days before.

By eleven o'clock we were back in Saint-Eugène, where we consecrated ourselves to preparing our chic "volunteers for death" outfits. I must say that mine was frankly quite pretty, an elegant summer dress with shoulder straps molding the bust, running my length, and coming to a stop a few inches above the ankles, where it flared out into a frill. It was a lavender blue, with small white stripes that perfectly matched my cork-wedge summer shoes in the same color. When trying it all on we had confirmed that, with our new haircuts and makeup, we would blend in perfectly among the European *jeunesse dorée*—even the most well-to-do among them. At noon we had lunch with Samia's parents, admiring their calm and serenity as our guts writhed with anxiety at the thought that maybe by the day's end they would learn that one of us had been killed or arrested. Or both of us. Or even all three, since Mama Zhor was to accompany her daughter to the Cafétéria. Poor Qadi Lakhdari! At one-thirty, we donned our outfits. Aware that we could not go out in the neighborhood dressed this way, we slipped long, loose, ordinary blouses over our fashionable dresses.

At the exact time of our appointment, we arrived at the second-floor apartment in the safe house that the police had failed to uncover even when they had arrested Djamila's former handler, Mukhtar Bouchafa. It was early afternoon. The day was warm and sunny, so perfect for lazing on the southern shores of the Mediterranean that we didn't pass a soul on the building's staircase or the second-floor landing as we headed to our rendezvous. We knocked, using the code chosen by Samia and Djamila. The door opened and we entered a seemingly unoccupied apartment. I quickly recognized the young woman who ushered us in: she was the one who had been waiting for Samia across from the Marché de la Lyre the morning of her meeting with El Kho. Samia and Djamila embraced like two old friends delighted to meet again. Samia introduced me to Djamila (as sister "Farida"); her ease, elegance, and friendliness seemed so natural, like we were already sisters. She welcomed me in a husky voice; her words seemed to flow in a luminous cascade. Djamila, who moved with confidence and serenity, asked us to follow her into the only lit room, a large salon where the shutters were drawn and the lights on. At one end was a dining table ringed with six chairs and at the other end a couch, in front of which kneeled a young man with brown eyes and black hair, busy with a task I couldn't make out well. Djamila presented him as Si Rachid (Rachid Kouache). After greeting us, he turned back around and resumed his crouch before the sofa. It took me a moment to understand what he was doing in that position. To get me to sit at the table, Samia had to tug at my dress and whisper, "Zohra, this is no time for daydreaming, we have to get ready to get into our roles." I wanted to reply, "But we're in our roles! What more do you want?" I said nothing, suddenly overcome by a strangely surreal feeling, as if I were watching myself in a film.

Two hours later, when Djamila opened the door on the second floor of 5 Rue Borely la Sapie in Bab El Oued, each of us was more elegant and classy than the last. It would be impossible for the Europeans, blinded by their racism, to detect in us the "Fatimas" of their fantasies. As soon as we sat around the table across from the couch, next to which Si Rachid and Djamila were crouched, Samia decided to make me repeat how I would enter the Milk Bar, sit down, hide my bomb, and sneak out at least ten minutes before the explosion. She even wanted to know what flavor of ice cream I was going to order (peach melba) and if I had prepared the exact change in advance, plus a tip to match the bourgeois outfit I was wearing, she specified. Exasperated, I rebuffed her, but Samia wouldn't hear of it. She insisted, explaining that my target was the most difficult of the three because of its small size and transparent walls, not to mention its proximity to the army headquarters. So, grudgingly and like a robot, I began to repeat everything that I was prepared to do in a very short while. But my friend, unsatisfied with my recitation, asked me to put more heart into it, to stand up and act out my movements, to act as if I were entering the Milk Bar, pretending that the table where we sat was the counter where I would plant my bomb. She kept repeating, "We have to foresee everything." I snapped that I had foreseen it all, even the probability of facing an unexpected situation. In that case, I would decide on the spot what to do; the important thing was to keep my composure, stay calm, and not let myself be overcome by fear and confusion.

I added that, to do this, we had to stop rehearsing. Djamila's and Si Rachid's laughter, which we hadn't even noticed, finally interrupted our surreal discussion. Standing with their arms crossed, they watched us with amused smiles, having just witnessed a spectacle that would long remain famous among the brothers, even the most senior among them. Then Si Rachid told us that the bombs were activated and stowed in the beach bags. Their timers were set, taking into account the time necessary for the journey to the target, our settling in and ordering, consuming, and paying the bill. Si Rachid reminded us that my bomb was set for 6:25, Samia's for 6:30, and finally Djamila's for 6:35. He insisted that it was absolutely necessary to leave the premises at least eight to ten minutes before the explosion and not to hang around the target. He concluded by reassuring us of his complete confidence in the three of us, and wished us good luck. Unlike Samia and Djamila, I only got to see our first bombs for the first time on that very day: they looked like long, wide wooden pencil boxes. Inside was a mechanical device—not the big round clock one imagines—that made no sound. The whole thing weighed six or seven pounds. Having never seen an explosive device in my life, I was proud to learn that the bombs were manufactured by our brothers.

The Air France terminal being the farthest target from Bab El Oued, Djamila left first. She squeezed us in her arms and said, "Good luck. May God be with you!" To Si Rachid, she said, "See you soon, *kho!*" Some twenty minutes later, it was Samia's turn to leave our refuge. She kissed us on the cheeks, took her purse and her bomb and said, "Good luck! See you soon, *inchallah!*" My emotions left me mute as I realized it might be the last time I saw her. To keep from crying, I turned to the window. I jumped when I heard Si Rachid say, "It's time, *khtou* (sister)!" Oh! This magic word, *khtou*! This word, full to the brim with such human solidarity and such tender brotherhood, whipped me up, reinvigorated me, and galvanized me all at once. Then, spontaneously, I turned back to my new *kho*, kissed him on the cheek, and said, "May Allah be with us!" I took my bomb, opened the door, and ran down the stairs, the beach bag slung behind my right shoulder like all the young girls did at that time. The word *khtou* was still dancing in my head and I felt like I was flying, buoyed by all the *khos* and *khtous* of the earth.

And We Became "Real *Moudjahidate*"

Today I have trouble recalling that walk from Bab El Oued to Place Bugeaud and Rue d'Isly, that epicenter of the European city, the French government, and the French army. Human existence seems to me to be interspersed with moments of such intensity and such violence that in truth we live them as if they weren't real, or as if we were drugged. I have lived these moments but have never known how to describe them. I know and am sure of one thing: what guided me that day was absolute necessity, the sacred duty to succeed in my mission so that my people would not despair.

Suddenly the Milk Bar was before me, all white, transparent, and shining: the hubbub of happy conversations, laughter, questions, youthful voices, summer colors, the smell of pastries, and even the distant twittering of birds in Bresson Square. All this enveloped me. I entered through the door facing the Rue d'Isly, which was closer to the counter and less crowded. Luckily, the center stool at the bar was free.

I walked calmly and perched myself atop it. I set my heavy beach bag on the ground in front of me, between my legs, my shoes braced on the metal circle that surrounded the stool's high legs. I set my handbag in front of me on the counter. I arranged my long bohemian dress to completely surround and conceal the stool. Look natural: those were my instructions.

I looked around: right at the Rue d'Isly entrance, a tiny table was wedged beside the ice cream bar. I could see two people sitting there. A dense, noisy crowd of men and women pressed against my back. In front of me were two servers dressed in white and at the end of the counter, sitting on a stool like mine, the cashier. The instructions were to leave at most eight to ten minutes before the explosion. I had arrived about twenty-five minutes before it. I estimated that fifteen minutes would be enough to set my beach bag in the right position, order, eat, pay, and leave. At the same time, I worried that fifteen minutes was too long for me not to be spotted. I ordered my peach melba and put my left forearm on my little bag, so that my watch would be constantly under my nose and I could watch it without being noticed. I didn't trust the wall clock in front of me. I was served promptly and set about attacking my ice cream.

I positioned my beach bag perfectly against the counter with my feet discreetly, all the while showing a barely perceptible smile to hint at the pleasure of tasting my dessert. I checked again that my beach bag was well secured and didn't risk moving when I rose. Panic began to overtake me when I realized how quickly the hands of my watch were turning. I had only nine minutes left to pay the bill, plus tip, for which I had the exact amount ready in my wallet, readily accessible in my handbag. I paid while repeating to myself, "Stoic. Stoic." At seven minutes before the explosion, I let myself slide gently off the stool, quietly picked up my handbag and made the few steps that separated me from the exit onto the Rue d'Isly. An invisible hand was crushing my neck, and I fought my legs and feet to force them to stay at the speed befitting a calm young girl on her way home. I turned right, skirted the lively outdoor terrace of the Milk Bar, and took the side alley that led me straight to the Rampe Bugeaud. I was forcing myself to walk normally, but my neck was getting more and more stiff, as if it were my head that was about to explode, and not the package that I had just left in the Milk Bar. I forced myself to finish descending the ramp to reach the seaside boulevard and catch the trolley to Saint-Eugène. I was walking, my head in a vise, when a huge explosion shook me, followed by the sound of shattering glass. My whole body was trembling and I realized that I was paralyzed, utterly unable to move forward. My head was empty, my limbs no longer obeyed me, and I no longer heard anything. I wanted to sit down right there in the street.

The sight of people screaming and running everywhere reanimated me and made me realize that I had reached the end of the Rampe Bugeaud, facing the stairs that led up the Rue de Tanger. I remembered that a friend of the family, Madame Caux, lived just a few meters away, on Rue de Tanger. Madame Caux ran a hotel where my parents stayed when they came to Algiers. Over the years, they became friends with her. Even after I joined the FLN, I occasionally shared Sunday dinner at Madame Caux's, especially when she mentioned that her friend Marguerite and her husband the colonel would be present. The colonel was part of the military's central staff and I would take advantage of the meal to guide the discussion toward "the events in Algeria." I asked questions that a young girl unacquainted with military life might ask. Then I would give the brothers a detailed report of the colonel's answers.

At that moment, a single idea pounded my brain: "I have to get back safe and sound to Saint-Eugène. That's part of my mission." Without thinking, I took the stairs leading up to the Rue de Tanger. Some of the street's inhabitants were at their windows, others outside, all talking and screaming at the same time. I passed through the noisy crowd without attracting anyone's gaze and threw myself into Madame Caux's building. She was at her living room window overlooking the street, saw me coming, recognized me, and ushered me in emphatically. She welcomed me by pulling me inside, then locked the door and worried aloud why I had been "wandering" around outside at such an hour in these troubled times. She led me to the kitchen, where she served me a glass of water and asked if I knew where the explosion had been.

"The explosion site can't have been very far," she said. "It made our window panes rattle. You are so pale, my child. Take this, drink. But where on earth were you?"

"Thank you. I was in the study hall and just as I left I heard an explosion. Then I got scared and . . ."

"You did well to come here. You should spend the night here," she said. "I am so worried about my nephew André, who still hasn't returned from the beach. He went to spend the day at my sister's in Castiglione. You know, the one who runs a beef and pork shop."

"Don't worry, Madame Caux, Castiglione is on the other side of Algiers, west of Saint-Eugène. André will return on the bus that drops off at the

Place du Gouvernement." I said all this while still floating in a cottony fog that separated me from the world and from my hostess.

Madame Caux excused herself, left me leaning against the kitchen table, and ran to open the living-room window to hear the news.

Shouts drifted up from the angry crowd, and were relayed to me by Madame Caux. "The bastards! The bastards! It was the Milk Bar! It's carnage!" "Do you hear the sirens? Oh! The Milk Bar! It's right in front of the army headquarters! Oh, the bastards! Murderers!" Madame Caux returned, leaving the window open. She kept talking, railing against "the bastards," the "gang of murderers" who dared to attack the "beautiful," "lovely" Milk Bar. Then she ran back to the window, having heard something new. She came back even more upset, wringing her hands: "Dear sweet little Jesus! It seems that another bomb exploded on Rue Michelet! They don't know where exactly. Wait, I'll call Marguerite. It seems that the army has joined the police. They have sealed all the entries to Rue d'Isly and Rue Michelet. I'll call Marguerite. I'm sure she'll have more information."

Upon hearing the phrase "another bomb exploded on Rue Michelet," I awoke from my numbness and, heart pounding, I said to myself that Samia and Mama Zhor must have succeeded, too. And Djamila? My God, the Maurétania was the most distant target. I prayed with all my might that Samia, Mama Zhor, and Djamila were safe and sound. Madame Caux, who hailed from mainland France and had only recently returned from her dear Île-de-France, was on the phone with her friend Marguerite, the wife of an officer in the colonial army! This fact finally brought me fully back to reality. I got up, went to Madame Caux, thanked her infinitely for her kindness, and explained that I had to get going to reach the bus by nightfall and return to the dormitory at Ben Aknoun, where I had to finish some urgent work.

She tried to dissuade me, informing me that Marguerite had confirmed the closure of all side streets surrounding the Rue d'Isly–Rue Michelet corridor. I reassured her that I would go in the opposite direction, toward the Place du Gouvernement, where there was another stop, just where her nephew André would be arriving from Castiglione. I thanked her again for her hospitality, bounded down the stairs and found myself in the Rue de Tanger, where a hysterical crowd of men and women of all ages rushed about.

Voices were yelling, "The bastards, the bastards, they sure wasted no time!"

"Dirty rats! They'll pay! They have to pay!"

"A-rabs, we'll smash them! We'll smash those dirty rats!"

"Arrests aren't good enough anymore, they've got to be exterminated! A good *fellaga* is a dead *fellaga*, I tell you! We should round 'em up and throw 'em into the sea, I say!"

The street was full of these venomous individuals; racism and hatred spilled out of them, sullying the walls and asphalt. I crept, shuddering, past the church at the end of the street, taking a side street that led to the Palais de Justice and then the Place du Gouvernement. The screams and threats of retaliation pursued me like a pack of wild dogs to the tribunal. I tried to escape them by walking briskly, head down, repeating to myself, "We too know how to manufacture and place bombs. We too know how to kill!" I was tense and shivering. Night began to envelop the city, filling me with fear that I might fail to complete the last phase of my mission: to return home safe and sound to Saint-Eugène.

Between the Palais de Justice and the Place du Gouvernement, on the waterfront, a chase. A man shot past me like an arrow. Shocked and frightened, I turned. Three Europeans ran in pursuit, trying to catch the fugitive. Terrified, I flattened myself into a doorway. The three Europeans paused a little further on, and the slimmest of them said, "Let's stop here. He went toward Bab Azzoun and in thirty seconds the dirty rat will be among his own kind. But I'll get him, and I'll smash his face in! I'll explode every last one of them! Not a single one will pass by the Hotel Aletti[11] alive!"

One of his friends noticed me standing petrified against the door and said, "Don't stand out here, Mademoiselle. Don't you know? Now they're targeting us with bombs, the bastards! Dogs! But we'll make them pay!"

Saying nothing, I quickly took up my route once more, eyes glued to the ground, clinging to my little purse as if my life depended on it, a voice inside me repeating, *What hatred! What hatred!* Another voice kept saying, *We are engaged in a thankless total war. Your bomb didn't amount to even a millionth of the damage they have caused, did not commit a thousandth of the crimes they commit every day against our people, or approach their napalm carpet bombing that destroys all in our countryside, human, fauna, or flora. Onward, onward! Get back safely to Saint-Eugène!*

I arrived at the bus and threw myself aboard. Not a free seat in sight. I stood, looking out at the Djamaâ El Kebir and Djamaâ El Djedid mosques. "Indestructible!" I told myself. The bus started up. It was maybe a quarter to

---

11. The Hotel Aletti, today's Hotel Safir, is located just several hundred yards from where this incident took place.

eight. I cast a glance around. No one spoke. A distressing silence enveloped the bus's interior. The passengers kept their eyes downcast, avoiding eye contact with one another. Fear seeped all around—the fear of the other. It was the last Sunday in September 1956, a beautiful warm Sunday, but the streets we crossed were nearly deserted. The Padovani and Saint-Eugène beaches and their terraces, usually crowded until ten o'clock, were empty. By the time we arrived at Saint-Eugène, few people remained in the trolley. I got off and hurried up the stairs leading to Rue Salvandy, where Samia lived at number nine. I saw Samia leaning on the balcony railing. Seeing me, she disappeared immediately to run downstairs and open the door for me. We fell into each other's arms, kissing and hugging, feeling each other as if to make sure that we were really alive, incapable of making the slightest sound. Mama Zhor joined us.

Just then, I collapsed at the base of the stairs, unable to speak or repress my sobs. With my legs no longer able to support my weight, Mama Zhor dragged me upright and pushed me down the hallway and into the sitting room, where she lay me down on a mattress set on a large rug. She asked Samia, who was crying along with me, to massage my temples, and went to find some orange flower water. She rubbed down my forehead and face and placed compresses on my eyes. I began to calm down.

She made me drink a glass of water, all the while repeating, "Serves them right! Allah be praised! You did it. We succeeded. Allah is with us." She added, "It's normal to cry. You just suffered a huge strain like you've never known before, and now comes the decompression. But you sure made us worry. Why did you take so much time to get back home? Did you have problems? Anyway, the important thing is you're here, safe and sound. Tell yourself that you have succeeded in your noble and difficult mission. Today, you are a true *moudjahida*, and your place is reserved in heaven." Then, without giving me time to reply, she continued, "My daughter, do you have any news from your other sister? Djamila, right? Do you know how it went for her? Poor child, her mission was so difficult. But I am sure she must have succeeded, too. May God preserve her and let her defeat our enemies, as you both have. Now, go wash up and change. We need to sit down to dinner." She returned to the kitchen, leaving us alone. My sobbing fit had lasted five good long minutes. We remained silent for a moment, sure that we were each thinking the same thing: *And what about Djamila?* We had no way besides Petit Mourad of getting in touch with her.

This meant having to wait until the next morning to go to the grocer for news. And that would require that we violate the strict instructions they had given us to hole up and not go out until "the organization" had signaled for us. Suddenly Samia rose, helped me to my feet and said, laughing: "Now we are real *moudjahidate*. We really are part of the guerrilla army."

Waiting for News

Samia pointed out that we had not planned a way to ensure that everyone was safe and sound in the end. It was a sign that she was doing well, despite the terrible strain we had just been through. To reassure her, I told her that Mourad and the brothers must certainly have been lurking in the vicinity of our targets, and that if something had happened to Djamila, they would have found a way to notify us. Despite these words of common sense, we were devoured by anxiety and devastating uncertainty. I asked Samia, "You were closer than I was to the Maurétania, and you didn't hear anything?"

She replied, "No, really nothing. Go figure, not even the explosion of my own bomb, or yours for that matter. When Mama Zhor and I were walking to the trolley stop, a noise reached us just as we passed by the Student Union, but it was fairly muffled. I thought maybe it was my bomb, since the Cafétéria was really an insulated place, all covered in wood and leather. But as we reached the stop, a European arrived from the other direction, waving and yelling, 'The bastards, the bastards, they blew up the Milk Bar!' That was when we realized the sound had been your bomb. From that moment on we had only one objective: to get home as fast as possible, hoping to find you there already. Why did you take so long to return? We were dying of worry."

I explained, "Unlike you two, I heard—felt, even—the explosion myself, down to my core, while I was at the end of the Rampe Bugeaud, about to cross to the Hotel Aletti and head to the Place du Gouvernement stop. I think I panicked, and when I realized that I couldn't proceed further without being spotted, I ran to Madame Caux's on Rue de Tanger."

Samia blanched in horror. "You poor miserable thing! What were you thinking? You're crazy! You went into the lion's den! And after we had practiced everything, over and over again, and after we had spent months imagining that moment!" I explained how I had found myself in a strangely unreal state, as if I had been doped, suddenly paralyzed, unable to go further, with my head clamped in a vise and a single idea pounding between my temples: *Do not get arrested.*

Aware of my abnormal state and afraid that my appearance might betray me, I had rushed to the nearest place I knew. I had found that one unforeseeable scenario. It was the kind of experience one can only really understand by living it, like burning one's hand or living as a "native" under the yoke of a system of settler colonialism. You can write a dissertation on it, fill the shelves of an entire library, but you will never know it in its deep and intimate reality, in its purest, truest form. "How could I really know what it is to plant a bomb, then feel it explode, before having that exact experience? How could I have known exactly how I would react to the blast until I had experienced what I experienced on the Rampe Bugeaud?"

I paused. "No woman is born a combatant; you must become one."

Samia admitted she did not know how she would have reacted if her mother hadn't been at her side. She told me how Mama Zhor had acted at the Cafétéria: "My mother will never cease to amaze me. When I arrived at the Cafétéria, thirty minutes before the time set for the explosion, I found her there, sitting right at the table we chose a few days ago, a cup of coffee in front of her and the *Algiers Dispatch* spread open before her. You should have seen her! You'd think she had been doing it her whole life, frequenting restaurants like that!

"With her straight grey hair impeccably styled in a classic bun, discreet, with her string of pearls and light-grey suit, she could have been mistaken for the Duchess of Parma! She seemed to radiate waves of maternal protection onto all those around her. She rose from her seat as she greeted me, gave me a kiss, and ordered me a cold drink. She paid for both drinks, after making sure that the beach bag was well stashed. Then, twelve minutes before the explosion, she motioned to me to get up and we left the place arm in arm. She was the one who set our pace: calm and serene, as if she had her whole life ahead of her. I was totally under her wing. I tried to imagine my aunts in Constantine, the aristocrats, seeing her sitting at the Cafétéria; *Lalla* Zhor as they call her, seated in a French café, her head uncovered, in a *gaouriate*'s dress! *Lahchouma*—for shame!" I laughed heartily at my friend's story but still felt a knot in my throat. I rose to go freshen up and change to be more comfortable in an indoor *gandoura*. Samia and I were settling down next to the large radio set that dominated the salon, to be sure not to miss the nine o'clock news, when we heard the sound of keys opening the front door.

My friend jumped up to greet her father and pry out the latest information, which he was undoubtedly carrying. Without waiting for our questions, he said: "Two bombs exploded late in the afternoon, one on Rue Michelet and the other on Rue d'Isly. There are many wounded and possibly dead. The Europeans are going crazy. Never before have our fighters hit them so hard, and especially so close to home, in the heart of "their areas" that they believed were protected. They are going crazy. *Allah yestor*! (May God protect us!) There is a constant stream coming and going from the Governor's Palace—civilians, soldiers, leaders. *Allah yestor, Allah yestor!*"

Samia interrupted, saying it must be another blow from the "Red Hand" to provoke more repression and "rat hunts" in the Arab neighborhoods like the Casbah, Belcourt, and others. But Monsieur Lakhdari did not seem to agree: "No, no, no! They seemed too distraught, genuinely surprised. No! This really must be our own fighters. But what are they thinking? The Europeans will react so fiercely and terribly. *Allah yestor!*"

But Samia wasn't easily discouraged: "How can they be so categorical in declaring that the culprits are our fighters? Haven't they falsely accused the FLN not long ago for the bombing at Rue de Thèbes in the heart of the Casbah, when the true culprits were the *ultras*? And with the complicity of the army and police, too."

"The Rue de Thèbes bombing, exactly. These last few weeks in Algiers, the only thing anyone talked about anymore was the FLN's vow to avenge the deaths at Rue de Thèbes. I think this idea of revenge is a mistake, a catastrophe. *Allah yestor!*"

With that, he turned on the radio to hear the nine o'clock news, and Mama Zhor poked her head through the door, asking us to prepare the *meïda* for dinner. Samia's father did not believe in human beings or their power to change the course of history, let alone free will. When he spoke of his childhood and youth in the Aurès Mountains or the path he had taken to become a *qadi* of Algiers, he always did so with great modesty, as if to say that he had nothing to do with his own ascent—that it was just his destiny, already written.

For him, the whole colonial system was a set of hardships that God made us suffer to test our faith; our liberation hinged on divine will. This philosophy constituted a major point of contention with his wife and daughter. Although she was very religious—or perhaps because she was—Mama Zhor felt that the fight against the occupier was more than just a simple duty. She believed that all good Muslims had an obligation to fight to liberate their land from its illegitimate occupiers, especially when they were non-believers.

That was why, when she stuck her head through the doorway of the salon, her husband ended the discussion with his daughter and turned on the large radio, which two minutes later broadcast a news flash. The journalist described the bombs at the Milk Bar and the Cafétéria and the damage. No word on the bomb at the Air France agency in the Maurétania. We ate quickly, trying as always to honor the meal prepared lovingly by Mama Zhor, but eager to get to bed. Our concern about Djamila's fate gnawed at us.

The eleven o'clock news again focused on the Milk Bar and Cafétéria explosions. The commentator talked at length about the victims and the wounded, explaining that at the Milk Bar, "the powerful blast blew out the glass walls, and these alone caused many injuries including among the passersby, who were many at that hour, at the end of a summer day at the beach." We cleared off the *meïda* and went up to Samia's room to take refuge. After slipping into our beds, we tried in vain to fall sleep. Despite our fatigue and the day's extreme strain, with the huge release of adrenaline and stress we had experienced since the afternoon, we remained awake until the dawn prayer, signaled by the sound of Mama Zhor's ablutions.

We waited for Samia's mother to finish her prayer, then went down to join her in the kitchen to prepare breakfast together: *mtaqba* and *msemen* flatbreads, coffee, milk, and honey.

Around seven-thirty, Qadi Lakhdari's driver Tahar brought the newspapers, and we jumped right into them. I took *La Dépêche Quotidienne d'Algérie*. Seized with pride mixed with profound unease, disbelief, and fear, I scanned the front page, looking for the bold headline splashed across the top, as was usually the case when our side hit their people or their interests. But no, there was none of that.

Information about the bombs was only announced at the bottom of the page, amid a series of other headlines, and most of the reporting was relegated to the interior pages, as if to minimize the event and mitigate its impact on the European population. This approach hardly surprised me, but some of the information in the article did—it expressly stated that the time bombs had been placed in the Cafétéria by two European women and in the Milk Bar by another European woman. I thought I had passed unnoticed in my disguise.

I returned to the article. They called our fighters "cowardly bandits," "godless, lawless criminals," "dirty assassins," "outlaw gangs," and "*fellagas*." The paper listed the people injured, their genders, ages, and where they lived, and paid homage to the speedy response and quality of care provided by the medical personnel. Two photos accompanied the article. One showed the devastation in the Milk Bar, which was "totally destroyed and saw a hail of broken glass propelled by the powerful blast, with devastating effects on the clients." The second showed a "native" waiter, his hand injured, being ushered into an ambulance, his face twisted in pain. I read and reread the article with a mad desire to scream. From my very depths, I refused to let myself feel guilty. I set about repeating to myself that Samia and I had chosen to participate in the national liberation struggle by joining the armed groups to fulfill our sacred duty to our country. We had consciously made that choice and accepted the blood price. Since November 1, 1954—without even counting the millions of "natives" killed between 1830 and 1945—our people and our fighters had never ceased to pay that blood price.

I reminded myself that the authors of the newspaper articles were part of this settlement by Europeans who had come to occupy the best parts of our territory, which were scrubbed of their legitimate children through massacres and genocides perpetrated by their army against our ancestors. I reminded myself that if we let them do it, we would end up like the American Indians.

It was only when Mama Zhor shook me that I realized I had gotten up and was standing in front of the window listing out my arguments aloud. She held me in her arms, walked me to the table, sat me down, and tore the

Bombing of the Milk Bar reported in Echo d'Alger

The Milk Bar after the bombing

newspapers away from us, throwing them in the trash and urging us not to read their lies. I explained that what bothered me was their double standard for indignation and their dirty work as a colonialist propaganda machine: "Why don't they tell the truth? What these papers call a 'civilian population' are these European settlers who their army brought by boat to colonize our country. Those they call a 'civilian population' are the agents without which our country would never be considered three French *départements* today! Those they call a 'civilian population'—and an 'innocent' one at that—they are the ones for whom the French Assembly passed the 'special powers' in order to bring us total war and exterminate us—us, the true innocent civilians, poor and defenseless—while their people lead the good life!" Mama Zhor held my hand as I spewed out my anger. I was suddenly ashamed of my unusual outbursts and looked up at Samia. Her head lowered, she raised her hands to her face, spreading her fingers wide to try to hide her bottled-up rage. We burst into sobs and fell into each other's arms, each of us burying her face in the crook of the other's neck.

When we were done, we took our seats at the kitchen table, once more calm and sure of ourselves, feeling that we had fully succeeded in our first mission.

In the articles that the colonial press dedicated to our two missions, the contents, form, and place reserved for them showed that the Europeans and their administration had suffered a blow to their certainties and their arrogance, that they had indeed been rattled and surprised. Their press, far from reassuring, couldn't manage to hide the confusion and panic among their people.

All this reaffirmed our conviction that our leaders' objective had been largely achieved: jar the Europeans out of the indecent tranquility and peace in which they had swooned, while only the "natives" had been subject to a total war since the outbreak of the national liberation struggle. "They want Algeria? Well! Algeria is at war, so let them taste the bitter reality!" That was our message to force them to open their eyes and realize that every day, thousands of "natives" were bombed, besieged, arrested, tortured, executed, or disappeared so that "peace, tranquility, innocence," the interests of the European population and the *status quo*, could be preserved and maintained. The FLN had achieved a major objective: to show our people that it was able to protect them, and especially to keep its word by striking blow for blow and hitting the heart of the European city.

In Algiers, particularly since March 1956 and the institution of the special powers, our helpless and unarmed people lived every night in anguish and fear, powerless against the fury and terror of the combined police and army forces, not to mention the *ultras*. So, yes, Samia and I were happy and proud to have participated in delivering justice for our innocent civilian population! Finally, we grasped the impact of our acts on international public opinion, including in France. Two bomb attacks on Rue Michelet and Rue d'Isly were not going to go unnoticed by the foreign correspondents, quite a few of whom were posted in the capital. By carrying the war to the heart of the enemy districts, the FLN created a situation in which the French could no longer apply their policy of ferocious repression and multiple atrocities against our people under the guise of "basic law enforcement operations." Only the lack of information on Djamila cast a shadow on our newfound happiness, even though we were sure she was all right, because otherwise— God forbid—we were equally certain that Petit Mourad would have crossed the land, the mountains, and the seas to inform us. Now all that was left was for us to follow instructions, shelter at home, and wait patiently, despite our gnawing impatience.

So we shamelessly pulled the newspapers from the trash and reread them while drinking a cup of coffee to the health of Djamila, Si Rachid, El Kho, and all our *khos* and *khtous* across the country. Settled comfortably on our cushions, less overwhelmed by our actions than we had been the night before, we devoured the remaining pages of the newspapers. Samia found the words to say aloud what reading all these papers inspired in me: "This is total war, and everywhere! Across the whole country!"

Indeed, the newspapers reported multiple attacks organized by our brothers in arms: the bomb that derailed the Algiers-Oran train, the clashes between "the armed forces" and the "outlaws" and other "*fellagas*" all across the country, or the arrests of "troublemakers" and the liquidation of some of our fighters.

I stopped reading. I wanted to understand the difference between all the events that the press relayed and those it didn't, and the bombs that we had placed yesterday at the heart of the European districts. The difference had nothing to do with the bravery and courage it took to commit those attacks. Obviously there was no one more brave and courageous than a fighter who, armed with a single pistol, killed a policeman or soldier in the streets of a European city with the near certainty of being shot down himself or lynched by the European civilian population, as had happened more than once. Nor did it have to do with the amount of damage caused by the attack. The difference between our acts and the others'—all of them necessary and full of admirable courage—was in their impact on the colonial population at all levels, on the regime, on France, and on international public opinion.

"Our bombs mark a decisive turning point in our liberation struggle. Bringing the war to Rue Michelet, to Rue d'Isly, and to the Air France agency in the Maurétania amounts to bringing the war to Paris, Lyon, or Marseille," I said to Samia. "Your father was right, they must be going crazy. Their response will be terrible and ferocious, but we must continue, because our country's liberation depends on bringing the war into 'their' territories. Now my father's words—'win or die'—take on their full meaning for us."

Shock Waves in Saint-Eugène

On the evening of October 1, 1956, I managed to fall asleep. My sleep was restless, haunted by the face of the terrible Madame Levaillant, my Latin teacher in my senior year. I dreamed of a European crowd, yelling and swarming around, tugging at me from all sides, with my former teacher among them. She kept talking, but I couldn't understand anything she said. Her eyes were fixed on me and her mouth kept opening and closing, terrifying me. I was roused awake in the morning by the sound of my own voice; I had been screaming.

The sound of water from Mama Zhor's morning ablutions managed to wrest me from the shivering torpor that numbed my body and my mind. I waited until I heard her descending the stairs, then ran to the bathroom to bathe myself from head to toe and purify myself from the nightmare's traces. Then I rejoined Mama Zhor in the kitchen and busied myself at her side. Without speaking, we sat side by side and had our breakfast. Only then did she tell me, in her soft voice, full of tenderness, "You didn't sleep well. It's because of Satan. May Allah punish him again and again. Invoke Allah and recite the *sourate Al Ikhlass*[12] eleven times. You will feel better afterward, you'll see." I did as she instructed without delay. Afterward, she added: "My dear child, you must absolutely believe that your parents will be proud of you, for you have honored your family and your whole noble lineage with your combat and your commitment. There is nothing nobler than to fight for your country and your religion. May Allah be with you all and protect you."

Samia joined us, carrying the day's newspapers—our only link with the outside world, since the brothers hadn't shown themselves. The papers finally gave us the answer as to why no one had said a word about Djamila's bomb. They all reported that the day before, an employee of the Air France agency at the Maurétania had found "a large beach bag," which he presumed a client had forgotten there. Upon opening the bag, the staff discovered the bomb, whose detonation system had failed. The ignition was linked to a large alarm clock that had stopped at five-thirty. Samia and I knew that Djamila's bomb was supposed to have exploded at six-thirty-five. This meant Djamila was safe and sound but that the police had the bomb, which gave them invaluable clues for their investigation and presented additional difficulties for our organization's future attacks.

We spent the day waiting for news from our leaders, and I began to wonder if they hadn't perhaps decided to leave us isolated for a long time.

That day, an unusual visitor arrived with alarming news: Mohamed Lakhdari, Samia's paternal uncle, freshly arrived the same day from Paris, where he lived and rubbed shoulders with the city's elites. (Three years later he became a senator, representing Algeria's eastern region in the French Senate). He informed us that a mobilization of all the police and army in Algiers had been decreed to "neutralize and dismantle" the bombing network. He explained that the European population was demanding that

---

12. The *sourate al Ikhlass* is the 112th *surah* of the Quran and is sometimes recited independently as a prayer.

the French government make every effort to arrest the perpetrators, make an example of them, and ensure that such attacks would never again be possible. As he spoke, Mama Zhor sat calmly beside her husband, her hair wrapped in a beautiful satin scarf with traditional long tassels. She asked her brother-in-law if the *roumis* already had an idea about who might have perpetrated the attacks.

He answered, "No, but only an organization with material means and experienced and trained personnel could undertake such bold actions. Such attacks require a sophisticated knowledge of explosives and fighters with unwavering resolve." Samia and I avoided looking at each other. Mama Zhor kept questioning her brother-in-law. Not one to pass up the opportunity to shine in front of a lady whose lineage led straight back to the Emir Abdelkader, he explained how the previous day all of Paris, its offices and its palaces, had spoken only of the attacks on the Milk Bar and the Cafétéria. He said the initial suspicions had fallen on Communist militants, since they had developed substantial expertise in explosives during the anti-Nazi resistance and even the Spanish War. He added that in Algiers, anxiety had spiked within the civil administration and the military, along with the European population, because no one had expected this kind of attack.

We were surprised, shocked even, by the effects that our bombs seemed to have caused in official circles. But that didn't prevent Samia from asking her uncle: "And what does all of Paris have to say about the attack on Rue de Thèbes?"

"Oh, stop it, Samia, with your tit-for-tat thinking!" he replied. "Of course I understand why you're asking this question and what you're after, but you must realize the enormous seriousness of the situation that Sunday's two bombings have caused. These bombs mean that it's a state of war in Algeria, not a mere disturbance in the public order! Anyway, you're a second-year law student, aren't you? You can understand these things." Then, addressing his brother the *qadi*, he added, "If the situation in Algiers ever becomes too dangerous, we shouldn't hesitate to send Samia to Paris. She will be fine with me and can finish her law studies quietly and under better conditions." Monsieur Lakhdari thanked his brother and explained that Algerian students had been on strike since May, and that his daughter was to be married soon anyway. He added that since the wedding date had already been postponed twice, it was now firmly set for December 24, 1956. Senator Lakhdari already knew his niece's fiancé, Anis, her maternal first cousin and a law student in Lyon. The two Lakhdari brothers decided that after the wedding, the young couple would go complete their studies in France.

Samia and I went up to her room, where we let fly all the laughter we had managed to restrain in the presence of the senator and his brother the *qadi*. We knew that, even in their wildest nightmares, they couldn't possibly imagine that the bombers were right there in front of them: the daughter of Qadi Drif, and the wife and daughter of Qadi Lakhdari. As crazy as it may seem today, it was the image of Mama Zhor—one moment in a conservative *gandoura* and scarf, one moment in a pearl-grey Chanel suit with matching shoes and handbag—that really had us writhing with laughter.

The next day, Wednesday, October 3, the newspapers confirmed for us what the senator had indicated the day before: that the explosions at the Milk Bar and Cafétéria were "the work of Communists, the only ones with sufficient know-how, mastery of bomb manufacturing techniques and seasoned fighters capable of planting them in places frequented by Europeans without causing suspicion." They went so far as to reveal the identity of the Milk Bar bomber: Raymonde Peschard, an activist known for her total commitment to and activities within the Algerian Communist Party. A photo of her, though not very clear, was published. The only similarity between us was the blonde hairstyle.

Samia and I were revolted and frightened by the ease with which the colonial authorities and their newspapers accused poor Raymonde Peschard—whom we didn't even know—without any evidence. The articles announced that she was wanted, since the police had been put onto her trail by eyewitness accounts. We were alarmed by the judicial system of a country that lauded itself as "the land of human rights and freedoms" yet didn't hesitate to violate the principle of the presumption of innocence by making a scapegoat of a perfectly innocent woman—and a French citizen to boot. We knew that the French system had never encumbered itself with scruples when it came to judging the "natives," since we had never been considered citizens or even full-fledged humans. But Raymonde Peschard was a French citizen. Moreover, she was not just suspected but outright charged. Without proof. Not for any act she allegedly committed, but for who she was: a Communist activist. We were staring straight at a clear case of totalitarian logic, in total violation of all legal principles. What a hypocritical state the French state was!

What's more, the media's reports and analyses were evidence of the deep ignorance and the contempt in which the French held our people—they were

essentially saying that the "natives" were incapable of knowledge and expertise, and that our women could never physically resemble European women.
In their eyes, we were nothing but "Fatimas and Mohameds," trained to
clean up their messes and carry their loads. Mama Zhor recited her verses,
invoking God the Almighty to let them rot in their racism and let it blind
them even more. We congratulated ourselves on our conduct while at the
university, which had been to stay discreet, anonymous, and self-effacing
and always refuse our dear Mimi's suggestions. We missed her so, but her
proposals would have led to us being noticed, and maybe even having a
police file on us opened. Being totally unknown to the police, the armed
services, and the *ultras* allowed us to be very useful to "the organization."
This conclusion filled us with great joy, and Samia proposed that we go to
the *hammam* to get a massage, relax, and listen to the *vox populi*. She added,
"Then we'll ask Tahar to take us to Roques to freshen up our haircuts!" Not
wanting under any circumstances to find myself at Roques or anywhere else
near the Europeans, I reminded her that we had to respect the instructions
to hole up and wait patiently. And, wisely, that was what we did.

One morning, we were in our room when we heard someone ring the
bell. We leapt up, but Samia beat me down the stairs to open the door.
From the exclamations of surprise, laughter, and audible joy, I understood
before even arriving that the visitor was for us. I knew it was Djamila from
her unmistakable voice. I rushed into the living room, where I found her
smiling and elegant, sitting opposite Samia and overflowing with happiness.
We kissed and Samia joined us in a three-way hug as if to ensure that, since
our last meeting on Rue Borely la Sapie, we were still all alive and ready to
continue the fight together.

Once the initial emotions had subsided, Djamila delivered a message
to us from our big brother: We were to come to the Casbah to remain there
for some time. She explained that it was a security measure imposed by the
circumstances. We asked her what that implied, but she replied that she
knew absolutely nothing. She said that she would be waiting for us the next
morning at ten o'clock at the location of her first meeting with Samia. Samia
tried to explain that it would be impossible for her to stay away from her
family home for several days, and that her father knew nothing of her activities. Djamila retorted that it was a question of "orders to be executed" and
that Samia could explain her situation to the big brother directly when she
met him. Djamila left as suddenly as she had come, refusing to stay with us
for lunch, since the brothers were awaiting her. Afterward, Samia remained

ill at ease, not knowing how to justify her absence to her father. We decided to present the problem to our wonderful accomplice, the only one capable of finding a solution. Mama Zhor listened to us and delivered her verdict. She insisted that her daughter follow her orders but suggested that she ask Monsieur Lakhdari's permission to spend two weeks with her sister Leïla, a married mother of three children, and assured her that she would make sure things worked out.

5

IN THE CASBAH

In the Casbah at Last

The next day, at ten o'clock sharp, we reached the rendezvous site and found Djamila waiting for us. We set off at a firm pace, but our progress was complicated by the thick crowd. The men were in all different outfits, from china-blue docker uniforms to Kabyle *gandoura* robes and *chéchia* caps. Some were bareheaded, others wearing a *chèche* turban or scarlet-red Turkish *fez*. Behind the stalls, young vendors hocked their wares to the women who passed, veiled in the white Algiers style. The smells clung to us: a penetrating mix of scents: spices, coriander leaf, fresh mint, cooked foods, and the stench of stagnant water. The hubbub prevented any discussion along the route. Djamila turned left and we took the Rue Porte Neuve, where the crowds thinned as we plunged into the bowels of the Casbah. We turned left again into a second lane, darker and lined with tall houses with no openings onto the street except for heavy studded doors squatting in solid wooden frames. Only a narrow stripe of blue sky was visible above. We followed Djamila, who advanced at a quick, confident pace, returning the greetings of veiled women and young children along the way. Everyone seemed to know and respect her. She stopped before one of the doors and knocked twice with a fist-shaped knocker. The door opened and we entered into the *sqifa*, a foyer darker and cooler than the street, broken by a ray of light that penetrated through a low door on the left. We stepped through that door into a dazzling light and found ourselves in a square courtyard with a floor of white marble slabs—*wast eddar*, the home's central courtyard. It was ringed by spiraled columns of white marble supporting open-air galleries with elegant wooden balustrades. From these overhead galleries, doors opened onto several rooms. The whitewashed walls were decorated halfway up in ceramic tiles with blue, yellow, and green motifs. Breathless before this beautiful symphony of light and color, I followed Djamila and Samia up the stairs to the second-floor gallery.

The stairs were capped with slabs of slate and the walls covered with the same ceramic tiles as the *wast eddar*. The upstairs gallery, open to the courtyard, had a ceiling of exposed wooden beams that seemed to rest on pairs of logs rising from each doorway. The heavy wooden doors themselves rose as high as the walls, but a smaller door the height of a man was set into each one. Djamila walked through one, and we entered a large rectangular room. On the wall facing the finely crafted door hung a large mirror in a wooden frame with floral mother-of-pearl inlays. A matching bench faced it. On the left, at the back of the room, a massive bed in forged iron dominated the entire wall. Across the room, the right wall was taken up by a large, beautiful armoire, again in wood and mother-of-pearl, with long mirrors. At the foot of the armoire, a carpet stretched across the entire room, topped with three mattresses covered with rich fabric and cushions, arranged in a U-shape. On either side of the door was a low window overlooking the open gallery outside. Samia and I were dazzled by so much beauty. After removing our shoes, we sat down on the mattresses, stretching out our legs on the soft carpet, silent lest our voices shatter the ambiance. The house was so quiet that it seemed uninhabited. We finally dared to whisper to Djamila our sincere gratitude for letting us discover such beauty and asked several questions, trying to gauge if all the houses of the Casbah were so elegant. It seemed unreal to me. It was the first time I had entered a house in the Casbah and the first time I saw a four-poster bed, surrounded by finely crafted wrought-iron gates and upholstered in blue satin. Everything around me was new, so different from the houses in my region, so refined, so harmonious. I smiled at the thought of living in a house that itself seemed to have resisted colonization and its misfortunes, for this must have been the style of our homes before the arrival of the French. Djamila laughed at how naïve we were, despite all our studies. It was all so luxurious that I asked Djamila if she slept in such a bed or if it was just for decoration. She stared at me, wide-eyed, and burst out laughing: "Of course! And we sleep tremendously well in it!"

Whispering now, Djamila asked me to refrain from talking too much in Arabic to our hostess because, she explained, in the Casbah women from the west of the country were not regarded highly. I confided to her that, in greater Oran, we looked down on the Casbah in the same way. We laughed heartily, then fell back into silence, letting the peace and tranquility of the place infuse us. A very young, pretty blonde girl with sapphire-blue eyes came in quietly to lay before us a *meïda* table and large copper tray. She greeted us and left to bring the lunch: dishes cooked with great care and gourmet presentation: salads, *chorba mqatfa* stew infused with coriander, and finally *elham beldolma*, vegetables stuffed with meat and rich in parsley and lemon. After lunch, a short woman of respectable age, wearing glasses and the traditional robes of Algiers, came to welcome us and inquire about our needs. She gave us each a prayer rug and, natural as could be, proposed that we accompany her to perform the ritual ablutions and complete the noon prayer. Djamila, who had shown great deference toward our hostess, now fixed her eyes on her feet and murmured something, but I didn't catch it. Samia followed with a "Me too." Then the old woman turned to me, still silent, and urged me to follow her. I realized that my two friends had elegantly refused what our hostess considered "the sacred duty of every *moudjahida.*"[1] I shot them a furious glare as they struggled to restrain their laughter, then followed the older woman out through the galleries.

Everything in this wonderful house appeared to have been carefully thought out, right down to the washroom. Nothing was missing: sandstone basins, buckets, and finely crafted copper bowls (polished to a shine) and piles of immaculate white towels. After performing our ritual ablutions, I followed Lalla—this was what everyone called our aged hostess—into a clean, fresh room every bit as elegant as the one where we had eaten lunch. In a sober, authoritative voice, Lalla led the prayer. I could only reproduce her movements mechanically, I was so anesthetized by all the events I had experienced in such a short time. Once our prayer was finished, we rejoined

---

1. The young women would have been exempted from performing their five daily prayers during their periods, according to traditional Islamic practice.

Djamila and Samia to share coffee. My friends gratified us with an *Allah yaqbal* ("May Allah accept your prayer"), aiming to mock me. Lalla replied that she hoped their "indisposition" would end soon so that the prayer could be spoken by four voices and not just two. After we had slurped down our coffees, Lalla asked us to follow her to show us our room.

We discovered a third floor, a perfect replica of the second, before continuing up to the flat rooftop terrace, a traditional feature of houses here. It overlooked the entire lower Casbah, part of the European city, and the marvelous Bay of Algiers beyond. At the horizon, the sea melded into the sky. Two newly constructed bedrooms, each facing the other, occupied part of the terrace. The other part was occupied by a spacious washroom. I learned that the people of the Casbah called this part of the house *el menzah*. The room that Lalla indicated to us was square, spacious, and sunny. A huge bed with a large mattress occupied three quarters of the room, and beside it squatted a nightstand with a large radio. Opposite the bed, a single desk and chair sat against the wall. Clean towels and soaps were arranged on the desk. "Here is your room. The bed is very large and all three of you are thin, so it will do," said Lalla. Addressing Djamila, she added: "If you need anything, call Zineb." She left us and disappeared.

Left alone, Samia and I asked Djamila, "What do we do now?"

She replied, laughing, "We wait!"

We let her know we were worried, since we had come without spare clothes. In fact, planning to return to Saint-Eugène in late afternoon to inform Mama Zhor, we had deliberately taken nothing with us except the clothes on our back. Djamila put us at ease by reassuring us that all the clothes we might need would be provided. And no sooner had she said it than it was done. Our friend returned a few minutes later with the little fairy Zineb, carrying *serouals el messelmine* (traditional trousers for women), *cassacates* (women's tops), and a mix of scarves. Just like that, Djamila, a worthy daughter of the Casbah, helped us to swap out our city clothes for these traditional garments. With no mirror in the room, we had to rely on each other's judgments, and soon came to agreement that the traditional clothes of Algiers suited us well. Djamila offered advice about social life in the Casbah. Our meals would be served in our room and Lalla came up to our abode regularly at prayer time, including for the dawn prayer. I came to dislike playing the actor in a comedy five times a day. There was nothing nice about the dawn prayer, especially since my two friends, whose heads were buried under the pillows and sheets, could hardly stifle their laughter at the sight of Lalla, serious, strict, absorbed in her prayer, and me behind her, constantly peeking my head up to mimic her movements. I spent my first day and night in the Casbah in this calm, silent little palace. My friends' warm presence and solidarity crowned my baptism as a *Casbadjia* (a resident of the Casbah) in joy.

The next morning, after breakfast, Djamila left us to execute a mission. Samia and I felt lost and disoriented, realizing that our first day of isolation had passed serenely thanks to her strong presence. We wouldn't even be able to find the route we had taken the day before with Djamila. We were totally dependent. The house encouraged us, chatterboxes that we were, to stop talking and learn to wait. Samia opened up to me, whispering, "I only have two and a half months at most to share with you. If God grants me life until that time, I have to get married on December twenty-fourth. The date was firmly set, as you know, and I can't push it back, since we have already postponed twice. Even Mama Zhor won't hear of it—she who is our accomplice, committed body and soul at our sides for the independence of our country, swore to me she would kill herself if the marriage doesn't take place on December twenty-fourth. She said that my father and my brothers would die of shame, since a third postponement would mean that I have lost my honor and that of my family, especially since Anis is my cousin. Do you understand this reasoning?"

I replied that I understood perfectly and that she faced a dilemma that could be summed up in a single question: "Can you tell the truth, that you are a bomber, and that is why you cannot marry? No, of course you can't. So, yes, Mama Zhor is right." Samia told me of the difficulties she was having in explaining all this to the big brothers. To which I replied: "Let it come, and then you'll explain. I'm sure they will understand."

My First Meeting with the Brothers

Suddenly a man filled the bedroom door. He was brown-skinned, tall, with an athletic build exuding presence and natural elegance. His face and eyes were still marked by the freshness of adolescence. Samia recognized him and bounded toward him. He wrapped her up in his broad arms and, continuing to talk and laugh, turned to me: "So you must be Farida! The one that nobody knew. *Marhba bik, ya khtou.*" (Welcome, sister.) "You have brought joy and dignity to the whole Casbah, *ya khtou!*" He wrapped me up too in his arms, which already felt fraternal and protective, repeating, "With sisters like you, I'm thrilled!"

Samia and I found ourselves under the protective wings of the man the colonial press called "the first-degree mob boss" and "the greatest villain the world has ever seen," whom all the French police and army forces were hunting, but whom the "native" people admired for his legendary courage and sharp sense of justice and dignity: Ali la Pointe. Popular legend held that he possessed the gift of omnipresence, since he was often reported to have appeared at the same time in different places, successfully executing several missions at once. However much the colonial press pursued him out of their vindictive hatred, charging him with every possible evil, the inhabitants of the Casbah revered and lionized him. In the Casbah it was said that as soon as he appeared, the enemy soldiers—including the sinister paratroopers who plied the old *medina* night and day—would turn against the wall, shielding their heads with their arms and crying "Mama! Help! Ali la Pointe!"

He took a seat on the edge of the bed and asked us to sit on either side of him. He rested his arms across our shoulders and hugged us toward him like a big brother or a father proud of his children. All the while, he called to someone we couldn't see, laughing and speaking in the language of the people of the Casbah: "Hey, come see the two fake *gaourias* who set off that party!" I felt tiny in Ali la Pointe's arms. I didn't know that I would soon live alongside him for months, protected by his immense affection, fed by his inexhaustible brotherhood, reassured by his legendary bravery and extraordinary courage. From the outset I felt very close to Ali, and sensed deep in my soul the word that suited him best: just. Later, during our life as fugitives, I would confirm that he had not an ounce of bitterness or hatred inside him.

Then El Kho came. I recognized him immediately from Samia's description. His face was all smiles, and his dark eyes—topped by thick eyebrows—sparkled with life and mischief. He reminded me of the Desert Fox. I couldn't believe it. I was next to Ali la Pointe and face to face with El Kho! I could hardly pay attention to their words. El Kho greeted us warmly and said bluntly: "They're going crazy. All the security services, the police and army, have dropped everything else and are on the bombing case. We learned that they've identified one of those who placed a bomb. So we didn't want to take any risks. Don't believe the press reports about Europeans and Communists. That's why we've decided to hide you out of sight, to give ourselves time to collect more reliable information."

We began talking like old friends. Samia, the jokester, participated actively in the discussion. I didn't speak much—because of the emotions that meeting these two great *moudjahidine*, these two great leaders, stirred in me, and because I was afraid that my western accent would betray my origins. But El Kho's mischievous eyes and casual laughter thoroughly thawed the atmosphere. Soon Djamila arrived and joined us on the edge of the huge bed. We were like five brothers and sisters meeting after a long separation.

El Kho addressed Samia and me: "You must not be impatient. For security reasons, you must stay here until further notice. If you want books or if you need anything at all, don't hesitate to ask Djamila. Every morning you will get the local and mainland French press, but don't let it poison your thinking. I see that you already have a radio—that's perfect." I piped up to say timidly that I couldn't stay long in the Casbah without passing by the university dorms, since my father might leave Vialar to come visit me. I explained that if he didn't find me there, he would panic and then surely contact Monsieur Lakhdari, who thought Samia was at her sister's.

El Kho, with his reassuring authority, said: "Don't worry. Regarding your father, everything is already taken care of." I didn't dare ask what he meant. And with that, they got up to leave, wishing us goodbye warmly.

Ali, still laughing, patted us on the back and exclaimed, "See you soon! Remember, you are safe here. We need you."

The two brothers wished us good luck and disappeared down the stairs, leaving us standing before the door, our hearts in a knot. Djamila ducked out, and a deep sense of loneliness came over me. The conviction that my life would never again be the same, that my daily routine would never again be so reassuring, made my throat clench up. I returned to our room and lay face down on the bed to hide the tears that flooded my face. Before long, Samia joined me, and Lalla's big bed became "the weeping bed."

We were lying there bawling in our new bedroom when the young blonde fairy Zineb came to announce that lunch was served. We followed her into the room opposite ours where salads were arranged on the *meïda* around a flat *sfiria*—a dish of lamb and bread meatballs, cheese, and golden eggs all fried together. After the delicious meal, Lalla came down to invite us for a bath in a *hammam*. I laughed to Samia with my eyes and whispered, "So much for being 'indisposed' for your prayer! Now Lalla will know!"

Samia dared an "I prefer to wait until tomorrow, if you do not mind, because I have no other clothes."

"Never mind that," Lalla retorted. Everything is ready downstairs in the *hammam*. There's a change of clothes for both of you, and everything you need for your bath. I invited Djamila to stay and join you, but she wasn't free."

We followed Lalla, who led us to the ground floor and then to another staircase we hadn't noticed the day we arrived, leading down to the *hammam* in the basement. We followed the steps to a low doorway with swinging doors that opened onto a rectangular room, where we found two mattresses covered in the orange- and black-striped fabric used in the *fouta* wraps from Kabylie. Everything we needed was laid out on the mattresses: cloths to wrap our bodies in, wooden clogs, thick wide towels, and smaller ones to wrap our wet hair. A second set of swinging doors separated us from the bathing room, where the walls were lined with ceramic tiles decorated with images of yellow, blue, and green tulips—as was typical for houses in Algiers—and the floor was paved with white marble. Hot and cold water flowed from copper faucets into marble bowls. Lying down with my back on the white marble, my mind empty, I let the heat overwhelm me and this moment of tranquility and contentment gently numb me. Much later, when I found myself stuck between Ali, Hassiba, and Petit Omar in one of our cramped refuges, barely much higher inside than the youngest among us, I would remember Lalla's *hammam*.

Even though Samia and I were surrounded by so much kindness—pampered, really—the *hammam* became a precious pause in our daily routines. Djamila, who always came at the end of the day with some treats, was our only living link with the outside world, with our earlier lives, with life itself. One day she brought us back some pretty, nicely tailored skirts and tops. "Why?" we asked. "Are we going out?" No, it was just an additional little kindness on her part, we learned, which sent us into hysterical giggling that filled the marvelous house. It wasn't long before Lalla came and lectured us to remember that our Prophet (peace be upon him) recommended total discretion for women, whose voices should stay inaudible even when they prayed! We teased her in response, recalling that our Prophet (peace be upon him) loved women and music, and fell into another fit of uncontained laughter, leaving her to conclude that we were three truly sorry *moudjahidate*.

Hassiba

We continued to respect our instructions never to leave the rooftop unless we were invited to do so. The pretty little fairy always served us and barely said a word. After a few days we discovered that other women and even men lived in the beautiful house. But all of them seemed to talk in whispers and tiptoe instead of walking, for no sound disrupted the house's monastic silence—except once, when we heard someone clap. We rushed to peer down into the central courtyard and discovered that clapping was how Lalla summoned the women of the house, who must have numbered three or four—we never knew exactly. To kill time, after airing out our room, cleaning, and reading the newspapers, Samia and I invented a game in which we tried to imagine the past lives of those we knew, including and especially our leaders. One afternoon, while we were enjoying ourselves imagining the former lives of El Kho and Ali and cackling aloud at our guesses, Djamila burst into our room. Behind her loomed a figure draped in a white *haïk*.

"You two seem to be having fun," Djamila commented. "I would like to introduce you to a sister." She turned toward the silhouette and told her, "Come in and take off your *haïk*. You're safe here. You're going to spend a few days with the sisters here." Then Djamila presented us by our nicknames. Our new sister crossed the threshold of the door, shed her veil, and lowered the *âadjar* from her face. She was slender, with a proud bearing, strawberry-blonde hair pulled back in a ponytail, and blue eyes that met our gaze directly. Samia and I immediately recognized her. It was the beautiful girl we had seen one day in August as she was leaving the Consolation grocery store. It was her look that had struck me that day. Her thin body, light-blue eyes, and round face suggested that she was still barely a teenager.

It was Hassiba Ben Bouali, our wonderful youngest sister, and we would learn that within her lay unwavering determination and firm convictions. Later, during the terrible period the French army baptized "the Battle of Algiers," Hassiba would tell us how she had escaped the security services, who had come to arrest her when she attended a cousin's wedding in Blida with her mother and sister. Around three in the morning, as the last guests were leaving the party, someone came to tip her off that the police were coming to arrest her. She immediately left the party, still dressed in her beautiful white lace evening dress, and finished the night in the house of a stranger.

In October 1956, Hassiba was working with Azzouz's team (the son of Si Lakhdar, the well-known herbalist in Belcourt) and the Timsit brothers, former Algerian Communist Party activists who joined the FLN after the July '56 agreement between our organization and the Communists. She was in charge of transport and routing from the Consolation to the villa belonging

Hassiba Ben Bouali

to Si Lakhdar and occupied by his son Azzouz, in the Birkhadem neighborhood. A few days before Hassiba's arrival at our shelter, the press had indeed reported the discovery of a bomb lab in Birkhadem run by the Timsit brothers, who were arrested there. Hassiba told us that she had escaped arrest that day thanks to the intelligence and vigilance of our wonderful brother Petit Mourad. As she spoke, she carefully folded her *haïk* and her *âadjar* and placed them on the table.

Lalla came to welcome her and scrutinized her with those beady eyes that always seemed to pat you down, even though Hassiba was not much older than the little house fairy who served us food morning, noon, and night. Hassiba passed Lalla's examination handily; though reserved, she responded to the words of welcome with the air, tone, and complicated formulas of young girls respectful of the age and rank of our hostess, who was charmed and didn't try to hide it. Hassiba clearly corresponded to Lalla's image of the perfect *moudjahida*. In truth, beneath the exterior of a frail young girl, she was very insightful, sensitive, and attentive to others. She chatted with Lalla and amazed us by winning her over. Following the afternoon prayer, the little fairy served us a wonderful coffee with all kinds of homemade breads, cakes, and unparalleled marmalade in our local style, with its big pulpy chunks. We sat around the beautifully prepared *meïda* and, just as the four of us were getting to know each other a little better, El Kho and Ali popped out of nowhere to meet our new "*bombiste*." It was an indescribable hubbub of words, laughter, exclamations, and uncontained joy. I was afraid Lalla would throw us all out, but I knew that as long as the big brothers were there, she wouldn't dare raise a fuss.

Of course, Ali couldn't help making us laugh by saying, "Hey look, *ya kho*, look at the little angel that the French army is searching for and calling the most dangerous person around!" He was talkative and kept expressing his surprise at discovering that the fighter presented by the colonial press as a "dangerous terrorist" was in fact so young, so fragile, so beautiful and refined. He couldn't get over it, and again and again expressed his astonishment and pride by repeating to El Kho, who was as happy as him, "It's better not to have sisters, if they're not like these!" Ali wanted to take a photo of all four of us there on the Belhaffaf's rooftop. Samia and I expressed our strong refusal, obsessed with the security rules and all that we had learned about clandestine living. But Ali insisted, declaring that he was the happiest of brothers and the proudest of men since God could not have sent him more wonderful sisters than the four of us. Eventually we gave in. Like a child enthralled by his toy, Ali officiated. He distributed a weapon to each of us, instructing us how best to hold and aim them. He took the photo, happy as a kid. Facing the camera, Samia, who hid her face behind the extended gun, couldn't stop ruminating throughout the following days about our incredible carelessness—especially that of our leaders.

Alas, fate would prove her right, because this picture would fall into the hands of the security services and help them to identify us. Before the photo betrayed us, nobody knew who we were, despite the arrests of brothers with whom we had worked. I tell the story of this photo because it expresses just how human, brotherly, and affectionate Ali la Pointe was. He saw Hassiba not just as a child but as a tender baby. One day I pointed it out to him and, clearly moved, he replied, "You see, *ya khtou*, normally you and Samia should be in university and this angel Hassiba in high school, but France has decided otherwise. Instead of being in school, she went to Azzouz's bomb lab. She could have been blown up like Rachid. And she's only a child. It's France who wants all this, *ya khtou*!"

All six of us sat around the *meïda* for afternoon coffee, and El Kho explained that Hassiba had been identified and was wanted by all the

Zohra, second from left, with gun, along with Samia Lakhdar, Djamila Bouhired, and Hassiba Ben Bouali

security services. He added that her photo had been circulated to all their agents, as well as to the informants and collaborators. As a result, until further notice, she was absolutely prohibited from leaving the house under any circumstances. El Kho continued, "Hassiba has indicated her wish to go underground in the *maquis*. She will need fake identity papers to get around. But before that, she needs makeup and a disguise."

Djamila peered silently at Hassiba, pondering, then said: "I think she should start by changing her hair color. If we apply henna to her hair a few times and darken her eyelashes and eyebrows, she'll have a totally different look. Because what strikes you first about her is the blond hair, eyelashes, and eyebrows. And then we'll see about getting her some glasses."

Djamila volunteered to buy the henna, which we used to coat Hassiba's hair from root to tip, as well as her eyebrows. Djamila ingeniously transformed the henna powder into a very fluid paste to coat Hassiba's eyelashes, and our subject stoically held her tongue when we used a hand mirror to show her the image of her turbaned head. I will never forget her, confident, disciplined, ramrod straight, her eyes closed. Her discomfort was evident, but she said nothing. Her rigid frame couldn't hide her anxiety, a feeling as difficult to express as it is to share. The feeling prompted by a dive into the unknown when they announce to you, even with a thousand forewarnings, even in the most loving way, that now that you no longer have a home, that you have to go elsewhere, that you don't know where or with whom or for how long. The feeling that prompts the total descent into the void—especially if, like Hassiba, you're marked, wanted, and pursued by all the enemy's forces, including its informants and collaborators. Especially if, like Hassiba, you are so young, still an adolescent, still legitimately and naturally needing the warmth of a family home. But, admirably, she let none of it show.

The next day, after the dawn and morning prayers—from which none escaped this time—and after breakfast, we asked Lalla to go to the *hammam*. Hassiba, to whom we had delivered a crash course in the rules governing "Lalla's palace," obediently followed instructions. We descended the two floors on our tiptoes, and since everything seemed deserted, Hassiba blurted out, "It's like Sleeping Beauty's palace!" Like us, she was captivated by Lalla's *hammam*. Once dried, Hassiba's long hair was a mahogany red and her eyelashes and eyebrows darker than they were naturally, which accentuated the contrast with her blue eyes. "Should we apply a second coat of henna?"

Hassiba finally expressed aloud what none of the three of us dared to say: "You have to cut my hair very short. I am sure that then my look will change completely. If we also find me some slightly tinted glasses, I'll be unrecognizable."

Djamila replied, "I don't think we'll be staying in this safe house for much longer. So there's no hurry, we'll do it in due course." Two or three days later, she arrived early in the morning to announce our leaders' decision to move us that very day, and handed us *haïks* and *âadjars* to wear. We quickly gathered our few belongings. Lalla came up to the rooftop to wish us farewell and good luck. We thanked her warmly and sincerely for her unforgettable hospitality and thoughtfulness. Her mask of authoritarian rigor burst. She took us in her arms and kissed us effusively, assuring us that she would never neglect to say a blessing for us each time she prayed. Beautiful little Zineb, always discreet, was waiting for us on the ground floor. With modesty but immense warmth, she wrapped each of us in her frail arms one by one, not saying a word so as not to cry. I was the last to say goodbye. I put her beautiful young face, which reminded me so much of my little sister

Leïla's, in the hollow of my shoulder and whispered, "Thank you. Thank you so much for everything. You too are a *moudjahida*. You have helped us tremendously and protected us wonderfully. We will never forget you."

With Djamila's Family

Veiled like the women of Algiers, all four of us walked out to the Rue de la Granada, which plunged into the depths of the Casbah. We followed Djamila, who veered quickly to the right, toward what appeared to be a dead-end alleyway: the Impasse de la Granada. With rapid steps, our sister led us to number 5, the last door in the alleyway. The heavy wooden door was not locked, as the Belhaffafs' had been. Djamila pushed open the door with an owner's authority and confidence, and we followed her into the *sqifa* and then the patio. The house was as beautiful, refined, and harmonious as that from which we had just come; the only difference was that it was filled with voices, laughter, and everyday sounds. This didn't prevent us from lingering in the courtyard, still in our veils, as if to soak up all this beauty, harmony, and life. Samia took the opportunity to whisper to me that we were in the house of our sister Djamila's family, the Bouhireds, where she had first met our big brothers. I followed our group toward the stairs and up to the first floor. We entered a large rectangular chamber designed just like those in the Belhaffafs' house, but furnished in a modern style.

Djamila and two women entered, carrying a *meïda* set with plates and steaming dishes. That roused us from our torpor. Samia rose to embrace the two young women, whom she had already met. Then Djamila presented Hassiba and me. Thanks to Samia's accurate description, I immediately recognized Oukhiti and Fettouma, whose family occupied the floor where we were now. Oukhiti, with her proud bearing, was tall, and her jet-black hair framed a face with fine features and beautiful dark eyes gleaming with intelligence. Her movements were quick and precise, yet welcoming and warm. It was hard to believe that this slender young woman, who was barely older than us, was already a mother of five. Fettouma had a squarer shape. I was struck by her immense eyes, bordered with long black lashes and topped with dark eyebrows in a well-drawn arc.

We had lunch together, honoring the delicious foods prepared for us: a selection of meat and fish dishes. My taste buds were conquered by both their exquisite refinement and by the novelty of some of them. I discovered the calamari that the women of the Casbah called *qamroun*. Our hostesses would not soon forget my astonishment and wonder. They had a good laugh when I explained that my knowledge of seafood was limited to sardines, whiting, and mullet. With a chuckle, they explained to me the richness and delicacy of seafood. They promised to make sure I tasted shrimp and many other varieties of seafood. It was difficult to remain indifferent to such kindness. At that very moment, I knew that whatever my future held, I would feel forever indebted to all those families that had opened wide their homes and hearts to us like one of their own and hoped they would one day consider me as such. From that point on, an indescribable link would tie me to the Casbah, which jealously guarded its treasures, offering them only to her children and to those who deserved them—that is to say, those who knew how to look upon her, discover her, respect her, and love her without holding anything against her.

Djamila informed us that El Kho had decided to allow us to return to Saint-Eugène, as he had verified that no one knew of us.

Samia, ever practical, asked, "Who will be our contact now?"

"You will work directly with El Kho, and I'll also be an intermediary," Djamila replied. While we could hardly hide our joy after waiting for this moment for nearly two weeks, Hassiba, still silent, caught my gaze. In her eyes, which were suddenly brighter than usual, I read all the anguish she felt at the thought of being left alone without us. It broke my heart, and I asked Djamila, "Do you think I can stay here with Hassiba? Samia absolutely must go home before her father launches a search party, but I just need to go show my face at the university dormitory once some afternoon." Djamila nodded, Samia said nothing, and a big smile lit up Hassiba's face. Before leaving us, I reminded Samia not to forget to propose to Mama Zhor the plan we had sketched out during our stay in Lalla's palace.

During our days of solitude and confinement, we had thought of possible targets in case the brothers decided to assign us new missions. Through this reflection, we had set our sights on the Préfecture—the regional seat of government and thus the quintessential symbol of the colonial regime. We had even gone so far as to concoct the perfect way to penetrate its defenses: dressing up as nuns. The Catholic Church was very present in colonial Algeria, with all its orders represented. We had noted which one's sisters wore very wide, long, heavy skirts and large head coverings that hid half the forehead, the cheeks, and the chin. Their caps had a high, hard edge, forming a large bell above the head. This outfit would be the perfect disguise to smuggle our bombs into the Préfecture. What's more, we knew that no security guard would dare search two nuns. Samia was supposed to outline our project to Mama Zhor (an excellent seamstress) and ask her to sew us those well-known uniforms.

All that remained was to propose our plan to El Kho for his approval. That was how Samia left us, already equipped with a mission. Djamila spared her from donning the *haïk*, which she was trying unsuccessfully to don like a true *Casbadjia*. Our hostess, after laughing uproariously at Samia's blunders, told her, "In the Casbah, you can't fool anyone, even the children. It's better that you go out unveiled. You will be less conspicuous." This remark left me thinking about the numerous, unfathomable secret codes that the old *medina* contained and that only the children of the Casbah knew.

With Samia gone, Hassiba and I remained alone the whole afternoon. Our youngest comrade assumed the posture she would adopt during her whole time with us: seated on a mattress, she brought her legs toward her chest, taking care to cover her feet with the swaths of her loose *seroual* pants. She wrapped her arms around her tucked-up legs and laid her head on her knees. In this posture, she resembled a kitten seeking caresses and protection. She seemed so young and frail, with such sad eyes, that I approached her to talk, as I knew she needed to do.

To encourage her to unburden herself, I began recounting to her how Samia and I had arrived in the Casbah under such catastrophic circumstances, and how my parents and Monsieur Lakhdari were totally unaware of our activities or where I was at that moment. Then she told me, "I think of my poor father. He knew nothing and suspected nothing about my activities. Yet it was he who had to face the police when they arrived at home to arrest me, while my mother and I were at a cousin's wedding. I feel horrible because I've always been very close to him. The police really did a number on the poor man. He doesn't even know where I am. He must be worried to death." I reassured her as best I could. She added that she felt guilty all the same because, as a senior official in the hydraulic services, her father worked among the Europeans and the *ultras*, who would certainly make him pay for his daughter's acts. But our parents were no fools, I suspected. When they came to warn her at her cousin's wedding, Hassiba told me, her mother hadn't asked a single question, as if she already knew of her daughter's activities. She had thought of only one thing: to get her child out immediately, without even leaving her time to change clothes.

Fettouma came to spend the end of the afternoon and part of the evening with us. Talkative, she allowed us to relax. She brought out part of her bridal trousseau—some linens and other beautifully hand-embroidered pieces—for us to admire. She informed us that Djamila was an expert in embroidery, fashion, and tailoring because she had taken courses. "Djamila is a real icon. Her pieces always get selected to be exhibited," she told us proudly. She explained to us that the house was occupied by several families besides the Bouhireds, and that the less the others saw of us the better. Fettouma told us the best times to use the toilets discreetly, when few people were out and about: the early morning, around three o'clock, and at night after nine o'clock. After dinner, which was served early, around seven-thirty, Djamila gave us two beautiful, impeccably ironed nightgowns and pretty slippers knitted by hand. Cloistered in Fettouma's room, only leaving late at night or before dawn to use the toilets, Hassiba and I spent our days combing through the newspapers, which, despite their best efforts, kept us informed on the continuing war of liberation across the country. We listened to the radio, and when we could no longer stand its dirty propaganda, we shared our childhood memories or tried to imagine our lives and our future in a free and independent Algeria. Hassiba never doubted that our country would be free, and I shared her faith.

One hot, rainy afternoon that autumn of 1956, Djamila and Samia came to surprise us. Samia brought me fresh linens and clothes. True to form, Mama Zhor sent treats for us and our hosts: her incomparable *maqrouts* and inimitable *taminet ellouz* (almond paste) from Constantine. All these loving gestures swept away our loneliness. While arranging my things in our hostess's mirrored armoire, I discovered a collection of outfits straight out of the rich cultural heritage of Algiers. A *qouiyet* (lady's outfit composed of traditional pants and a fine matching vest) in dark red velvet, embroidered with gold thread weathered by time; some satin *seroual* paints in all shapes and sizes; and *carakous* and other tops cut from pure silk, all decorated with pearls and other glittery things and embroidered in the finest style. Multiple head coverings and *maharmates el ftoul* (satin scarves with long fringes) completed this splendid collection. Dazzled, I stood speechless before the treasure trove passed down by the women of the family for generations to Fettouma. Someone had the idea to try on the outfits to see them on our bodies. Within an hour, we were all made up and dressed like true women of Algiers. Hassiba proved to be a great makeup artist—especially with the eyes—Djamila a great beautician, and Fettouma an irreplaceable costume artist. Those with divine voices began to sing Fadhéla Dziria's song "Ana Touiri," and all four of us began to dance under the watchful eye of

Fettouma, who corrected the awkward ones' missteps. It was a moment of profound joy.

An insistent knock at the door brought us back to reality. Fettouma opened the smaller door, stuck out her head, then turned to Djamila. "It's for you."

We Meet Ben M'hidi

Our sister stepped out for a few minutes, then returned and instructed us to remove our makeup, put our usual clothes back on, and straighten the place up as quickly as possible. She asked Fettouma to leave the room and informed us in a barely audible whisper that El Kho and Ali were arriving with a brother we hadn't met before. She added in another hushed whisper that this new one was a very senior official, but that El Kho had asked us to act natural and treat him like any other activist. For obvious security reasons, at no time could we afford to betray any official's rank by our conduct. Disciplined, we followed the instructions. A moment later, there we were dressed like any other girls in the Casbah, the room tidy and clean, sitting and chatting quietly like girls from respectable families when someone knocked at the door.

We rose as if we'd been stung by a swarm of bees. El Kho entered first, with his flirtatious smile, followed by a man of average height with slightly crimped chestnut brown hair, combed back, and an impeccably shaved face. This detail struck me because it contrasted with El Kho, whose cheeks and chin were often covered with stubble. Ali, bringing up the rear, had to stoop to pass through the little door and immediately filled the room with his big, childlike laughter. He embraced and teased us.

El Kho introduced us to the new brother, Si Mohamed, who greeted us with a calm and serene face, barely showing an imperceptible smile. Physically, Si Mohamed was the model of an ordinary Algerian; he could have gone completely unnoticed were it not for a certain something that lent him an aura even before he spoke. He had a sharp gaze, deep and concentrated yet tender. All at once, it conferred the authority and perspective derived from a life of organizing and combat, the tranquil assurance that arises from faith in a supreme plan built on unshakable convictions, and the eminence of someone with an acute sense of responsibility and dignity—but also a fraternal generosity implying self-detachment and deep love for his people. Such was the look of Ben M'hidi: I would later learn that Si Mohamed was none other than the great Larbi Ben M'hidi.

Djamila, Samia, Hassiba, and I stood silent and intimidated before this leader. He greeted us very warmly, expressing his pleasure at meeting "young Algerian women worthy of the name." Si Mohamed seemed to hold sincere consideration—I would even say proud admiration—for the four of us. I was amazed by it. I shot a quick glance at Samia. Disciplined, she had adopted her prudish air, haughty and falsely detached—something I was incapable of, being so overwhelmed with emotion. Taking the lead, El Kho invited us to sit down. Ali set his machine gun down at his side and sat on the bed. Si Mohamed, wearing blue denim, sat on the mattress at the foot of the armoire, alongside Hassiba and Samia. El Kho, Djamila, and I sat on a second mattress set at a right angle to the first. I sat facing Si Mohamed and could observe him as I wished. Ali kept up his teasing and Djamila responded with some of her own. El Kho turned to Hassiba to tell her that everything was in place to transport her to the *maquis*. He asked Djamila to arrange a visit by the photographer to prepare Hassiba's ID photos, and suggested that Hassiba think up a first and last name herself, so that in case she was stopped she would react naturally. I observed Si Mohamed, noticing that at no point did he shed his natural air, eloquent silence, imperceptible

Larbi Ben M'hidi, one of top leaders of the FLN

smile, or his deep gaze, so full of humanity. The *meïda* was set and El Kho invited Si Mohamed to serve himself. Everyone was seated around the delicious white chicken soup, but I was paralyzed at the thought of having to eat with the three big brothers. Apart from my time at Samia's, where I felt at home, it was the first time I had sat down for a meal with men from outside my family.

After the soup, next was *chtitha djadj* (garlic chicken in red sauce) served in a large deep pan that held plenty for all of us and gave off an aroma that made our mouths water. Intimidated, I hardly dared to reach out my hand, even as the others ate heartily—and with good reason, as the dish was divinely good. After the meal, Djamila asked Si Mohamed to play *yadess* with her. Smiling, he replied, "I don't know this game. How does it work?"

"It's a popular game in the Casbah," our hostess explained. "It's simple. You see that Y-shaped chicken bone? We'll break it and each keep a half. From then on, as soon as one of us hands an object to another, the one who takes it must say *'Âala bali'* ['I know']. If he doesn't, the one who handed it over shouts *'Yadess!'* and wins." She immediately handed the bone to Si Mohamed; they broke it in two and each kept a piece. I was so stunned by our sister's audacity—to dare to casually propose a game to one of our revolution's senior leaders—that I remained frozen, a chunk of bread in my hand, not daring to make the slightest movement. Suddenly Djamila shouted triumphantly, *"Yadess!"* Indeed, as soon as the bone had broken, she had handed her half to Si Mohamed, who took it without saying *'Âala bali.'* Djamila had indeed won, as she explained to our leader, who listened, calm and serene. Ali laughed uproariously, El Kho's face was split by a broad smile, and Djamila celebrated, while Hassiba, Samia, and I were petrified by our sister's audacity. Si Mohamed quietly conceded defeat. I wanted to disappear, to evaporate right there, but Ali, who missed nothing, called to me, "And where are you? So you're not eating a thing?"

"Alhamdoulillah! [Praise be to God!] I ate well," I whispered, never expecting what would follow. Ali dipped a piece of bread in the sauce, stuck a piece of chicken on it and reached it toward me. At my gesture of refusal, he exclaimed: "Yes, yes. You are going to eat this piece, for the health of the great Ramdane Abane. You don't want any misfortune to befall such a great leader, so eat!" I had to swallow the piece he handed me, without daring to look up. He continued to reel off the names of our great leaders, from Benboulaïd to Ben M'hidi, Bitat to Boudiaf and Krim Belkacem, to whose health Hassiba, Samia, Djamila, and I had to swallow huge portions

of bread and chicken soaked in sauce, all amid cascades of laughter from Ali and a smile from Si Mohamed, who seemed to be enjoying the mood. I was furious with Ali. I no longer dared to look at Si Mohamed, convinced that he was no fool. He knew that we knew. Finally, El Kho put an end to our agony by announcing their departure. Ali, euphoric and loudly affectionate, wished us well and left first, his machine gun under his shoulder, pressed against his torso. Si Mohamed wished us good night and good luck, then followed him out. El Kho lingered a few seconds to tell us that we would soon be put back to work.

The door had hardly closed behind him when I exploded: "Why this farce? Acting as if the great leader was a simple activist! Tell me! I'm sure he wasn't fooled. What was all that for?"

Samia took it further: "We could have taken the opportunity to discuss things with our big brother instead of playing at this burlesque comedy!"

Hassiba pushed further still, saying: "This was such a missed opportunity!"

We felt ridiculous and were on the verge of tears. Djamila managed to calm us by explaining, "I didn't have time to give you some details because things went very fast. But after the Rue de Thèbes bombing, the senior leaders agreed that 'the organization' had to respond. But they didn't know which 'volunteers for death' El Kho had selected for the task. After the Milk Bar and Cafétéria attacks, and before being informed by our people, they only had the French press's version of events, which accused European Communist militants with certainty. When they were informed that it was in fact young, homegrown Algerian girls, FLN activists, who had brought the war into the European quarters, they were surprised. Pleasantly surprised, but surprised. Si Mohamed then asked El Kho to introduce him to these girls without revealing his identity or his role in 'the organization.'"

We accepted Djamila's explanation but kept our anger in reserve, still resenting El Kho a bit. We were, in fact, a little bitter at having been trained in rigid discipline to the point that we had appeared before Si Mohamed as shy, awkward young girls incapable of playing along with the act.

New Missions

The next morning, Djamila announced that El Kho had summoned her, Samia, and me. We met him at the Belhaffafs', where he was staying in our old rooftop refuge. In corduroy pants and a black shirt, he sat cross-legged on the big bed, a machine gun placed just to his right and a pistol on the nightstand. He greeted us with that big smile that creased his whole face, leaving just the two bright slits of his eyes. Inviting us to sit, he began by explaining that we needed to keep up the pressure on the colonial regime and exploit the disarray in which the colonists and their security services found themselves. "Are you ready to strike again in the European neighborhoods?" he asked us. All three of us answered in the affirmative without the slightest hesitation. Released from my crippling shyness, I dared to share with him the plan that Samia and I had been devising in recent days. I explained why the Préfecture made a wise target: success in this attack would have an immense impact on the European population—whose fundamental certainties would be seriously shaken—as well as on the colonial regime and its arrogance. The Préfecture was an essential institution of the colonial regime, not to mention the impact such an attack could have for our people, who were recognizing more and more the FLN's capabilities to render justice.

El Kho listened, picking at his left thumb the whole time. I had already noticed that when he was preoccupied, he attacked his left thumbnail, which he had worn down by half, giving it the curious shape of a flattened bird's beak.

Djamila asked, "The Préfecture? But how will you get inside? How will you escape? It's fortified inside and out!"

Then Samia explained our plan in detail, emphasizing that we had left nothing to chance. El Kho remained silent throughout the exchange. Only his right hand tweaking his left thumb betrayed the intensity of his thoughts.

"What do you say, *Kho*?" I asked him.

He took his time before answering, then said, "Keep thinking about it. I have to ponder it myself."

Then it was Djamila's turn to present her plan. She pointed out that the trolley descending from Yusuf Way to the Place du Gouvernement crossed both Rue Michelet and Rue d'Isly, two streets frequented mainly by the *ultras*, since the more modest Europeans lived mostly in Bab El Oued. She had recorded the busiest periods: between nine-thirty and eleven-thirty in the morning and between three and five in the afternoon. She proposed to set the bomb to explode at the Grande Poste stop. This way, she explained, we would be targeting "the big fish," who then would know that Algeria was at war and understand that they could no longer sit back and enjoy life while watching us die. El Kho gave her the same answer he had given us.

That day, I left with Samia for Saint-Eugène. We had to pass by the Préfecture, observe the security measures around the building, and note the comings and goings—in short, refine our reconnaissance of the place and its surroundings. We decided to spend the next two days studying when and how the police and military teams stationed around the building changed shifts. We were increasingly convinced of the significance of our target, given what it represented as a strategic center of the colonial regime. None of our leaders could tell us otherwise, not even Si Mohamed. I was overjoyed to regain my freedom to walk about and move wherever I pleased. At the same time, I felt sad for Hassiba, who was condemned to live in secret, hounded by all the intelligence agencies, official and otherwise. I could only imagine just how profoundly shaken our youngest sister felt by the terrifying, indescribable feeling of knowing that, apart from those few people assigned to hide and protect you, anyone else might be among those targeting you.

In such case, how could one not notice the disproportion and imbalance of forces? Secular France, its army and police, on the heels of a frail girl whose crime was wanting the independence of her country. I tried to put myself in our younger sister's shoes, which was easy enough, and the ridiculousness of it leapt out at me: France, heir to an empire, was mobilized against little old me.

Me who was nothing, who knew nothing except that I was in my country with the right to want to live freely and independently, rid of the colonial system. I told Samia my thoughts, which she shared. We decided to take full advantage of our freedom of movement by throwing off the shackles of our education and the rigid rules erected between us and life, between us and the freedom to be, say, do, come and go. We agreed to go to the university campus, to open wide my balcony door overlooking the green lawn, to clean the place, to walk down the walkways and avoid no one. We even hoped to meet some of the French students with whom we had forged a camaraderie during the two years spent together at the university and who could have become friends. It was mid-October, with the start of the academic year in full swing. Our European comrades from second year were all there, boys and girls alike. They were beginning the third and final year of their degrees in law. Going up the wide avenue lined with leafy trees leading to the dorms, we met two classmates, Raymond Lafarge and Jean-Marc Perrin. We all greeted one another and walked a stretch together, talking about the rain and nice weather. They made no allusion to the political positions that we had assumed, nor to "the events," as the Europeans liked to call them. Upon arriving at the small crossroads where the walkway split to lead toward the boys' and girls' dorms, we went our separate ways, wishing each other good luck. We asked ourselves if these two classmates could imagine our true beliefs or if they might suspect us of being in the armed groups and concluded that they weren't suspicious in the least. First, because while they were liberals, they were sure of their right to live like the master's sons here in our country. They might concede that some among us, the "educated" ones, could coexist with them. Nothing more. The Algeria conquered by their great-grandparents was theirs. So they didn't think about us in terms of citizens with rights and duties. They thought us incapable of even feeling a sense of duty toward our country and our people.

The girls' dormitory was animated; the students, back from vacation, were busy cleaning. We greeted those we knew and made our way to my room. It was as I had left it the day my father had dropped me off. With a heavy heart, I sat down at my table and wrote at length to my parents. Brazenly lying, I confirmed to them my registration for my third year of law studies. Merciful God, forgive me—but it was for the cause and I didn't want them to worry. After the dorm, we headed to the area around the Préfecture. On the sidewalk across the boulevard, we leaned on the seaside railing, facing the main entrance of this beautiful building with its imposing mass and harmonious architecture. We crossed the street to get a closer look at the facade.

A patrol of soldiers paced the sidewalk, while police stood in booths flanking the door. We exchanged a few words with the soldiers, laughing together at their boredom, promising them that we would come back and, why not, go enjoy an ice cream with them when they got off duty. We left them and circled the Préfecture, noting the position of the doors, the number and locations of the guard booths and movements of the patrols. We continued to the rear entrance facing Rue Alfred Lelluch (today's Rue Asselah Hocine). The door there was as well guarded as the front one, with police stationed on both sides, and by a military patrol. It was clear that it wasn't easy to enter or leave the Préfecture. But we were sure that two nuns would not appear unusual. Except we were still stuck, because we couldn't think of a reason why two nuns would need to enter the building. We decided to focus that day's lunchtime conversation on the Préfecture and its relations with citizens, to see what insights Samia's father might provide.

The next day, early in the afternoon, Djamila rang at 9 Rue Salvandy. Mama Zhor invited us to sit around her *meïda*, which was as sumptuous as ever, and recounted some of her mother's childhood memories. (Her mother, Mama Hanana, was still alive back in Constantine.) It was about the last battles of her great-grandfather, the Emir Abdelkader, and his betrayal by the King of Morocco, who imprisoned his envoy Bouhamidi and blocked the delivery of provisions to his fighters and their families. She reminded us what came next: the Emir Abdelkader's forced exile and Bouhamidi's murder in a Moroccan prison. As a moral to this story, she insisted that the "big brothers" should count only on our valiant and courageous people to liberate the country. I was moved and full of gratitude for this sacred lady who, until the end, was always keen to remind us of the greatness of our people despite the poverty into which colonialism had plunged them. We left the house galvanized, happy to exist and giving thanks to God for having positioned us to participate in a great moment in our history.

We took the trolley to the Place du Gouvernement, then followed the route to the Belhaffafs' at a brisk pace, aware of our youth and our vitality, secure in our justification, and above all convinced that we were marching decisively toward our mythical independence. We reached the rooftop to find El Kho sitting cross-legged on the bed in the same position as the day before. We understood the limits of our power when he told us that our idea of targeting the Préfecture was excellent, but that the symbolic importance of this colonial institution demanded that the mission be an absolute success. However, he added, too many hazards stood in the way. The proposal therefore required more thought, more preparation, and more time, though "the organization" would not shy away from lending a strong hand.

"In the meantime, the situation demands that we keep up the pressure on the Europeans," he explained. "That's why we have selected the plan Djamila proposed. Sister Farida, the two of you are appointed to prepare and execute the mission. You must determine the schedules of peak times and the part of the trolley's journey where the greatest percentage of the passengers are well-to-do. Remember that since the Milk Bar and Cafétéria attacks, the French have put new security measures in place. Every European is responsible for his own safety and the others', and every 'native' is suspect. It will be very difficult for you to leave an object behind without attracting attention. The hardest problem to solve is how to plant the bomb while diverting all the passengers' attention. Finally, as you know, if one of you were to be arrested it would be a blow with huge consequences for our organization."

We listened like good schoolgirls. Then Djamila asked, "When do we start the reconnaissance?"

"Tomorrow," El Kho said. "In a week, we put it into action."

The Uncommon Courage of Djamila Bouhired

The next day, Djamila and I left at half past eight, when the street was still dark. The strip of sky that we could see was a dirty off-white. Some elderly women were heading, baskets in hand, toward the market. On their feet they wore a kind of black ballet flats with dun-colored soles. (I would wear the same kind later on, when we would need to always be ready to jump silently from rooftop to rooftop, scale walls, and reach small openings to slip inside.) We reached Rue Randon and cut a path through the packed crowd, not hesitating to jostle those who blocked our way. I had walked a good amount in the Casbah since I first "disembarked" there; I was starting to feel at home there and tried to adopt the residents' way of life. With a turn onto Rue Henri Martin, we reached Rue d'Isly and picked up our pace to catch the trolley to the last stop at Yusuf Way, passing by Rue Michelet en route.

We set our watches to the same second and began our work of observing everyone who rode the trolley—their age, gender, looks, and number. We timed the trip between every two stations and the time we stopped at each one, until we returned to the Grande Poste, where we were to get off. To write down our observations, we had each taken a book with a large sheet of paper folded inside. At that time, the trolley had three doors: at the front beside the driver, at the middle, and at the rear. We each boarded through a different door. From the very first reconnaissance mission, we decided that on the D-Day, we would each make the return trip to the Belhaffafs' in the Casbah alone, by different paths. We had to repeat our observations all week to identify the peak day and time. To avoid being recognized by the drivers and conductors, we regularly changed clothes, hairstyles, and looks. We wore the veil every which way, from the most sophisticated style of the Algiers bourgeois to the humblest manner of the women worn down by hard work and poverty. One morning, while preparing for our mission, as we were taking the trolley from the top of Rue d'Isly we saw Didi Omar, Djamila's father, sit down near the driver.

We looked at each other, frozen in stupor, one terrifying thought in my head: what if this had been the day we placed the bomb? What would we have done? We were both veiled, each in a separate trolley car, and Didi Omar was immersed in reading the *Echo d'Alger*. We got off while he continued his journey. Still reeling with emotion, I told my sister of the immense gratitude I was addressing to the heavens that this wasn't yet the D-Day, and suggested that she ask her father to stop passing through the European quarters and using the trolley. Calm and determined, Djamila explained that in that case, we would need to warn all our people, which was impossible. She reminded me that our people didn't need to take the trolley to die. They died every day, in every part of the country, simply from France's raids and fierce repression. By living in the Casbah, she added, her father, like all the other inhabitants of the *medina*, spent his nights in fear and terror of the French police and army. The Casbah was surrounded, subject to the curfew since August and transformed into an open-air concentration camp for the "natives"—all while the Europeans lived in peace and quiet.

"Our actions aim to take the war to them, to let the whole world know that the Algerian people are leading a war of liberation against their European occupiers. It begs the question: what responsibility must each of us assume in this war of liberation, recognizing that the fight isn't an even one? That's why I always complete my mission without pausing to ponder the imponderables, which as you know well can be numerous. But we have no other choice. This is what France has imposed on us!" Djamila left me stunned but appreciative of her sincere and total commitment to our cause. It was in the course of this mission that I discovered the uncommon—nay, superhuman—courage of my sister in combat. I also discovered that supreme sacrifice could be embodied by a young woman named Djamila.

Indeed, on the day of the attack, we found ourselves in the Belhaffafs' house, where El Kho, Ali, and Abderrahmane Taleb (whom I was meeting for the first time) handed us the basket containing the bomb. I preferred to carry the basket since it seemed safer for Djamila—who knew the Casbah inside and out—to lead the way while we followed several steps behind, in case we needed to avoid an army patrol. But our sister didn't see it that way. Categorical, she grabbed the basket and refused any discussion. With a wave of her hand and complete confidence, she told the brothers: "See you in a while, *inchallah*!" And we left the room.

We descended quietly to the patio, then the *sqifa*, where we took a moment to collect our strength, energy, and attention before confronting the street. Once outside the Casbah, we decided to walk side by side and converse calmly, stopping now and then before a shop window like the rest of the pedestrians. We checked our watches to take the trolley to the top of Rue Michelet at ten-thirty. We had decided that each of us would enter by a different door and stand far enough apart to monitor the other passengers and spot any problems that might throw a wrench in the plans we had so carefully laid.

Djamila entered via the front door while I took the middle one. My heart was pounding as I tried to look naturally at my fellow passengers. The majority were middle-aged Europeans, except for some "natives," recognizable by their *haïks*. I had a heavy heart, but as my sister would say, we were at war. At the next stop, few people got off even as many others pushed to get on board. It was harder for me to see Djamila and keep track of her movements. We planned to get off at the university stop before the bomb was to explode ten minutes later at the Grande Poste. My gaze sought out my sister's from the other side of the car. With an imperceptible movement of the head and eyes, she informed me that everything was going as planned and that it was time to head for the door to get off. I forged a path through the compact mass of the crowd and reached the center door where, leaning against one of the rails, I looked in the direction of Djamila, who was standing near the front door. She signaled to me that everything was all right and that we should get off. I did so as soon as the trolley stopped, heading slightly away from the flood of passengers commuting at this hour.

The doors closed again and the trolley headed off with the ding of a bell toward our target, the Grande Poste stop. I searched for Djamila's white veil among the passengers who had just disembarked and were already walking away from the station. There was no *haïk* in sight. I waited patiently for the station to empty, sure that she would appear, but nothing. No Djamila. It took me a few seconds to realize that she had stayed with her bomb in the trolley—and would be the first person it would shred to bits. I began to run, sprinting like crazy to catch the trolley. No longer able to see or hear a thing, I pushed everything and everyone in my way. I ran, I ran to the Grande Poste, where the bomb was set to detonate. I ran toward the terrible noise that, I knew from the Milk Bar, would explode within me. I ran, screaming, "Why? Why did she do it? She has no right!" When I finally arrived at the Grande Poste, there was no trolley. I continued my frantic race, convinced that it must have accelerated its pace and that the bomb would explode before the last stop, the Place du Gouvernement. I was still running, not in the city but in a nightmare, my heart in my throat, my face and my *âadjar* flooded with tears of despair. When I reached the last stop, at the Place du Gouvernement, I saw no trace of an explosion.

I looked all around, distraught, and saw mostly veiled women with baskets in hand, men in blue denim sailor's outfits, bareheaded or wearing a fez, and some modestly dressed Europeans. So panicked that I wondered whether I hadn't gone mad, I literally pinched myself to make sure I was really where I thought I was. I told myself that in my mad rush, I must have missed where the bomb had exploded. I reversed my course, but when I reached the university stop I realized that the bomb hadn't gone off. But what had become of Djamila? Arrested in the trolley by plainclothes police? I hated myself to my very core for having gotten off without her. I should have waited for everyone to disembark so I could have stayed by her. Dying from guilt, not knowing what to say to the brothers when I returned home, I stumbled about in indescribable confusion. What would I say to Djamila's mother, Auntie Baya? To Oukhiti? To the whole Bouhired family? I began making my way back to the Place du Gouvernement in tears. A woman— one of our own—shook me and said, "Don't cry my girl, I hope it's nothing serious. Can I help you? Wait, I'll ask for some water for you. Hold fast to Allah, He will open all doors for you."

I looked up at her and realized that I was standing below the vaulted arches of the Bab Azzoun arcade. I thanked her and turned toward the Casbah, determined to go and confront the terrible truth. Having never before entered and walked the *medina*'s streets without a guide, I will never know how I found myself in front of the Belhaffafs' house, where I knocked twice like Djamila did. It opened immediately, as if they had been expecting me. Without looking around me, I trudged up to the terrace, ready to suffer all the brothers' rebukes, and for good reason. As I reached the rooftop, half conscious, Djamila's arms greeted me. A tumultuous commotion ensued, with loud voices and laughter, while someone made me sit on the bed and withdrew my veil and *âadjar*. In a total daze, I looked at all the faces coming and going and talking, though I understood nothing. I was in shock when someone's hands gently shook me and handed me a glass of water. I burst into tears and Djamila, also crying, took me in her arms, asking, "Where did you go? I was worried sick. Were you lost in the Casbah?"

I stared at her, incredulous, then heard myself say, "What about the bomb? It exploded? Where?"

"I wouldn't be alive here in front of you if it had," she said. Then, her voice choked with rage and sobs, she exclaimed, *"Ana mak' houssa!* [I'm jinxed!] The bomb didn't explode!"

Finally, I recognized the voice of Ali, who was consoling her, thanking God that things had happened as they did, avoiding what would have been her certain death. Gradually, the discussion came into focus. Djamila recounted having slipped the bomb under a seat, ensuring that no one noticed it, or so she thought. She was adjusting her *haïk* and had nearly reached the trolley door when a voice behind her called out aggressively, "Hey! You, madame! You forget your package!"

Djamila, who had only taken a few steps, turned toward the voice, a European woman's, and replied in a French mixed with Arabic words: "I haven't forgotten it. You see, I'm just arranging my veil!" She leaned over, took the bomb from the basket, which she kicked under the seat, and hugged the package conspicuously to her chest with her left hand while clutching the folds of her *haïk* with the other. She faced the woman who had challenged and looked her in the eye. The European shrugged her shoulders and turned her back. Djamila, well aware that she was under scrutiny, decided not to get off at the university stop as we had agreed but to continue, resolved to go down with the bomb. The only precaution she took was to edge toward the largest group of Europeans in the area and to move away from some veiled women, hoping that the explosion would not mortally wound them. She spoke the profession of faith, clutched her bomb tighter against her chest and waited for the explosion. She rode like that, seated all the way to the last stop. The bomb didn't go off.

At this point in her story, her voice failed. No one spoke. The silence was heavy. Suddenly, her low voice slightly hoarse, she repeated, *"Ana mak' houssa!"* She paused again, eyes open, face frozen and flooded with an uninterrupted torrent of tears. I've never seen anyone cry like that. Looking straight ahead, her wide-open eyes shed an impressive stream of tears that slid down her motionless face. Motionless and without any expression, she seemed absent, devastated by an immense sorrow on which no words seemed to make an impression. No one dared to move or speak. I was overwhelmed at the sight of such profound distress, and thought to myself, "This isn't Djamila crying. These tears have come from the depths of time. They express all the misfortune that has befallen us since the arrival of the French."

Still silent, she ran her hands all over her face, took out a tissue, wiped her eyes, blew her nose, breathed, and repeated several times, *"Astaghfirou Allah"* (I ask forgiveness of God). We sat all around her, hypnotized. I couldn't take my eyes off her face, which was still swollen from the torrential tears that had run all the way down her neck.

She broke the silence by shouting to me, "And where were you? You had us so worried!" How could I explain to her the panic and anxiety that had

seized me when I didn't see her get off the trolley? How could I explain my
mad dash between the university and the last trolley stop—twice—literally
mad with fear that she had been shredded to bits or arrested? How could I
tell her of my wandering and my confusion?

So I simply said, "Why did you do this to me? You should have kept me
with you!"

She hugged me against her again, and it was Ali who, by wrapping his
arm around her, finally managed to get a smile out of her by saying, "*Ya
khtou*, thousands of Frenchmen aren't worth one hair on your head. What
would have become of us if you had been killed?"

I discovered that day what the word *courage* meant—and just how far a
commitment to serve our cause could go. I knew that day that Djamila was
not only ready to sacrifice her life for our country's independence, but had
already dedicated her whole being. In addition, Ali, the most just of the just,
by asking her that final question, reminded us all of Djamila's commitment,
as well as that of the whole Bouhired family, in service to the revolution.
Her parents, Uncle Omar and Auntie Baya, had transformed their home
into a makeshift field hospital and refuge for our leaders and activists—men
and women alike—while their rooftop terrace housed a veritable explosives
laboratory. Djamila's uncle, Uncle Mustapha, and his wife Oukhiti (born
Fatiha Hattali), were engaged body and soul in the liberation struggle. It
went all the way up to her paternal grandmother, Yemma. Despite being
elderly, crippled by arthritis, and only able to move with great difficulty, she
reigned as an Algerian queen, sovereign in her own country, never waver-
ing, always inspiring bravery, valor, and unwavering faith in our revolution
and its sacred goal. What could France do, even with its state, its army,
its police, its informants, its torture and ferocious repression, against all
the Yemmas, the Auntie Bayas, the Oukhitis, the Lalla Belhaffafs, and the
Zinebs? Nothing. The racist, arrogant, and contemptuous colonial system
knew precious little of our people, our culture, and our codes. As for the
world of women, they knew nothing at all. After 126 years of colonialism,
the Algerian woman remained the impregnable citadel.

I had come to know Djamila bit by bit. The first time, I just saw her
image reflected in the bay window of the Boukerdouna Pharmacy in July
1956, when she had a rendezvous with Samia. I had been struck by her allure,
her elegance, and the impressive mass of hair cascading over the shoulders.
On September 30, 1956, when she welcomed Samia and me at 5 Rue Borely
la Sapie, we were captivated by her fine facial features, the particular timbre

of her voice, and her frank and resounding laugh, as well as her keen sense of humor and self-deprecation. I had found her authentic and reassuring, all of which made her, in my eyes, delightful. Then at the Belhaffafs', I discovered an accomplished young woman—the kind all mothers dreamed of in those days. Besides her beauty and natural elegance, she also held a delicate refinement, tremendous concern for others, and profound empathy. The attempted bombing on the trolley revealed other facets of her character. The sweet, urbane, caring Djamila could turn into a very direct person with a firmness bordering on rigidity, refusing even to imagine the possibility of retreat. She had the kind of exceptional courage that I call superhuman, because it could push her to go straight to her death with open eyes, knowing it and accepting it. By embracing the object that would bring her certain death and reciting the profession of faith, she proved her transcendent courage and total sincerity. She became my sister and my friend.

From that day on, we settled in at the Bouhireds', and regularly went down the street to the Belhaffafs' for our activities. Samia stayed in Saint-Eugène and joined us when El Kho called her in for a mission. It was a difficult time in her personal life; she was torn between her commitment to the revolution and her wedding. Very shy about expressing her innermost feelings, my friend suffered a great deal in silence. She was convinced that neither the sisters nor brothers in arms would understand what she called her "disengagement." I lectured her, reminding her that our sisters, as women, knew very well the limits imposed by our society, simply because they themselves lived with these limitations too.

As for the brothers, I committed to handling at least two of them: Si Mohamed and Ali. I told her my deep conviction that her generosity, her openness to others, her worth, her temperance, and her real consideration for us would lead Si Mohamed to understand her situation perfectly. I added that Ali would not only understand but would even go so far as to stand up to anyone who cast a stone at her. That was how I managed to cheer her up and convince her to open up to El Kho and inform him of her upcoming wedding. She promised to do it by mid-November, because she wanted to continue working with us until then.

After the death of our brother Rachid Kouache in the Villa des Roses laboratory explosion in Tagarins due to a mishandling of materials, the decision was made to reconstruct the workshop in the Casbah, on the Bouhireds' rooftop. The survivors of the terrible accident—Abdelghani Marsali, Chérif Debbih, and Abderrahmane Taleb—had settled at 5 Impasse de la Granada and gotten right back to work, with Hassiba at their side. Our sister Hassiba was under strict orders never to go outside—not even to take the stairs from one floor of the house to another. Her hair had been cut and was now dark red, along with her eyebrows, making her eyes seem a deeper blue. She looked more mature than the frail teenager who had come to take refuge at the Belhaffafs', but her serious, thoughtful air still clashed with her young age and frail figure. Although she was hidden away, she somehow seemed calmer, less closed, less guarded than in the early days. Hassiba had joined the group of bomb makers who lived and worked in the laboratory built on the terrace of 5 Impasse de la Granada. Obviously, there was no longer any discussion of her heading to the *maquis*. So beautiful, so young, so frail: we were proud of our first woman bomb-maker!

Little by little, I spaced out my comings and goings between the Casbah and Saint-Eugène. Thousands of French soldiers were posted across Algiers, verifying the papers of every passerby, searching bags, baskets, and even people. In the European city, the atmosphere of fear pervaded everywhere, even down to the worried, inquisitive looks from fellow passengers on public transport. Alert and wary, they scrutinized their environment constantly, going so far as to check under their seats. Finally, war and her hateful companion, fear—who until September 1956 had only stalked the "natives" and their neighborhoods—had begun to infect the European city. The more afraid they grew, the more military patrols they deployed in town and the more they demonstrated that Algeria was not a set of French *départements* but in fact a country that was foreign to them and under their occupation.

Obviously, our political goal was to bring fear to the European city. Therefore, we had to redouble our precautions. Samia only came to the Casbah when her missions required it. On these occasions, she found Hassiba and the brothers there, but Djamila and I were often absent in the course of our duties.

On the morning of October 23 while we were eating breakfast, Petit Omar burst in brandishing several copies of the *Echo d'Alger*, *Dépêche Quotidienne*, and *Alger Républicain*. The terrible news was splayed across the front pages in bold, capital letters: a plane carrying five FLN leaders—Mohamed Khider, Mohamed Boudiaf, Ahmed Ben Bella, Hocine Aït Ahmed, and Mostefa Lacheraf—had been intercepted by French army fighter jets, who forced the pilot to land at Maison Blanche Airport in Algiers. A photo showed the men standing, handcuffed to one another. We joined El Kho and Si Mohamed, with whom we had an appointment. They greeted us and immediately raised the issue of the plane's abduction.

Si Mohamed explained: "The five leaders of our FLN external delegation had flown to Rabat in Morocco, and were headed for Tunis to participate in a North African peace conference and discuss with President Bourguiba and King Mohamed V the conditions of a potential future negotiation with France. Give me your opinion on what happened."

I worked up my resolve before saying that, even if the newspapers talked of this as a serious setback for our organization, it was worth asking whether this setback wasn't Morocco's instead—it was their sovereignty that had been attacked, since the plane had been flying under a Moroccan flag. In addition, I explained that France, while acting in violation of international rules, had given our organization a sort of *de facto* recognition.

I added that I was proud to belong to an organization that—just seventeen months after the launch of our war of national liberation—had managed to establish a political committee, military leadership, and an international delegation charged with exporting our struggle abroad—and that it was already the embryo of our state. I concluded that France's shameless recourse to airplane hijacking proved that, rather than negotiate with us, they preferred war.

Djamila added that nothing the French did surprised her, since they had shown us what they were willing to do to stay in our country. "France has behaved like a pariah state. They might even have shot down the plane. I would expect nothing less from them. But what I don't understand is our external delegation's approach. Why did all five of them take the same plane with everyone's full knowledge? And a plane flown by a Frenchman, who some newspapers are even saying is a reserve officer? I think our leaders behaved with unforgivable carelessness. We're at war, not on vacation!"

Eager to hear from Si Mohamed, I took the floor to say, "Djamila is right. And also, our external delegation's attitude raises the question of just how much confidence we should place in the Moroccan and Tunisian regimes."

A huge smile creased El Kho's face and he turned to address Si Mohamed: "You see? They've got it all figured out."

Si Mohamed, calm and serious, replied: "We can also interpret these events as our sisters do. But for us here, what we must concentrate on is knowing what our people think of this event, the gravity of which we cannot ignore. What the people think of our organization is very important."

El Kho picked up the thread and charged us to go out, listen to the people, and prepare a report.

"A written report?" I asked.

"Of course! And it's very important," replied El Kho. Si Mohamed left the room to retire to his room. As soon as he closed the door, we besieged El Kho with questions about our senior leader's real state of mind. We wanted to know what he thought of our external delegation and their evident negligence, if we were already planning reprisals to go blow for blow with France, and if we ourselves would participate.

El Kho confirmed what we already knew, namely that the abduction of the five officials traveling on an official mission under the protection of the king of Morocco and the president of Tunisia was nothing if not extremely serious. He explained that everyone would be held responsible for their actions. Our responsibility was to learn what our people were thinking—not of France and its army, but of our organization and its leaders. Djamila replied, "Message received, 100 percent. You mean Si Mohamed is very critical of those who organized this unfortunate expedition."

Furious, El Kho yelled at us, "I never said anything like that! And now that's enough. Get out there and listen to people and draft your report!"

We decided that Djamila would go collect information in the Casbah and Belcourt and I would do so in Saint-Eugène and Climat de France, with Samia's help. We plunged in immediately, and through our survey found the following:

First, the midair takeover in international airspace did not surprise the Algerians, who knew the real nature of colonial France. For them, France was no better than Nazi Germany.

Second, our people unequivocally condemned the carelessness that our external delegation had shown by deciding to travel with all five officials in the same plane. Everyone thought that by not taking extra precautions, they had given the enemy an opportunity to deal a serious blow to the entire "organization."

Third, many of those surveyed had questioned just how much confidence we could put in the Moroccan regime. Former activists from the PPA, UDMA, and other groups went so far as to remind us of the king of Morocco's betrayal of the Emir Abdelkader in the nineteenth century, at a crucial moment in his resistance against the French occupation. Former MTLD activists reminded us that an agreement had been reached in the fifties between the three liberation parties of the Maghreb—Istiqlal in Morocco, Destour in Tunisia, and our MTLD—to launch the liberation struggle simultaneously in all three countries. But our Maghreb brothers had then gone it alone, preferring instead to negotiate with France on the side.

Fourth, at the same time, all those we spoke to were proud that their organization had forced France to behave as a pariah state and its army as veritable bandits. They added that the disgraceful methods used by France to arrest our five officials showed the fear that the FLN inspired in the French administration and army. It was, in their eyes, the clearest recognition of the FLN as representatives of the Algerian people.

Fifth, our people's faith in the FLN was intact. They were proud that their organization could lead the fight on all fronts—military, political, diplomatic—and to mobilize so many officials to negotiate. However, they demanded more rigorous security rules for the officials to better protect and strengthen "the organization."

Sixth and lastly, while our people were well aware of the extreme brutality of the French regime, they were impervious to its propaganda. Better yet: the more the French media tried to hit the external delegation and the FLN, the more our people's faith in their organization and their leaders grew. We all saw it as a mark of pride: the French would only lash out at a credible threat.

We drafted our report and went to deliver it to El Kho.

Couriers for the Cause

All throughout the last week of October 1956, the colonial press gloated that, after the five officials' abduction, the FLN was done for. We wanted to show that the opposite was true. The more bent the colonial regime was on transforming the Casbah and other "native" sectors into open-air concentration camps, the more our organization was compelled to carry the war into enemy territory. France's aim was to reduce us to nothing more than a band of notorious outlaws that threatened public order within its territory, from Dunkirk to Tamanrasset. We spent the month of November working to demonstrate that the FLN remained intact and stronger than ever. Not a day passed that Algerians—whether our activists or otherwise—were not arrested or executed. Just like not a day passed where our side didn't carry out an operation.

We were charged with transporting the bombs manufactured at 5 Impasse de la Granada out of the Casbah and into the European city. The exercise proved increasingly difficult, since the Casbah was surrounded and closely surveilled. We adapted to the new realities. Gone were the casual, improvised methods used to transport the first bombs. The enemy was searching ever more aggressively, even rummaging through bags carried by young Western-looking women reentering the European city. The Casbah's few remaining exits bristled with barricades and barbed wire, but we headed for them fearlessly—though always followed by one or two armed brothers ready to fire, in case we were searched. (In this case, we had been instructed to throw ourselves to the ground and crawl away from the shooting.) We prepared our special transport runs thoroughly, studying all the Casbah's exits and developing a particular *modus operandi* for each one. We left nothing to chance and scrutinized everything, from the number and times of the patrol shift changes to how they were conducted. I confess that the *baraka*, or good fortune, that we felt blessed by had never abandoned us. I must also confess that this *baraka* was aided by Djamila's exceptional knowledge of the Casbah and all its entry and exit points, including—and especially—those that very few people knew.

In addition to the bombs, we had to carry various packages and letters out of the old *medina* to addresses around greater Algiers. The rest of the city held no secrets that our sister didn't already know. That was why Djamila was also charged with escorting the wanted activists in town to the Casbah, where they could take refuge while awaiting their transfer to the *maquis*.

In November 1956, our sister left alone on a mission and returned in late afternoon accompanied by a teenage girl of clearly European complexion. Her features were still marked with the imprint of childhood: her smile, her eyes, her complexion, and very fine hair, gathered in a long, thick braid behind the ears. It was Djamila Amrane, whose real name is Danielle Mine, daughter of Jacqueline Guerroudj, the great activist I would later come to know in prison. As the colonial press reported it, Danielle Mine's network had been dismantled. Under the responsibility of Djilali Guerroudj (her stepfather; Danielle was Jacqueline's daughter from an earlier relationship), they brought together a number of former Communist activists who had joined the ranks of the ALN after the July 1956 agreement. Danielle would stay with us at the Bouhireds' until the conditions were right for her to escape to the *maquis*.

Simple and affable by nature, Danielle quickly became the mascot of the group. Her youthful, crystalline laugh, her efforts to speak Arabic despite her very "old French" accent, and her total and sincere commitment alongside us softened us and filled our room with gaiety. Auntie Baya, perhaps because she was a mother, was most touched by Danielle. With a smile tinged with sadness, she—for whom every European was by default Christian—whispered to us in Arabic so only we would understand: "Too bad she is not Muslim, because she has all the qualities she'd need to be a *moudjahida*. You absolutely must protect this child, with your lives if necessary." Later, I would encounter Danielle and her mother, Jacqueline, in prison. But at that point we were still expected to uphold the rules of complete secrecy and our compartmentalized structure, and so we would never speak of the moments we spent together at 5 Impasse de la Granada or any other moments of our life in the organization. I could have learned at the time that, from October 1956 onward, Raymonde Peschard, condemned by the colonial press and its puppetmasters for the Milk Bar attack, lived in the *maquis*. There, she cared for the wounded and assisted families driven from their villages, all with exemplary dedication as an FLN fighter—side by side with Danielle Mine and many other brothers and sisters.

To Raymonde, Danielle, and all the Europeans who took up the cause of our liberation struggle and participated actively, I would like to express our infinite gratitude and our eternal appreciation. Danielle Mine, Raymonde Peschard, and their whole group were in the eastern *maquis*, near Constantine. In November 1957, Raymonde would fall as a true martyr of our revolution, and Danielle would be arrested alongside N'fissa Hamoud. I must note that Danielle and her mother Jacqueline are full-fledged Algerians, if not more Algerian than most—because, along with dozens of other activists like them, they chose Algeria and its cause. They would serve its liberation, then its construction and development, with unrivaled loyalty and devotion.

A Surprise Visit in the Casbah

One afternoon on a dull day, while Hassiba was busy with Abdelghani, Si Mourad (Chérif Debbih), and Dahmane (Abderrahmane Taleb) in their laboratory on the terrace, Djamila and I had just returned from a mission in town when Petit Omar appeared—as usual, without warning. His round, childlike face and dark almond-shaped eyes glowed with intelligence and mischief. He informed Djamila that there was a visitor who had been waiting alone for us for several hours down on the ground floor. We hurried down the stairs. Arriving at the threshold of the room, Djamila pushed open the door and I recognized my younger brother Kader sitting quietly on the bench. Shocked and incredulous, I was overwhelmed with happiness and indescribable emotion. I leapt toward him, wrapped him in my arms, and hung myself around his neck, all the while asking how he had managed to reach me, how our parents were, whether they still hated me, and more.

Meanwhile, a turkey—of which only the head protruded from the opening of the basket woven by my mother—gobbled loudly. I recognized my mother's handiwork; as a good daughter of the High Plains, she had sent a bird and a thick carpet to thank her daughter's hosts. (The talkative turkey would endure in the annals of our group, since Ali la Pointe never hesitated to recall my reunion with my brother every time he wanted to break a painful or tense atmosphere; when, in the heart of July and August, we were crammed into a shelter, suffocating and dripping with sweat, Ali would raise our spirits and encourage us to transcend our inhuman conditions by reminding us of the story of the turkey's journey from Vialar to be recruited into the ranks of the *fidayine* of the Casbah. In a barely audible murmur, he would imitate the turkey, forcing us to concentrate on not laughing aloud and in doing so managing to make us forget the terrible conditions we subsisted in.) Bombarded with my questions, Kader told me how brother Nafaâ Belhaffaf had come to Vialar, sent by "the organization" to meet my father. Fifty-seven years later, I relay the account that my brother, Abdelkader Drif, gave of his visit:

> Si Nafaâ's meeting with my father took place at the tribunal; he informed him of Zohra's new situation, which hardly pleased him.
>
> Mother was with me visiting Tiaret. Mihoub the taxi driver was dispatched to bring us immediately back to Vialar. When she heard the news, my mother's face went so pale I will never forget it. It was a thunderbolt that led to the decision, after some discussion, to task me with traveling to Algiers to examine the conditions of my sister's new life, and especially to learn about her host family. Our brother Si Nafaâ Belhaffaf proposed a visit within the next two weeks. After careful preparations, I took the bus to Affreville [today's Khemis Miliana] and then the train to Algiers. As my companions on the voyage I had the turkey and carpet that I was to give to the family hosting my sister. When I arrived in Algiers, I quickly established contact with Belhaffaf, who came to meet me at the hotel. I

followed him along a route that I didn't know, maintaining a safe distance as he requested. Only the gobbles of my august traveling companion—which made my guide's head spin around in bewilderment—reminded me of the importance of my mission. Si Belhaffaf led me to a beautiful Moorish-style house located in the Impasse de la Granada. I was greeted with warmth but also curiosity, thanks to my turkey and my carpet, by the hostess, Fatiha Hattali [Oukhiti], wife of Mustapha Bouhired [whom we now know as a brave *chahid*, or martyr]. My sister, who arrived a few hours later, found me sitting still on a bench in an elegant Oriental salon, sweating profusely. I probably looked something like a Buddha statue. She was accompanied by two beautiful young girls who resembled virgins of paradise. I found myself thinking about the rumor going around about the *moudjahidine* freedom fighters and their supernatural powers. Zohra was with her comrades, as if in a paradise called the Casbah of Algiers.

I cannot recount how we learned of Zohra's presence in this clandestine world and my own journey without mentioning one particular anecdote. The day of my visit to the paradise of these three nymphs, Coincidence also invited herself to the rendezvous. Zohra peppered me with questions, asking me if everything was fine. Having been her close accomplice, I knew where she was heading. I reassured her as best I could. With a discreet glance, I recognized the nymph with short, red hair as Hassiba Ben Bouali, whose hand was promised to her first cousin Mehdi Bentekkou, my inseparable friend and high school classmate. Abdelkader Ben Bouali, Hassiba's father, was the brother of Mehdi's mother. They had promised one another to consider a common destiny for their two children—a well-established tradition within some large Muslim families. Thanks to my friendship with Hassiba's future husband, I was in on the secret. I had recognized Hassiba despite her new look. Her new red hairstyle made her even more beautiful, but if the other nymph (Djamila Bouhired) had asked me anything about her I would have feigned ignorance to show that I knew how to keep a secret, this great virtue of clandestine life. I stayed for a while alone with Zohra, whom I eagerly reassured about our mother's reaction to the news of her daughter's new circumstances.

After a royal dinner together, my sister and her companions kept me for the night. But when I thought about being in the Casbah, certainly surrounded by plenty of *moudjahidine* (to whom the *vox populi* ascribed supernatural powers), and about the possibility that I might experience a French army raid like those our co-religionists were often subjected to, I couldn't sleep a wink. I jumped at every creak of wood and tried to analyze and locate every little noise. At dawn, I poked my nose out of my room, hoping in vain to see my sister arriving, and regretted that I hadn't invented some excuse to ask her to stay with me. Finally, the house awoke. I heard doors opening and children crying, and the smell of coffee with milk tickled my nose and made my mouth water. I dared not go out on my own until invited, and no one came to invite me, even to allow me to go freshen up. Sitting on the bench, I squeezed my legs together, tortured by an urgent call of nature and not daring to flinch. Around ten o'clock, the door slowly opened and I heard Zohra whisper, "Kader, Kader, are you still asleep?" I sprang up, afraid she might leave. She showed me to the toilet, then once my business was done, we had a long morning full of laughter, with Djamila and Hassiba showering a thousand kindnesses upon me. When I departed, a part of me stayed behind with them. Auntie Baya asked me to pass an invitation to my mother to come see Zohra, then Si Nafaâ walked me back to the station and stayed nearby until the train departed. I returned to Vialar bearing the pride of having fulfilled my mission, reassuring my father and especially my mother that their daughter was living in a revolutionary family and surrounded with affection. And that was the truth.

I would not see my brother Kader again until independence, after the signing of the Évian Accords, when he, my father, and my brothers Mohamed and Boumediene came to wait at the site where the buses arrived to drop off the Algerians detained at Rennes prison.

Long before that date, he would escape to the *maquis* in the Ouarsenis Mountains, where he was arrested after a clash with French paratroopers. As a prisoner in a secret detention camp—in violation of all international laws and rules of war—he would survive only thanks to the obstinacy and stubbornness of our mother. When she learned of her son's arrest, she harassed the entire military hierarchy in Algiers, not forgetting to offer lavish gifts to the infamous General Massu's wife who, at that time, was attempting to "get closer" to the "native" women. In her frantic search, my mother had the good fortune—without knowing it—to be received by Général de la Bollardière, a former resistance fighter and practicing Catholic who had spoken out against the Nazi-like methods that the "great French army" was using. Kader and one of his best friends, Ahmed, were saved from death just moments before their scheduled execution thanks to my mother's struggles and admirable tenacity—but that is a story for another book.

6

BRINGING THE ALGERIAN QUESTION TO THE GLOBAL STAGE

Planning an Assassination

One day in early December 1956, Petit Omar came to inform us that El Kho wanted to see me and Djamila. We met him most often at the Belhaffafs', where the whole family had appeared to us little by little. In this large, beautiful house, centered around the marvelous and vigorous Lalla, lived brothers, sisters, and cousins, some married and others not yet. We crossed paths with them when we climbed up to the rooftop, where El Kho, Ali, and intermittently Ben M'hidi stayed. We often ran into the Belhaffaf brothers Abderrezak, Abdallah, Amokrane, and Nafaâ, all of whom were engaged body and soul in the revolution. Like the Bouhireds, the Belhaffafs put everything they had toward liberating our country: their home, their belongings, their sons, and their wives. Discreet and virtually invisible, the wives, under Lalla's direction, faced the fury of the paratroopers and their devastating searches repeatedly and with dignity and heroism. Never would the unworthy French soldiers manage to get the slightest information from any Belhaffaf.

On that early December day, we found El Kho sitting cross-legged on the bed as usual, a machine gun close at hand. He immediately got to the heart of the matter by assigning us the mission of preparing a bomb attack to eliminate a traitor, Bachagha Aït Ali. He explained that the Franco-Muslim Circle—a club we didn't even know existed—was mostly frequented by the members of the Algerian Assembly, who stopped there between legislative sessions for lunch or drinks. The result was a mixed clientele of Europeans and Algerians, most of whom our people considered traitors, and the worst of these was the Bachagha Aït Ali. [1]

This sinister individual was not only an Assembly member but also the chair of the Algiers city council. He was notorious for his public condemnation of our national liberation struggle and for his participation in France's fierce repression against our people. The report sent by our brothers from Wilaya III in Kabylie [2] was unequivocal, citing the many arrests and executions this traitor had enabled over many years. As an example, they cited the case of activist Mohamed Said Mazouzi, who had been languishing in prison since 1945, falsely accused of attempting to assassinate Bachagha Aït Ali.

The Wilaya III leaders had sentenced the Bachagha to death, but since he took refuge in Algiers, where he continued to frequent the Franco-Muslim Circle, our brothers had transferred the execution order to the Algiers Autonomous Zone. By planting a bomb in the club, we would kill two birds with one stone: we would eliminate a great traitor and strike an important blow against a symbolic site of collaboration with the enemy. After thanking El Kho for the trust he showed in us, we set out to surveil the Franco-Muslim Circle. It was not far from the Palais Carnot—seat of the Algerian Assembly—and Bresson Square. We had to study the site and its surroundings carefully and choose the best table for planting the bomb. In addition, we had to determine the best route with the fewest patrols for us to

---

1. Building on Ottoman tradition and borrowing their term, the French designated *bachaghas* throughout Algeria to serve as intermediaries between the colonial administration and the population. Often drawn from local elites (i.e., major landowning families, tribal chiefs, or *zawiya* leaders) the *bachaghas* came to be detested for their betrayal of the liberation struggle. Many, like the Bachagha Aït Ali, were also awarded political posts.

2. The FLN's organizational structure divided the Algerian territory into six *wilayas*, or regions: Aurès, the North Constantinois, Kabylie, Algiers, the Oranie, and the South. The third *wilaya*, Kabylie, covered the majority Berber-speaking mountainous region just east of Algiers, from where Bachagha Aït Ali hailed.

bring the explosive device from the Casbah. We decided to eat lunch in the Franco-Muslim Circle several times to familiarize ourselves with the layout and the staff, but not so much that they could give an exact description of us in case things went wrong.

On the day of our first reconnaisance, it was winter; the sky was overcast and it was cold. We began by changing our hairstyles. Djamila straightened her heavy, voluptuous hair, pulled it back into a tight bun just above her neck, and wore glasses with slightly tinted lenses and metal frames. That gave her the sour, pinched look of a very "old-school" teacher, which was accentuated by the navy pencil skirt, wool sweater, almond-green vest, and square-heeled lace-up shoes. I also changed my hair, but Djamila found it insufficient. We decided to visit the row of hat stores in the Galeries de France to find the perfect hat or beret to clasp all my hair and prevent any possible resemblance to Raymonde Peschard, whose picture had been published in all the newspapers in October. I darkened the brown of my eyebrows and used mascara to darken my lashes and enlarge my eyes. A grey pleated skirt, red turtleneck sweater, and red heels completed my disguise. Djamila said, "I hope there isn't another Communist sister who looks like you in this get-up, or they'll start to really despise the FLN!" Briefcases in hand and purses over our shoulder, we walked confidently toward the Franco-Muslim Circle. As soon as we entered, a waiter came to take our coats from us. The place was well kept and decked entirely in red: the carpet, the velvet bench seats, the matching scarlet armchairs, and even the drapes framing the windows, while thin white curtains protected customers from pedestrians' prying eyes.

Glittering copper plates sat atop finely crafted coffee tables, ready to welcome customers. Natural as could be, we asked the waiter if we could have the corner table facing the window, since El Kho had specified that Bachagha Aït Ali had a reserved table near a window, at the corner where the two bench seats met. We sat at the table facing the one the Bachagha usually occupied, with only one other table between us. Given how narrow the place was, our position was ideal: close enough to the traitor's table, but not so close that he could get a good look and recognize us as fellow "natives." No one seemed to pay us much attention; the waiters were attentive without being invasive. While chatting in low voices, we explored the space under the benches with our feet to assess the depth, all the while watching the comings and goings and very casually scanning the other guests. It wasn't crowded; only three clients, each at a separate table, lunched in silence. The servers seemed to know them. We asked for the bill, expressed our satisfaction at the quality of the menu and the service, and left a generous tip. As we left, to the side I noticed a small florist's kiosk that hadn't been there when we arrived. A beefy blonde woman with European features stood there with her arms crossed against her chest and hands tucked into her armpits, waiting in vain for clients. I made a mental note to discuss her later with Djamila.

El Kho had asked Hassiba to tell us that he was waiting for us at his usual safe house. As soon as we arrived, he informed us that Bachagha Aït Ali went for lunch at the Franco-Muslim Circle every Thursday at noon. We reported all our findings to El Kho and assured him that the mission didn't involve any major difficulties. By the following Thursday, with Hassiba's help, we were transformed and unrecognizable.

Around half past twelve, we pushed open the Circle's front door and immediately spotted our target. He was dressed all in white, in a traditional *âabaya* robe embroidered up the front and open at the chest to reveal a beaded cotton vest. He wore traditional wide-legged pants, and on his head the *tabani* headdress of a tribal chief. He cut a fine figure, the old Bachagha Aït Ali. Looking at him, I couldn't comprehend the rage that drove him to cause such harm to our brothers. He in turn looked at us as we headed to the table we requested in the opposite corner. With a disarming ease and confident smile, Djamila said to the server: "Last time, we had such a nice time. The meal was delicious, with such a friendly welcome and impeccable service! We finally found the restaurant that we've been searching for, with great food and fast service!" The server was on cloud nine. We sat down and, while perusing the menu, I shot a glance toward the Bachagha, trying not to meet his gaze.

A moment later, I decided to stop looking at him or hearing his voice, and instead to carefully observe the surroundings, the other clients, and the servers' movements—and to focus in particular on the space under the seat, still not forgetting to time how long the old traitor took to have lunch, since he hadn't yet been served when we arrived. We were to stay until he departed, so why not go for a starter, main course, dessert, and coffee? Two men seated at a table near the front door caught my attention. They were European, but clearly not Assembly members. They wore suits and ties, but in their attitude when the door opened, in the way they waved to the servers, there was a tension. Several times I caught their gaze landing on us. They were in my line of vision and our eyes met a few times. Plainclothes police? I admit I shuddered at the thought that they might have noticed a resemblance to Raymonde Peschard. I gave Djamila's foot a nudge; she understood. I found myself wanting to hide part of my face by leaning it on my open hand and pretending to chat and laugh. The Bachagha was sipping his coffee when the two men got up. One walked to the door and the other stood by the table, continuing to talk to their waiter. I risked a glance at the Bachagha. He was slowly getting up as a server rushed to pull aside the table and clear him a path. The first man had left. The Bachagha headed for the door. He exited and the second man followed him. So they were his bodyguards. El Kho had warned us that the traitor enjoyed a personal protection detail from the colonial authorities—and for good reason.

Back at 5 Impasse de la Granada, we removed our disguises and began to pool all our observations and findings in an orderly and methodical way, so as not to forget anything or leave anything to chance. We came to the conclusion that we needed one more visit to the Franco-Muslim Circle before declaring ourselves fully ready.

A Change of Plans

Two or three days later, Petit Omar burst into our room to inform us that El Kho was waiting for us. We walked to the meeting site expecting that El Kho would give us the date for executing the mission. Probably the next Thursday, we figured. A few more days to turn over all the plans in our minds and identify any weak points, then the big day would be upon us.

To our great surprise it was not El Kho who greeted us, but Si Mohamed. True to form, smiling, polite, with that peaceful strength, he intimidated us and imposed his personality without even needing to talk. He invited us to sit down. After the usual greetings, he surprised us by saying bluntly, "El Kho told me that you are in charge of a very sensitive mission?"

His question was rhetorical, seeking only our confirmation. I looked at Djamila and she understood my question: Was he trying to test us? Since we were not supposed to know his rank, having been instructed to treat him like a simple activist, was he seeking to test our discipline, our seriousness, and our compliance with the rules of discipline and our organization's compartmentalized structure? I looked down to avoid his gaze and not let myself be destabilized.

"What operation are you alluding to?" we asked after a moment of heavy silence.

"Let's not play cat and mouse. I'm talking about the operation planned against the Franco-Muslim Circle." Then he asked us to put an end to the childish rapport that we continued to adopt around him, pretending not to know but knowing full well who he really was. He still didn't tell us his name, though.

Freed from the obligation to continue El Kho's farce, we threw ourselves into describing the mission and its preparation in minute detail. We took turns presenting, sometimes cutting each other off and then, realizing our ridiculousness, resuming our discussion more calmly. He listened to us without reacting or interrupting, impassive, but with his face lit by that famous, barely visible smile. He seemed to approve the thoroughness and rigor with which we had prepared our operation. Finally, we announced that the next day we were planning to go to the Franco-Muslim Circle one last time before the big day.

In his calm, deep voice, he crushed us: "This mission is canceled."

Incredulous, Djamila and I looked at one another, repeating: "Canceled? Canceled? But why?" Then, one after another, we reiterated that everything had been carefully studied and prepared. That the operation presented no danger to us. That the only risk was that the bomb would not explode, as had happened several times recently. Believing we understood the reasons for our leader's reservations, I told him, "If you crossed paths with us the way we disguise ourselves to go to the Circle, even you yourself wouldn't recognize us."

Si Mohamed let us outline all our arguments. He let us speak our fill, listening to us until not a single justification remained. When we were silent, he said simply, "You must understand that if the slightest event befell the laboratory, the impact on the course of our revolution would be incalculable and would delay the war's end and the arrival of our independence."

Just like that, Djamila and I burst out laughing, saying that if the end of the war depended entirely on our small laboratory, then neither we nor our children—if we were to have them one day—would ever see independence. Growing more aggressive, we began comparing the modesty of our means to the immensity of our goal for independence. Then we turned to recalling all Bachagha Aït Ali's misdeeds against our brothers. We needed to finish him off to put an end to his poisonous betrayal.

Si Mohamed, ever patient, let us spill out all our nonsense without losing his calm or his famous half-smile. He simply said, "As far as you are concerned, the operation is canceled. There are other ways to silence this traitor with manageable risks."

Instead of complying, we seized on the term "manageable risks" and analyzed it aloud before our great leader in order to show him that our proposal was the only viable one! Based on our perfect knowledge of the Franco-Muslim Circle and its hyper-secure surroundings, we explained that sending a *fidaï* to take down the Bachagha was doomed from the start, not to mention that it would amount to sending a brother to certain death. Stubbornly, we looked Si Mohamed straight in the eye and shot back at him virulently, "If a brother dies trying to accomplish this mission with its 'manageable risks,' you and El Kho will be solely responsible. You won't be able to say that you didn't know, because we've warned you!" We were unaware just how serious our words had grown. Our plan was the only thing that counted. We had to make our leader change his mind.

Suddenly a dry voice that we did not recognize shook us: "That is enough. Do you not know that you're out of line, and subject to the military tribunal? The operation is canceled. That's an order. It's final and no one may question it!" Taken aback, flooded with shame and despair, Djamila and I fought with all our strength not to burst into tears and aggravate our situation.

The leader must have realized it because, after a moment of silence, he said, "Djamila and Zohra, I want you to know that your courage, your determination, and your commitment are admirable. Not just in my eyes and in the eyes of all the brothers, but in our people's eyes, too. However, you must remember that you are not—that none of us are—ordinary soldiers in a conventional army. You and all of us are, above all, activists for a highly political cause: the independence of our country and the liberation of our people. Do you think we are in a war between two states with more or less equal power? Do you think we are in a war between two conventional armies that act on behalf of their states?

"Never lose sight of what we are: political activists whom the colonial regime's arrogance has forced to become fighters in a war of national liberation. How are the battle lines drawn? On one side is the colonial regime with its old state and its army, one of the most powerful in the world, outfitted with the heaviest and most sophisticated weapons. On the other side are fighters born from a population reduced to living as miserable 'natives,' given no choice in life except the method and weapon to be used by their executioner. Our first duty, if we are to defeat them, is to never lose sight of this abominably unjust and completely asymmetrical configuration. Only with this reality in mind will we understand France's objective: to defeat us militarily by literally crushing us, physically eliminating us, and holding all the means to do so: raids, arrests, torture, executions, and ferocious repression.

"Meanwhile, it is by keeping this configuration in mind that we will oblige France to meet us on a different battlefield: the political one, where it can never win. That is why our ambushes, our attacks, our bombs, and all the rest must help us to defeat France politically and to diminish it morally and symbolically. We are not killers. We are fighters for a just cause, moved by the most sacred of duties: to liberate our land and our people. It is the colonial regime that kills—torturing, oppressing, and repressing to perpetuate its system of occupation on our land and our people, trying to convince everyone that Algeria is French. That is why each of our attacks, each of our ambushes, each of our lives sacrificed must serve to unmask France before the world, to show that our people are at war against a foreign power occupying us by force. To do this, our people have established a political organization, the FLN, and an armed organization, the ALN. *That* is the meaning of the primacy of the political over the military, which is a fundamental principle of our revolution. To that point, I invite you to read and analyze the platform of the Soummam Congress, which explains our revolution's aims and philosophy.[3]

"Before letting you go, I want to ask you to stand by to lead a crucial awareness campaign to mobilize our people, as the Algerian question will soon be debated at the UN. The challenge is to demonstrate that the FLN legitimately represents our people. You see, it is thanks to the struggle of our brothers in the ALN in the *maquis* and in the cities, and also thanks to the bombs in the European city, that the world has become aware of our cause and that the UN has agreed to include the Algerian question in the General Assembly's agenda. This is a great first victory for the FLN, and hence for all our people. It is the meaning of the primacy of the interior over the exterior, the other fundamental principle of our revolution. So go, and know that I am counting on you. Until next time, good luck."

When we returned to our safe house at 5 Impasse de la Granada, we burst into tears. For two weeks our preparations had been driving us. Now that they were dead in the water, we felt suddenly drained of our energy. Seeing our tears, Hassiba worried that something terrible had happened. We reassured her and explained that we had experienced a setback because we were women: "Whatever we do, they will always look at us as weak

---

3. The Soummmam Congress, organized in August 1956 in Kabylie, the mountainous region east of Algiers, established the tenets that guided the liberation struggle and the foundations of the eventual Algerian state.

creatures who need to be protected!" Hassiba didn't probe any further into the reasons for our revolt.

We spent the next day helping Auntie Baya and Oukhiti with household chores, trying to forget our disappointment. In the afternoon, we were sitting in Oukhiti's room reading the papers when Hassiba, immersed in reading one of the dailies, exclaimed, "There's a great film at the cinema, not far from the Rue Rovigo! It's called *Operation Swallow: The Battle for Heavy Water* and it takes place during the resistance, in Nazi-occupied France. If I wasn't wanted, I would have gone to see it."

Djamila and I looked at each other without saying a word; the same idea had sprouted in our heads and our decision was instantaneous. We were free. We arrived just in time to buy our tickets and to find our seats as the projector began showing the newsreels—those veritable propaganda pieces. Then, for nearly an hour and forty minutes, we were immersed in the world of the shadow war, eagerly following each scene. We saw something of ourselves in the resistance fighters, leaving the role of the Nazis to our French occupiers. As we watched, we promised ourselves to draw inspiration from the film for our own future missions. The film ended with the Germans' demise, which we took to be a wonderful omen for our cause. When the lights came on, Djamila sighed: *"Inchallah hadha falna!"* (God willing, that will be our destiny!)

Once outside, we discovered that the December night had already fallen. We rushed through the streets, frantic at the thought that the brothers might have been looking for us. We emerged on an illuminated Rue d'Isly, with its brightly lit shopfronts and teeming crowds happily going about their Christmas shopping. Heads down, we hustled toward the Rue Rovigo, where the winding uphill route to the Casbah was much quieter, with just a few passersby hurrying to return home. As soon as we passed the Marché de la Lyre, a black and silent urban desert welcomed us. The further we walked along Rue Randon, then Rue Porte Neuve, then Rue de la Granada, the more the darkness and silence thickened and grew ominous. We quickened our pace. It was only seven o'clock, but there wasn't a soul in sight, nor a glimmer of light to guide a newcomer. But the residents of the Casbah seemed alert, monitoring the slightest movement, trying to identify the slightest sound. It seemed like we could almost hear their breathing.

Arriving at the Bouhireds', we went directly to Oukhiti's room, where we found Hassiba. Djamila threw her bag on a bench and sank down, sobbing breathlessly. Our youngest sister rushed to her and hugged her close, asking me with her eyes what had caused all these tears. With my eyes, I confessed my ignorance. Worried, Hassiba began to shake our sobbing sister and asked her, "What happened? Was a brother arrested? Or killed?" But Djamila was spilling tears from somewhere deep within, just like the day of the failed trolley bombing.

When at last she finished crying, she wiped her face and said, "The bastards! It's only us who are living this war! Us 'rats'! At seven in the evening we are forced to hole up while their people live their lives, since the war doesn't apply to them, doesn't touch them." At that point I explained to Hassiba where we had come from: from Rue d'Isly glittering with lights and teeming with men, women, and children. All European. All busy and happy to buy their year-end gifts and prepare their feasts in peace. Just a ten-minute walk from the Casbah, which was transformed by their police, their army, their spies, and their regime into a ghetto, subject to curfew, surrounded and besieged by barricades, barbed wire, and patrols.

We Loved Life So Much

At the end of December 1956, Hassiba and I had been sheltered, fed, and protected for more than two months by the Bouhired family, who had completely integrated us as their own daughters. We had grown used to sharing breakfast and lunch with Oukhiti, Uncle Mustapha, and Djamila and dining with the brothers from the laboratory. Sometimes Ali and El Kho joined us for a night when they happened to change safe houses. When we were not busy completing a mission, Djamila and I helped Oukhiti and Auntie Baya with the housework. Auntie Baya never ceased to chide her daughter and sister-in-law for committing an inexcusable breach of the rules of hospitality—in her eyes, at least—by accepting our help. Personally, I was particularly fond of those moments when, forgetting the reasons that had brought me to the Casbah, I could joyfully help with washing out the hallways.

Our favorite delight was splashing in the water when we helped Oukhiti do the laundry. Sometimes, after completing the chores on the top floor at the Bouhireds', we descended to the Mezianes' to lend a hand to our friend Fettouma. I loved those precious moments and acts of feminine solidarity where, even as we put our hearts into our work, our exchanges often led to wild fits of laughter. The women of the Casbah fascinated me—their way of doing and saying things, their discussions, their stories and dialogues, all filled with adages, proverbs, maxims, and flowery parables whose meaning was not always clear to me. Sometimes the meaning completely escaped me, which got my friends writhing in laughter at my bewilderment. These wonderful days often finished with afternoon coffee served on a *meïda* with a copper tray full of homemade cakes. But even then the women were not inactive—their fingers were busy embroidering, crocheting, knitting, or preparing homemade *mqatfa* noodles. No one was surprised by my presence nor asked any questions. On the contrary, all showed us openness, affection, and friendship. I was acutely aware of how privileged I was to experience these magical moments.

At nightfall, we met the brothers for dinner in the square room. The eldest of our group, Si Mourad, half lying on the bench, his pipe in his mouth, followed our conversations or smiled at the unexpected jokes that Ali couldn't help but make about one of us (sometimes angering us). When he was present, El Kho imagined the wonderful cruises that he would organize for us throughout the Mediterranean once we had our independence. Then we would all begin to choose different ports of call. When we asked him on what vessel he intended to organize the cruise, he gave a mysterious answer: "The yacht is there waiting for us." To bring Si Mourad into our collective daydreams, one or another of us would ask, "And you, Si Mourad, will you come with us?" We never managed to drag Si Mourad in our flights of fancy because, as usual, he smiled his narrow eyes and continued to smoke his pipe calmly, the understanding older brother in the face of our caprices.

Ghani and Djamila, both children of the Casbah, born and raised in two adjoining houses on the Impasse de la Granada, were thick as thieves and understood each other at a glance. Dahmane, with his thick glasses and frail body, seemed eternally preoccupied by some chemical formula or another. He and Hassiba formed our scientific duo. Since my talents lay in arts and letters, I looked at our scientists with tender admiration. Sometimes we played cards, dominoes and, of course, *yadess*, always with a cake as the prize. We also tried never to forget to celebrate birthdays—a way to ward off bad luck and make sure each one would not be the last. We all knew that each day we lived was a victory over a possible arrest or a probable death. This was what made our relationships so strong. There were, of course, sad evenings when we learned of a brother's death or arrest. The rule—unspoken and unwritten, but followed by everyone in these cases—was to fight against despair, against despondency, against death. And it was from the group that we each drew the energy to stay standing. It was from the most generous one, the most human and fraternal one—Ali—that we greedily sought a breath of fresh air, a burst of energy, and the will to pick ourselves up and continue fighting harder than ever.

A Voice on the Radio

I had gone to the Belhaffafs' house to meet Si Mohamed at his request. When I reached the terrace, I found the door to his room open, the radio on, and Si Mohamed crouched down beside it, pinching the skin of his forearm, asking himself out loud: "How could his body betray the most dedicated of wills?" Evidently, he didn't realize I was there. From the radio came the voice of a man, his accent clearly marking him as Algerian.

The voice called on our people to condemn the FLN, to denounce them as a gang of "scum and miscreants," and to look to France and her army for protection. This tape was broadcast all day long—not just on the radio and in the newspapers, but by Jeeps armed with megaphones circulating in and around all the "native" quarters. We all knew full well by what cruel means these statements had been extracted. The man to whom Si Mohamed listened now, stupefied, was none other than Ben Alla El Hadj, deputy leader of Wilaya V, which Ben M'hidi commanded. Absorbed in concentration as he was, Ben M'hidi's entire body showed just how overwhelmed this voice had left him, this voice he thought he knew so well.

I took several steps back, cleared my throat and entered, announcing my arrival by joking, "Hello, hello! Anyone home?" The terrible nasal voice filled the room, listing out its *mea culpa*s and entreaties to the natives. To try to lighten the mood, I exclaimed, "This guy again? He's all over town. But everyone knows his story, none of us are fools. It's a complete farce!"

Si Mohamed raised his eyes and, fixing me with his gaze like always, responded calmly, "You're wrong. That's Ben Alla El Hadj, a brother in arms, one of our first activists, battle hardened, and one who pledged his life to our cause. I know him very well. He's also my deputy at the head of Wilaya V."

I hadn't expected him to share all that. After a short silence, the time to regain my composure, I tried to react to this news like someone unaware of just who she was addressing. I started to stammer, but Si Mohamed cut me short at the first words: "This game is over! You know—all three of you, just like all the brothers—exactly who I am: Larbi Ben M'hidi. We have serious problems, and that's why I brought you here." He was angry. Presuming it best to act surprised, like someone who hadn't a clue who Larbi Ben M'hidi was, I continued to play dumb, hopelessly dumb. This seemed to have the effect of irritating him beyond belief, and he flung up his hands.

Not knowing that I was only making things worse, I adopted the most appropriate attitude for a young activist before her superior officer, her chief (and what a chief! A leader of November 1954, who was already a hero to me): I started calling him "sir." This, of course, only aggravated him further, earning me a tongue-lashing: "What has just changed between us? I was never a fool, but you play this routine so poorly, all three of you!" Now completely unsure how to escape, I stared at him speechless, realizing just how presumptuous we had been to imagine that Si Mohamed had been fooled by our act for a single instant.

My confusion must have pained him, because he began to explain how happy he was to live among his people in the Casbah, protected by them, and how proud he was to work beside us. Then he dictated several letters to me, which I transcribed with all the devotion I could muster.

When I had finished, he reread the text, looking satisfied, then said, "I need to return to Oran. We both know your father is a judge in Vialar but that you're from the Oran region, where your father has friends and family. Listen closely, Zohra. I'm going to ask you a question you must answer honestly, with no other consideration but the truth: Do you think your father, Qadi Drif, would agree to drive me to Oran? We both know he has a vehicle and goes often to Tiaret and Oran."

Without hesitating, I responded, "Of course he'll drive you. It's the least he can do." Of course: Si Mohamed had to get to Oran urgently, since the Wilaya V had just been decapitated by the arrest of Ben Alla El Hadj. Surely the combatants there were disoriented, maybe even demoralized.

"Listen to me closely. It's not about what you think or want personally. It's about your father, and he alone can decide for himself. We know he has a large family to care for, and that transporting me could put him in grave danger. Besides, he's a civil servant."

I understood that he wanted to know if I had any reliable way of contacting my father and passing him this question. But I insisted, "I know my father well, and I know him as a man of duty, guided by his conscience. He will accept and drive you to Oran. You speak of danger. But what danger is there? My father drives my mother, brothers, and sisters regularly and is rarely stopped at the roadblocks in our region. It only happens sometimes when he comes to Algiers, after he passes Blida."

He listened, following my words with evident interest. I explained how my father had helped me to return to Algiers in July '56 during the student strike, knowing full well what choices I had made and in violation of my mother's wishes.

Encouraged by his close attention, undoubtedly flattered and honored by the confidence he was placing in me and in my father, I began to reflect aloud on the practical aspects of the mission, outlining the various obstacles and risks and listing all the possible solutions. I mentioned the possibility of an ID check of all the passengers, and countered, sure of myself: "It's simple. You'll wear a dress from Oran over your pants and shirt, and we'll wrap you in a *haïk* in the Vialar style, which luckily covers the entire face, with just an eye peeking out—not a single eyelash! With you dressed like this, I'd love to meet anyone who could imagine the great Ben M'hidi disguised as a housewife, sitting beside her husband, Qadi Drif, and carrying her youngest daughter on her lap." I could already taste the joy of yet again outfoxing the colonial authorities and their thugs.

But Ben M'hidi, calm until that point, cut me off sharply: "Never, never at all!"

My enthusiasm disappeared and I replied, dumbfounded, "Never? Never what? Disguise yourself as a woman?"

He looked me straight in the eyes and said, "Exactly!"

I was stunned, floored—a punch couldn't have hit me harder. Arising from my emotional knockout, I flung back at him in Arabic, *"Âallach ya Si Mohamed? Khayef tetih men serdjek?"* (Why, Si Mohamed? Afraid of falling off your high horse?) I continued, "What's the matter? What's going to happen? Where is the dishonor in disguising yourself as a woman to fool the enemy for the sake of our struggle? You're afraid of getting caught while dressed as a woman, aren't you? Is it so dishonorable to be a woman in your eyes?"

My diatribe was cut short by the tears that choked my throat and filled my eyes. Ben M'hidi stopped me by grasping my hand and repeating, "No, no! That's not what I wanted to say! It's not what you think! Let me explain. Or, if you prefer, we can discuss it, calmly and peacefully, but first sit down." I did.

"Imagine the reaction of our people if they learned that one of their leaders was arrested in women's clothing. The question isn't 'How does Ben M'hidi view women?', especially the *moudjahidate* like you. I assure you, I have nothing but respect and endless admiration for all my sisters in this fight. The real question is about our society's taboos. These taboos die hard, because colonialism has deprived our people of the chance to evolve and instead relegated them to almost universal illiteracy and total destitution. These are facts we can't ignore. We need to organize ourselves and act according to our sociological and cultural realities, but we also need to push these realities to evolve, especially through your participation—you, the women—at all levels of responsibility. It's a long road, and a task we can't really take up until we are independent. Today, our only task is the struggle for our country's independence. That's my point of view. What do you think?"

My voice still uncertain, I gave him my opinion: "Si Mohamed, I want you to know that after November 1, 1954, Samia and I never stopped looking for the Novembristes, yourself included. You all were our heroes. The respect and dedication I have for you and the others, there is nothing like it. But I have to disagree with you on this question. All the sisters engaged in our fight, myself included, have had to endure those rules that you call 'sociological and cultural realities.' We have had to butt up against and even violate all the taboos that had been drilled into us, even break the ultimate taboo by going to live far from our families in mixed quarters with our brothers in arms. We were fully conscious of the risk that our society might condemn us for that. What's more, we knew that if our own people condemned us, the French would not hesitate to exploit that against us and our revolution. But our contempt for colonialism and our commitment to liberating the country were always far stronger than the taboos. And you know what we discovered? Our people did not condemn us. They did not reject us. On the contrary, they respect us, they are proud of us, they aid and protect us. You want proof? In this very moment, you and I in this room are welcomed, protected, respected—and in your case I would even say idolized, and rightly so—by the Belhaffafs, a conservative family like all the others, but one that decided to put the revolution above our taboos."

I stopped there, not daring to say aloud to him that the taboos endured more strongly in our leaders' heads than among the people. Likewise, I didn't dare tell him that my pain was that much worse because it was he—the great Ben M'hidi, whom I viewed as nearly divine—who had provoked that pain. With my eyes lowered, I let a line from my favorite poet, René Char, escape from my lips: "Clarity is the closest wound to the sun."

Si Mohamed laughed aloud and asked, "Who's that from? You still read so much? Where do you find the time for it?"

"It's a line from René Char, a French Resistance poet," I replied. "You know, fighting against taboos leads to anxiety and insomnia. I read like a maniac as a kind of therapy, to stay sane. Some fight the anxiety by nourishing their stomach—I do it by nourishing my mind."

He laughed again and said, "We need to wrap up our debate. I think you're right, but only in the absolute sense. For you to be entirely right, young ladies like you would need to be much more numerous and work to change all of us, including all the brothers. But in the meantime, know that you have come to command the utmost respect and admiration from all of us, through your total commitment and courage. You owe that to no one but yourselves. And that's already a revolution in many of our minds. I know already that it's thanks to you, the *moudjahidate*, that no father will deprive his daughters of schooling upon independence. Don't forget our main objective: independence. As for the trip to Oran, we'll discuss it again later.

"You should know that I too have insomnia, though honestly I must say that it's for different reasons than your own. But I would like to try this therapy of yours. Could you get me a book the next time you go to stock up?"

"Of course," I replied, and rose to leave.

It must have been eleven in the morning and I decided to go to the National Library. But once among the shelves, I realized that I hadn't asked Si Mohamed what kind of books he liked to read. Economics? Political science? Classic literature? Novels? Essays? Poetry? Apparently it was up to me. I finally decided to get him a book on constitutional law, state institutions, and electoral systems, figuring that he would need to start preparing now to lead our future independent state.

Several hours later, when I handed him the book, a hefty volume whose title and author I've forgotten, Si Mohamed took it, furrowed his brow as he read the back cover, then raised his eyes to mine and burst out laughing. "Couldn't you have found something a little more serious?" he joked. I explained to him the dilemma that I had, staring at the rows of books in the National Library, and the thinking behind my choice. He assured me that, to fight his insomnia, he would make do with my tome, though he would have preferred a lighter novel or some poetry or theater, since he couldn't go out and escape his refuge like I could. Then he took on such a serious air that he suddenly seemed sad. "Today, our only goal is our country's independence. Our duty is to unite our people, to continue to win more to our cause. Never lose sight of that. Once we achieve our independence, those of us who remain will face new challenges. Will I be alive or dead? No one can say. And besides, we have so much to do now to liberate Algeria. The enemy is ferocious, the sacrifices immense. The only question I care about is 'Am I ready to sacrifice myself?' To you, I answer simply, 'Yes, I am ready.'

"So, I'm going to give you back this monstrous book and take the one you chose for yourself. Dostoyevsky, I believe. That will work just fine."

I left, my hefty volume in hand, sheepish but more than ever admiring, fascinated, and appreciative of Ben M'hidi. As for the trip to Oran, we never spoke of it again.

The Casbah Holds Its Breath

That Christmas Eve, the day of Samia's wedding, would see several bombings, including on the Boulevard de Provence in Bab El Oued and at the Pergola Café near Saint Augustine Church in Hussein Dey. "Consider this bonfire our wedding present," El Kho wrote to Samia. In the house there were incessant comings and goings, forcing the occupants to clear out of the galleries, patio, and stairs, return to their rooms, and lower the curtains each time one of the brothers went up or down. Even that wasn't enough to hide their anxiety. It was the first time I saw a young fighter with Germanic features visit our safe house, in a hurry to talk to El Kho. It was Habib Réda, who would go on after the war to have a long, illustrious acting and production career—he had organized and coordinated all those attacks.

As we readied for bed, Hassiba explained that the laboratory had just received a more reliable and powerful material for making the bombs. "Dahmane was thrilled. He promised great bonfires for the French army and their 'innocent civilian population.'"

It is worth remembering that we experienced many disappointments when bombs failed to explode. When the press announced triumphantly that their bomb squad had defused one of our bombs, we knew that really they had discovered it intact, with a faulty detonator. After Fernand Iveton[4] was sold out and arrested and his bomb confiscated, Dahmane withdrew into himself, mumbling constantly and isolating himself to the point that

---

4. In November 1956, a fellow worker witnessed Fernand Iveton plant a bomb (prepared by Abderrahmane "Dahmane" Taleb) in the gas factory where they both worked and turned him in. Police defused the bomb, and no casualties resulted. Less than three months after his arrest and torture, the FLN sympathizer Iveton would become the only *pied-noir* guillotined by the French during Algeria's liberation war.

Ghani, who was very close to him, grew seriously worried. Hassiba concluded her update by saying that she understood Dahmane's state, since with the old materials only three out of every eight bombs exploded. She explained that in addition to the hard work in the laboratory, you also had to consider the hours of labor needed to conceal the bombs in the newspapers and baskets before entrusting them to the young *fidayine* who planted them.

I will never forget the evening of December 24, 1956, which we spent together, trying to make it less overwhelming, less stifling. The whole Casbah had spent the afternoon with bated breath, praying that a brother I didn't know, Louni Arezki, one of our organization's most committed and formidable fighters, would not fall into the French army's hands. He was facing down dozens of soldiers from all of the French armed services, who had closed off a residential block between Rue Dupuch—not far from Rue Rovigo—and the Marché de la Lyre. El Kho, Ali, and Alilou had come to join us at 5 Impasse de la Granada, where Ghani, Si Mourad, and Dahmane had already arrived. Alilou, El Kho's liaison officer, knew the Casbah like no one else: every time he walked out the door he came back with the latest news. Our brother Louni had decided to attack the guards of the Tenth Military Region, the army headquarters for Algiers, in the heart of the European city.

But in those final days of 1956, the army and police, on red alert, were everywhere, searching everyone and everything, even as the European neighborhoods buzzed with preparations for the next day's Christmas holiday. Louni had submitted his plan of attack to El Kho, who had tried to dissuade him. But he had so meticulously prepared his operation that he managed to convince El Kho. Unfortunately, unforeseen circumstances had arisen and Louni, wounded in the leg, had tried to retreat into the Casbah. Chased by a large pack of soldiers, he had holed up in a building as the entire Casbah held its breath. The rooftop terraces were full of people following the hunt by dozens of enemy soldiers for this wounded fighter. El Kho and Ali were beside themselves: it was absolutely impossible for them to rescue their brother, with all his exits blocked off. We listened as Ali and El Kho examined the possibility of creating a diversion. But Alilou was adamant: the block and building where Louni was holed up were inaccessible. With my brothers and sisters, I experienced firsthand the asymmetry of forces and the imbalance of resources that Si Mohamed had spoken of to Djamila and me: a huge deployment of French military and police against an injured "native." The unbearable injustice of the situation left us revolted, and the powerlessness we felt tormented our very hearts and souls. The tension stiffened our limbs, compressed our throats, and beat at our temples. Louni was doomed.

That night nobody could sleep, especially Ali, who had long been very close with brother Louni. Other brothers had been arrested too. We all knew what France, "Land of the Rights of Man and of the Citizen," was holding in store for them: torture, then capital punishment. Indeed, after he was arrested Louni was immediately subjected to torture, including all the "newest" techniques. Later we would learn that they made him lie on a board covered with nails, dragged him by his feet, and whipped his back into shreds. But we also knew that with each life sacrificed, dozens more would rise, ready to offer themselves up so that Algeria might live.

The Taste of Death

The morning of December 26, all the colonial press announced that an "outlaw" had shot and seriously injured the Bachagha Aït Ali while he was eating lunch at the Franco-Muslim Circle. The reports noted that the attack was the work of a young man who, after shooting the traitor, had left the restaurant and walked toward Bresson Square. The corner florist had picked him out and began shouting out to bystanders. A patrol stationed nearby took chase and shot him down under the arches of the Bab Azzoun arcade, just below the Casbah. For the Europeans, he was a "criminal" and "outlaw," but for us he was a *fidaï* and a *chahid*.

Djamila and I were very angry because the job of eliminating the traitor Bachagha Aït Ali should have been entrusted to us rather than to a novice young brother. But what increased our rage tenfold was that we had vainly tried to explain that the only possible operation in this hyper-protected club, constantly surrounded by patrols, was the bombing attack we had carefully planned. We decided to go see El Kho, despite the strict rules governing communication between us that prohibited such initiatives. It was about nine o'clock when we burst into the Belhaffafs', furious, our eyes welling with tears of rage. We found El Kho seated in his shelter on the rooftop, a sheet of paper torn from a notebook in his hand. Oddly, he didn't seem surprised to see us. Without a word, he handed us the sheet. His eyes had an unusual glow and he kept picking at his thumbnail. Looking down at the awkward, childlike handwriting, we could see just how much whoever had drafted it had struggled to do so meticulously. The words, written phonetically in French, attempted to translate literally a thought conceived in Arabic. The short letter was addressed to El Kho and signed by the slain *fidaï*. In it he expressed his pride at having been chosen to put an end to the treachery of Bachagha Aït Ali. He was aware of the danger that his mission carried and accepted the supreme sacrifice so that his brothers might live in dignity. He wrote, "Today, I might learn the taste of death, but I accept it for our dignity." He concluded by thanking El Kho for having granted him this privilege.

We were overcome by sobs. El Kho got up and went outside—probably to cry too. We hadn't exchanged a word. This young man's death at the end of 1956 inspired us to launch a project Djamila and I had been discussing ever since we'd begun feeling reduced to inaction. We imagined preparing to head for the *maquis*, aware that the ALN was lacking medical and paramedical staff there. Djamila took up the case and arranged for us to visit the Mustapha Pacha Hospital to start a nursing training course.

One afternoon in the last days of December, we presented ourselves at one of the hospital's departments, which at first seemed deserted. A young man in a white coat with blue eyes and combed-back brown hair graciously showed us into an office that looked like a monk's cell. He asked us about our medical knowledge—we admitted we had none—and gave us several handwritten index cards. We plunged straight into reading them, but he asked us to put them away and memorize them at home. He took us into a room with test tubes and other laboratory equipment lined up atop a white ceramic lab table. There, we proceeded on to some practical exercises: how to apply a tourniquet, how to administer an injection, and the like. He freed us after a very intensive hour, but not without setting our next appointment. Djamila and I learned our cards by heart in the meantime.

At the next meeting, we arrived at the department at the same time as an ambulance, from which the nurses pulled a person completely covered with what looked to me like aluminum foil. Our professor ran outside, instructing the nurses, and asked us to follow them. Inside, the nurses set down the stretcher and left. Once we were alone, our professor parted the metallic sheets enveloping the patient, warning us that it was a severe burn case. I just barely had enough time to turn my head. Then, paralyzed, I began to shake, refusing to look at the charred mass before me. The young doctor handed me a syringe and asked me to apply what we had learned by giving the burn victim a shot. Instead of taking the syringe, however, I covered my face in my hands to avoid falling, since the whole room had begun to spin around me. I knew then that I could never, ever, do it, despite our professor's encouragement to administer the injection and relieve the patient's pain.

Braver than me, Djamila put the lesson into practice and injected the victim without the slightest tremble of her hand. Our doctor, faced with my hangdog demeanor, tried to reassure me that my reaction was common among many beginners. He added that, unfortunately, you get used to it. But my case was hopeless beyond repair; I concluded that I could never be a nurse. I would later learn that this young doctor was Pierre Chaulet, a brother in arms. I would only see him again after the country's liberation.

At the end of December 1956, events accelerated. Djamila and I hid the index cards in the dresser, as no one in the group knew of our nursing initiative. As we shall see, this serious violation of the organization's disciplinary rules would nearly have dramatic consequences on the morning of February 2, 1957.

Surprised By an Honor

Another day that month stands among the most wonderful and intense of my life. Si Mohamed had arrived accompanied by El Kho and Ali. He surprised us by saying he had come to fulfill a mission given to him by the CCE. El Kho handed him a small package. With slow, meticulous movements he extracted four objects wrapped in paper.

"These," he said in a grave voice, "are the National Liberation Army's first medals of honor."

My throat knotted up with emotion and tears filled my eyes as I asked, "Medals? Our military makes medals?"

He then presented us one medal for us to admire. It was rectangular and seemed large for a medal, maybe two inches by an inch and a quarter, and was cast in a metal the color of molten lead. Inlaid at the center was our national emblem. When Si Mohamed gave me my medal, I was in heaven, thinking, *This will be the most beautiful jewel of my life!*

He did the same with Samia, Djamila, and Hassiba, and suggested that we not show them to anyone and hide them in an undetectable place. All four of us felt such happiness, such privilege, an emotion so powerful that, to try to swallow the tears that overwhelmed us, we teased El Kho and especially Ali while laughing awkwardly like little girls. I will never forget Si Mohamed's face before us. He looked at us, smiling, his eyes shining as if they were wet, and full of compassion, amusement, emotion, tenderness, fraternity, and—my God—a pride that could have split the walls! El Kho and Ali were perfect, standing silent, serious, and solemn, almost as if at attention.

We gave our medals to Alilou for safekeeping, and he put them somewhere that would be impossible to find. Years later, I would learn that he had sealed them in a wall in the Casbah; only he knew the spot. He promised to give them to us at independence. Unfortunately, Massu's paratroopers and torturers decided otherwise.

Sometimes I find myself dreaming that during the restoration of this citadel of the resistance, full of dignity and courage, this bastion of our war of liberation that is the Casbah, our children, those brilliant architects of heritage in whom I believe, will find our precious medals. Let them never forget that these rectangles of coarse metal symbolize the suffering of our people and the huge sacrifices they made to recover their dignity and freedom. Let them never forget that freedom and dignity can only exist through national independence and sovereignty.

The Algerian Question Before the UN

In November 1956, France named General Raoul Salan to oversee its forces in the country. He was presented by the press as "an expert in anti-guerrilla warfare," "a great warrior who earned his stripes in Indochina," and "one who can put an end to the misdeeds of the outlaws and *fellagas*."

In truth, after their humiliating defeat in Indochina, France and her army had just lost another war: the war of the Suez Canal, led by a Franco-British-Israeli coalition against Egypt. In total blindness that led them to believe that Nasser and his regime bore the true responsibility for triggering the November 1, 1954, revolt in Algeria, France mistakenly believed that by crushing Egypt, they would finish off our revolution. Pressure from the Russians and Americans ended the Suez expedition, leaving a French army and government more frustrated than ever and desperate to regain their prestige. It was at us that they would throw all their destructive force and hatred, carried by officers like Salan, Massu, Trinquier, and their men, at the orders of a French political regime whose sole purpose was to keep Algeria in France's sphere by any means necessary. But despite all this, thanks to our struggle and determination, the Algerian question was scheduled for discussion and debate in January 1957, placing the Algerian drama at the heart of the discussion at the United Nations.

In those final days of 1956, Ben M'hidi—known to us as our respected commander Si Mohamed and living with us in the Casbah—supervised our political and military operations in Algiers. He oversaw all the armed groups El Kho commanded. He also led our political branches, unions, and professional guilds, and liaised with the Coordination and Execution Committee (CCE), our revolution's highest governing body, created following the Soummam Congress. Besides Ben M'hidi, the CCE consisted of Ramdane Abane, Benyoucef Benkhedda, Krim Belkacem, and Sâad Dahlab—all fighters, all living among our people within the country. Even if Si Mohamed was all we knew of the CCE, to us it represented more than just the leadership of our revolution; it was simultaneously our dream for a national government and the manifestation of that dream. We were so proud to have transitioned in just twenty-six months from an armed insurgency to a genuine national liberation war, led by a quasi-state with a political institution (the FLN), a military institution representing the Algerian people in the struggle (the ALN), and international representation.

As was decided at the Soummam Congress, the country at war was organized into six *wilayas*, or regions, and the capital configured as the Algiers Autonomous Zone (AAZ) under the CCE's direct control. There was also the external delegation—of which five members had been arrested on October 20, 1956, in the aerial seizure by the French military—as well as the FLN federations in France, Tunisia, and Morocco. In any event, the AAZ and its armed groups, political branch, and intelligence branch were under the direction of the immense Ben M'hidi, whom we had the chance to get to know since he had elected to take up residence with us in the Casbah, among his people. Djamila and I were aware of the privilege this represented. It was he who explained to us our revolution's doctrine and ultimate objectives. He pushed us to "read and meditate on" the Soummam platform. Patiently, he explained to us the political, social, cultural, and economic aims as well as the principles in which our revolution and its strategy were rooted. He repeated that we must keep up our action on multiple fronts: political and military, interior and exterior—but always respecting the primacy of the interior over the exterior and the political over the military.

We learned from Si Mohamed that every military operation must serve our ultimate political objective of full independence by obliging France to agree to negotiate. At the same time, we had to prevent France from solving its challenges militarily, by fierce repression, as it dreamed of doing. To do this, he insisted on the necessary work of building our people's awareness and political understanding—through our commitment and our arguments—in order to affirm the FLN's role as the people's sole legitimate representative. It was as if, in anticipation of the Eight-Day Strike of January 1957, Ben M'hidi had seen to it personally that we explain the objectives and their importance to our people, even if it meant going door to door in the Casbah and preparing to cover needy families' costs during eight days without work.

After more than two years at war, our leaders had managed to make Algeria the central issue of the UN session. Now both sides were preparing for the debate. Based on a decision by our leaders in the CCE, our camp—the people and activists united around the FLN—had chosen a massive, civil, and peaceful mobilization: an Eight-Day Strike. The general strike was designed to demonstrate our people's full support for our delegation at the UN, where the Algerian question was to be debated peacefully, and to affirm the FLN as our sole legitimate representative. Everybody had been talking about it, and the street had buzzed about it since late December 1956, but no one knew either the date or the duration. These two pieces of information depended on the date that the United Nations would set for the debate.

Contrary to what some think, my belief is that the Eight-Day Strike was decisive in advancing our revolution: it made "the Algerian question" an international issue and and enabled international recognition of the FLN as the sole legitimate representative of our people. It unmasked the true nature of the French presence in Algeria to the world, while also showing our people's deep commitment to freedom, dignity, and independence. With its total war, torture factory, and forced disappearances by the thousands, France offered the world—and its own domestic audience—evidence that Algeria was not France, that its army was behaving as an occupying colonial army on foreign soil, and that our independence was the only solution.

We Get Our "Eight-Day Strike," Massu Gets His "Battle of Algiers"

The enemy camp—that is to say, the government of Guy Mollet, Minister of Algeria Robert Lacoste and his army; and the settlers and *ultras* of French Algeria—were also preparing for the UN debate. First were the proponents of a hard line for French Algeria; they were found throughout Algeria but also back in metropolitan France, among the civilians and soldiers alike. Recruiting their thugs from among the ranks of the *ultras* organizations in

Algeria, they organized the assassination, on December 28, 1956, of Amédée Froger, president of the Association of Mayors of Algeria, and several attacks on December 29 against churches, temples, and even a cemetery crypt—all of which they blamed on the FLN. By committing these attacks and attributing them to our fighters, they hoped to prevent negotiations with the FLN and force the French government to give the army full powers in Algeria.

Froger was an important figure in the European colonial population, one of the key settlers of the Mitidja plain, hostile to all reform. He was said to have been one of the fiercest perpetrators in the massacres of our people on May 8, 1945. The news of his assassination, greeted with joy by our people, provoked reactions of suspicion and vigilance on the part of our leaders, who quickly recognized the manipulation and its purpose. Surprised by the news, El Kho summoned the leaders of all the local zones. They confirmed that Froger's assassination was not the work of our *fidayine*. Our brother sent Alilou immediately, and Petit Omar later that day, to make the rounds of the Casbah and other "native" neighborhoods and instruct residents to avoid visiting the European city the next day, when Froger was to be buried. The brothers had immediately understood that the great colonist's assassination was the work of the *ultras* organizations, and therefore readied themselves for all sorts of provocations. The funeral day was one of the most agonizing days I have ever experienced. The entire Casbah was on alert; all its exits were under the control of our *fidayine*.

On the rooftop, a continuous hubbub reached us, as well as sporadic gunshots, screams, and an unceasing blare of car horns. El Kho sent activists to observe the funeral and report back. They all returned with vivid stories of the unprecedented violence that the gangs of Europeans young and old had visited upon any "native" in their path. We were left to mourn the deaths of dozens of our people, victims of the outburst of hate that accompanied the funeral. This was how the settlers and their *ultras*—with the complicity of the army, police, and French politicians—prepared to debate the Algerian question at the UN.

They created the conditions for the transfer of all powers to the army in order to crush our revolution and its goals by "cleansing" the country—particularly Algiers—of its fighters. Guy Mollet's public address, reported by the press throughout the first ten days of January 1957, confirmed our fears even as it confirmed our analyses. As part of its preparation for the UN's debate on our country, the French government decided not to recognize the FLN but instead to fight it to the death, and to grant full powers to the army in greater Algiers. This would kill two birds with one stone: break our strike and wipe out the AAZ. To justify its decision, the French government pointed to the attacks led by the *ultras* on December 28 and 29, which were unjustly blamed on our organization, as well as to the atmosphere of fear, terror, and racial hatred that had resulted.

That was how, on January 7, 1957, General Massu—freshly arrived from Egypt, where his army had suffered their historic setback—came to be granted full civil and military powers in greater Algiers. He paraded through the city with thousands of paratroopers, applauded by a crowd of "innocent European civilians" happy to know that the land would finally be cleansed of all the "natives" and "outlaws." To justify the total war he intended to lead, Massu decreed that our Eight-Day Strike was "insurrectionary." Massu the war criminal, beaten in Indochina and humiliated in Suez, would invent his "Battle of Algiers" against an impoverished, empty-handed indigenous civilian population reduced to subhuman status. Massu the war criminal would conjure up this "battle" to help everyone forget all the battles France and its army had lost to other states and armies. What cowardice, to call it a "battle," this operation carried out by the army, the police, and their torturers against a people unprotected by any law or any rights—a long war of ethnic cleansing right in the capital.

Massu would divide up the city, encircle the "native" districts to the point of suffocation, conduct daily and nightly raids, thousands of searches, roundups by the thousands, and put in place a system of torture on an industrial scale: nobody would escape, not children nor women nor the elderly. Not content to torture in their interrogation centers and walled-off villas, Massu's army would practice these vile methods in the very homes of those they tortured, especially in the Casbah. That's not even counting the forced disappearances by the thousands. With such methods, it was easy for France and its war criminals to win a "battle" against a helpless people. That may be why, sixty years later, France still doesn't admit the crimes it committed here. As for us, our enemy's arrogance, hatred, and blindness only strengthened our determination to continue fighting while remaining doubly vigilant.

We had to keep fighting to refute France and its war criminals, who trumpeted that this was the end of the FLN. We had to be vigilant in adapting to the new conditions of repression and total war. Thus, despite the enemy's pressure, Djamila and I continued to ferry bombs and other packages outside the old *medina*. We had to use all our ingenuity to get past the checkpoints that blocked each exit. But the children of the Casbah knew their city all too well: they detected the flaws in the enemy's system and exploited them. Hidden exits were left unguarded, and the residents became experts in the timing of the soldiers' patrols. Each time a patrol was slow to take up its shift, or paused in its rounds to question some poor "native" or just take a cigarette break, "the organization" was watching. The information traveled swiftly through our network, and our fighters and couriers would seize the chance to dash in or out of the Casbah, our labyrinthine refuge.

First Raid at the Bouhireds'

Given how it started, 1957 promised to be the year of all-out confrontation.

Not only was Algiers surrounded and locked down—especially the Casbah—but the old city swarmed with patrols of seven to ten soldiers, who now grew bolder. They moved in single file, guns loaded, ready to fire. On our transport runs we were obliged to go two at a time.

I didn't know the Casbah and I would have been hard pressed to locate the addresses where we had to drop our packages. That was why Damila or Petit Omar generally served as my scouts. They led the way and I followed a few steps behind, usually with a basket of groceries in hand. If my guide gave the signal, I was to take shelter in a house bordering the street and immediately climb to the rooftop for maximum safety.

Ultimately, that was how I would learn to orient myself in the Casbah: by the rooftop terraces.

In addition to the increased army presence throughout the city, Robert Lacoste, the Resident Minister, had advocated a simultaneous, comprehensive military and political attack: "This is the price to be paid for liquidating the outlaws' political and military infrastructure." So Massu poured his thousands of paratroopers, police, informants, and torturers into the "native" neighborhoods, then began sweeps and raids in the Casbah.

This was how one day in January, at about three in the morning, a relative of Fettouma Meziane who worked as a bus driver was pushed back into the house as he left for work by a patrol that had blocked the alleyway. Showing his ID card, he tried to explain that he needed to get to his job. But he was shoved brutally back into the house and one of the paratroopers replied to him, "Today, nobody from the Casbah will make it to work. That's an order." He returned home and, as soon as the door was shut, woke his wife, who came to notify Djamila, Hassiba, and me. Only Djamila and I were not yet identified or wanted, and we hadn't yet built a shelter for hiding at the Bouhireds'. The brothers—Si Mourad, Dahmane, Ghani, El Kho, and Ali—were still sleeping in their room. Djamila went to wake them.

It was immediately decided that all the brothers, plus Hassiba, would go from rooftop to rooftop to the Belhaffafs' house, where there was already a functional shelter. After confirming that the soldiers hadn't yet taken up positions on the rooftop terraces (probably while waiting for all the lanes and alleys to be blocked off so as not to lose the element of surprise), Hassiba and the brothers set off. They left with heavy hearts; even if their chances of evading the search were very good, the bomb lab was likely to be discovered if the soldiers climbed up to the Bouhireds' rooftop. The life of every inhabitant of 5 Impasse de la Granada—including those who were totally unaware of our activities—was in danger.

Djamila and I quickly understood that our challenge would be to do everything possible to prevent the soldiers from climbing up to the rooftop, where the brothers stored their equipment and raw materials in a small outhouse. The cache was accessed by sliding aside the mirror over the sink; it was a perfect spot, but the work wasn't yet complete. Hence the risk that the soldiers could discover it. How could we keep them from climbing up to the rooftop? That was our chief problem. We went to wake Oukhiti and her husband, Uncle Mustapha, then decided to do a full spring cleaning of the house right then and there, starting with dumping water all over. We attacked the square room where the brothers had slept. The ashtrays were overflowing and the blankets and mattresses were infused with the smell of tobacco. We set about erasing every last trace that the room had been occupied. By four in the morning, the bedding and towels were hung out along the gallery railings. We washed down the room's every nook and cranny, its windows and doors, and even wiped the walls with towels soaked in orange blossom water. We made up the two couches with flowered slipcovers and cushions that matched the room's colors.

On the shelves, we placed books taken from Uncle Mustapha's library: Victor Hugo, Lamartine, and other well-known authors. Oukhiti was heating a large pot of water and was ready to pour in coffee grounds and fill the air with the smell of Turkish coffee the moment Djamila gave her the signal. Trays were set with coffee cups and sugar spoons and placed close at hand.

It was January and very cold. Restless, we waited for the sunrise. We climbed up to the rooftop to scan the surroundings and listen for noises. Not a soul in sight, though we knew that the enemy was all around, just a few meters from us, on Rue Porte Neuve, on Rue Randon, and on Rue de la Granada.

The sun finally rose in the blue sky, flooding the brothers' room and all the galleries with light. Even though everyone was awake, an unusual silence hung in the air, increasing my anxiety. On the alert, we awaited them, imploring heaven "to blind them," as Auntie Baya said while murmuring prayers. "*Echedda fi Allah! Allah yaâmi bsarhoum!*" (Hold fast to God. May he blind their sight!) We had tidied up all around, and of course in our own blue room, so welcoming with its cheerful and harmonious colors. Suddenly we heard a voice, followed by the sound of boots. They had entered the patio below. Two soldiers soon stationed themselves on the second floor, their loaded machine guns pointed toward the ground floor. We were on the third floor, listening closely, but all we heard was the crunch of their boots on the marble. They were still on the second floor. Djamila and I had our radio on fairly loud, on a station broadcasting classical music. Viennese waltzes, including "The Blue Danube," spilled out, and the soldiers must have heard them since we had purposely left the door slightly ajar. In the kitchen, the water was already boiling. Spoon in hand, Oukhiti awaited the signal to pour in the coffee grounds and prepare a steaming brew for our uninvited guests, who we hoped to occupy on the second floor long enough to make them lose interest in inspecting the rooftop. Suddenly they invaded our floor: fifteen paratroopers in camouflage fatigues, armed to the teeth, the same as on the other floors. We were waiting, ready to welcome them with hot coffee, delicious *maqrouts*, and coy smiles, knowing we had to prevent them at all costs from going higher.

They were young, with accents from metropolitan France, probably draftees. We knew the *pied-noir* accent perfectly but didn't hear it from them. One exclaimed, "Wow, it's nice here! 'The Blue Danube!' My word! I never thought I would hear that in the heart of the Casbah!"

"Why is that?" I replied, smiling with all my teeth as I led him toward the brothers' room, where he and five or six others followed me as another group looked elsewhere.

"Ah, it's the radio! What station?" he asked.

"Radio Luxembourg," I said. They entered and began turning around the room, some looking out the window and other flipping the books on the shelves. A strong smell of coffee filled the room.

"Say, it smells like good coffee in your home!" exclaimed one of the paratroopers.

"Yes, but we are deprived of milk and croissants today thanks to you!" one of the girls said with a smile.

"And what should we say to that? We haven't slept all night and the day is just beginning," he replied.

"Well! We'll share what we have. A nice hot black coffee will wake us up!" I replied.

Djamila was already in the kitchen alongside Oukhiti, filling the serving pots with steaming coffee. The young paratrooper, seeming to take our bait, shouted out: "Captain! Captain! These beautiful girls are offering us a hot coffee. We're all invited!" The captain stepped out from the group and eyed us with suspicion. But the young soldier with the metropolitan accent added, "Captain, we've already inspected the room. Come see, we were even greeted with some Johann Strauss in the Casbah! It's nothing like the other houses where we've been!"

The captain, surrounded by his soldiers, all of them probably exhausted from their filthy work of raiding and repressing the "natives," gave the green light and the whole column of fifteen young men, laughing and joking between themselves, followed me into Oukhiti's room. Djamila laughed along with one of the soldiers' jokes, and then at another who raved about the "hidden treasures of the Casbah." She arranged the coffee cups on the main table, accompanied by Oukhiti, who, with a wide smile that brightened her dark features, offered them a plate of *maqrouts* in one hand and another with pieces of Russian cake bought the day before for El Kho's birthday. Delighted, the eager young soldiers let their astonishment pour forth. "This sure isn't how we imagined the Casbah!" one of them said.

"What were you expecting here? A bunch of women languishing about, trapped in their harem?" asked Djamila. Oukhiti refilled coffee cups as they were emptied, and circulated the *maqrouts*—those "divine honey cakes," as one of the enraptured paratroopers dubbed them. Everyone was talking and laughing. Behind the table, facing the door, stood the captain, who certainly wasn't being shy around the coffee and cakes. Djamila faced him across the table, amid the lively hubbub of the room full of soldiers.

Abruptly, the captain fixed his gaze on Djamila and said, "I would like to know what lies behind those eyes."

Sharp as a tack, she flirted back, turning her head and sliding her long, thick hair over her shoulder. Running her fingers through the cascade with a smile, she replied: "My hair, as you can see."

A burst of laughter filled the room, followed by admiring looks in my sister's direction. At that very moment, Djamila and I noticed the plate, where a few last pieces of cake had escaped the soldiers' gluttony.

Among them was a piece that El Kho had bitten into the night before. We looked at each other and instantly had the same idea. Since I was closest to the captain, whose empty cup *Oukhiti* had just refilled, I smiled and presented him the plate, with El Kho's piece from the previous night facing him, and said, "Don't leave any cake unfinished. The honor is yours, Captain. You get this nice big piece here." He reached out, took the piece that I indicated, and shoved it whole into his mouth.

Oukhiti, Djamila, and I were relishing the pleasure of making him eat our commander's leftovers, when the captain called out, "Come on, men! Recess is over! Back to work!"

I asked innocently, "Is our presence keeping you from doing your work?" While expressing our readiness to help them in their search, we continued stoking the conversation with the soldiers on the Casbah and its lifestyle. They didn't know where to turn and faltered, utterly lost and hesitating. The captain put an end to that, ordering some of the men out to search the other upstairs rooms. Our hearts beat wildly, petrified that we had only delayed, but not totally prevented, their search of the rooftop terrace where our lab was located. I hurried to catch the soldiers who were already preparing to recommence their search at the blue room. We had to delay them as much as possible.

As casually as I could, I stepped in front of the door and clapped my back against it. With a giggle and smile, I told them, "This is the girls' room. It's sacred! No boys allowed!"

They laughed. A few played along, and one of them laughed back, "After coffee, where better for a warrior to rest than in the Vestal Virgins' chamber?"

"You have to do your duty!" Djamila told them, as she heaved open the large doors and swung them against the wall, inviting the soldiers to enter the room. The first few advanced timidly and stopped to look around. Djamila played hostess, opening the great armoire, where our laundry was tidily arranged, then stepping aside and urging those who hesitated at the threshold to enter. Comments, a few of them bawdy, rang out here and there as they shuffled through without really searching and headed for Auntie Baya's room, where her young boys Aziouez and Nadir were still sleeping. Opening the cupboards wide, Djamila's mother encouraged them to search well, while her husband stood back, leaning on the railing. Throughout the whole search, we didn't leave them alone, continuing to laugh and chatter about this and that, first with some, then with others. A moment later, we were in front of the stairs leading up to the rooftop. The soldiers asked where it led.

"To the terrace. Shall we?" Djamila asked with perfect composure, beckoning them with an inviting smile to go bask in the morning sun.

"What's up on the terrace?" asked the captain.

Just then, an impatient and exasperated voice reached us from the patio below, shouting, "Hey! You up there! What are you doing? We still have work to do!"

"On our way, chief! On our way," the captain replied.

Donning disappointed looks, we said, "So you aren't coming up on the terrace? What a shame! We have a splendid view of the Bay of Algiers and part of the Casbah. And it's so nice out today."

The captain ordered his men downstairs immediately. "We've dragged things out enough here already!"

"Too bad," we repeated to each soldier who thanked us for the warm welcome as he left.

One of them told us, "This wasn't the case in the other houses we visited. People threw us dirty looks and barely responded when we talked to them."

When the last paratrooper finally left the house, we collapsed, devoid of all energy. After nervous laughter and hugs, Oukhiti, Djamila, and I burst into tears under the placid eye of Auntie Baya, who, in a barely audible whisper, wished them all the ills of the earth. I sought refuge in the brothers' room. My sisters joined me, a tray in hand, carrying three large bowls of *café au lait* and a plate of *maqrouts*.

We wanted to celebrate this great victory over Massu's forces. We had just managed to save not only our laboratory but, above all, the inhabitants of the first and second floors, on whom the French army would have had no qualms in applying their systematic rule of collective liability. After finishing our coffees, we climbed up the rooftop to try to observe the progress of the raids. We didn't know what had happened to the brothers or the Belhaffafs' home. We reassured ourselves that if the shelter had been discovered, we would certainly have heard a firefight: Ali, El Kho, Ghani, and Si Mourad were all armed and would never have gone down without a fight. The whole area was eerily silent. No screaming children, no shouting, no trash collectors prodding their faithful donkeys overloaded with saddlebags full of garbage ever onward. Nothing. All we made out, here and there, was the faint crackling of the radios carried by the sentries posted at the end of each street. The entire Casbah was waiting for the raid to end.

Hassiba, Si Mourad, Ghani, and Dahmane returned to 5 Impasse de la Granada at nightfall. According to them, the enemy's search of the Casbah with a fine-toothed comb had yielded little despite all their efforts.

7

THE EIGHT-DAY STRIKE

Preparations

The general strike that set Algiers and the Casbah humming took shape gradually.

A few days after the intense sweeps of January 8, 1957, El Kho and the brothers explained the CCE's instructions, the strike's context, and the eminently political objectives of the peaceful activities that "the organization" had chosen and was requiring of all FLN/ALN activists. The general strike was meant to demonstrate the Algerian people's unanimous will for freedom and independence, as well as its total support for the FLN, to demolish the French regime's arguments that Algeria was "a part of France's territory," the armed uprising "an internal challenge to public order," and the FLN/ALN fighters "a band of outlaws disconnected from the Algerian people." The instructions explicitly specified the need to establish strike committees at all levels. They also asked that we recommend to families that they stock up on eight days' worth of essentials, and authorized the strike committee leaders to supply needy families at the FLN's expense.

211

Implementing these directives demanded detailed knowledge of the city and its neighborhoods, with a level of organization proportional to the ambitious objectives. El Kho had the brilliant idea to appeal to women singers and other artists for the work of mobilizing people, identifying the needy, and organizing families. It was an excellent proposal because they were popular, even celebrities, and could enter the homes, where women reigned and where men were forbidden to enter, according to our society's strict rules of gender segregation. This genius idea was made possible by exceptional outreach and organization in the arts and culture community by Habib Réda, an artist and brother in arms with extraordinary talents. That was how El Kho, accompanied by Ali, Djamila, and me, came to chair a meeting with a dozen women artists in the sumptuous home of the Bachagha Boutaleb, located in the Impasse Kléber. The greatest women from the worlds of theater and song were there.

El Kho took the floor to explain the objectives of the strike. Then he tasked the women present to explain them, in turn, to the women they would go out and meet. Next, he broached the question of identifying families who could not afford to stock up for the duration of the strike and would need FLN assistance. Finally, he proposed dividing the Casbah into districts, to be supervised by committees and teams who would cover every street, block, and household. He selected the team leaders on the spot, informing the women artists that they could request help from other women whom they trusted. El Kho insisted on the importance of outreach and explanation. The teams would fan out across the whole old *medina*. At the same time, he recommended never trying to intimidate recalcitrant families but instead seeking to understand the reasons for their distrust, and told us to note their reasons as accurately as possible and forward them to the team leaders. At the end of the mission, the team leaders were to transmit to committee leaders an activity report with a list of addresses of all families in need, their numbers, and the head of household's profession. He ended by stating that each of the designated leaders would be informed of the date and place of the meeting where the mission reports should be submitted, and emphasized the critical importance of respecting the deadlines.

With the brothers, we busied ourselves managing the strike preparations in coordination with our labor unions and professional guilds. CCE leaflets flooded all of Algiers and the whole country, calling our people to join a general Eight-Day Strike beginning Monday, January 28, 1957, at midnight.

The FLN's leaflet was clear, instructive, and concise, and addressed the Algerian people directly, ending with:

> For the eradication of the colonial regime;
> For the liberation of the Algerian homeland;
> For the establishment of a democratic and social Algerian republic;
> Forward toward the eight-day general strike, starting January 28, 1957, at midnight! Long live free and independent Algeria.

While the FLN/ALN—in perfect concert with our people—prepared our peaceful mass strike, Massu and his thousands of paratroopers, police, torturers, and psychological warfare experts were actively building a formidable repression mechanism and a vast, shameless propaganda operation with the dual aim of breaking our general strike and annihilating our organization.

From the day he arrived in Algeria, Massu had *carte blanche* to use any means necessary to break, subdue, terrorize, torture, kill, and clean up. To do this, and to justify the hellfire that he would rain down upon our people, he began by unilaterally labeling the strike "insurrectionary." This term he chose was a deplorable trick for justifying the hatred and fury with which he would confront it. Completely free and unfettered by laws, regulations, and scruples, he would transform the "native" districts into lawless territory—special zones for committing all imaginable violations. With high barbed-wire fencing, barricades, and military checkpoints, he surrounded the "native" districts to the point of suffocation. He swept and raided morning, noon, and night. His thousands of paratroopers yelled at, insulted, mistreated, and threw men, women, and children to the ground. They forced open doors with their boots and machine-gun butts, smashed furniture and dishes, and made off with jewelry and money. They rounded up tens of thousands of people, cramming them into trucks and leaving their families to wonder where they were being taken. Their sole crime was to have been born "native."

To them every "native" was guilty and therefore eligible for "questioning." Massu made our capital city into the global capital of torture, torment, and abuse—a terrible distinction for which Algiers would pay dearly, in the form of the thousands "disappeared" and hundreds of extrajudicial executions, not to mention the thousands imprisoned and dozens executed by guillotine. During that month of January, that year 1957, and well after, Massu and his torturers, paratroopers, cops, and reservists tormented in the basements of police stations, detention centers, prefecture headquarters, villas equipped for this horrible work, settler farms, and more. But as the torture factory took on industrial proportions, Massu was "obliged" to torture in the "natives'" own homes. And as if that system of terror didn't suffice, Massu drew up fliers that he dumped across Algiers by the thousands, which were picked up by the colonialist press—both radio and newspapers. These called on and threatened the "natives" not to strike. Yet despite all this, Massu was nonetheless unable to prevent strikes organized by our brothers and sisters against army patrols on January 23 and 26, or against the European city on January 26. That day, three of our sisters—Djamila Bouazza, Fadhila Attia, and Djamila Amrane (Danielle Mine)—planted three bombs that shook Le Coq Hardi, L'Otomatic, and (once again) La Cafétéria, right in the heart of the European quarter.

Although this notorious general had failed to stop our attacks, he hadn't even tried to thwart the bazooka attack that the *ultras* organized against General Salan's offices at the Tenth Military Region headquarters. These die hard supporters of French Algeria and its apartheid system, draped in the most sickening cowardice, which allowed them to blame their actions on the FLN without any qualms, wanted to exploit the extremely tense climate in Algiers to bring down Guy Mollet's government. And so Parisian politics were carried out in Algiers by the *ultras*, whose members were ensured total impunity for their excesses, since the unarmed "natives" constituted an inexhaustible reservoir of scapegoats and sacrificial victims. All this to say that on the eve of the strike Algiers was on the verge of exploding, crushed between two irreconcilable wills: ours, which wanted to turn it into a ghost town by ceasing all activity—even the most ordinary errands, like buying bread and milk—and Massu's, which aimed only to break our strike by any means available.

Algiers, the Ghost Town

At last, the fateful day arrived. El Kho charged Djamila and me with monitoring the strike's impact on the residents of the Casbah, especially the women and children.

From the rooftops we witnessed the most distressing spectacle that an army could present. Each morning, dozens of military trucks took up positions on Rue Marengo, Rue Randon, and at Bab Jdid at the top of the Casbah. Then thousands of paratroopers descended, spilling throughout the old *medina*. They flooded the old city, machine guns in hand, occupying all the streets and rooftop terraces, leaping from one rooftop to another while firing bursts into the air. As helicopters carrying soldiers flew low overhead, rattling the Casbah with the terrible noise of their rotors, paratroopers on the ground yelled and knocked violently on doors. As soon as the doors opened, they unceremoniously shoved the residents aside, insulting them and ordering the men to get outside with their hands on their heads. They lined them up in front of the houses, then did the same with the children. When the women tried to intervene, crying, they were thrown to the ground, insulted, and stomped on. First the men, then the children were led like cattle in a chute, hands on their heads, menaced by the guns and the helicopters whirring infernally overhead, to the streets where the trucks were parked. There they were herded like animals into the beds of large military vehicles: the children were taken to school and the adults to idle work sites or to some unknown destination.

As soon as the paratroopers and their trucks disappeared, the men and children who were not held set out for home, taking long back routes. Since all the "natives," even the merchants, were following the call to strike, we watched from the terraces as the "Land of Rights and Liberties" put on another shameful spectacle. With a deafening din, soldiers smashed the iron shutters of the "native"-owned shops and ransacked the interiors. All this happened under the watchful eye of the Europeans, these "innocent civilians" who came to admire the cowardly and vile labor of their soldiers, armed to the teeth against poor unarmed shopkeepers. How they were ugly, hideous, barbarous, and savage, these Europeans who came to live in our land—and supposedly to civilize us! Djamila and I watched with revulsion and fear.

Despite the fierce and monstrous repressive machine put in place by Massu, the strike was a success. Even the French newspapers recognized Algiers as a "dead city" and a "ghost town." The neighborhood markets were deserted and the central wholesale market empty. (Through the reports addressed to El Kho, we would later learn that Massu had gone so far as to send his paratroopers into the surrounding countryside to harvest vegetables and stock the markets for the Europeans.) The construction sites were all at a standstill, as was public transport. Even the cafés belonging to our people—despite being opened by force by paratroopers—remained hopelessly empty. Massu's leaflets—dumped from helicopters by the thousands—had changed nothing. Nor had the Jeeps carrying specialists in psychological warfare, who used megaphones to call on the "natives" not to respect the strike or risk reprisals. Algiers was a dead city, deaf to Massu and his legions.

However, around eleven in the morning on the fourth day of the strike, we noticed two or three men who looked to be sneaking along with milk jugs in hand. Djamila and I quickly understood that they were family bread-winners trying shamefully to go buy some milk for their children in secret. It was understandable and legitimate, but very dangerous for the future of the strike. We looked at each other and decided to respond immediately by speaking with the wives because if fathers were sneaking out to get milk for the children, it was certainly under pressure from the mothers.

Meetings from Rooftop to Rooftop

Around noon, we decided to climb over the wall separating us from the adjoining terrace. Once atop the neighbors' house, Djamila addressed the occupants in her powerful, husky voice, "*Ya mwalin eddar, sbah el khir âalik-oum!*" (Hello, neighbors, good morning to you all!) The children were the first to scramble up to the terrace, followed by women of all ages. We dove right into our impromptu meeting. In awe, I was all ears as Djamila, an unparalleled orator, punctuated her speech with references to the struggles of our Prophet (peace be upon him) against the infidels. She peppered her remarks with popular sayings, reproaching all those who betray their camp to satisfy their hunger: "*Âala kerchou, khla âarchou!*" (He who follows his stomach abandons his kingdom!) The women expressed their agreement and support by belting out strident *you-you-yous,* while the older ones cried out blessings for us and all the *moudjahidine* and wished the worst evils on the infidels. But our gathering soon drew the attention of paratroop-ers stationed on some of the terraces, and they began hopping from roof-top to rooftop to reach us. In response, the women and children led us and the whole gathering to the most distant terraces. All the rooftops that didn't contain enemy soldiers were filled with women and children wailing out *you-yous.* Guided by our countless accomplices, Djamila and I jumped from rooftop to rooftop, explaining again and again the justifications for our strike and how we must remain united in solidarity around the FLN out of loyalty to our people, our homeland, and our Prophet.

Among the bright memories I hold of my life in the Casbah, that after-noon among our sisters and mothers stays with me as if engraved in stone. Even today, I sometimes remind myself of that warm solidarity and perfect synergy with those women, their eyes feverish and bright, expressing all at once their sense of awe and brotherhood, solidarity, and faith in our cause and in this mythical FLN that knew everything, saw everything, was everywhere, and was calling on them to stymie our enemy. It was the afternoon of January 31, 1957. Two days later, on February 2, 1957, the sixth day of the strike, our refuge at 5 Impasse de la Granada would witness a very unsettling day.

Public Torture in the Home

Over the course of the day, the feverish atmosphere would leave me with a vague feeling of anxiety, on top of the fatigue that came from my guard duties—a measure put in place by El Kho since the infamous January 8 raid. Every night from eleven o'clock on, we stood guard two at a time for three-hour shifts. This way we could follow the paratroopers' movements in the streets and alleys of the Casbah by listening for the rubbing of the fabric of their camouflage uniforms and the steady tread of their boots on the cobblestones. Despite their precautions to surprise—the better to terrorize—the sleeping residents, these sounds were amplified by the dead silence that reigned over the Casbah as our population, subjected to a regimen of fear and repression, holed up at home. We could hear them so well that El Kho and Ali could pinpoint exactly where they were and even guess which house was bearing the brunt of their fury.

That February 2, El Kho and Ali had arrived, contrary to their usual routine, early in the afternoon at 5 Impasse de la Granada. Evidently, the situation was troubling. Djamila had asked the first- and second-floor tenants to return to their apartments and not come out until she signaled them. We spent the whole afternoon emptying the laboratory, tightly wrapping all the materials and objects stored there in wax paper and plastic sheets. Alilou, Ghani, and Si Mourad had carried the packages downstairs, where everything was carefully hidden in the *djeb*—the underground cistern where rainwater was collected. Over dinner, each of the brothers seemed deep in thought, even the usually exuberant Ali. A sullen air hung over the evening. Around eleven o'clock, the two selected for guard duty climbed up to the terrace while the rest of us got into bed.

At about two in the morning, the door to our room shook. The muffled voice of one of the brothers called, "Girls, girls, wake up!" Someone jumped out of bed and opened the door. Our brother's muffled voice grew insistent and reached me even in my half-slumber. "Hassiba must immediately come into the room next door, near the roof. The house is surrounded. Quick, quick! And don't turn on a light!"

We rushed with Hassiba to the room where Fettouma Meziane and her mother usually slept. El Kho, Ali, Ghani, and Taleb were standing, weapons at the ready, waiting for Si Mourad to finish clearing the opening of the secret refuge, which was tucked behind a large copper plate under the wrought-iron four-poster bed. Fettouma and her mother both sat on a mattress, staring at the brothers. Si Mourad bent over and lit his flashlight, illuminating the pitch-black hideaway.

He slipped inside first, followed by Hassiba, Ghani, Dahmane, Ali, and finally El Kho. They were all wanted. They piled onto one another in this small, dark refuge carefully constructed on the house's second story. Inside, they would spend some of the most interminable hours—the longest (and undoubtedly the cruelest) night—of their lives. That night would scar us and torment us forever. As soon as Hassiba and the brothers were in the refuge, we rolled the great copper plate back into place over the opening. Then we pushed the four-poster bed against the plate. Djamila and I returned to our room, leaving Fettouma and her mother nestled on their mattresses. We were on alert, listening carefully in the silence, which hung thick with anxiety and the noise of the paratroopers. They overran the terrace above, but as long as they didn't announce their presence with their customary brutality, we could keep hoping.

We didn't wait long before the heavy front door shuddered from the violent strikes of machine-gun butts. Despite the ferocity of the blows, the door held. One of the ground-floor tenants went to open it and was immediately shoved aside and thrown to the ground. In a second, every floor was filled with paratroopers. With kicks and jabs of their rifle butts, they smashed open the bedroom doors, hurled invectives, and barked through megaphones, "Everyone out! Everyone downstairs to the patio! Right now! Make it snappy!"

When I reached the patio, I gasped. Djamila's father Uncle Omar, her Uncle Mustapha, and all the other neighbors, some in *gandoura* robes and others in pajamas, were being held, seated on the patio floor with their hands tied behind their backs, by paratroopers pointing loaded guns at them. Silent, they shivered with cold: a terrible damp chill cut through the skin and penetrated to the bone. I joined the other women in one of the rooms that opened onto the patio, with the door closed. Auntie Baya and

Oukhiti followed me inside, supporting Djamila's grandmother Yemma, who was bent double, leaning on her cane. This wasn't going at all like the previous searches. Why had they emptied all the adult occupants from the upper floors? Why had they tied up the men? None of this boded well.

We needed to inform the brothers holed up in the second-floor wall of how things had turned, so that they would remain vigilant. But how to get back upstairs? The paratroopers had forbidden us from moving. Then we had an idea: the women from the upper floors needed to go get their young children and babies, who had stayed asleep in their beds. We all set about shouting at once: "We want our children! We want our children!" Screaming in unison, banging our fists on the door and window facing the patio, we generated an impressive racket, unsettling the paratroopers, who arrived ready to interrogate and threaten, spitting back at us, "Why? Why?" We responded by shouting our request louder and pouring out our best dramatic tears until they finally gave in, more to silence us than to satisfy our request. As they crossed the patio on the way to the stairs, the women bent over their men and showered words of encouragement on them. They were shivering on the icy marble. Djamila and I hurried upstairs. When we reached the skylight, we began to talk aloud in Arabic, using code words to transmit as much information as possible to the brothers in the hideaway. We also wanted to retrieve the index cards that the young doctor had given us in our brief nursing training. Once we had hidden them carefully under our clothes, we helped the mothers bring down their sleeping children.

Auntie Baya returned anxious because, despite her protests, the paratroopers had refused to let her bring her sons Lyes and El Hadi, aged fourteen and eight. What did these soldiers want? Obviously, they weren't looking to search the rooms. They were holding positions on the rooftop terrace and each upper floor, and on the ground level they were posted at the base of the stairs and outside each room ringing the central courtyard. While the women finished chewing and swallowing our incriminating index cards, which we had torn to small pieces, Oukhiti pulled down the shutters and stood by the window. She stared out at the patio, where the men had now been forced to lie flat. The paratroopers stood above them. Oukhiti rose onto her tiptoes, twisted this way and that, and craned her neck to try to see what was going on all around the patio and the second-floor gallery. Suddenly she exclaimed: "Djamila, Zohra, come see. They're taking Mustapha toward the upper floors! They'll torture him!" Everyone knew the love that bound Oukhiti and her husband. That was why we sincerely believed that she was just being dramatic. Neither Djamila nor I could believe that France would turn a home upside down in front of its inhabitants, much less commit torture in that very home. I knew they had made an industry of it in our land, against our people. The victims numbered in the tens of thousands, despite France's denials. Killing in every possible way—thrown into the sea, buried alive, smoked out (this horrid technique borrowed from the gas chambers), executed on the spot, killed individually or collectively, heaped in a pile and "treated" with quicklime, hundreds of villages bombed with napalm, the poor unarmed "natives" hunted like prey, strangled by bare hands, decapitated in the guillotine, exploded along with a whole block of houses. Killed alone or killed in bulk. Killed secretly or killed publicly. Yes. I knew of it all. But that night at 5 Impasse de la Granada, I had—we all had—the cruel and horrible privilege of experiencing the latest sophisticated French technique for crimes against humanity: public torture in one's own home. As I came to stand beside Oukhiti and comfort her, a terrifying wail made our hearts skip a beat. It started up again, stronger than before, filling the whole room, our whole beings, and leaving us petrified and shivering.

Oukhiti began screaming with all her might: "Mustapha! Mustapha! *Echedda fi Allah! Echedda fi Allah!*" (Hold fast to God!) She rushed to throw open the door and found herself face to face with two monstrous paratroopers, who drove her back with their loaded guns. My tears were flowing and my blood pounding at my temples when a wave of unbearable cries shook me anew. They were the shrieks of wounded animals, cries of the tormented that will never fade from my memory. I gripped the window bars with both hands, stuck my head through, and as if in a trance, I screamed with all my might at the horror that this criminal treatment that the French army was inflicting on these men inspired in me.

I went off on a long diatribe, denouncing the supposed "Land of the Rights of Man." I let out a sarcastic laugh when I recalled the words of such-and-such poet glorifying France and its humanism. I called them assassins, criminals, and Nazis. I couldn't shut up. I didn't want to shut up. To keep quiet would have meant agreeing to die in silence. I spat forth my deepest contempt for how they built their famous principles of "liberty, equality, and fraternity" upon the corpses of millions of the colonized. No longer willing to contain these feelings that inspired such demons within me, I screamed out my hatred until I could hardly breathe. I screamed so I wouldn't have to hear the victims' tormented cries. I didn't want to hear the inhuman screams of those men being tortured, exhibited like beasts before their families, their wives, their children. They all had their eyes closed, as if hoping to banish the humiliation they were suffering, which others' looks rekindled. Among the tortured, silence reigned, and with it anxiety.

We watched the stairs, where the torturers descended in search of their prey. While the vile work continued on the second floor and while down below we breathed to the rhythm of the screams, groans, and whimpers of our brothers, a group of paratroopers began a systematic search of the third-floor rooms, where the Bouhired family lived. One of the assailants shouted an order at us: "One of the women living on the third floor, get up here immediately!" Oukhiti, still stunned by the torment inflicted on her husband, wanted to go. But we kept her back and Djamila ascended to the third floor, an anxious Auntie Baya urging her to stay calm and reminding her that the only way to dominate "these dogs" was to show them contemptuous composure. As soon as Djamila left us, we began to listen and pray that nothing dreadful would befall her. All that reached us were the groans of the tormented on the second floor, the endless noise of the paratroopers' boots coming and going, and their shouting. We began a gloomy wait and began to discuss what to do if she took too long to return. We had no confidence in this army of sadists. We decided together to wait a few more minutes and, if she didn't reappear, to all push our way out together toward the stairs, screaming and wailing *you-you-yous*: we knew our *you-yous* terrorized them. Beyond that, we would see what happened. Three of us posted ourselves at the window overlooking the patio to watch. Just as we were about to put our plan into action, Djamila reappeared, walking calmly. She crossed the patio, stopping before those who had already suffered. She leaned over her uncle and her father stretched out on the icy slabs and, ignoring a barking paratrooper ordering her back to the room where we were waiting, laid a kiss on each of the tortured men, like a balm to heal their bodies and souls.

The soldier was still barking, and Djamila was still ignoring him. There was a defiance in her attitude. We grew scared for her. Impatient, we followed her progress from the window, ready to tell her to hurry up. Oukhiti couldn't help but cry out, in a voice that betrayed her anxiety, to get back into the room. She finally returned. We rushed to her. Stony-faced, she mumbled, "I'm alive. Rest assured, those dogs did nothing to me!"

Turning to me, she said: *"Allah ma habch el khsara!* [God doesn't want us to lose!] In a book where I'd slipped them, they found the IOUs that Si Mohamed had written out for the three of us. Do you see? Thanks to this carelessness, we could have caused a disaster!" They were IOUs written in

Si Mohamed's own hand, dated and signed! The way events had accelerated, it already felt like a century ago. Those blessed moments when Hassiba, Djamila, and I used to sit around the *meïda* with Si Mohamed, El Kho, Ali, and the other brothers from the laboratory were already a distant memory! We had been so happy to be back home after accomplishing the day's missions and had decided to play *yadess* again. Someone had called out to our senior leader: "Si Mohamed, whenever we played *yadess* with you, you lose. But you've never paid your debts!" Our great leader made no effort to hide his surprise: "Debts? But what debts?" Together, like magpies, we had recounted the *yadess* rules to him and explained that, having lost every time, he was in debt to each of us. We were joking, but Si Mohamed took things very seriously and admitted that he was indeed indebted to each of us, but nothing belonged to him—not even the shirt he wore. Everything belonged to the FLN, he said, and thus to the people. Ashamed, we tried to defuse the situation by explaining that it was only a game, and that the "debts" had never been anything more than a simple pastry or ice cream cone. We added that the most important thing for us was the game itself, and relaxing, and not the settling of debts that we had joked about. But *Si* Mohamed wouldn't hear it that way. Still serious, he continued: "To be honest, I have three objects: a pen, a nail clipper, and a watch." He showed them to us, then continued: "But those three objects are very dear to my heart, since they were given to me by three brothers who are precious to me. Two of them died as *chouhada*—may God preserve them: Mourad Didouche and Youcef Zighout. The third, Rabah Bitat, is in prison." I stared, transfixed, at the objects he showed us. But Si Mohamed had continued calmly, "However, I always pay my debts, so I will write out an IOU to each of you. At independence, if Allah sees fit to let us live to see it, I will repay you my debts. And I if I die, you will present these IOUs to any member of my family, and they will take care of them." He took up his pen, the one given by one of the brothers he held dear, and immediately wrote out three IOUs in perfect French, signed and dated them, and handed one to each of us. Djamila had collected them and slipped them between the pages of an encyclopedia on a shelf in Uncle Mustapha's library.

Now a paratrooper held those IOUs in his hand and demanded that Djamila explain their meaning. Aware that at that moment she held in her hands the fate of us all, she replied confidently, "Oh! Yes, of course! These are the IOUs that my brother had to write out to me and my two cousins,

Six of the historical leaders of the FLN: Back row (l. to r.) Rabah Bitat, Mostefa Ben Boulaïd, Didouche Mourad, Mohammed Boudiaf. Front row (l. to r.) Krim Belkacem and Larbi Ben M'Hidi.

Zohra and Hassiba. We beat him a few times playing pinochle but, since he was broke, he had to give us IOUs. You know, he's a student. He studied in France. You can check." She told me that soldier's gaze was locked on her eyes, trying to read whatever was inside her. Looking him straight in the eyes, without hesitation, she continued: "Do you want me to get our family registry?" The paratrooper read and reread the IOUs, turning them over and over and seeming to hesitate—probably because he couldn't imagine "lawless Arabs" who could write in French so clearly, let alone care about honoring their debts. Unable to do more, he waved Djamila off.

Suddenly, just when we thought that the French army had reached the outer limits of indecency, a scream rent the air, the sky, the earth, and the gut of every woman present—first and foremost those of the victim's mother, Auntie Baya. She had stayed silent since the torture began, but now she fervently implored God to give the men the strength and courage to face the most inhumane and degrading ordeal that a human being can suffer. Then she cried out, "That's Lyes's voice! It's him, I recognize it." Then she was silent. She didn't utter a word. Perhaps she was praying. He was only fourteen!

A terrifying silence fell over the patio, intermittently torn by Lyes's screams or his childlike voice crying to his torturers: "Stop! Stop! I have the right to speak! Stop!" Then there was silence. We all craned our necks toward the second floor, the makeshift torture chamber, the room that also held the hideaway where Hassiba and the brothers waited behind the huge copper tray and four-poster bed. Oukhiti, Djamila, Fettouma and her mother, and I had the same thought at once. We began to pray to God that Lyes, despite his youth, could withstand the torment without talking. Otherwise, it would be carnage for the whole household, the whole block, and the whole neighborhood. Applying their principle of collective responsibility, the paratroopers would blow it all sky-high.

Again, Lyes's young voice, full of tormented sobs, cried out: "Stop! Stop! Yes, I saw Ali la Pointe! Just stop, I'll tell you where he is!" We heard him clearly because he wasn't speaking the words, he was screaming them. I began to breathe to the rhythm of his voice, not knowing what to do, feeling guilty to the point of death because it was our fault the boy was being tortured. We had never asked him if he wanted us using his house as our shelter. Then I worked through the same reasoning in the other way: Did the French ask his opinion or our people's before colonizing us? Did they ask before making him and all of us into "natives" that they could freely and publicly torture in our own homes simply because we held a strike? My blood beat hard at my temples.

Suddenly a crude European voice rang out, "Stop! Can't you see that he's delirious and just spouting nonsense?" The silence hung heavy and thick. We no longer heard Lyes's screams, but we heard several paratroopers trudge down the stairs. We pressed ourselves to the window again. Dazed by the extent of the horror, we thought we had reached a state of anesthetized numbness. But then we saw ten paratroopers surrounding two little boys, forcing them to descend to the patio: it was El Hadi, Djamila's eight-year-old little brother, and Mohamed Amor, the ten-year-old son of our ground-floor neighbor, Auntie Zohra! God, what would they do to them? There were only two small boys. The paratroopers called to one another, conversed with their commander, and came and went between the floors. Soon, they came down with ropes and began searching for a power outlet around the cistern in the central patio. Eventually we grasped the reasons for the sudden commotion: they wanted to bring the two little boys down to the cistern in order to search it. Djamila and I looked at one another, the same thought crossing our minds: *We cannot let the two boys go into the cistern without warning them*. We quickly explained to Auntie Baya that she had to tell El Hadi not to bring anything up from the cistern because of the danger it would mean for the whole household. She gave her approval for our plan.

The paratroopers, having lit up the opening with powerful spotlights, began to fix ropes around El Hadi's chest and under his arms to lower him into the cistern. Just then, all together, we began beating furiously on the door and shouting with all our might. We created such a racket that they came and opened the door threateningly, to make us shut up. While all the others continued to scream and cry, Djamila and I shouted with all our fury, "We will not stay silent! We women want to kiss our children before you drown them! Kill us all if you want, but we will not be silent so long as they have not embraced their boys."

The commanders, wanting to do away with "the unbearable din of 'the Fatimas,'" gave in to our request. El Hadi, stared, frightened, at this crowd around him, but soon found himself in his mother's arms. Auntie Baya hugged him to her chest and whispered in Arabic in his ear: "My boy, be a man! Be worthy of the *moudjahidine*. If you touch anything, push it back as far as possible with your foot. Bring nothing back up to the surface. Nothing!" We couldn't tell if El Hadi had understood; we continued to make noise to prevent the enemy from catching on. His big sister Djamila took him in her arms in turn, embraced him, and whispered, repeating: "Be a man! There is nothing in the cistern! You don't bring a thing up! You don't say a thing!" Then the paratroopers, incensed with our "backward Arab women" ways, took back the boy they had tied up like a parcel and lowered him into the deep reservoir's frigid water. Once at the bottom, soaked up to his armpits in the icy water, he cried out: "There he is! Right in front of me!" All the soldiers crowded around the edge of the cistern, pointing their guns down to where El Hadi continued screaming in terror. Then one of the paratroopers understood why the boy was screaming and said to the others, "Stop! Don't shoot! It's just his shadow that has him scared. Don't shoot!"

The men watched, prostrate and motionless, as this horde swarmed around the cistern's opening. Silence settled once more. All our eyes were fixed on Auntie Baya. She held her beautiful delicate hands across her cheeks and mouth, leaving visible her eyes staring at the door. Motionless, silent, she prayed. The door was still open. Finally, they pulled El Hadi up and untied him. He was soaked, blue with cold, his teeth chattering. Dawn was breaking, but the house was still plunged in darkness.

We were waiting for El Hadi when a conversation echoed down from overhead, on the second floor, chilling us to our bones. One of the paratroopers suggested to another, probably his superior, to submit some women to "the question." "Maybe they'll speak, since the men didn't say a word?" Immediately, we closed the door again and, in a whisper, informed our sisters-in-suffering, while recalling that the men—even young Lyes—had resisted in the face of the worst tortures. We explained that it was our duty to be worthy and never betray anyone. We added that Djamila and I would behave in such a way toward the paratroopers that they would choose one or both of us. We called for calm, solidarity, dignity, and resistance through tenacious endurance. Never talk. Finally, we touched on the supreme punishment reserved for women: rape. We reminded every woman how unwise it would be to believe that she would be spared if she gave up information. It would be the opposite. So, in every case, stick to a single line of conduct: never talk, and repeat to yourself *Echedda fi Allah*.

We were all seated, silent, tense, listening for the footsteps that would herald our torment. El Hadi entered instead, and we huddled around him, stripping off his wet, icy cold clothes. Each of us gave up a warm piece of clothing and we covered him from head to toe, proud that he hadn't brought a thing up from the cistern's depths. We took advantage of the chance to galvanize the women, presenting them the example of this eight-year-old boy's strength. We resumed preparing ourselves mentally, praying to God to give us strength and courage to face torture. Suddenly, we heard a voice ordering the paratroopers into formation. The day had dawned. It was seven o'clock and our ordeal had lasted since two. Paratroopers came to free the men from the binds they had endured all night. Each of them was trying to get up without showing how difficult it was to move his limbs. Only the repeated opening and closing movements of their hands and their difficult steps betrayed their extreme suffering. Oukhiti rushed toward her husband, supported him, and helped him climb to the third floor. The families returned to their rooms.

Everything had been upended: dishes broken and thrown to the ground, clothes strewn, valuable furniture broken, flour mixed with sugar and coffee, oil poured all over the kitchen floor. A tornado couldn't have caused so much damage. While the paratroopers wrapped up their ropes and collected their vile torture equipment, Oukhiti's voice echoed out: "I can't find the money I had hidden in my closet. Who's the commander? I want my money back!" We rejoined Oukhiti on the third floor. Everything there was devastated. Auntie Baya, always placid, walked to her room, where her husband Uncle Omar already stood. From the second floor, Fettouma's sister cried out, lamenting: "They robbed me! They stole my jewelry!" The paratroopers were preparing to leave, their kits on their backs. Their commander pretended to question them, without conviction.

In a whisper, Auntie Baya told her sister-in-law: "Just stop! Let them go. To hell with them and all the money. What's wrong with you? Let them leave!" Then she turned to address Fettouma's sister in Kabyle, the local Berber dialect. Everyone returned to their ransacked rooms. We heard nothing more.

After having verified that the paratroopers had completely left the house, the terrace, and the whole area, we rushed to free Hassiba and the brothers, who were half asphyxiated and still reeling from the horrors of the torture they had heard from just a few steps away. These "outlaws," these "terrorists," were stunned by the sadism and cruelty of these foreigners who claimed to offer the world "respect for human rights."

Oukhiti, ever thoughtful, came to offer us coffee, then begged us to rest.

The Safe House Is Safe No More

It was February 3, 1957, the seventh day of the strike. El Kho called us together to give the order to leave the Bouhireds' house, which was now "blown." It was clear, he said, that the paratroopers were in possession of some information and would soon return. He instructed the brothers to move the whole lab, including the equipment and supplies hidden in the cistern, to a new address that he would give them. Finally, he ordered us to separate into two groups so as not to "put all our eggs in one basket," and urged us to rest while awaiting instructions. As for the brothers, they spent the day packing up the laboratory equipment, and by late afternoon an unusual silence filled the house. El Kho and Ali left in the late morning. They took a moment to mark their immense appreciation to all the house's residents and convey their infinite gratitude, soberly, without grandiosity. Hassiba, Djamila, and I each had a lump in our throats and tears in our eyes.

We decided to overcome the trauma by joining Auntie Baya and Oukhiti in cleaning up the rooms devastated by Massu's abominable soldiers. The indescribable mess of the kitchen alone required a whole day's hard labor. We threw ourselves into cleaning up, throwing out, washing, polishing, and putting everything back in order as if to announce that we were fully alive, both inside and out, and that our love of freedom and dignity was stronger than the death and terror sown everywhere by Massu and his troops.

At the end of the day, Uncle Mustapha called for me. He was seated, facing the wide-open door. His battered face testified to the previous night's suffering. "Starting from tomorrow, I will be joining the brothers in the *maquis*," he stated in a hollow voice. I stood speechless with astonishment. But Uncle Mustapha, fearing that I had misunderstood, replied: "No! If you think I'm incapable of going to fight because of what I suffered yesterday, no! It's just what the French have been making us suffer for so long now already; it changes nothing for me. Fatiha and El Kho will confirm it for you—everything was prepared before that cursed night." This news took me aback, and I was unable to answer. I simply looked back at him through my tears. He handed me his handkerchief, raised his sympathetic but authoritative gaze and said, "I wanted to inform you of my decision because now you're a lady of this house and a sister in arms. I leave at ease because I know that Fatiha is courageous. She has so much strength and inner resolve, and she can see to the children's education. I also know that you and Djamila will be at her side and that she can count on you both. In truth, I wanted to talk to you because I wanted to confide Djamila to your care."

Surprised and stunned by Uncle Mustapha's words, I tried to interrupt him to reassure him of my sister's strength, energy, and courage. But he insisted that I pipe down and let him finish: "You heard me right. Yes, I am asking you to watch over Djamila. Yes, I am asking you to be for her what I was for her: a moderating force. Because to anyone who doesn't know her well, Djamila seems like the most determined, the strongest, the one with solid experience and excellent insight into others. But think again. I who raised her, I know her uncommon courage, but I also know that her excesses make her fragile. I am counting on you to bring her back to reality when you feel she's being too extreme. Moderate her; she needs it."

Night fell on the house, which was missing many of its inhabitants. Even children matched their games to the heavy, sullen atmosphere that swathed the area and the entire Casbah. We were still living—surviving, really— under the supervision of machine guns set up on the terraces, hemmed in by a profusion of repressive colonial forces and their arms.

Assessment of the Eight-Day Strike: Total Success

We learned, after the end of the strike on February 4, 1957, that Massu and his paratroopers had tried every available means to break our population's will to fight and adherence to the FLN's orders. The systematic torture that they elevated to an industry was blessed by the French political authorities and even by officers of the Catholic Church, including Father Delarue, who issued a veritable Christian *fatwa* to sanction the torturers' crimes. During the mass arrests, some of our key activists were taken and subjected to electroshock torture in bathtubs, among other monstrous treatments. The confessions they wrenched out enabled the enemy to deal our organization some heavy blows.

Nonetheless, despite the orgy of repression, our strike was a total success. The serious press, French and foreign alike, had to acknowledge it. *Le Monde*'s February 3–4 edition read, "The strike's success, despite official statements, is not questionable. . . . A fact is established before all the world: the confirmation of the FLN's steady strengthening, as much among immigrant workers as among the urban Algerian masses." The international and mainland French press—the entire world, really—discovered that "the events in Algeria" could not be boiled down to "internal disturbances to the public order," as Guy Mollet had just trumpeted at the UN. They discovered that the FLN was not what the French authorities called it ("a handful of outlaws"). On the contrary, thanks to our people's mobilization and total adherence to the FLN's call for a general strike, we managed to show the entire world that, on the one hand, the conflict that pitted us against France was a conflict between a colonized people and its colonizer, and, on the other hand, that the FLN was the Algerian people's only legitimate representative in our struggle for independence.

The Eight-Day Strike gave our national liberation war the international dimension that it had been missing. From now on, neither states nor unions nor the UN nor the media—no one—could speak or act on the "Algerian question" without going through the FLN. We had unmasked France and its human rights violations before the whole world. It was a decisive turning point in our national liberation war. It was then that we "internationalized" our struggle, much to France's chagrin.

For all these reasons, I stand convinced that the Eight-Day Strike was the major national political event that forever shattered France's plan to keep Algeria as its settler colony. Because of the strike, France and her army would enter a mad, blind spiral that would take them, five years later, straight to a defeat (not yet digested even today) against a people determined never to bend, whatever the price.

After February 8, El Kho instructed the teams of *fidayine* who had escaped Massu's meat grinder to attack the military and continue to take our armed conflict into the midst of the "innocent" European population, who continued to live peacefully as if the war didn't concern them. It was as if the fierce repression that fell upon our neighborhoods day and night was the condition for their happiness.

The reports that continued to reach El Kho confirmed the carnage in our ranks, particularly among our rank-and-file activists, where the partitioning system was not applied rigorously. It was so serious that new rules were enacted. Djamila and I were never to leave except draped in *haïks*; when delivering packages, we had to be preceded by a scout. All liaison officers were to be recruited from our host families. In addition, we learned that the paratroopers were fixated on 5 Impasse de la Granada because they had found the house empty of any occupants two days after the horrible night of torture they had conducted there. The reports indicated that they had searched it from top to bottom.

That was why we concluded that the paratroopers had information— but that it was incomplete. Who had spoken of 5 Impasse de la Granada? El Kho decided to send some brothers to remove and bring back the bombs that we had not been able to carry when we left this blessed safe house. They were still hidden in the camouflaged laboratory on the terrace. On their third visit, the paratroopers discovered the laboratory—but without the bombs. The press announced that Massu's men had seized several bombs at the home of fellow freedom fighter Bachagha Boutaleb.

After these two blows to our organization, the brothers thought to check whether the mason who had built the caches and laboratories and camouflaged them with such talent and ingenuity had not been swept up in the recent raids and "subject to questioning." Indeed he had been. The mason, known as "Mathurin Popeye," had been picked up by chance along with dozens of other "natives." Subjected to the worst torture, he had spit it out. Who could cast blame on a torture victim? We didn't. The terror is still etched in my memory from those raids. Sixty years later, there are times when my children wake me at night to tear me from the clutches of the same nightmares, haunted by the screams and moans of the tortured.

In February 1957, Massu and his paratroopers led their "Battle of Algiers" by applying a horrific strategy: "If the FLN lives like a fish in water among the natives, then we must drain the water to kill the fish!" It was a terrifying strategy that aimed for pure extermination. We had no choice but to win or die. We were obliged to adopt a nomadic lifestyle, roving from safe house to safe house while continuing to fight and rebuild our organization.

Today there are street names that resonate in my head: Rue des Abderames, Rue Sidi Ramdane, Rue de la Grue, Rue du Lion, Rue du Sphinx, Impasse Kléber, Impasse Lavoisier, Rue du Nil, Rue Cato—all home to safe houses through which we passed. Sometimes we had to flee just hours or minutes after arriving. El Kho, without giving us any explanation, would stand up, give the order to collect what few weapons we had in our possession—revolvers, bombs, plastic explosives—and abandon a home that, moments later, would be overrun by paratroopers. I particularly remember one grey February afternoon when we had arrived—after an eventful crossing of a part of the Casbah infested with paratroopers—in a beautiful house with a vast patio centered around a fountain tumbling into a white marble basin. Under our *haïks*, clutched against our stomachs, Djamila, Hassiba, and I carried the bombs that had survived multiple searches by the paratroopers. Petit Omar led the way, Djamila behind him, followed by El Kho, Hassiba, and me, with Ali bringing up the rear. Since it was cold, the brothers wore wool hats and scarves that enveloped their necks and lower faces, rendering them more or less unrecognizable.

As soon as we reached the beautiful house, the moment the door of the vast and beautiful salon was closed, we ripped off our sweaty *haïks*, *âadjars*, caps, and scarves and then dropped onto the cushions, legs stretched out on the wide carpet. Nobody wanted to talk. I was enjoying this unexpected moment of calm and peace. To no longer be walking, to no longer be jumping from terrace to terrace, to stop running, to sleep my fill—it was my one and only wish. I pressed against Hassiba, set my head on her shoulder, and whispered in her ear: "I am dreaming of stretching out on this mattress. I'm so tired of walking." Hassiba smiled and encouraged me to lie down. The brothers sat silent. Suddenly El Kho stood up and hissed, "Quick! We must leave quickly! Do not leave anything behind!"

Desperate, I looked at Djamila and Hassiba, who calmly helped each other repack the bombs against their stomachs with a long shawl. Then they helped me do the same. We left as we had come—in single file. No sooner had we left the alley and turned onto a side street than the last two in our line saw paratroopers arriving at the other end of the alley. Before reaching our refuge, on the Rue du Nil, we learned from some passersby that Bachagha Boutaleb's house had been surrounded and invaded by a swarm of paratroopers. So much for stretching out to sleep my fill!

8

DESPERATE TIMES

Ben M'hidi's Fate

Just as we were starting to grasp our new circumstances and adapt to the terrible conditions imposed upon us, a bombshell dropped, leaving us all devastated: Ben M'hidi had been arrested! On February 23, the front page of every paper announced the news, with the photo to prove it. I stared, incredulous, at the newspapers, refusing to believe the disaster that had befallen us. But it was surely him. He looked straight ahead calmly, his face lit by an imperceptible smile. His whole demeanor expressed the serene confidence of a leader, a man convinced that the cause for which he fought would triumph. I focused on that look I knew so well, and I cried. I told myself, "He must be thinking of Ben Alla El Hadj and preparing himself to learn, at last, the answer to the question that has kept tormenting him."

I understood that at that very moment, as the photographers' flashes bombarded him, he had wanted to send one final message to us, to our people. He used the enemy's own photo to speak to us and guide us one final time by communicating a serene confidence through the cheerful light of his eyes and the slight smile that illuminated his face. His message was clear

Arrest of Ben M'hidi

and compelling: brute force will never triumph over moral force. With their strength and composure, his eyes told us that no force in the world could break a people's will to be free.

For several hours, the news plunged me into a paralyzing despair. Then I regained control and even allowed myself to hope. Through some exercises in self-persuasion, I told myself that if the French regime had wanted to torture him to death or "liquidate" him, they would have refrained from presenting him to the photographers upon his arrest. The photo published in all the newspapers clearly showed a man handcuffed but with a vigorous and determined air.

Again, the French launched a propaganda campaign around the arrest of a prestigious leader, in hopes of delegitimizing the FLN in the eyes of our people and implying that the colonial army was omnipotent and invincible. But a completely new, unusual element struck and intrigued me: the daily papers reported that Massu and Bigeard had confided to several reporters the respect and admiration that Ben M'hidi inspired in them. The two war criminals praised our leader's intelligence, his political acumen, his courage, his finesse, and his intellectual capabilities, as well as the visionary nature of his analyses. They recounted what Ben M'hidi had fearlessly predicted—"The FLN will expand the war from Dunkirk to Tamanrasset"—to remind the French of the certainty of their eventual defeat. It seemed they could hardly find enough words to praise Ben M'hidi. I sensed something fishy, which I tried to coax out by reading and re-reading the articles. But no sooner had the media barrage about him begun than it was followed by an airtight silence, as if he had never existed.

Since his arrest, El Kho and the entire organization had mobilized day and night to figure out where Ben M'hidi was being held, but still we knew nothing either of where he was detained or under what conditions. In vain. During those terrible days, I sometimes found myself saying to Djamila and Hassiba, "Maybe they transferred him to France and he is with the other big brothers."[1]

On the morning of March 6, the newspapers brought us the dark and terrible news: Ben M'hidi was dead. He had "committed suicide by hanging himself with strips torn from his shirt," according to one cynical headline. Not a single one of us believed this story for a second. Speechless with pain, we all knew that our leader had been eliminated by the French regime.

I still consider Ben M'hidi's death an immeasurable loss. His absence hurt us terribly throughout the rest of our revolution, just as it would after independence. A man of honor and conviction, he held a faith in his people and their revolution that bordered on the religious. He had nobility and humility in equal parts, just as he had the simplicity of the greatest leaders that rendered him accessible to ordinary people. He was a true undisputed leader, a fellow combatant, respectful of the other activists, a visionary strategist, and a formidable politician—exactly what his country would need once it was finally independent. Having had the honor and privilege to be part of the group that rubbed shoulders with him in the Casbah, I can testify that, beyond his attributes as a senior commander, Ben M'hidi had uncommon virtues. Until the end, even once he was gone, he would remain my leader, my guide, and my inspiration. How often, faced with crises or difficult situations, I asked myself how Ben M'hidi would have thought or acted! But at the same time, my God, how difficult to emulate him, whose moral rigor and honesty were as demanding and sharp as a razor blade! He

---

1. After the French military captured their plane in October 1956, the five FLN leaders were arrested, questioned, and then transferred to prison in France, where they were held for the remainder of the war.

was one of those men and women to whom humanity only gives birth once every few centuries.

The "garbageman's work," as the bloodthirsty Massu called it, would be amplified along with the practice of "netting fish"—bringing in thousands of people at random, all systematically subjected to torture. Massu later wrote, "Torture is effective. Most people crack and talk. Then, most of the time, we finish them off." Combatants of European origin weren't spared the horror, especially if they were Communists. In the end, the entire Communist network would be virtually dismantled. Every day saw its share of sisters and brothers killed through torture or otherwise liquidated, and to date the resting places of thousands of women and men remain unknown. All these disappeared, those who had the sea as their grave, those for whom a tomb was improvised in a cellar, those who were buried at the base of a garden in a pit dug at night, and the hundreds of thousands of others, may they rest in peace. This land—its plains, its mountains, and its sea, all of Algeria—is bathed in the blood of her children, who gave their country their very bodies and souls.

Angels in the Mosque

Starting from mid-February 1957, we were lodged on the Rue du Nil with a family of two old spinsters raising their nephew, Mahfoudh, and his sister, Nacéra, who had lost both parents. Barely eighteen, Mahfoudh behaved like the head of the household with his maternal aunts and little sister. He was a disciplined activist, completing his missions with precision and discretion. This had allowed him, until that point, to escape Massu's paratroopers. The safe house—which only Alilou, Si Mourad, El Kho, Djamila, Hassiba, and I knew—had the best security measures, allowing our leader to take stock of the fierce repression suffered during the Eight-Day Strike and begin to rebuild our networks, then redeploy them.

Ali la Pointe and another brother, Atmane Hadji, known as Ramel, were housed in a beautiful cozy house located on the Impasse Lavoisier, overlooking Rue Randon. Their safe house was the home of a great-uncle of Djamila's whose widow, Auntie Zaghla, lived there with her children.

Under the new measures announced by El Kho, no activist was to know the address or occupants of a safe house unless he or she was staying there. Djamila and I were therefore responsible for serving as liaisons from Rue du Nil to the Impasse Lavoisier. Djamila was suffering from severe gastrointestinal problems that had left her bedridden for an entire week. During her illness, I accompanied her to Auntie Zaghla's house on Impasse Lavoisier, since her condition required medical assistance.

There we received the awful news that Oukhiti's husband, Uncle Mustapha Bouhired, had been captured in the *maquis* outside Algiers, tortured, and then dragged in the night back to his home for more punishment. There in front of 5 Impasse de la Granada, he tried to escape but was shot down by a burst of machine gun fire, his spilled blood forever permeating those walls we knew so well.

As soon as the curfew ended, Oukhiti, accompanied by her father, Uncle Lâarbi, harassed the French authorities to turn over her husband's body so she could bury him according to our traditions.[2] But they refused, preventing her from doing the customary washing ritual or organizing the funeral vigil. The body was only returned to her at the cemetery to be buried directly. Djamila and I, hidden in our veils, joined the family and friends gathered at the El Kettar Cemetery overlooking the Bay of Algiers, surrounded by a swarm of well-armed paratroopers. Covered by a simple sheet, Uncle Mustapha's body lay next to the grave. His mother, Djamila's grandmother Yemma, uncovered her martyred son's head and shoulders, revealing his ALN military fatigues and a recent haircut. His eyes were wide open. It was the first time I ever saw a dead person's face. God, he looked young! Wrapped in their *haïks*, the women wept in silence. An inconsolable Oukhiti sat beside her husband's head, moaning in pain. She bent over him and then lifted her head in sync with her heartrending groans.

Across from her, Yemma sat cross-legged, upright, her eyes dry and lips chanting in silence as she fingered her prayer beads. Her impressive, dignified presence was like a gauntlet thrown at the feet of the paratroopers who had defiled the sacred mourning rites. They stared at her as if hypnotized, with a glimmer of fear in their eyes. She seemed to be telling them, "I am unbreakable Algeria! You killed my son, but you remain the foreign army of occupation. I will bury as many children as it takes to throw you out! And out you will go!"

When Mustapha's body was lowered into the ground, above the sobs a long, deep, crystalline *you-you* tore the clear air. It was Yemma's way of wishing farewell to her youngest child, who died as a martyr so that his

---

2. In the Islamic tradition, burial should be carried out within twenty-four hours of a death. The body is laid to rest facing Mecca as particular prayers are recited.

country might live free. All the women followed her in a shrill, uninter-rupted concert of burning *you-yous*, giving the men goosebumps and the foreign soldiers the fright of their lives, reminding them that they would forever exist beyond the impassable borders of our culture—those borders so well guarded by our women.

Ramadan began soon after, on April 1 that year. Like the Bouhireds, the majority of families entered the holy month[3] with the pain and grief of a dead, disappeared, arrested, or wanted relative. But the people of the Casbah refused to abdicate. They welcomed Ramadan with fervor and piety. After the breaking of the fast, even if the nights didn't hold their former glory, they didn't lack for activity.

On April 8, 1957, El Kho summoned us to the Rue du Nil. I arrived with Djamila, still recovering, to find an unsettling silence and an ambiance so heavy you could have sliced it with a knife. Si Mourad, El Kho, Alilou, and Hassiba were as mute as goldfish, each one lost in his thoughts.

El Kho brought us up to speed. That morning, at dawn, three brothers had been guillotined: Arezki Louni, Saïd Badouche, and Amar Mameri. It wasn't so much their deaths that overwhelmed us but the cruelty with which it had been dispensed with a guillotine, that quintessentially French instrument of torture and death. We knew that France tied the hands of each activist behind his back and stretched him out full length on his stom-ach to bare his neck, defenseless, at the mouth of the guillotine so that the blade would separate the head from our brother's body. Our brother's head would then drop into a basket to be collected as the barbaric trophy, bloody and shameful, of a NATO power engaged in massacring an impoverished people. With these executions, the French regime was denying our broth-ers a dignified death, the death of a combatant, a death upright and staring into the eyes of their executioners. This aspect of our brothers' execution by guillotine drove us mad with pain.

I didn't know Arezki, whose terrible tracking and capture, encircled by a myriad of paratroopers, we had witnessed on December 24, 1956. We knew that he had been tortured; now we heard about his execution.

---

3. In the Muslim lunar calendar, believers observe the holy month of Ramadan by fasting from sunrise to sunset, eating no food and drinking no water in order to better understand the suffering of the poor and destitute throughout the whole year. The fast is one of the five central "pillars" of the Muslim faith.

The day of his execution, he woke early in the morning, rose from his pallet, and concealed in his sleeve a metal object he had whittled as sharp as a razor. As he was marched to his death, he struck the guards around him in the neck, gravely injuring them in a final mission as a *fidaï*. With a cry of "*Vive l'Algérie*" and "*Allahu Akbar*," he strode definitively toward the guillotine. And that was how our brother Arezki Louni died a martyr.

That evening of April 8, 1957, after breaking our fast, we were having coffee when a burst of loud voices reached us. Mahfoudh was struggling with his two aunts, who had been traumatized by the executions. They were screaming in fear because they had realized that their nephew, the only man of the house, was involved in the fight against the French soldiers. They were terrified to know that Massu's cruel horde might cut him and his family down at any time. They cried and begged him to save himself, his sister, and his old aunts. He owed it to his departed parents, they said. We looked at one another, understanding that it was time for us to leave the house at 14 Rue du Nil. Our rule, which El Kho had never transgressed, was to never oblige a family to host us. At the end of the evening, El Kho informed us that we were scheduled to depart the next morning at dawn. It was the best moment to move, since the streets would be deserted.

At four-thirty, after checking every nook and cranny to erase any trace of our presence, we were finally ready. El Kho's liaison officer Alilou arrived and we left our refuge in the order prescribed by El Kho. Mahfoudh led. He was instructed to go straight when we reached the intersection of Rue N'Fissa and Rue Sidi Ben Ali. Behind him came Hassiba, followed by El Kho and me. Alilou came behind me, with Djamila bringing up the rear. She was tasked with carrying a large briefcase bulging with important documents, one or two guns, and some clips. El Kho advised her to turn back if anything happened. Si Mourad was to remain back at 14 Rue du Nil. Rue N'Fissa, consisted of a long upward staircase swathed in semi-darkness. Arriving at the corner of Rue Sidi Ben Ali, Mahfoudh continued straight. Just as Hassiba reached the street, followed by El Kho, Mahfoudh suddenly retraced his steps and hissed, "A patrol! A patrol!"

"Scatter!" El Kho shouted to us, before jumping up and pressing himself against the far corner of the intersection. I heard bursts of machine guns as I ran behind Hassiba without taking my eyes off her, because I didn't know the address where we were heading. Suddenly I fell. The shock was so violent that I lay dazed, my whole body seeming dislocated. Alilou, who was following me, had a hard time bringing me back to reality. He shook me, begging me to continue fleeing. But I didn't move, as if my body couldn't or didn't want to follow me in my life as a hunted animal, as if it were abandoning me there.

I resigned myself to waiting for the enemy to come put an end to me. But Alilou wouldn't hear of it; he shook me again and again. I shouted at him to leave me, to save his own skin. But he sat down next to me and swore he wouldn't move until I was back upright. In a split second, the image of Alilou being arrested provoked something like an electric shock in my brain, pushing me to heave myself up, lean on my brother, and resume our flight. In a daze, I passed out again.

When I regained consciousness, I was sitting cross-legged, my *haïk* wrapped tightly around my right forearm, my *âadjar* hanging around my neck, in a room with low ceilings and whitewashed walls, like a small prayer room. The ceiling and the upper half of the walls were white and the rest painted forest green. As if emerging from a coma, I looked around wildly. I was not alone. Six or seven elderly men in white *gandouras* surrounded me, fingering their prayer beads, their lips moving, immersed in prayer. I was in a tiny mosque. I got up suddenly, without saying a word, unfurled my *haïk*, wrapped myself up, and stepped out quietly. I did not dare speak to these men, these angels, who had certainly protected me for hours with their bodies, their prayers, and their silence. They asked me nothing, continuing to pray silently. I did not tell them anything. Only my eyes conveyed to them my infinite and eternal gratitude.

Outside it was broad daylight. I was on Rue des Sarassins. So I had been in the little Bourkissa Mosque, though I would never know when or how I had arrived there. My last memories were back at dawn and included machine-gun bursts, my sudden fall, and Alilou shaking me to continue our escape. I managed to reorient myself and find my way to 14 Rue du Nil. That was the rule: if something unexpected happens during an outing, return to the starting point. When I reached Mahfoudh's house, the door opened as if someone inside was watching me. Si Mourad snatched me inside and closed the door, "Where have you been? Alilou and Mahfoudh left to search for you." I was unable to utter a word. Unable to ask the one question that burned on my lips: What had become of El Kho?

I heard Si Mourad's voice bludgeon me with the only terrible possibility that had not crossed my mind: "Djamila was wounded and arrested." I heard, but didn't understand what Si Mourad kept telling me. Djamila arrested? But that was absurd, impossible. She had been bringing up the rear, far from the shooting, and had instructions to turn straight back in case of problems. Leading me inside the house, Si Mourad struggled to calm me down. He tried to make me drink some water, but I refused. It was Ramadan, the holy month of fasting, and I thought of the little mosque that had sheltered and protected me. He left me even more confused when he asked me if I knew where El Kho and Hassiba were, even as he reassured me that they hadn't been arrested. I felt a duty to warn the family that had been housing Djamila and Ali la Pointe, whose address Si Mourad didn't know. I put my *haïk* back on and left the Rue du Nil to head for the Impasse Lavoisier.

When I arrived, I pounded on the door, slamming the knocker like a madwoman. It took an eternity for the door to open. When she saw me, Auntie Zaghla exclaimed, "Why did you knock like that? The paratroopers aren't chasing you, are they?" I shook my head and rushed to the room where the brothers usually were. Recognizing the seriousness of the situation, Auntie Zaghla lifted a corner of the large rug that covered the room's entire floor, revealing a perfectly smooth surface. She leaned forward, pounded the floor and exclaimed, "Lift the door, lift the door!" The perfectly invisible trapdoor opened and out came Ramel, then Ali. They had taken my frantic knocking for a raid by the paratroopers! I told them right away that Djamila had been wounded and arrested and was now being taken to the Second District Commissariat. I told them everything I had seen, heard, and survived since dawn. I added that Si Mourad was informed and ready, but couldn't get in touch with El Kho.

Ali picked up his gun and was preparing to leave when Petit Omar arrived, followed by Hassiba. They confirmed Djamila's arrest. Due to her wounds, she had been transferred to the Mustapha Pacha Hospital. El Kho, who had managed to reach the refuge safely, was doing everything possible to determine her exact location. They added that the Bouhired family had been informed. Before breaking the fast, we learned that Djamila had been transferred to the Maillot Military Hospital. Uncle Lâarbi, Oukhiti's father, worked there as a nurse. We hoped for more news later in the evening.

Today, after sixty years in which I never mentioned these terrible events, the surreal feeling that overwhelmed me that day remains undiminished. Nothing foreshadowed Djamila's arrest. My feeling of disbelief was born of refusal—not refusal to confront the injustice and misfortune we suffered, but refusal to accept and surrender to them. Yet when I listened to my logical side, I knew that arrest and death were the possible—if not almost certain—consequences of our choices and our commitment. Even if our country's independence was inevitable, the chances we combatants would survive to taste the happiness of that achievement were nearly zero.

When I thought about the total war France and her army were waging against us, I knew that our future would hold prison or death. So why this feeling of bafflement, verging on denial? For several reasons, but the first and most terrifying one, even worse than the fear of death, was the fear of torture. Even though she was wounded, I knew she would not escape torture and abuse.

I tried in my distress to reconstruct the events of that cursed dawn. When the shooting started, I had just followed Hassiba onto the Rue Sidi Ben Ali, with Alilou and Djamila trailing me. They were still on Rue N'Fissa and should have turned back when the skirmish broke out. What had happened? We learned only later: one of the French bullets had hit Djamila directly in the shoulder, passing just a few centimeters from her heart, knocking her to the ground and leaving her to bleed out. In that state, she couldn't get up and turn back. The patrol found her wrapped in her haïk, lying in her own blood, protecting under her veil the precious briefcase containing the mail addressed to the CCE, the money, the pistols, and the clips.

At first the soldiers took her for an old lady, the victim of a stray bullet. When they tried to take her to the hospital, not knowing who she was, she refused, explaining with difficulty that she preferred to return home alone, all the while trying to hide the precious briefcase. But the soldiers, taken aback, seized the briefcase, opened it, and quickly grasped that they had before them "a dangerous individual." They hustled her off immediately.

An Escape Attempt

Later that same evening, after the breaking of the fast, Oukhiti joined us. Her mere presence reinvigorated us and brought us back to life. She reminded us of the enormous sacrifices made thus far and those that remained to be made. She recounted the news from her father: after being taken to the Mustapha Pacha civilian hospital, where she spent nearly an hour in surgery, Djamila was transferred—by a guard of elite "red-beret" paratroopers—to the Maillot Military Hospital, where she had been placed in a guarded cell. Only the attending physician and a nurse had access to her, and only when accompanied by a paratrooper captain. Djamila's wound was serious and no one could say how long she would need to stay hospitalized.

After Oukhiti's departure, I reminded Hassiba of our last discussion with Djamila the previous night. Still feeble from a week of illness, tired of not being able to fight like she wanted to, she had informed us, "I made contact with someone who could get us to the *maquis*. If you're up for it, all he needs is some time to prepare the false papers. I think we'll be more helpful in the *maquis* than here, where we can hardly do anything and where we may even have become a burden to El Kho. In the *maquis* the brothers need everything—weapons, nurses, secretaries, and more. What do you think?"

Of course we were keen on going, especially Hassiba, who had been wanted for much longer than the two of us and had been living in complete secrecy, even when inside the safe houses, since her arrival in the Casbah in October 1956. In addition, aside from Si Mourad, who now handled the political mission of reorganizing the Algiers Autonomous Zone, others had been arrested and the laboratory dismantled.

Hassiba now found herself a veritable orphan. So we had not only been keen on going, we had been grateful to Djamila for opening a new option for continuing our liberation struggle.

Hassiba and I spent an almost sleepless night. El Kho, who knew how shaken we were and probably wanted to lift our morale, began discussing preparations for the upcoming jailbreak openly before us. Uncle Lâarbi continued to send him information regularly. El Kho explained to us that Djamila had to be informed and give her consent to be rescued. Uncle Lâarbi had to smuggle in a note, dictated by El Kho, who transcribed it onto a thin sheet of tobacco rolling paper. Djamila knew El Kho's style, and to give credibility to the message he used key words and phrases known exclusively to our group. El Kho then charged the irreplaceable Habib Réda to scout the site and select brothers capable of successfully executing the escape plan.

The obstacles were numerous. First, there was the problem of how to enter the military hospital grounds, with all the exits guarded by armed soldiers who controlled access strictly. Only accredited personnel had access—medical staff, often military, or civilians like Uncle Lâarbi, who had to show an ID badge with a photo and detailed information on the holder. Next, there was the question of what to do inside the hospital and how to locate the cell where Djamila was being held around the clock under the watchful eye of soldiers, without forgetting the exit plan and while mapping the different positions of the guard posts.

Finally, we would have to set the plan for ferrying our sister out, remembering that she was gravely injured and very weak, having lost a great deal of blood. We were assured that she could move, albeit with great difficulty.

Once all these issues were sorted out, we would have to determine the right time to reach the cell where Djamila was locked up, get her out, then exfiltrate her from the hospital and transport her to a waiting refuge. The preparation lasted almost a week. It was decided to execute the escape plan between eight-thirty and eight forty-five in the evening, during the changing of the guards. In that window, no soldiers, doctors, or nurses would be prowling around Djamila's cell.

On the D-Day, having lived for nothing but this moment for over a week, Ali, Hassiba, Si Mourad, and I sat with El Kho around the *meïda* after breaking our fast, waiting for news of the escape. We were all silent. Starting at nine o'clock, I began to discreetly check the hands of my watch. Mentally, I calculated the time required to execute the escape plan, including the time required to reach the refuge and get our sister settled there. Knowing she was in bad shape, I added some more time for the care that would be required after moving her. But the hand on my watch turned mercilessly and no news came. I decided it was a good sign; if it had not worked, we would have known right away. Then I began to pray that the silence would persist, for fear of hearing those terrible ominous words. Sealed in this bubble of silence, I hadn't noticed when El Kho was called out of the room. His muffled voice brought me back to reality: "It didn't work." The abyss sucked me in.

I refused to listen to words that would just twist my soul and break my heart further, and it took me some time to realize and understand the idea that my sister in arms and in life was truly and definitively arrested. Assisted by Hassiba and Ali, I gradually returned to the world. El Kho, who kept picking at his beak-shaped thumbnail—his unconscious sign of great distress—was saying that everything had gone as planned. The armed brothers tasked with jailbreaking Djamila had managed to enter the hospital without incident and reach a room near our sister's cell, where they waited amid a jumble of storage boxes for the attending nurse—one of our own—to come for them the moment the guards began their shift change. They had entered around eight o'clock, nearly half an hour before the time set. Behind the wall that ringed the hospital, along the road leading to the Notre Dame d'Afrique Basilica, two vehicles were parked, drivers at the wheel, ready to transport Djamila as soon as she was exfiltrated from the hospital.

Suddenly everything was in disarray—whether by coincidence or because of a leak we will never know. At the very instant the operation to rescue our sister from the enemy's clutches was supposed to begin, the Maillot Hospital was surrounded by a sea of red-beret paratroopers. The brothers, hidden in the room near Djamila's cell, had a front-row seat and watched helplessly as our sister was abducted and placed into a closed military truck that drove off at once, leaving the hospital for an unknown destination. If up to that point Djamila's injury had allowed her to escape interrogation, we knew that now she was about to learn what thousands of our brothers and sisters had already experienced in their flesh and their souls: the French army's "advanced civilizing methods."

A Lawyer for Djamila

From that moment, a single idea consumed me, keeping me from sleeping: at dawn I would go and recruit her one of the lawyers who had come to Algiers from mainland France to defend our activists.

Every day in the press I read reports on the trials of brothers and sisters facing the Permanent Armed Forces Tribunal. Certain lawyers' names came up often—all of them, the reports stressed, members of the Paris bar. Some of them, like the couple Pierre and Renée Stibbe, had been defending nationalist activists since 1945. Even if I didn't know any of them, I at least knew where to find them: according to the press, they all stayed at the Hotel Aletti. The prospect that Massu's men might torture Djamila to death, or simply kill her, haunted me. The night was long, very long.

Then I saw the sun rise and the newspapers arrive. While the house was still shrouded in silence, I plunged myself feverishly into reading the papers to find out if any of our fighters' defense attorneys were in Algiers. A certain Mr. Zavarro's name kept coming up. What's more, the journalists already won over to the "French Algeria" side were vilifying him. It took nothing more to persuade me to head out immediately to contact and convince him to defend Djamila. Since I hadn't informed El Kho of my decision nor asked for his approval, I tasked Hassiba, who was aware of my plan, to cover for me by inventing whatever reasons she wanted to explain my absence to the brothers. I promised her I would be back around noon; if I wasn't back by twelve-thirty, she could alert the brothers. I donned my *haïk* and my *âadjar* and told Hassiba the plan: "I'll go first to Uncle Lâarbi's to ask Oukhiti to accompany me, with her family registry in hand." (After her husband's death, Oukhiti and her children had moved back to her parents' home.) "Then we'll go take Auntie Baya's family registry from Impasse de la Granada. So, to get the lawyer, Oukhiti will pretend to be Djamila's mother and I'll pretend to be Oukhiti. With our *haïks* and our *âadjars*, it will look plausible. And in the case of a search along the way, Oukhiti and I will each have a family registry to show as identification. The police are used to the 'Fatimas' not showing their faces. You see, I've thought of everything, don't worry. Nothing will happen to me. I'm counting on you to handle the brothers in case they ask about my absence."

And with that I left. I walked quickly, lost in my thoughts, seeing nothing around me. Soon I was standing face to face with Oukhiti, who was busy dressing her children. She was surprised to see me out so early. I grabbed her, asking her to put on her *haïk* and *âadjar* without further delay and fetch her family registry. I promised her that along the way, I would explain my plan to help Djamila. At these words, she passed her children off to her mother and sister, grabbed her family registry, and slipped into her *haïk*. We headed for the exit with her still adjusting her *âadjar*.

We ran at full tilt to 5 Impasse de la Granada, where I hadn't set foot since early February. As soon as we entered, we took the stairs two at a time, arriving breathless on the second floor where Djamila's parents lived. The house seemed deserted and almost shabby. Massu's destructive pack had passed over and over again through the place and ransacked every surface: ceramic tiles were torn out, walls gouged, wrought iron twisted.

Auntie Baya was in her room. She came out to welcome Oukhiti, her sister-in-law, who had announced her arrival. When she saw me, she flinched in fright and shouted, "What are you doing here? One girl arrested, don't you think that's enough?" I explained that I had to get her family registry since the brothers had entrusted me to get a lawyer for Djamila as soon as possible—otherwise she would be killed. She handed us her precious registry and we left right away. We soon reached Rue d'Isly, which I hadn't walked since early January.

The European city seemed even more foreign and hostile. I had wrapped my hair in a scarf that covered a good half of my forehead. I held the two sides of my *haïk* tightly under my chin, my eyes probing, inspecting passersby and looking out for paratrooper patrols. We arrived safely at the Hotel Aletti. As I pushed the revolving door, my heart heavy and a lump in my throat, I remembered coming here as a young girl, accompanied by my father. If he could have guessed that I would end up in the Casbah, hunted by all the police under the sun, he would certainly have hesitated before leaving me in Algiers. But this wasn't the moment to turn back time.

When we reached the Aletti's reception desk, I addressed the clerk calmly. "Please inform Mr. Zavarro that we are waiting for him."

"But Mr. Zavarro checked out of the hotel yesterday."

His sentence clanged in my ears and despite my *haïk*, my headscarf pulled down over my forehead, and my *âadjar*, my dismay and disappointment were visible to the receptionist, who was evidently Algerian. I was deflated, having staked everything on this Mr. Zavarro I didn't even know. With him gone, I didn't know what to do or where to go. Lost, I stared at Oukhiti, who waited silently. The receptionist quickly brought me back to life, however, by saying: "Mr. Zavarro is gone, but another lawyer from Paris is here, Mr. Vergès. Would you like me to call him?" I accepted, full of gratitude, then looked around. Across from the reception desk I saw a small sitting area with benches and leather armchairs and a small table. We headed there. Oukhiti slid onto a bench and I sat down beside her. The reception area, which was filled with small sofas, was very lively.

Men with briefcases in hand came and went; waiters passed back and forth with white dishtowels folded over their forearms, balancing trays of glasses and mugs. A man of Asian appearance, quite young, approached and greeted us, then sat down facing us and introduced himself: "Mr. Vergès. The receptionist informed me that you were looking for me."

I looked at him, dumbstruck. The name Vergès sounded so typically French that I had expected a Frenchman to show up. Mr. Vergès was of medium height, with an ivory complexion, high forehead, and narrow eyes that sparkled with intelligence behind thick glasses. A wide smile spread across his face. Back then, I mistook all Asians for Indochinese, so I thought to myself, "Oh, an Indochinese! Diên Biên Phu! He must surely sympathize with our cause and will take good care of Djamila."

I tried to remember if I had seen his name in the papers and trial reports. I couldn't recall. In Arabic, Oukhiti exhorted me to speak, pointing out that the gentleman was waiting. I decided to trust him and threw myself in. I started with the introductions, taking on Oukhiti's identity and presenting her as Auntie Baya. I explained that we had come to request Mr. Zavarro's services because my niece had been in the red-beret paratroopers' clutches since April 9. He kept smiling, his eyes fixed on mine. He explained that the lawyers of the Paris bar took turns assisting Algerian prisoners being tried in the military courts. He added that Mr. Zavarro had left Algiers after assisting several prisoners and that he had come to carry on the work. He said this calmly and clearly, in a deep, pleasant voice.

I turned to Oukhiti for advice. Just as unfamiliar with Asians as I was, she said, in Arabic, "*Ya tafla* [my girl], this man is Chinese. Do you really think he can overcome these French savages?" He stared at me, attentive and still smiling. In any case, we had no choice. So I told him what had happened to Djamila, and that we didn't know where they were holding her and feared she might succumb to the paratroopers' torments, knowing full well that torture had become a systematic practice. Mr. Vergès let me speak, his eyes focused on me. Waiters came and went. When I finished, he stayed silent for a long moment. He ordered a coffee and invited us to have whatever we liked, handing us the menu. I pointed out that we were still fasting. He took out a notebook and wrote down Djamila's name, date and place of birth, and family's address. He explained that he was ready to inform the prosecutor about this case that very morning, but that to do so, her mother or father would need to provide a letter designating him as their representative.

I proposed that we do it right away, since her mother was present, and that's just what we did. Mr. Vergès dictated the letter to me and Oukhiti, still pretending to be Djamila's mother, signed it. I asked him to tell us what his fee would be, so we could pay part of it immediately. He asked us more questions about the paratroopers' activities in the Casbah and their treatment of the population. What a godsend! A French Indochinese man, a lawyer from the Paris bar—this was not a chance to be missed! So we recounted to him the cruel night of February 2, 1957: the sweeps, the raids, the violent searches. We emphasized the systematic torture—including in homes. When we finished, a silence fell over us.

Then Mr. Vergès took the authorization letter, skimmed it, and asked me, "'Djamila' means 'beautiful' in Arabic?"

Surprised, I nodded, not understanding where he was going with his question.

Vergès, motionless in his chair, his gaze steady, said: "Djamila is a common name in Algeria."

Annoyed, I began to get up, asking Oukhiti to do the same while whispering in Arabic, "I think we've come across a pervert who, like the French, sees us as lustful Moors." But Mr. Vergès didn't move. He kept staring at me, and suddenly I realized that he was trying to convey an important message to me.

I sat back down and met his gaze as he repeated, "Djamila is a common name in Algeria." The message clicked in my brain and I grasped what he wanted to share with me: another sister, another Djamila, had also been arrested.

I turned to Oukhiti and just had time to start, "Oukhiti—"

Vergès interrupted me by conspicuously raising his voice and saying, "So, I will speak to the Prosecutor of the Republic this very morning about your daughter Djamila's case." Then he stared just as conspicuously at the table. I fell silent. He wanted to warn me that we were in a place riddled with rats of all kinds, both human and inanimate.

In parting, I thanked him and indicated that from now on it would be Djamila's mother—I pointed to Oukhiti—who would contact him. Her address was included in the authorization letter. He saw us out, walking with us down the hotel's front steps, through the small garden, and out the entrance. Once outside, he spoke to us in a hushed voice: "I am going right this moment to file the complaint about your daughter's disappearance. I understand that there are many missing persons and that torture is a common and systematic practice. We must condemn all of this, and publicly."

I asked him, "Would you do that?"

"Yes, but I need records with as much information and evidence as possible. You will have to collect them."

"Okay, I will. Goodbye. You have Djamila's mother's address. Contact us."

We left him and began walking back to the Casbah. Along the way, we prepared our version of events to present to El Kho. I left Oukhiti at her father's home and kept my word by arriving at our safe house by eleven-thirty.

I arrived to find Hassiba worried sick. Thank God she hadn't needed to lie to cover for me. The brothers, who had stood guard all night, were still sleeping. I told Hassiba about my expedition, giving every detail, and concluded by telling her of the full confidence Mr. Vergès had inspired. I had agreed with Oukhiti to come back to break the fast together and finalize the version we would tell El Kho.

Shortly before the cannons fired to signal the breaking of the fast, we arrived at Uncle Lâarbi's. Oukhiti informed us that Mr. Vergès had contacted her that afternoon with more information about his plans, including the address of an apartment where we could get in touch with him and bring him documents. He also asked to receive the first set of documents needed for Djamila's defense, especially testimonies about the torture committed at 5 Impasse de la Granada, in the next two days. I agreed with my friends to spend the next day working to prepare the case files.

When Oukhiti delivered her report to El Kho, she insisted emphatically on how well the Bouhired family regarded Vergès. She noted that he was a Communist and had declared his willingness to form a group of lawyers for the FLN; he was ready to launch a public campaign in France and around the world to denounce French repression and torture. Our organization needed only to give him the green light and provide some well-documented cases.

She finished by explaining that he was awaiting the first set of documents within two days. She handed the address to El Kho, who gave his consent and charged Si Mourad and me with collecting the records of all our brothers and sisters who had been arrested, tortured, executed, or disappeared. Again, I promised El Kho that I would spend the next day on the first case. Behind his approving smile, I perceived some hint of anxiety or tense sadness. Indeed, the next morning, El Kho told us that we absolutely had to leave our refuge at Impasse Lavoisier. He added: "We should have done this as soon as the paratroopers kidnapped Djamila from the Maillot Hospital."

On the Run in the Casbah

El Kho had sent Petit Omar to find us new accommodation, but there had been no response. Thanks to Massu's policy of terror, we were seeing our possibilities for refuge dry up. Finally, a departure plan was set. But it was Ramadan, and at this hour the streets of the Casbah were swarming with people and patrols. They decided that Ali and El Kho would wrap themselves in *haïks* to try to conceal their identity. Despite our fatigue, despite the dejection and sorrow we felt, the process of Hassiba and me trying to fix a *haïk* onto Ali's athletic frame cheered us all up. Thanks to his faces and jokes, the whole house resounded with our alternating laughter and playful bickering, since Ali insisted on keeping his hands free in order to handle his gun easily in the event of an inopportune encounter with the enemy soldiers. We called on Auntie Zaghla to help us sort him out. She sat him down on the couch, wrapped his head in a patterned white scarf, passed a second one wrapped in cord around his waist, and tied it securely. With safety pins, she affixed the *haïk* so it would cover his forehead, gather under his chin, and attach at several points on his belt. Then she added the *âadjar*. Like this, the veil wouldn't slip off, yet it still left Ali the option to carry his machine gun as usual. Throughout the whole exercise, Auntie Zaghla had trouble keeping her cool and laughed loudly with us. This interlude reinvigorated us, giving us the strength we needed to go out and face the hostile streets.

With Auntie Zaghla's help, Hassiba and I strapped bombs to ourselves, each pressing one against our belly and another in the small of the back, and securing them by wrapping a long, fine shawl several turns around the midsection. Each of us also had to carry a briefcase under her arm—all hidden under our *haïks*, which we now knew how to don deftly. But despite Auntie Zaghla's talents, the woman that Ali wished to become in the eyes of passersby was as curious as she was imposing. El Kho, smaller and thinner, pulled off the illusion better. But war is war, and you do what you have to do! We had to go, so off we went.

El Kho hadn't succeeded in finding us a shelter, but Hassiba and I didn't know that. Around four o'clock, we left the Impasse Lavoisier with Petit Omar leading the way. I came behind him, followed by El Kho, then Hassiba, and Ali in the rear. Before exiting, El Kho had given us strict instructions. If Petit Omar saw a patrol, he would drop a handkerchief and then continue straight on his path. If that happened, I was to go into the nearest house, where the others would follow me, or branch off into the first adjoining alley I saw. On this Ramadan afternoon, Rue Randon was so crowded that we bumped into some of those walking toward us, heads down, bent double under their burdens. Some stopped to throw a puzzled glance to this large, horse-like woman before quickly diverting their gaze, dropping their heads back down, and hastening their steps. From time to time, El Kho caught up to me to instruct me to slow the pace. He did it each time Petit Omar, to my great distress, disappeared from my view. In these cases, I slowed down, advancing with short steps like a blind woman, since I didn't know where we were headed. Then, like a leprechaun playing with us, Petit Omar would suddenly reappear, head over to whisper something to his uncle, then resume his place in the lead before disappearing again, forcing us to walk with measured steps. He led us on a tour of the Casbah several times over. Thanks to our scout—who was alert and knew every place and person in the Casbah, especially the children his age—we managed to avoid the frequent patrols. But as dusk (and with it the breaking of the fast) approached and the streets emptied, our situation grew more precarious.

El Kho called to his nephew and spoke to him briefly. Petit Omar resumed walking, swerved into an alley, and then led us deeper into the Casbah's upper reaches. We came to a small square—the kind that are all throughout the old *medina*—onto which a few houses fronted, split by streets leading off in different directions. Petit Omar headed to one of the houses and opened the door, with us on his heels. At the same moment, we heard the cannon that announced the breaking of the fast. We stayed standing in the entryway while El Kho stepped into the central courtyard. As soon as he crossed the doorstep, Ali whipped off the *haïk* and scarves enveloping him to wipe off his sweat: he was drenched! Our young scout returned and asked us to follow him. We were in the central patio, about to enter one of the ground-floor rooms, when the yelling of several women tore through the house. The cries came from the second floor, and we instantly understood why. They were demanding that the head of family, a certain Omar, throw us out and lock the door behind us.

In the quiet neighborhood, the women's cries would likely draw attention to the house. Ali, pale, leapt in a single bound to the center of the patio, aiming his gun at the second floor. In a harsh voice, he ordered them to be quiet and reminded them that all of us had nothing to lose since we had long rubbed shoulders with death. He added, "I'm warning you. If your screams attract the paratroopers or alert their rats, you'll be the first victims. I swear it on the blood of our martyrs!"

It worked. We gathered in the doorway to the room that we no longer wanted to enter. Inside, El Kho spoke with his friend Omar. Ali, his face flushed, could hardly contain his distress and pressed his forehead against his forearm, leaning on a pillar. I looked at him and cried. Deep in my soul, I felt his confusion, grief, and anger, all laid bare by a horribly vivid realization—the realization that, that day, the fear and terror inspired by the French army had surpassed our people's hatred of them. At one time, hosting Ali la Pointe or El Kho would have been a great honor. But Massu and his paratroopers had passed through here, and the terror and annihilation were stronger than people's real and sincere commitment to the ideal of independence and the FLN. El Kho introduced Ali to Omar, the master of the house, who wished him welcome and beseeched him not to dwell too much on the women's reaction when we arrived. "You know, they're emotional, and to be honest they like the *moudjahidine*. But their fear of the paratroopers makes them nervous." Ali didn't comment.

We entered the room, which was dimly lit by a small ceiling lamp, leaving the corners in shadow. Hassiba and I ached in our stomachs and our backs. The heavy metal charges that had been pressed tightly against our bodies for hours had inflamed our skin and hurt our spines. We found a corner where we helped one another unload our burdens then massage each other's backs. We could finally sit down and stretch our legs.

Omar returned, carrying a *meïda* table. El Kho thanked him and asked for some strong coffee to revive us, since we were exhausted. With my back propped against the wall and legs outstretched, I fell asleep. El Kho's voice woke me. He was speaking sharply to his friend, saying: "Don't change anything about your habits. Go outside and play your dominoes like always. But I'm warning you, if the paratroopers surround the block or approach the house, you will be responsible for whatever happens!" Later, Petit Omar arrived with a well-stocked basket. We were famished and devoured the hearty meal sent by El Kho's family, apart from Ali, who ate very little, but poured himself coffee and smoked cigarette after cigarette.

I had an appointment the next morning to give Mr. Vergès the first dossier, so after dinner, I set about working, and wrote all night. I wrote three documents. The first described the circumstances of Djamila's arrest, her injury, the one-hour stay at the Mustapha Pacha Hospital, and her transfer to the Maillot Hospital, from where she disappeared, stolen away by the "red berets." The second document recounted in minute detail the horrible paratrooper raid of February 2. Finally, I wrote a letter in which I communicated our organization's enthusiastic approval of Vergès's defense of Djamila and the convening of a group of lawyers for the FLN. I finished by thanking him for his commitment to stand by our side, and affirmed our commitment to provide the documents and records essential to the campaign to denounce the French colonial regime's repression and torture in Algeria.

The alarm clock woke me: seven o'clock already! I had to go out to face the silent, empty streets of a Ramadan morning. Without its usual colorful, noisy, and cheerful crowds, the Casbah became an unreal space from another time, another world. I got up, slipped the files between my belly and my underwear, and wrapped my waistline with a long shawl just to be safe. I threw on my *âadjar* and my *haïk* and glanced at Ali, who was still awake. He said, "Sister, be careful! May God protect you!" Outside, I started to leave the Casbah. Just as I turned onto a street of wide, low stairs, I heard laughter and loud voices: a patrol of paratroopers walking merrily down the street, with machine guns and coils of rope in tow. They reminded me of the ones who had tortured the residents of the Bouhireds' house. Had they come to finish off that same dirty work? I turned right back to the nearest house and pushed against the door, which, to my great relief, was open.

I took the stairs two by two to the terrace, which I quickly scanned before jumping to a neighboring terrace overlooking another street. Among the many rooftops, I spotted one with an open door and a curtain half raised, and decided to take refuge there. When I crossed the threshold and ducked my head beneath the curtain, before me was a woman, her head wrapped in a wide white shawl bound by a narrow band with black spots, sitting cross-legged beside an elongated shape covered by a white sheet. At the end of this form, two candles were burning. A corpse. I sat down beside this woman draped in silent grief, keeping my *haïk* on as I had seen at funeral vigils in the Casbah. The woman didn't move or speak to me; her eyes were absorbed by the body before her. She was observing the greatest of solitudes—that of a loved one departed. After a moment of stillness, with infinite care, I slowly slid out the envelopes pressed against my stomach and slipped them under the carpet on which the deceased was laid. In case the paratroopers showed up . . .

We remained like this, all three of us, the lonely woman in mourning, the deceased, and I, all silent, motionless, frozen in our positions. This moment of absolute calm and meditation drove away the stress and anxiety that had gnawed at me for weeks. I surrendered myself to the moment. I had to make a considerable effort to tear myself away from the peaceful atmosphere and remove the envelopes, sliding them with infinite delicacy. I concentrated on making myself as light, invisible, and silent as the shadow of the deceased, in order to slip out without disrupting the aura of peace. In the light, my heart sank, and with it the shawl that I had wrapped around my waist. I descended stealthily, like a thief with soft steps, toward the door of this unknown house still plunged in sleep. When I arrived on the street, it was quiet, with no patrol in sight.

I hurried to the rendezvous site, which I reached an hour late. Mr. Vergès was gone but a lady, obviously Algerian, was waiting for me. Taking me for Auntie Baya, she explained that my daughter's lawyer had a hearing scheduled, and so had to return to the tribunal and had left her to recover the files. I gave her the two envelopes, thanked her, and left to return to Hassiba and the brothers.

I found my way back without incident. The brothers were waiting for me, on alert and worried sick. They had decided to leave this cursed home upon the breaking of the fast. Huddled like abandoned orphans in the gloomy underground room, we waited, gnawed by anxiety, for Petit Omar to return from his mission to find us somewhere else to stay. The most grueling aspect of this clandestine lifestyle was the uncertainty: we could go for hours, sometimes days, without clarity on aspects of life that were critical for our survival.

Omar, the owner, burst in to announce in a barely audible whisper that the sector was being sealed off by the paratroopers. We looked at one another, the same thought in our eyes: Had one of them given us up to the enemy? El Kho calmly ordered him to go lock himself in with the women on the second floor. Then he asked Ali to go to the terrace to assess our chances of using the rooftop to escape.

Ali reported back: "There's no chance of escaping by the roof. We're completely surrounded. A fight is inevitable. I locked the door leading to the terrace to prevent the paratroopers from surprising us from above." Hassiba reappeared, gesturing to me to follow her. She brought me to one of the central patio's walls, under which I made out a rectangular gap about three by two feet that opened onto a kind of storeroom packed with a large heap of random objects piled up to the arched ceiling.

"What if we slide behind this thick pile of junk covered in cobwebs?" she asked. Her idea struck me as ingenious, and we immediately proposed it to El Kho and Ali, who agreed. We crept one after the other behind the massive pile, deep into the storage room. El Kho and I stood flat against the wall while Ali and Hassiba crouched behind the mountain of spider-infested junk.

Finally, they arrived. We heard them overrun the hallways, calling out as they advanced. We hung onto their every shout and every tread of their boots. A nearby voice barked, "What's that?"

A second, frightened one replied: "A storeroom, as you can see. It's always been there. Each family just dumps their old stuff in it."

We held our breath, motionless, ready for an all-out battle. Fortunately, the voice faded away. The paratroopers raised their siege around three in the afternoon. No sooner had they gone than Petit Omar reappeared, bearing good news: we would finally be leaving.

The Blues

We were no longer dreaming of withdrawing to the *maquis*. It was clear to us: We had to overcome this challenge right here in the AAZ, where there was so much suffering all around us. We were reminded each day when we saw all the survivors—the men whose arms Massu's men lashed behind their backs, pushing them forward with uncertain steps, their heads hooded in a burlap bag with just one eyehole. After the torture, the paratroopers led these hooded men on leashes down the middle of the busy streets. The men only had two choices: cooperate and keep their bodies alive, knowing they would die in everyone's eyes, or refuse to cooperate and be slaughtered, but with eternal dignity. Death in indignity or death in honor.

We wrote tracts to flood the "native" sectors, particularly the Casbah, to affirm the strength and indestructible character of the FLN. Si Mourad and Ramel reorganized the armed groups and bomb networks. El Kho now took charge of the military network and political organization and tightened the rules on organizational separation. Each officer was now forbidden from calling on liaison officers not living in his own refuge. Thus Hassiba and I became the only links between Ali la Pointe and El Kho in one refuge and Si Mourad and Ramel in another. Houria, Ramel's wife, was his liaison officer.

El Kho, Ali, Hassiba, and I found shelter in the center of the Casbah, in an unusual house with just two floors, simple whitewashed walls, and columns and arcades connected by rough-hewn beams. A gnarled fig tree stood in the middle of the courtyard, providing shade. The house's name was well chosen: *Dar Essdjour* (the house of trees). Our host Dahmane, a fellow activist (not to be confused with our senior bomb-maker, Abderrahmane Taleb, alias Dahmane), showed Ali and El Kho something bordering on religious adoration.

After breaking the fast, Dahmane went out to join his friends to play dominoes at their usual spot and gather the latest information about arrests or deaths of our activists. It was essential not to depart from normal habits, to avoid attracting attention or raising questions, particularly from the "rats" and "blues." The latter were former activists born and raised in the Casbah who, broken by torture, had been reduced to the lowly status of informants. By dressing them up in blue workers' outfits recognizable to all, even at a distance, and forcing them to roam the Casbah, the enemy sought to discredit the FLN in the eyes of the people by destroying its majestic aura. In fact, no one was deceived about who was responsible for the terrible situation or about who the enemy was. Everyone knew that the "blues" treatment was the cruelest and most demeaning method Massu had invented to continue the torture and destruction of beings, souls, wills, and human dignity. It continued even beyond the death of each "blue."

The cruelest, most dramatic such case was that of our poor brother Alilou. Until the dawn of April 9 and Djamila's arrest, Alilou had been the most devoted of El Kho's liaison officers. Starting that day, as I have explained, El Kho had imposed new rules of separation by assigning each survivor of Massu's terror a mission and sometimes a destination. As such, El Kho ordered Alilou—whom the French had recently picked up, questioned, and released—to go underground and cut all ties with other activists in preparation for departing to the *maquis*. Alilou took this decision very hard. He came to me, looking for an explanation. Ever since the beginning of the revolution, he explained, he had always worked under El Kho's command with unflinching loyalty and had even come to believe that El Kho could do without any one of us except him. I acknowledged that he had grown irreplaceable but reminded him that the terrible conditions of Massu's repression obliged us to adapt.

Alilou wouldn't listen. He began to cry, and I realized that he interpreted El Kho's decision as a form of banishment and an unbearable loss of confidence and was having a nervous breakdown. His whole life centered on El Kho, our group, and the revolution. When we parted, he was still profoundly hurt by his isolation, and I feared he might commit suicide. Little did I know that he would suffer much worse. Arrested on July 24, 1957, after having been wanted for many months, Alilou was subjected to the most horrible tortures: electroshock, the bath, the bottle, the blowtorch—even having his nails and chunks of skin ripped off with pliers. The next time we saw him, our brother was shattered and reduced to hobbling through the Casbah on his torn feet as one of the "blues." And for nothing, because on that April day when El Kho sent Alilou into isolation, he also completely restructured "the organization," leaving Alilou ignorant of the new safe houses, liaison officers, mailboxes, and everything else.

While the horrible tortures he suffered failed to extract any information, they did succeed in destroying our brother forever, until his death well after our independence. Until then, slandered as a traitor for supposedly having divulged information under torture, Alilou continued to suffer the painful consequences of the French colonizers' systemic torture. To me, he was no traitor but a victim pure and simple. He was never the cause of any of our brothers' or sisters' arrests or deaths. He knew where Oukhiti lived and what Hassiba and I looked like even in our *haïks*, but he never sold us out.

After living through that staggering night of February 2 on Impasse de la Granada—that horrible night when human beings, torturers and the tortured alike, were reduced to a beastly state—I came away with the deep conviction that no one can predict in advance his own capacity to resist torture, nor the reaction of anyone else subjected to torture. But above all I came away convinced that to judge the victims of torture is to forgive the act and exonerate the torturers, which turns you yourself into an accomplice of the criminals and extends the crime even beyond the victim's death. To consider Alilou a traitor and excuse his torturers and the colonial system would be the true betrayal.

Another Victim

One night after our kind host Dahmane had left to meet his friends, El Kho, Hassiba, Ali, and I went up on the *Dar Essdjour* terrace to spend the evening there. We needed to breathe, to see Algiers and its lights, to imagine the Rue Randon and its crowds, the Djamaâ Lihoud synagogue, the Place du Gouvernement, the cafés all lit up, and vendors selling special Ramadan sweets. We needed to reconnect with "normal" life, with the everyday monotony that one yearns for deeply when it is lost. We escaped by evoking memories of the past, memories of another life. El Kho and Ali told us of their youthful escapades, as if we were already old.

We also dreamed of our future. Obviously, we all imagined we would experience it together, in independent Algeria. El Kho was sailing on the waves of the Mediterranean aboard his famous yacht, provoking laughs from Ali, who teased that he would end up at the bottom of the sea. While talking, we scanned the surrounding terraces and alleys, keeping watch for paratroopers, elite Zouave troops, and infantry, who roamed together in groups of ten or twelve, machine guns in hand, cartridge belts slung over the shoulder.

Around midnight, Hassiba and I went to bed, leaving the brothers to continue their vigil. It was broad daylight when a volley of loud pounding on the front door woke me. We scarcely had time to leap out of bed and dress before El Kho burst through into our room, asking us to go immediately to the Impasse Lavoisier, where Dahmane was in an awful state. He had been picked up the night before in a sweep and horribly tortured but had miraculously escaped. He needed help and Hassiba, who had taken first-aid courses, might be able to patch him up while awaiting better treatment. I would serve as the scout to avoid patrols. It was Auntie Zaghla who ushered us toward the room where Dahmane lay. He was naked, visibly burned, and spread full length in the wide four-poster bed. We recoiled.

Dahmane moaned, "My sisters, oh my sisters, they burned my whole body. Look! Come see. Please help me." Shamefully, I admit today that his large body lying spread-eagled, his head buried between in two pillows in the majestic bed lined with pale pink satin, formed a comical picture; such was my shock and Hassiba's that nervous guffaws spontaneously spilled from our lips. Dahmane continued to moan and called to us, "My sisters, come, help me! Why are you laughing?"

We passed from awkward laughter to uncontrolled tears in the face of such cruelty imposed upon a man. I told Hassiba, "You're the nurse, you have to go try." She walked to the bed, suppressing her tears, and tried to cover Dahmane's naked body with a sheet. But he cried out, "No! Please, don't cover me. Everything burns me! Everything burns me!"

Hassiba tried to calm him and reassured him that El Kho was doing everything possible to get him treated swiftly. His poor body was entirely covered with large, bright pink patches that looked as if the skin had been torn off. His lips were swollen and his ears puffed up. Hassiba had brought some *barham*, an artisanal ointment, which she smeared on his entire body. Then she placed compresses soaked in orange flower water on his eyelids and lips. Dahmane was moaning in pain, but he found the strength and courage to tell us what had happened:

"After we broke our fast yesterday, I went to Rue de la Lyre. I had just turned when a paratrooper patrol stopped me and asked me to smile, to open my mouth. I smiled and opened my mouth. Then, without explanation, they put me in handcuffs and pushed me into a vehicle where they already had four or five people. They blindfolded us and started off. The ride was short. They made us get out, beat us violently with their clubs, and took our IDs. They put me in a room and left me there waiting for what seemed like an interminably long time. I was afraid, my teeth chattered, and I kept telling myself that I had to be worthy of Ali la Pointe, to be brave just like him. I kept telling myself that neither he nor El Kho nor Ramel knew that I was in their hands. I had to resist and never betray them, no matter what might happen to me. Then a very loud voice cried out, 'Come on, you bastard, let's go!' They grabbed me, made me climb some stairs, and then made me walk and walk. I heard a door close and realized we were in a room. I was still blindfolded. They ordered me to strip naked, and then they made me sit on a chair and took off my blindfold. They started slapping me violently while showing me a man's picture. I recognized him right away. He was a merchant, a butcher—my contact. His store was one of our drop points. I had dropped him a letter just before we broke the fast. When I denied knowing him, they began to beat me like maniacs. The more they hit me, the more I repeated to myself: 'You cannot betray Ali la Pointe. You have to be worthy of his trust. He does not even know you were arrested. He is counting on you.' And them screaming and beating like crazy, repeating that, under interrogation, the butcher had formally identified me as the man with the gold teeth. During questioning, the butcher had stated that the mail was dropped at his place by a man with all his upper teeth in gold. But I, I denied it again and again." Dahmane had been subjected to electric shock torture for hours, on all parts of his body, from head to toe—on his chest, on his genitals, on his face, on his ears, on his lips, everywhere.

"I kept screaming, but they continued. The worst was when they put the cloth in my mouth and my cries stayed stuck in my chest and throat and choked me. I couldn't hear anything, didn't know anymore who I was. When they stopped, it was only to scream in my face, 'Where is Ali la Pointe? Where is Yacef? Where is Ramel? You'll die slowly, you son of a bitch! We'll make you spit out everything you've got!' Anyway, even if I had wanted to talk, I wouldn't have been able to, since I could not feel my tongue, my lips, or my uselessly hoarse throat. A single sentence kept turning around in my head: 'He doesn't know, they don't know. I can't betray them!' Then they started up again even harder, all over my body, everywhere. I was nothing but pain and suffering. I didn't even know who I was. Then finally they stopped, exhausted from torturing. They tied my arms to the back of the chair and left me naked, promising to slash up my body and rub salt in the wounds. 'Then we'll see how you wriggle, how you'll beg us to listen to you, you bastard! We'll have the last laugh!' And they left.

"After a while, I began to notice my surroundings. I was in a small room, tied to a chair, my body on fire from the pain, my throat tormented by burning thirst. I shuffled over to face the door, which let in a ray of light. I began to moan, 'Water! Water!' A young soldier's head appeared in the opening and looked at me. I begged him with my eyes and moaned again, 'Water! Water!' The head disappeared. A bit later, the young soldier returned and, his gun still clutched firmly in his other hand, extended a canteen of water to me. I looked back at him, pleading. He set the canteen down and untied the ropes securing my arms to the back of the chair and binding my wrists. Then he stepped out, leaving the door ajar. Oh, my sisters, what a relief! Even if my whole body was screaming in pain. I drank every last drop of water and began the most agonizing wait of my life. They had promised to come back and slash my body with a knife and rub salt in my wounds. Having heard that, how could I stay under control? How could I keep from betraying my comrades? With all my soul, I begged God to take pity on me and give me the strength to resist and not betray them. I turned all this over for a long time but found only silence and anguish. At least the monsters still hadn't returned. Then God took pity on me, because he gave me the strength and courage to stand up, move toward the door, push it halfway open, stretch my head out, and look: straight ahead, far away, was a light. Squinting into the darkness, I realized that my torture chamber opened onto an immense, long room at the end of which was a doorway—the source of the light. Everything was silent. I worked up my courage, opened the door wider, and took a step forward. My eyes adapted to the darkness, and to my surprise, I stood in a wide corridor separating two rows of beds. I was in a military dormitory where French soldiers were sleeping, one to a bed, each with his gun against the wall near the headboard, a clip loaded.

"Supported by some divine force, I advanced silently toward the light coming through the partially open door. There, I found the proof that God had heard my prayers, since I realized I was inside the Ketchaoua Mosque, which I know well. I knew Massu had requisitioned the building. Every day while passing by, I had seen sentries posted on either side of its imposing door. And now I was just beside that same door, from the inside. I was just getting ready to open the door and run like mad to escape the sentries when my eye caught sight of the machine gun propped against the wall at the head of the last bed, where a soldier was sleeping. I approached slowly, grabbed the weapon, and headed as fast as I could for the exit. I don't know how, but a burst of shots rang out—from me, who had never handled a gun in his life. Then I ran. Ran like a naked fool, with my machine gun. I ran across the Djamaâ Lihoud market. I could hear the paratroopers' shouts and their bootsteps on my heels. To escape them, I threw myself under a stall with a big wicker basket. I hid inside the basket, under a bunch of empty burlap sacks I found stowed under the stall. I stayed there, suffering like a martyr from my posture and the wicker spikes poking my already raw, burned body. The paratroopers sprinted across the market, barking their orders and insults, then continued to the top of the Casbah."

Dahmane was crying as he spoke. He was still in shock, stunned to have discovered the capacity for infinite cruelty that his fellow men could exhibit against him. He expressed total and complete astonishment—not just mental, but physical. As recounted his story, he repeated a phrase like some sort of mantra: "I don't understand how you can treat a man like this. Even the infidels shouldn't be able to treat a man like that. The paratroopers aren't men, they are demons."

Crying along with him, I told him that torture had been invented by humans. Massu and his paratroopers had elevated it to the level of an industrial system in order to destroy us, individually and collectively, and to enslave us. I added that Massu had failed in his case because he, Dahmane, had resisted. He was a hero. But Dahmane was suffering and needed to talk. He spoke with a shattered voice, sobbing while blotting his eyes with a tissue to prevent the heavy tears from running down his burned face. Hassiba made him drink something, comforted him, and told him how proud we all were of him. But he didn't seem to be listening to us, for he resumed his story right where he had stopped:

"As soon as I was sure that the paratroopers were gone, I pulled myself out of the basket and resumed my wild escape. I was in an alley, facing a closed door that I began to pound with all my strength, begging someone to come to my rescue. A man opened the door. I threw myself into his arms and clung to him with all the energy I had left as he tried to extricate himself, not understanding what was happening. But I clung to him, crying and begging him not to throw me out because I had a pack of paratroopers on my heels. I was naked, mad with fear and pain. Then I heard a woman's voice urging the man to lead me to a room off the patio. There I was given a glass of water and a *gandoura* robe. The woman brought a pot of *barham* salve, which the man spread over my whole body. I fell asleep, the machine gun still in my arms, and didn't wake until daybreak. My hosts wrapped me in a white *burnous* cloak, wrapped my head in a *chèche* of the same color, and wished me good luck. I didn't know them and didn't know how to thank them. They saved my life. I pray to God to preserve them from all evil, especially from Massu and his paratroopers. As I left, I realized I was just steps from Ramel and his wife Houria's safe house at 7 Rue Porte Neuve. I headed there. When I reached the door, I clung to it and began drumming away incessantly. But the door stayed closed. Fearing that a patrol might suddenly appear, I started hitting the door with the butt of the gun, shouting in French, 'Open up! Police!' Houria opened the door. I threw myself into her arms and held onto her, but she pushed me back violently, shouting without listening to me, 'Who are you?! Have you no shame?!' Houria only recognized me once I lowered the cloak's hood and unwrapped the *chèche* from my head. She then started lecturing me, thinking that I had been playing a prank. But she quickly noticed the burns and wounds stamped upon my body by the torturers, and then she understood why I had clung to her, sobbing. She closed the door, supported me at arm's length, and brought me into a room.

"Thinking, just like Houria had, that it was paratroopers when they heard me knocking, Ramel had taken refuge in the shelter while his wife had tried to hide all evidence of his existence in the house. He was, after all, a wanted man. Houria put me on a mattress and went to find her husband. He came to me and began to comfort and console me. I told him the main points of what had happened to me, assured him that I hadn't been followed, and asked him to warn El Kho and Ali la Pointe. But I was in agony; my whole body felt aflame like a bright torch, and I begged Ramel to do something to soothe my pain. He consoled me, congratulated me, and thanked me for saving the entire organization through my sacrifice and courage, he said, because neither he nor El Kho nor Ali had suspected that I had been arrested. Ramel repeated that what had happened was a real miracle—made possible by courage and faith in the FLN. He let me rest, giving him time to inform El Kho and find me another refuge where I could be treated. That's how I ended up here a few hours later."

Hassiba and I cried as we listened to him, not even trying to hide it. She put another layer of *barham* on his body, all of which was skinned raw, and replenished the orange-flower-water compresses on his eyelids and lips.

Our traditional ointment finally tamed Dahmane's physical trauma. But our poor brother was not out of the woods yet; he would have to pull out all his gold teeth before we could get him false papers and send him to the *maquis*. With no dentists among our ranks nor among our supporters, Dahmane again demonstrated unparalleled courage and endurance by accepting a raw extraction by hand. As soon as his jaw healed, he got his false papers and escaped to the *maquis*, where he later died as a martyr. I will never forget Dahmane: his kindness, sincerity, generosity, and uncommon courage. Whenever I go into a museum and find myself facing a painting of a tortured Christ, the image of my brother Dahmane comes back to me: lying naked, burned from head to toe, arms outstretched like a man crucified, trembling with pain. And without fail, tears come to my eyes.

Ali la Pointe's Unparalleled Courage, and the Women's Active Solidarity

After tending to Dahmane's wounds, Hassiba and I returned to *Dar Essdjour,* where El Kho and Ali had already gathered our few belongings and cleaned our rooms to remove any sign that might betray our passage. A little boy living in the house came to tell us that a squad of paratroopers was heading toward the area. *Dar Essdjour* was a low two-story house with rooms all facing onto the central patio. The boy had hardly finished telling us when the house was shaken by a salvo of violent knocks at the front door. We were sitting ducks. We all gathered in a room with a skylight no bigger than two feet across that led to the adjoining terrace. Ali ordered us to remove the mattresses from the room, push the table against the wall, and to place the chair on top of it. We would have to escape through the window, since all other exits were blocked. While monitoring the progress of the paratroopers, who had just overrun the patio, Ali jumped onto the table and gave El Kho a leg up. After clambering onto Ali's shoulders, he managed to climb up and grip the window sill and from there jumped out, landing on the terrace.

Meanwhile, from behind the curtain that separated our room from the patio, I monitored the paratroopers. They were still clustered together in the courtyard, waiting for some unknown signal. Ali, still on the table, squatted and ordered Hassiba to climb onto his shoulders. He stood, El Kho grabbed Hassiba by the arms, and they hoisted and hauled her onto the terrace. Still surveilling the paratroopers, I warned Ali that they had started moving toward us. He jumped down from the table, calmly took up his gun, came to stand behind the curtain, and motioned for me to climb on the table and chair and get ready to slip through the skylight. He watched the paratroopers, who were now on the upper gallery, making their way toward our room in a group. Ali didn't move. I watched him. He was standing still. His machine gun, with the safety off, was pointed out at the gallery. His face was serene and his whole being radiated calm, assurance, and self-control. With his arms stretched out toward me, El Kho couldn't follow the scene unfolding below and kept waving at me to grab his hands. But I didn't move; I couldn't take my eyes off Ali. I waited motionless, like him. Suddenly, he pushed back the curtain with the barrel of the machine gun, took a step forward until his body filled the entrance and, without moving, showered the paratroopers before him with bullets.

Not one of them could strike back or fire a shot. Ali walked forward calmly, his back straight, his machine gun spitting intense fire, met by the paratroopers' screams of terror. He returned, jumped onto the table, and grabbed me like a bale of hay. I'll never know how I ended up rolling along the terrace as Ali's athletic chest emerged from the skylight. El Kho collected us, all the while shouting, "Watch out! Don't stand up! The paratroopers are all over the terraces!"

But we had to leave this rooftop. Ali had already fired several bursts through the skylight into the room we had just escaped, which the remaining paratroopers were attempting to enter. Other soldiers would soon surround us and attack from the neighboring terraces, so we had to act very quickly. Hassiba and I were responsible for the large briefcases stuffed with documents.

As soon as we all ran across the terrace, machine gun bursts rang out. We threw ourselves flat, on orders from Ali, who then leapt up and began sweeping the neighboring terraces with bursts from his gun, while yelling at us to jump to the next rooftop. El Kho disappeared with Hassiba, whose baggy *seroual* pants had been riddled with bullets that miraculously had not actually touched her. Ali and I jumped and found ourselves surrounded by dozens of women. They were everywhere, on all the terraces. They trilled out their *you-you-yous* and guided us: "Over here! Watch out, they're up ahead!" or "They're on the left, go right!" They protected us, too, by forming a barrier with their bodies. The paratroopers were looking for us but saw only the women, gesticulating wildly and wailing out their *you-yous*. Oh! The *you-yous*. The *you-yous* that galvanized us as much as they frightened and destabilized the paratroopers—especially the draftees. After we had crossed a few terraces, I found myself alone with Ali, who pushed me toward a doorway that led down some stairs and into a courtyard.

We stopped to catch our breath. We were drenched. Strangers' hands extended to us with cups of water, urging us to drink, though we were fasting. They insisted, "You are *moudjahidine*, you can drink, God allows you to." Others wiped the sweat that dripped from Ali's face. Still others ran up and down to signal to us where the paratroopers were. We were in an area some distance away from *Dar Essdjour*, but Ali decided that we should return to our safe house. "But they're blocking all the streets!" a woman cried. Another one told us, "We closed the door to keep them from reaching the terrace." Ali thanked them and said simply, "Let's go, sister! Let's count on God." I had no fear and felt like we were invincible. I calmly followed Ali after thanking the women, whose words followed us: *"Allah yestarkoum! Maâkoum Allah!"* (God bless you! God is with you!)

When we reached the door, Ali bent down and rolled up his pants. Then he stood, hugged his gun to his right side, looked at me, smiled, and said, "Let's go!" I pulled the latch and opened the door wide. At the crackling of Ali's machine gun, young soldiers cried out, "Mama! Mama!" Bent double, they wrapped their heads in their arms, forming a bizarre honor guard for us. We followed the street without even running, Ali carrying his gun, ready to shoot, and me with my bulging briefcase clutched tightly against my chest. Ali ordered all the pedestrians we encountered to face the wall to prevent them from staring and recognizing us. They complied. Arriving at the Impasse Lavoisier, I noticed my outfit: I had just crossed half the Casbah dressed in *seroual* pants, a traditional blouse, and no veil. My *haïk* had been left behind in our now-abandoned shelter at the *Dar Essdjour*.

Not long after, the paratroopers were on our heels once more when we were again saved by the women of the Casbah, who occupied the terraces *en masse*, wailing out their *you-yous* to disrupt the soldiers while at the same time guiding us to escape. Our group got separated in the process of escaping over the rooftops, with Ali, Si Mourad, and Hassiba going in one direction and El Kho and I in another. All the surrounding terraces were occupied by French soldiers.

Yelling to us to duck to avoid the bullets, the women on the terrace we had just jumped onto waved us toward a door that led into the house. Inside, an old woman welcomed us and quickly explained that our only chance to escape the paratroopers' onslaught was to take refuge in the *djeb*—the family's water cistern—where she led us, urging us to hurry. A long ladder had already been lowered into the *djeb* by two young ladies who stood nearby, stabilizing it against the stone walls. They helped me down. When I reached the last bar of the ladder, I felt around with my foot for the cistern's bottom, but El Kho was descending fast and I had to release the ladder. I let go. I could stand, but the water came up to my shoulders. I warned El Kho and, before sliding into the water, he handed me the gun, the clips, and a pistol so we could keep them dry. Then the women hauled up the ladder and slid back the marble slab that covered the *djeb*, leaving us in pitch blackness. We remained submerged in the water, our arms aloft, for what seemed like an eternity. We took turns holding the guns overhead, arms extended, whispering to one another when our arms grew tired and we needed to hand them off. Each time El Kho took over, I dropped my stiff arms into the icy water and pedaled my feet to avoid hypothermia. The wait was interminable and I struggled with all my energy not to slip under the water. Finally, the marble slab slid aside and the women lowered the ladder back down to rescue us. That day, these anonymous, admirably united women saved our lives without asking anything in return.

It was in these terrible conditions, hunted ceaselessly, that we would work with Si Mourad and the other sector chiefs to reveal the truth of the French army to our people, to mainland France, and to international opinion. At the same time, Ramel was reconstructing the networks of *fidayine*, who would begin attacking the paratroopers as soon as Ramadan ended. El Kho had charged Si Mourad and Ramel with reconstructing an explosives lab. But another problem was worrying our leader: how to rebuild a network of safe houses with secure refuges.

A New Safe House on Rue Cato

Having narrowly escaped several of the paratroopers' sweeps that April, we went to seek refuge in the lower Casbah. The day was well under way. We advanced as usual in single file, with Petit Omar leading the way. Since we had to cross a good portion of the Casbah, El Kho and Ali hid themselves under *haïks* once again. We were a few days away from the Eid holiday that would mark the end of Ramadan, and despite all the misfortunes the people were suffering, no family planned to deviate from the ancestral traditions and rites. The streets were bustling. Men and women, weighed down with purchases, zigzagged to avoid children carrying trays of cakes to and from the public ovens. Ali and El Kho advanced, their eyes scanning every last corner, ignoring the men, who diverted their eyes from their unusual silhouettes.

Only the children were enjoying themselves openly. But none of us followed them, not even with our eyes. Petit Omar finally stopped at 4 Rue Cato, the last house on a lane that opened onto a square in front of the Djamaâ Lihoud synagogue, near the busiest and most popular market in the Casbah. Though smaller than the Belhaffafs', the house was just as beautiful and elegant. Late in the afternoon in those last few days of April, its multicolored ceramics, white marble, and slate sparkled with the sunlight flooding inside.

A man in his thirties, who seemed to know El Kho, came to welcome us. We followed him upstairs, where he opened a door and addressed Hassiba and me plainly: "This is your room." After so many stays in cobweb-infested hovels where all kinds of bugs stung us, crawled up our necks, and crunched under our feet, we found ourselves in a room decked out in pink and purple, scented with jasmine and dominated by a huge bed. Not a single wrinkle was visible on the bedspread. A young woman came to welcome us and offer us a bath. She opened her armoire and pulled out everything we needed for the *hammam* and two outfits (*seroual* pants and traditional blouses). Khoukha (Arabic for "peach"), who was barely eighteen, had a pretty face, big black eyes hemmed with long lashes, a fine nose, and a petite mouth. She exuded gentleness and generosity. After our bath, we slipped between the perfumed sheets, exhausted, and immediately fell dead asleep.

The next morning, Ali began constructing an undetectable shelter in case of a paratrooper raid. Assisting him was Mahmoud, the owner's nineteen-year-old nephew, who would soon become one of El Kho's liaison officers. Ali mobilized all his ingenuity and know-how as a former bricklayer to design and build a truly undetectable cache that opened onto the courtyard through a tiny portal. Before squeezing through, we had to decide which part of the body to start with. Ali, with his athletic build, naturally had the most difficulty. Once inside, we had to stay seated, our legs drawn tightly to the body. Given the shelter's configuration, how difficult it was to access, and our desire to avoid endangering or disturbing our hosts, we decided that we would take refuge there every night after dinner, apart from whoever was chosen to stand guard on the terrace.

We spent those last days of April 1957 sheltered in this home at 4 Rue Cato. The owner's store adjoined the house, under a window where El Kho sat all afternoon behind the lattice, chain-smoking and sipping coffee endlessly and watching the comings and goings of people jostling through the vegetable market. After three months of this life without respite, hounded by Massu from shelter to shelter, after the setbacks and killings and arrests, we found a semblance of stability in this safe house. El Kho took the time to reorganize our work and our networks. We had to react to the enemy's sustained propaganda campaigns and conduct a rigorous and complete census of those arrested, tortured, executed, or disappeared. Along with that, we had to catalog all the French army's systematic torture methods. Last but not least, we had to relaunch our recruitment and restructuring amid a people besieged by colonial repression and terror.

Oukhiti Overcomes

Across the street from 4 Rue Cato, the house at number 3 had just been put up for sale. Oukhiti, with whom we kept in contact, wanted to leave her father's house but didn't want to return to the Bouhireds'. Ever since that terrible raid at their house, all the members of the Bouhired family had been persecuted ceaselessly by the paratroopers. The French subjected the family home to nearly daily unannounced raids under the pretext of visiting "the house with the bomb lab" long after they had already sacked and desecrated it.

Oukhiti hoped to mourn the assassination of her husband, Uncle Mustapha, in a quieter place. She visited the house at 3 Rue Cato and liked it, especially since it was well away from the Impasse de la Granada and her parents' home. All of us were happy the day she moved in at 3 Rue Cato, where the second-floor windows faced onto those of our own safe house at a close distance, allowing us to communicate easily. Assembling our group for a meeting was as simple as crossing the narrow lane discreetly around the start or end of the curfew, or in full night.

Oukhiti also gave her accord for Ali to build a shelter in her house. Nobody besides her and our small group would know of its existence. We decided that this emergency refuge would hold the documents we needed to save, plus any other objects of importance. We built it quickly. It was spacious but unlit and difficult to access. The only way to enter was with a ladder set between the opening and the staircase below. Once inside, it was impossible to exit unless someone outside placed the ladder there.

One night when we were at Oukhiti's, around two in the morning, paratroopers flooded the area, stormed the terraces, and began to invade homes. We barely had time to slip into our shelter. Oukhiti put away the ladder and ran to open the door, which shuddered with the blows from the soldiers' machine-gun butts. We listened to their muffled sounds and waited for them to finish their search, certain that the refuge was completely undetectable.

When the house again fell silent, we began to prepare to return to the light and fresh air. In the shelter, it was so dark that we couldn't even make each other out. The total darkness and silence in which we were plunged was stifling. A deep anguish twisted my guts, suffocating me. I groped around until I found Hassiba, who gripped my hand tightly. Time seemed to stand still. Oukhiti was taking forever to come let us out. A voice reached our ears, at first muffled and hardly audible, then louder, clearly addressing us: "Hey you all! Come out! Where are you? The paratroopers took Fatiha."

The voice was Uncle Lâarbi's.

Once we had clambered down, he he filled us in: After searching the house meticulously, the paratroopers had hauled off poor Oukhiti! By buying this little house, she had hoped to keep her children safe from the brutal aggression of Massu and his henchmen, but they had evidently found it curious to see her leave the Impasse de la Granada and settle into a new house, so they came to surprise her in the night. Uncle Lâarbi urged us to leave, repeating: "They'll certainly torture her, and as you know, the torture victim is in God's hands. How long will she hold out? Nobody knows. So go!"

To allay his fears, we decided to leave—but just across the street to 4 Rue Cato, which Oukhiti knew too. We spent the rest of the night keeping watch from the rooftop terrace, scrutinizing every unusual noise. The day dawned with neither Oukhiti nor the paratroopers reappearing. Soon the market in front of the house was invaded by a boisterous crowd. Hassiba and I watched daily life proceed as normal from behind the latticed window facing the window of Oukhiti's house. Around eleven o'clock, a silhouette appeared behind the window facing us, and our sister's muffled voice brought us back to life. It was Oukhiti. She asked us to join her later, when she gave us a signal. But our patience was exhausted. In a rush to see her and reassure ourselves that she was all right, we went straight to her house.

She was sitting on the couch, hands flat on her knees, head down, absorbed in her thoughts. She looked up at the sound of the door closing. She was unrecognizable, with huge dark circles around her eyes and her face stained a dirty ash grey. Her hair, usually a beautiful jet black, hung from her head in clumps, as if it had been lathered with soap and then poorly rinsed.

"Those dogs, they tortured you!" we cried out, before surrounding her and smothering her in our arms, desperately showering her with kisses and affection. Oukhiti didn't speak, didn't cry. She just sat there, hands flat on her thighs, looking down, as if she needed some time to restore herself and all those around her. We pressed around her, holding her hands to communicate our sisterly warmth, to communicate our solidarity with her body and soul—both of them abused and tortured. Leïla, her youngest daughter, just three years old, came in in tears, calling for her mother. She came to nestle against Oukhiti, who laid her hand on her head, quickly resuming her motherly role and comforting her. Oukhiti rocked back and forth and simply said, "Tell El Kho that their Captain Chabannes proposed that I collaborate with them. He asked me to provide information, especially on you two girls. Tell him that I eventually accepted so that they would release me."

We stayed a little longer with her, then went to update El Kho. He instructed us to go back to Oukhiti, reassure her, and inform her that he and Ali would visit the next day after the curfew. He added, to our great disappointment, "Go tell her and then come back. We must let her rest among her children and her family."

The next day, around one in the morning, Oukhiti opened the door and El Kho, Ali, Hassiba, and I dove inside. Her five children were sleeping with their grandmother, Yemma. Oukhiti seemed to have overcome the ordeal, helped by a good bath and a night's sleep with her children. Indomitable, she sat straight, like a reed after the storm.

Although the torture's traces were clearly visible on her face and arms, she didn't want to discuss her ordeal. She barely alluded to it, announcing that she would prepare a *ouaâda*—a meal offered to friends and family to celebrate important occasions—at noon the next day to thank God for letting her live for her children's sake. She invited us to stay and share this meal with the family. At midday, Oukhiti's brothers took a wide wooden bowl heaped with couscous, garnished with meat, chickpeas, and vegetable sauce, to the shrine of Sidi Abderrahmane as an offering and charity, as is the custom for such celebrations. That day, our meal was a lighthearted one.

We were enjoying our coffee after lunch when El Kho addressed Oukhiti: "You were right to accept Captain Chabannes's deal. This way, we'll have a refuge under the French army's protection. But you should ask him to issue you a written directive safeguarding you from raids from the other security forces."

Seeing an opening for some fun, Ali added, "Why don't you do it now? They love our food. Bring him his portion of the *ouaâda*—it will make his knees buckle!"

No sooner was it said than it was done. We prepared a large plate filled with meat and vegetables. Djamel, Oukhiti's eleven-year-old little brother, accompanied her all the way to Captain Chabannes's command post, carrying the platter in a basket. Oukhiti was received with open arms and her couscous proved a great hit. She returned carrying a document declaring the house and its occupants safe from sudden raids, thereby rendering our refuge inviolable. This way, we managed to continue our work for several months under the captain's protection—all without his knowledge and at his expense.

The Massacre on Vauban Way

Meanwhile, the French regime continued its policy of total war. Every month the guillotine was paraded from Constantine to Oran, passing through Algiers en route. At each stop, brothers were executed over two days. Every month, the French regime took the heads of twenty-seven brothers in the most macabre way. And as if the orgy of crimes and repression wasn't enough, the colonial regime worked to outdo itself with daily propaganda proclaiming the FLN's imminent demise and calling on the people to throw themselves into the arms of their persecutors.

El Kho decided to retaliate. We drafted a leaflet announcing our intention to counter the executions of our brothers with bombs targeting the European population and inundated Algiers with them. On May 1, the day of the *Eid* celebrating the end of Ramadan, we launched a successful armed attack against the Fifth Arrondissement police station, located on Boulevard Bru. The following days saw attacks targeting the paratroopers and other French armed services, all of them successful. Our people heard the message loud and clear: contrary to the propaganda the French was hammering frantically and continuously, our organization was not destroyed. Our people found their confidence and hope again. Best of all, the press didn't even hide the anxiety of the political and military leaders. The French forces of repression, of course, responded with their customary brutality. The massacre on Vauban Way constituted just one of the many cruel examples.

Our *fidayine* carried out an attack on May 17 against a barracks on Vauban Way, where a detachment of the First Paratrooper Regiment was stationed. Two of the three guards were killed; the third one, though wounded, managed to escape and raise the alarm. Another detachment of the same regiment, a "local unit"—that is to say, a unit comprised entirely of *pieds-noirs* civilians—retaliated by rushing to a nearby *hammam*, which at that time of night lodged poor travelers from different parts of the country and the homeless. Under their *pied-noir* commander, the paratroopers forced out all the bath's occupants, lined them up against the wall and machine-gunned them at point-blank range. It was a massacre justified by "collective responsibility." Dozens of men, all civilians, fell atop one another in a pile.

Later, trucks arrived: the dead would disappear forever, and some of the injured would be transported to the hospital. Among our people, the Vauban Way massacre stirred the same anger, the same feeling of revolt, the same demand for a response, as the one that followed the bombing at Rue de Thèbes in 1956. Our people didn't understand why, when the FLN/ALN targeted the occupying army, the latter massacred indigenous civilians. They demanded that the European "innocent civilian population" be plunged into anguish and death—especially since the colonial regime didn't initiate even a semblance of judicial procedure against those responsible for the massacre.

And so the brothers took things into their own hands. On June 3, 1957, three bombs placed in lampposts exploded near the Grande Poste, at the Place Lagha, and near the Maurétania, doing considerable damage. Six days later, late in the afternoon of June 9, a bomb exploded at the Casino de la Corniche, one of the most famous cabarets, causing many casualties.

We didn't have to wait long for the reaction. Starting on June 11, the day of the Casino attack victims' funeral, Algiers would experience some of its darkest days. Dozens of "natives" were lynched and shot. In Bab El Oued, Algerian butchers were even impaled on meat hooks in front of their shops. Massu flooded Algiers with several thousand more paratroopers and, with the help of the *ultras* groups and territorial guards, restored things to his liking by strengthening the devastating vise last seen back in January and February.

As for us, while we were pleased to see our activists' resilience, courage, and willingness to continue fighting no matter the price, we were deeply worried. Through their endless brutal sweeps of the Casbah, the paratroopers had seized hundreds of bombs and almost all our supplies. What's more, Massu had managed to trace our supply chain for explosive materials and squeeze it dry. The central problem worrying the brothers that month was how to rebuild our plastic explosives stock, since we only had a very limited number of bombs left. But we had made a commitment to our people to respond to every capital execution of a brother with bomb attacks in the European city. We had distributed leaflets saying as much over and over in Algiers, so that nobody could miss it—especially not the French civil and military authorities.

Meeting Germaine Tillion

One evening in mid-June, after dinner and the cumbersome process of settling into our shelter for the night, El Kho informed us that a former French resistance fighter close to General de Gaulle was in Algiers and wanted to meet us. She was accompanying a mission of the International Commission on Concentration Camp Practices (ICCCP), which had come to investigate the detention conditions of FLN/ALN prisoners in the French prisons and camps. Her name, he told us, was Germaine Tillion. Her name echoed in my head, taking me back to my college years with Samia and Mimi—a previous life. We had talked together about Germaine Tillion. As Mimi had recounted to us, while researching her anthropology thesis, Tillion had lived for several years in Algeria's Aurès Mountains to study the social organization and customs of our Chaoui peoples. We especially admired her courage for resisting the Nazi occupation, a commitment that had landed her first into prison and then into the Ravensbrück concentration camp, from which she had been liberated in 1945.

Our point of contention with Mimi had been the "social centers" and the "appeal for a civil truce" initiated by Camus and supported by Tillion, who had come to Algiers in early 1956 to attend the public conference organized to explain the appeal's scope and meaning. I have already recounted our falling-out with Mimi over Camus's initiative. It was then, while trying to convince us of the initiative's merits, that our friend told us of Tillion's "centers." Speaking to Governor-General Jacques Soustelle, Tillion had proposed establishing centers to combat the extreme misery in which the overwhelming majority of the "natives" lived. These centers would provide them with medical care in clinics, literacy courses, and vocational training, as well as assistance with the onerous paperwork requirements of the French bureaucracy. Mimi had praised the centers' objectives and benefits for our people and the sincerity of their initiator, a signatory to the "appeal for a civil truce." Samia and I had nothing against such initiatives, but had wanted to show how futile they were in the face of the ocean of misery our people lived in, dispossessed and impoverished as they were by the colonial system. We even jokingly asked Mimi if the Governor-General was ready to build a million social centers to dry up this ocean.

In truth, we had never really tried to understand these "social centers," convinced that the deep and absolute poverty in which our people were held went hand in hand with the system of settler colonialism. Mimi had retorted that this was not a reason to refuse the help of people of goodwill while awaiting the "hypothetical liberation" of our country. We responded to our friend, "When Madame Tillion joined the resistance against German occupation in 1940, the liberation of France was just as hypothetical, since the Nazis had decided to stay a thousand years! Fortunately, the Americans and Churchill didn't abandon France!"

Little more than a year after that debate with our beloved Mimi abruptly ended our friendship, I sat in our refuge at 4 Rue Cato thinking of her, transported back by the mention of this famous ethnologist, resistance fighter, and prisoner. I wished I could tell her that she had been right to welcome the "help of people of good will." We seriously needed it in order to reach—and why not?—a truce that would allow us to reorganize our explosives supply chain. What's more, I imagined that someone like Tillion—a former freedom fighter who resisted the foreign occupation of her own country and suffered for it in a concentration camp—would be nothing if not understanding. I thought about all this while El Kho emphasized the great esteem in which academic, literary, and political personalities held her—including General de Gaulle, to whose family she was close. Hassiba asked El Kho how we had established contact with her. He explained that one of our activists who wasn't yet wanted by the police had been approached by mutual friends.

Later I would meet this brother, Ali Bouzourène, who is still alive today but very ill. I visited him recently and asked him to recount this episode of his life, which he did plainly and generously. Ali Bouzourène had managed to leave the Casbah after the Eight-Day Strike to escape the French soldiers who had invaded the old city and begun the "netting fish" operation so dear to Massu, and took refuge for three months with his family outside Algiers. He had returned to the *medina* in early May and reestablished contact with FLN activists and friends, including Hadj Smaïn, deputy judge at the court of Algiers, and his relative Fatima Hamdiken, both of whom were above all suspicion. Smaïn adjudicated in the system's highest court, handling litigation over marriage, divorce, and all questions tied to inheritance among the "natives." Hamdiken was university educated and a close collaborator of Germaine Tillion. The FLN tasked these two with persuading Bouzourène to testify before the ICCCP commission that Germaine Tillion was accompanying to help with their investigative work. They encouraged him to present the most accurate information possible, neglecting neither full names nor dates nor addresses, to allow the commission members to verify his statements.

Fifty-six years later, he confided to me: "I informed brother Yacef [El Kho] of my meetings with the ICCCP commission and suggested that he meet Germaine Tillion. I thought that way he might be able to sketch for her a more complete picture and tell her about events that I hadn't experienced. He heard me out and promised to think about it. Hadj Smaïn and Fatima concurred with my idea and agreed to convince her. I met El Kho several times and explained that these two activists vouched for Germaine Tillion's intellectual honesty, moral rectitude, and great personal virtues. I reiterated her past as a resistance fighter and that she was ready to meet him. I guess El Kho probably conducted his own investigation; one day he called me to give his consent. I had *carte blanche* to organize the meeting"

As soon as El Kho gave the green light, Hadj Smaïn and Fatima Hamdiken informed Madame Tillion. That afternoon around four o'clock, she arrived with Ali Bouzourène at 3 Rue Cato. He had taken precautions to ensure that they had not been trailed. I remember well this lady of a certain age, medium height, with black hair, soberly dressed and wearing eyeglasses. When she greeted us, her face was impassive. Her eyes scanned each of us in turn. Ali la Pointe had a very serious look, as if he were sulking. El Kho, his face split by a wide smile that creased his eyes, looked relaxed and confident. Hassiba, as usual, was distant and reserved, and stared straight into Germaine Tillion's eyes. As for me, I was both curious and delighted to meet a French Resistance fighter in the flesh for the first time.

Germaine Tillion sat facing El Kho and Ali, who laid their guns on the bench behind them. Hassiba and I took seats flanking them. Oukhiti, always lively and considerate, didn't let a silence settle. With her natural charm, she welcomed our guest and asked if the journey through the Casbah's alleyways had not tired her out too much, especially with the heat. Oukhiti spoke an improvised French, meaning that whenever she didn't know a word in French she would just put a French-sounding twist on the Arabic word. Madame Tillion thanked her, smiling, while Hassiba and I struggled to maintain straight faces at the sound of Oukhiti's French, especially when our eyes met Ali's. She left the room to fetch cold drinks, tea, and pastries she had spent all morning preparing. We made small talk for a while. Then, after a short silence, Madame Tillion looked at El Kho and Ali and asked them, "So, you were wishing to meet me?"

Ever smiling and fussing with his thumbnail, El Kho looked at her and said in a playful tone: "Oh yeah? I thought it was you, as a member of the ICCCP, who had been wishing to meet us to get more information."

Our guest looked at him again, no doubt beginning to identify with whom she was speaking. After another short silence, she said, "Let's just say that each of us needs to see more clearly and to examine all the facts together."

Since El Kho had encouraged us to participate in the discussion, I couldn't help but ask, "What facts are you speaking of? The war against the occupier? You know it, having lived it yourself."

El Kho explained everything that the people of the Casbah and the other "native" areas had suffered for months—the serious and multiple violations of their most basic rights. Encouraged by El Kho, we gave as much detail and information as possible on the many abuses of the French police and army, as well as the *ultras* organizations. We emphasized that the situation had worsened since General Massu and his paratroopers had been entrusted with full powers to break the general strike ahead of the UN General Assembly debate on "the Algerian question." Young and perhaps naive, we spoke by first addressing the resistance fighter who had struggled against a foreign occupation of her own country, and second, the supposedly impartial person come to investigate the conditions of Algerians in the detention camps.

Was it because she was French that she couldn't bear to hear us compare an Algeria occupied by her people to France occupied by the Germans? Was it because she had herself been a resistance fighter that she couldn't stand to hear us compare the French army's atrocities in Algeria designed to break the resistance to those of the German army in France? She interrupted us in a dry, powerful voice: "You are killers, too!"

The silence fell abruptly, intensifying in my brain the echo of those words she had just thrown into our faces, multiplying the terrible injustice and unbearable asymmetry between colonized and colonizer, between national liberation fighters and an army of colonial occupation, between the right to freedom and dignity and the denial of these same rights. In my eyes her words betrayed her bias and her determination to defend France and its regime, even in the face of her fellow resistance fighters.

I retorted, with no trace of a smile: "Killers? Yes, just like you yourself were during the German occupation of your country!"

I resented her for having destroyed my last illusions about some Europeans' humanity. I resented her for confirming for me with a simple, clear, and unambiguous phrase that which I had repressed because I need to believe in the human race. Because I already knew, at twenty-two years old, that one could resist occupation in France and then commit massacres to continue occupying Algeria. I especially resented her for telling me so clearly the only truth that is worth knowing: whatever the reasons, historical or otherwise, in the eyes of the French we would never be full humans. Then, with emotion, passion, and violence, I let fly at her all that I had crammed into my young brain.

Suddenly, El Kho cut me off with a look I knew was an order to keep quiet, while Madame Tillion patted my arm and said, "Shush, now, you're still a child!"

Despite El Kho's fierce eyes, I replied: "And paternalistic, to boot!"

That day, I finally understood that someone who had resisted German occupation was not necessarily an anti-colonialist. Fortunately, El Kho was calmer, and continued to explain to Germaine Tillion that as a people attacked on their own land and occupied by another people and its army, it was our right and duty to fight to liberate ourselves. Then he explained how the FLN had been obliged to use bombs in the European city. Citing the many examples, he showed her that our violence was the answer to the original violence—which continued in many forms—employed by the police, the army, and the *ultras* against the entire indigenous population "without distinguishing between innocent civilians and the killers, to use your term."

Germaine Tillion asked: "And what must we do to stop this infernal cycle of violence?"

A long silence greeted her question. I looked at El Kho. He was jubilant, and his eyes flashed me an imperceptible message asking me not to say anything. He let the silence thicken and grow heavy before speaking, slowly, as if thinking aloud.

"You know, whatever you may think of them, our activists and our people are determined to fight to the bitter end despite the suffering they have endured and that which is yet to come. The French army has felt our men's courage and continues to want to debase them. I don't know if you have followed what's happened in Algiers since the beginning of the war of liberation. It was the day when France decided to guillotine our fighters that the FLN and ALN decided to escalate the fight. Denying us dignity, even in death, is the ultimate provocation. We want to face death. We want to die standing up, not cut in two!"

Germaine Tillion listened to him, her face serious. She had probably never viewed execution by guillotine from the angle El Kho described: as the supreme human debasement. Then she said: "Would you be willing to stop using bombs against the civilian population if we put an end to the executions?"

El Kho consulted us with a glance, then seemed to sink into a deep reflection. Ali fiddled with a button on his shirt. Hassiba, her hands resting daintily on her knees, looked back and forth between El Kho and Madame Tillion. As for me, I was admiring El Kho's new skills as a negotiator and praying for this to work, since we had almost no plastic explosives left to continue honoring our promise to our people.

Finally, El Kho asked, "What guarantees would I have that the French government would honor this pledge?"

Germaine Tillion, in response, stated that her visit to the Casbah was a personal initiative. She reminded us that she was in Algeria because the

French government had selected her to accompany the "foreign" members of the ICCCP.

"Precisely," replied El Kho, giving me a look to tell me to join back in. "Your proximity to some members of the Government allows you to testify to the nature of the Algerian struggle and to explain that we are not bloodthirsty, but rather fighters put in a situation that hardly leaves us any choice of means."

Germaine Tillion listened, unblinking, but with full attention. Her look shifted from one to another; perhaps she was trying to perceive what each of us thought of such a proposition? Another silence.

Then I ventured, "You know, Madame, nothing other than the colonial regime and its violence and unspeakable injustices led us to the situation where we are today. I know it is difficult to 'humanize' war, but I actually think that if the French government stopped inflicting the indignity of death by guillotine on our fighters, our entire population would support the initiative you are offering: to stop bombing the European city in exchange for an end to executions by guillotine. However, and excuse me for repeating it, we were forced by your side, by its system and its methods, to go to these ends."

I spoke slowly, trying to tame the tremor in my voice and the sobs that threatened to crush my windpipe. I didn't want to cry, but the tears began to flow nonetheless. My eyes met El Kho's. Like me, he seemed to be praying for this to work since, as our leader, he certainly knew better than me just how exhausted was our capacity to fight back.

After a long silence, Germaine Tillion simply said, "I promise to faithfully report what I have seen and heard. Yes, if we can, as you say, 'humanize' this confrontation, then all of us will perhaps have contributed to mitigating the hatred that is in the process of overwhelming our peoples."

Madame Tillion's expression "our peoples" led me to conclude that she was fundamentally honest and loyal, since she recognized the fact that we were two populations in confrontation. Her honesty and loyalty would not prevent her, however, from believing that Algeria should remain under France's thumb. Nor did she shy away from showing us that she shared neither our ideas nor our struggle, much less our means of carrying out that struggle. We were on equal terms when it came to loyalty and honesty, since we didn't shy away from clearly explaining to her our ideas and our ultimate goal: the independence of Algeria, whatever the price.

Next, we passed to the practical questions: How would we keep in contact, given the need for strict secrecy? It was decided that brother Ali

Bouzourène would send her a sealed letter, without knowing its content, and the name and address where she could reply. On the spot, we agreed on a code and nicknames to designate certain people, including those to whom she intended to send detailed minutes of our exchanges. The time had come for our guest to take her leave; Ali Bouzourène was waiting for her in the entry hall. She let her gaze wander over each of us—as if to engrave our faces into her mind. Was it because she knew we were condemned to arrest or death? I do not remember her wishing us good luck. Oukhiti accompanied her to the door, then returned a few minutes later to the room where we were still sitting silently, each in his place. Germaine Tillion had asked her why, she recounted, after all the misfortunes that had befallen her, when she was still responsible for five young orphans, why did she continue to assist the FLN? Oukhiti had answered simply and clearly: "I'm fighting, and I will keep fighting, to liberate my country from foreign occupation." And with that, Madame Tillion left with clear and simple messages to deliver to the powerbrokers in France.

El Kho exulted, "We are going to enter into negotiations with the French government. This will be a de facto recognition of the FLN, all thanks to our struggle!"

A few days later, she kept her word. She let us know by a coded letter that our proposal seemed to have been welcomed favorably! Subsequently, she informed us that she had also faithfully reported the content of our meeting to General de Gaulle. Each time we received a letter, we sent a confirmation and then responded by renewing, solemnly, the terms of our accord and the absolute necessity to inform "our parents in Tunis."

Then Germaine Tillion announced her next visit. It hit us like a cold shower! She had come to announce the French government's refusal to order a stay of execution for our brothers on death row. She was still in Algiers when three brothers were executed at the Barberousse Prison on July 25, 1957.

They Had Their Marianne, We Had Our Djamila

Since the start of the French occupation and especially between 1881 and 1944, Algeria had been subjected to an exceptional judicial framework. The Indigenous Law subjected those it called "natives" to disciplinary prison sentences set by the administrators of mixed "Algerian-European" communes. This amounted to a sort of repression, since there were some offenses that only "natives" could commit, such as "daring to look in the eyes of Monsieur the Prefect." The "natives" were not brought before the standard circuit court, but instead before a court composed of a judge and two assessors who applied the procedure of *flagrante delicto*, eliminating the need for an independent judicial investigation.[4] Furthermore, before being presented to these courts, the "natives" were naturally subjected to "questioning," as the Commission of Inquiry on Torture established in January 1956 by François Mitterrand, then Minister of the Interior, reported under pressure from a wing of the mainland French press: *l'Humanité*, *l'Express*, *Témoignage Chrétien*, and *France-Observateur*. This commission's report stated, "During their interrogations all police, gendarmes, judicial police, and intelligence police services use, more or less: beatings, the bathtub, the water hose, and electricity." The same report noted what the police had told the commission: "These methods, like basic blows, would not be particularly effective in countries where individuals have an extraordinary resistance to all kinds of hardships."

Also, to reduce resistance from the "natives," the French National Assembly adopted new judicial provisions—proposed by the leftist government of Guy Mollet. Algeria, the favorite testing ground for exceptional legal frameworks, would see the application, starting in 1956, of the infamous "special powers" enabling the executive to govern by "decree laws" signed by the Council President, Guy Mollet, the Minister of National Defense, Bourges Maunaury, and François Mitterrand, now Minister of Justice. The latter, as a lawyer, couldn't claim that he didn't know these texts violated the French constitution and constituted a system of absolute illegality.

These laws—which would give Massu the power of life and death over greater Algiers from January 1957 onward—were passed overwhelmingly in March 1956, by a National Assembly dominated by the left and where the Communist Party was well represented. With this new legal mechanism, executive power over the three departments that constituted Algeria would be transmitted to the Resident Minister, henceforth "custodian of the powers of the Government of the French Republic."

---

4. Whereas standard procedure under the French legal system would require an independent investigation by the judiciary to complement the initial police investigation before proceeding to trial, this step could be bypassed in cases where the defendant was caught "red-handed" in the act of a crime or had confessed.

Measures were then taken to reorganize the justice system in Algeria: military courts replaced civil courts. They could issue rulings directly—without a prior independent investigation—on anyone supposedly caught in the act of a crime against persons or property, even for offenses punishable by death. Scandalized lawyers would qualify this battery of new texts as a "negation of defense." The first consequence of this transfer would be the boom in "permanent armed forces tribunals": hundreds of fighters were brought before the courts for expedited prosecutions. The results were terrible and immediate: a dramatic increase in the number of death sentences and a surge in executions by guillotine.

In January 1957, on the eve of the Eight-Day Strike called by the FLN, Guy Mollet's government decided to entrust police powers to the army, as the so-called "special powers" allowed it to do. "The Battle of Algiers" could thus begin—a "battle" that consisted of a crazy proliferation of police activity, of the mass arrest of tens of thousands of "natives" at random, of the desperate and systematic use of all forms of torture to "make them talk fast, very fast," and of the liquidation of thousands of "natives." "Massu's methods were torture," Colonel Argoud would write in 1999.

> He liquidated everyone, even the innocent. The Bay of Algiers was an underwater cemetery. . . . I have said that torture was unacceptable and we used it. Employed well, it has no consequence. When the guy was a criminal, we would take him to the village square and shoot him there, just like we did a century or two before. I never felt any regret. I was the commander of my sector for two years, and we shot two hundred people. We will never know how many summary executions there were; the count would be in the thousands, the tens of thousands.[5]

Faced with this profusion of repression and torture, the FLN instructed us, if arrested, to "hold out" for forty-eight hours—the time needed to reorganize our networks. Many brothers and sisters lost their lives before the forty-eight hours were up. Or after. They never spoke. The CCE also instructed all activists who were arrested to challenge the courts before which they appeared with the legitimacy of their struggle to free their country from

---

5. From Georgette El Gey, *Histoire de la IVième république: La république des tourmentes (1954–1959)* (Paris: Fayard, 1992 [2010]).

foreign occupation, thereby transforming the court into a platform serving our national liberation struggle.

To defend the arrested activists, the FLN convened an initial group of Algerian lawyers. But this group had no time to implement the CCE's new strategy, as they were themselves arrested and sent to internment camps in March 1957; one was even murdered. It was the second group, formed by Mr. Vergès, with the FLN's agreement, that would implement this strategy in what the press called "the bombs trial," in which Djamila Bouhired appeared alongside Djamila Bouazza, Abderrahmane Taleb, Abdelghani Marsali, and Abderrahmane Hamened before the Algiers military tribunal on July 11, 1957.

Here I will recount in brief this scandalous and unjust operation of the French justice system, which served as the colonial state's right-hand man, justifying its repression and depleting the ranks of our fighters. The courtroom more closely resembled a Roman colosseum—complete with wild beasts and with the aristocrats playing military judges—than it did a theater of lessons on human rights. In such circumstances, what choice did the defendants and their lawyers have? Either they accepted the logic of this parody of justice and its eminently colonialist essence while using all legal means to make the best of it, or they set themselves in opposition to this logic and the colonial regime it served. The latter amounted to continuing our liberation struggle in the courtroom, with a division of roles between the accused activists and their lawyers. The former had to admit their membership in the FLN/ALN, confess their actions, then proclaim the legitimacy of the liberation struggle and the inevitability of its success in achieving Algeria's independence. They had to transform the French courts into a forum for denouncing colonialism. As for the lawyers, they had to expose this travesty of justice, its iniquity, and its bias and demonstrate that the French justice applied to the Algerians was an integral part of the colonial system, against which the accused fighters had arisen to liberate their country. Because of that, this "justice" was incompetent and unfit to judge them; it could not be both a judge and a party to the case.

This was the disruption strategy conceived, developed, and implemented by Jacques Vergès before the Algiers military tribunal.

On the morning of July 11, 1957, the trial opened against a backdrop of exceptional violence. Djamila Bouhired took her fight to heart, even down to the very clothes she wore: a bright green skirt, a stylish white blouse, and in her hand a silk scarf in scarlet red that she brandished like a fan or used to wipe the sweat from her brow in the sweltering courtroom. All the local press described Djamila's outfit without any comment, but the audience, composed on the trial's first day almost exclusively of the families of the accused, was not deceived: The green, white, and red—the colors of our national flag—were thrust right into the face of Colonel Gardon, the terrible Principal Public Prosecutor,[6] famous for having established a "list of measures to be taken in the context of the special powers" and for professing that Algerian fighters were not entitled to combatant status because "they were monsters, wild beasts" who "should be disposed of without the hassle of any ethics." The colors were thrust too in the face of the presiding justice, President Roynard, who later that year would chair the Permanent Tribunal of the Armed Forces of Algiers and mark his rule by his intransigence and severity. (Death sentences that the court, under his leadership, pronounced during his vile career in Algeria represented 26 percent of its total judgments![7])

Djamila Bouhired, Abderrahmane Taleb, and Abdelghani Marsali had been brought to trial barely three months after their arrest to answer charges of "criminal conspiracy, endangering state security, assassinations, and destruction of buildings by explosives," based on a single police record, which everyone knew contained confessions extracted under torture. Likewise, everyone knew the purpose of these trials: demonstrating to the "innocent European civilian population" that all means necessary were being used to protect them—including the most despicable of all, execution.

When it opened on July 11, 1957, our brothers' and sisters' trial attracted a strong presence of local and mainland press curious to discover the "women terrorists" and the bomb builders. From the start of the proceedings, Djamila refused to participate and wouldn't offer a word, except when the tribunal was to withdraw for deliberation. Then she expressed her "faith in our fight for freedom, in our country and its people, and in our independent future."

Abderrahmane Taleb addressed the court to confess and confirm his status as an ALN officer, recalling that "my country is at war with France"

---

6. In the French legal system, the Principal Public Prosecutor (*Procureur de la République*) is the senior prosecutor, responsible for prosecuting cases and monitoring judicial outcomes in the public interest.

7. In Sylvie Thevenot, *A Strange Justice: Judges in the War in Algeria* (Paris: La Découverte, 2001).

and making one single request: "that the court issue a much-needed summons for the French army officer who arrested me at the foot of the mountains in Blida." He warned that he would not participate in the proceedings if the court were to reject his demand—which, of course, it did.

Without ever losing his Olympian calm, Abdelghani Marsali freely admitted his status as a member of the ALN, the crowning of his commitment to the national cause from a young age.

Thus, the three main defendants demonstrated unmistakably that they were not the "wild beasts" and "criminals" the newspapers described at length, but instead patriots, fighters who defended—with the rudimentary weapons available to them—their people's right to live freely in their own country, free of colonialism.

The first day of the trial ended amid an electric atmosphere thanks also to Vergès's new "disruption strategy," which was as innovative as it was disconcerting, and saw the defense attorneys and the magistrates battling at length. The local press didn't understand it in the slightest and chalked the clashes up to "the inexperience of the young Parisian lawyers"! It's true that this was the first time Jacques Vergès would apply his theory of the "disruption trial," the one that would later make him one of the few giants of the bar worldwide. Yet this same press did not fail to emphasize the calm and assurance of those who stood accused, including Djamila Bouhired.

This media coverage stimulated so much interest that the second day of the trial saw a wave of European men and women jostling in the cramped hall of the military tribunal on Rue Cavaignac. They made no effort to hide their curiosity, staring and pointing openly at the defendants. They were visibly surprised to discover two beautiful young women, well groomed and elegant, one of whom in particular demonstrated a profound serenity, openly laughing at the remarks of one or the other co-defendants. They discovered that the two girls didn't come close to matching the fantasies they had been trafficking in about the "native" women, and that the "Fatimas" had transformed into "Djamilas"—young women of conviction and commitment, confidence and beauty. They drove the families of the accused to the back of the room, hurling threats and jeers at them.

The families didn't respond to the provocations. Ever calm, they continued to send signs of encouragement to their children and—through our language of the eyes and of discreet gestures—communicated news that they deemed important. When the court reopened the session, Vergès and his collective of Parisian lawyers continued—through procedural objections—to disclose to the public the true and grossly unfair nature of the "justice" applied to Algerian fighters. The European audience inserted themselves into the proceedings and—in response to the audacity of the young lawyers—replied by shouting, swearing, and hurling threats at the defense and the defendants without the presiding justice even attempting to impose order. Besides our brothers and sisters, the target of the most racist and threatening abuse was clearly Vergès. It grew so bad that, in a room of white-hot angry French spectators spewing hatred and heckling his every word, slandering him as a "little Chinese man" and other jeers—the lawyer asked Roynard, "Shall I remind them that my ancestors were building palaces while theirs were still eating acorns?"

President Roynard didn't lift a finger to restore order. The defense, Vergès, Moutet, and Gautherat, announced their decision to leave the bar, noting that the order required for the trial to be properly conducted was absent, though they did not suspend their defense of their clients. The court, however, decided to continue the trial and designated other lawyers for our three defendants. The prosecution unsurprisingly requested the death penalty against Djamila Bouhired, Abderrahmane Taleb, Abdelghani Marsali, Abderrahmane Hamened, and Djamila Bouazza. Lifetime forced labor and twenty-year sentences were requested against four other defendants. The court also demanded death sentences *in absentia* against Yacef Saâdi, Amar Ali (Ali la Pointe), Hassiba Ben Bouali, Mahmoud Bouhamidi, Samia Lakhdari, and me.

In the dock, our brothers and sisters met the prosecution's indictments with calm. Moutet snuck quietly back in to sit beside the appointed defendants and confront the court. He pleaded for Abdelghani Marsali, then left the room while Lainné, the lawyer appointed to Djamila Bouhired, took the floor. He began his sincere argument by noting: "The most difficult thing is that I wasn't even given a look or a gesture, much less an approval or disapproval, from the one I am supposed to defend. The two of us remain complete strangers to one another."

Equally honest, Mr. Haddou, appointed to defend Abderrahmane Taleb, didn't fail to point out that he would be pleading our brother's case "without ever having opened his file" and "without ever having spoken to him."

Djamila, Dahmane, and Ghani remained calm. Through their silence, stoicism, and serenity despite the cries of the European spectators calling for their execution, our brothers and sisters continued leading their fight on a new battleground. Even the conservative *Le Figaro* didn't fail to emphasize this in its account of the trial, writing, "This is an opponent that we are judging."

Before the debate ended, Vergès and Gautherat reappeared in the court, requesting that the tribunal should verify several crucial facts before oral arguments, to ensure that the truth was shown. The tribunal rejected this request. The crowd of screaming Europeans shoved this way and that, as if trying to grab the lawyers and lynch them right there before the presiding justice—who abstained, again, from any attempt to restore order.

Mr. Vergès cried out, "Mr. President, are we here for a military tribunal or a mob lynching?" This the tribunal judged offensive to the court, earning the lawyer a warning and precipitously raising the excitement of the bloodthirsty European spectators. At that point, Vergès and Gautherat recognized the impossibility of continuing the discussions. Totally blocked from defending their clients, they declared that they were definitively leaving the bar but not before they had strongly denounced "the scandalous nature of this justice that has no interest in the facts" and the apparent desire to simply "render the politically necessary executions legal." Before removing his lawyer's gown, Vergès warned the court, "The trial has just begun, and it will be carried out elsewhere."

With that, the security services had to intercede between the mob of *pieds-noirs* and the lawyers to allow them to leave the tribunal. But this didn't prevent the court from continuing its scandalous trial. A silence as heavy as lead fell when the government commissioner took the floor to announce his harsh indictment.

Then the president spoke to the accused, one by one by name, asking if they had anything to add in their defense before the tribunal retired to deliberate. He gave the floor to Djamila Bouhired, who stood and enunciated calmly, "My only crime is the love I have for my country. Yes, I love my country and I want to see it free. Nothing can prevent it from becoming so, *inchallah!*"

The *pieds-noirs* immediately began shouting vulgar insults at her, with some chanting "Death! Death!" while others looked ready to leap the benches and barriers to execute her themselves. There, for once, the presiding justice had to threaten to summon the security forces to restore order. As for the families of the accused, they were huddled close together, all eyes turned toward their children, striving to transmit to them the strength and energy necessary to continue their combat. Then the president called out Dahmane: "Defendant Abderrahmane Taleb, have you anything to add in your defense?"

Silence fell once more. Dahmane rose slowly, scanned the room, and said: "Mr. President, I am an officer of the National Liberation Army and we are at war against France. Whatever sentence you might pronounce, even if it is the death penalty, it will change nothing. Algeria will be free, despite them all." Everyone present remained silent, even the *pieds-noirs*, who seemed shocked.

Next it was Ghani's turn. He stood, gazed at length toward the Algerian families, grinned at them, then he—the one so often silent—said: "My people are at war against France. In my capacity as an Algerian, I have done nothing but fulfill my duty."

Finally, even Djamila Bouazza—whose family had insisted that her lawyer plead insanity—declared: "What I did, I did out of patriotism."

When the court withdrew for deliberations, the *pieds-noirs* left the room silently. Only the families of the accused remained in the gloomy, dimly lit courtroom. Then the tribunal members returned, stiff in their military uniforms emblazoned with their many medals. Each one took his place, and with his gavel, the president rapped a sharp blow on the desk and declared the session open. Then he took the floor for a very long speech in which he cited figures and mentioned each of the accused, one after the other, and their charges. He announced that the tribunal had determined them all guilty without exception. Finally, the presiding justice turned to address the accused, asking them all to rise.

"Defendant Bouhired, rise!" Djamila rose, standing straight—calm, serene, and beautiful as freedom. The president repeated aloud each of the five charges before the tribunal, and the verdicts. Then he announced that she was sentenced to death. She sat back down calmly, without flinching.

Next up were Djamila Bouazza, Dahmane, and Ghani. They all received their death sentences without showing any feeling, almost with indifference. Throughout the president's litany, the families took refuge in prayer and contemplation.

It was the evening of July 14, 1957, the anniversary of the storming of the Bastille. Oukhiti, the best reporter the earth has ever seen, brought us a detailed account of the trial's close, as she had each day. Then she sat silent for a long time. None of us could manage to restart the conversation for fear of bursting into tears. We avoided looking at one another while drinking sip after sip of water to swallow our tears and loosen the knots in our throats. Ali got up and went up to the terrace, no doubt to vent his profound grief.

As for me, I was overwhelmed, crushed with grief. I couldn't believe that Djamila, Ghani, and Dahmane would die. That night, paradoxically, the word *death* felt hollow. Having already experienced the deaths of some of my brothers and knowing what crimes colonial France was capable of toward our people, I couldn't deny reality.

Oukhiti continued, informing us that the previous morning, while the trial was in full swing, Mr. Vergès had dispatched a young messenger to lead her and Auntie Baya outside to him. He asked them to trust him and assured them that Djamila agreed with his defense strategy. Then, turning to Auntie Baya and putting a hand on her shoulder, he said: "She will be sentenced to death, you know. But, *inchallah,* nothing will happen to her, I promise."

Auntie Baya had replied: "She's like all her brothers and sisters. All that happens to her is what God has decided. And you, my son, be blessed, because you are behaving like a true *moudjahid.*" Oukhiti swore she had seen Vergès's eyes fill with tears as he left them.

The first consequence of Vergès's strategy was that, unlike other trials that had pitted us against the colonial regime—so expeditious that they never lasted more than half a day—Djamila's trial had lasted four days. A first! The second consequence was the media coverage. Our brothers and sisters had managed—despite everything—to transmit the image of a people's war of national liberation against a foreign occupier, and the image of fighters with unprecedented courage and just and legitimate objectives, inhabited by unwavering determination and a strong will to prevail. No doubt about it: this new image had only emerged thanks to Vergès's disruption strategy.

The next day I got up very early to join the brothers, who were already awake and had read all the press. While drinking a strong coffee with milk, I threw myself on the newspapers, separating them into two piles. The Algerian dailies had all devoted their front pages to the "bombs trial." Some announced the four death sentences in bold letters, while the others highlighted "the death sentences for the two Djamilas." All fell tooth and nail on Vergès and Gautherat. In contrast, the mainland French press highlighted the trial's unprecedented nature, given the presence of two young women "prosecuted for acts of terrorism" and the new defense strategy. *Le Monde* wrote that it was "the most important case the Permanent Armed Forces Tribunal of Algiers had ever seen." The metropolitan press didn't fail to note that the violence of the outbursts had made the trial impossible. It also noted that the accused were not viewed as defendants but "as opponents"— enemies to defeat.

Other than discovering for the first time the faces of young Algerian women among those engaged in the urban armed struggle as *bombistes*, the metropolitan press was also struck by the clashes between Vergès's group and both the court and the *pieds-noirs*, who were as hateful as they were vindictive. Indeed, having come to see what a "Fatima-turned-terrorist" looked like, the crowd had been taken aback to discover in Djamila Bouhired a beautiful woman fully and calmly admitting her actions, her combat, and her membership in the FLN/ALN, all with confidence and disconcerting determination. That made the *pieds-noirs* crazy. *Le Monde* wrote, "She displayed a moral superiority that made her the soul of terrorism." Algeria, at war for its independence, now had a name and a face: Djamila!

They had their Marianne, we had our Djamila.[8] This was the beginning of the legend. Djamila—her face, body, and name—became, rightly, an icon for people worldwide in their struggles for liberation, and the object of crippling hatred from all the disciples of colonial systems.

The day after the trial, Si Mourad arrived in the afternoon with Oukhiti. She reported that Vergès had told her and Auntie Baya, before his departure for Paris, that "the real trial would now begin" and would reveal to the world all the crimes and violations France had committed in Algeria. None of us could have imagined that day that this young lawyer would commit himself body and soul to our fight. He saved dozens of those on death row and never had the terrible task of accompanying one of his brothers to the guillotine. The future would reveal what an amazing hero of the bar Vergès would become. He was our brother in his anticolonial convictions, in our liberation struggle, and in his unwavering faith in victory whatever the risks, threats, or torments. We will always know our brother by the Algerian name he chose for himself, Jacques "Mansour" ("the Victorious") Vergès.

But that day after the trial in July 1957, none of us suspected all that— except perhaps for our big brother Si Mourad, our brilliant and insightful union leader, El Kho's right-hand officer. Asked his opinion on the trial, he said: "It's clear that this young lawyer is an anticolonialist activist. He has solid convictions and has forged his own strategy, consisting of transforming the accused into the accuser. In mainland France, I'm sure it will make a lot

---

8. Dating back to the time of the French Revolution, depictions of a goddess of Liberty known as Marianne have been used to symbolize the French Republic and its ideals. Today Marianne remains enshrined on the French government seal and in many other official depictions.

of noise. Just like I'm sure that if we offered to let him join us in the organization, he would. In fact, he is already an FLN activist."

But once the excitement aroused in us by Oukhiti's account and the various analyses had passed, we were seized with anguish: the two Djamilas, Ghani, and Dahmane had spent their first night on death row. I knew that for the men, a section of the Barberousse prison was reserved for those "promised" to the guillotine and that Ghani and Dahmane would share death and the long wait beforehand with dozens of other brothers, surrounded in their fraternal solidarity and affection. But the two Djamilas were the first two women on death row. Was there a section for them? Had they locked them up together, or each one to her own cell? How would they survive the wait for death? I shuddered, and all the tears I had contained these last few days gushed out. I took refuge on the terrace, overlooking the sea, and invoked all the saints to protect my sisters and brothers.

Today, sixty years later and after the death of my brother Jacques Mansour Vergès, I feel a duty to him and to our youth—particularly those who dream of embracing the law—to emphasize the turning point that Djamila's trial constituted in the history of defense strategies on a global scale. Vergès's trial strategy and his demonization by the colonial press offered an icon to an Algeria at war and to the independent Algeria still in gestation its female emblem in Djamila. For colonial France, she was "the soul of terrorism." For us and for all freedom-loving peoples, she became the soul of liberation and the symbol of Algeria at war, beautiful and rebellious. This image was reinforced by the fact that at the trial there was not one but two Djamilas, and that the death sentence was pronounced *in absentia* against three other girls, fighters on the run, Hassiba Ben Bouali, Samia Lakhdari, and me.

France, Massu, and their "Battle of Algiers" were stripped bare before the world: they were unleashing their hundreds of thousands of heavily armed soldiers against women and girls whose only crime was to love their country to the point of fighting to liberate it. For the first time, the world discovered that Algerian women were full participants in our liberation struggle. Vergès's strategy also helped show that the tribunal was arbitrary and incompetent by definition, being that of an occupying power. Likewise, it helped strip the masks off the local media and the "innocent civilian population," the *pieds-noirs* whose true face was now revealed before the international press.

A stubborn, spirited lawyer full of dignity and baffling to his enemies, Vergès mobilized a coalition against the denial of rights. He faced the Red

Hand everywhere, all while maintaining the panache and dignity so dear to his heart despite not always having a roof over his head or bread to eat. He was a tender being, gifted with extraordinary sensitivity and immense erudition. In times of hardship, such as the arrest or loss of a brother, we found solace and affection in him. I have often regretted that Vergès never met Ben M'hidi and Ramdane Abane. But how lucky we were to count among our ranks this brilliant lawyer, thanks to whom freedom and human dignity would conquer new territory in the war against injustice and subjugation.

9

THE ARREST

Another Meeting with Germaine Tillion

Our second meeting with Germaine Tillion took place on August 9, 1957. Our hope that the French authorities might commit to suspending our brothers' executions, as Madame Tillion had communicated back in July, had lasted only long enough for them to set the guillotine in motion.

In fact, from July 24 to 25, 1957, several executions plunged our people into mourning, releasing us from the pledge to stop setting bombs in public places in the European city. Unfortunately, given our lack of supplies, we had to react urgently to keep our word to our people. As a result, our *fiday-ine* set several bombs the next afternoon without having the time to prepare the attacks properly. Some only damaged property, while others were defused by the enemy. Nonetheless, even if we were far from satisfied, we felt that we had kept our promise; our people—and our enemy too—understood perfectly well that the FLN/ALN was alive and well, still in their midst, still active and fighting.

On August 8, El Kho informed us that Germaine Tillion would visit the next day. Early in the afternoon of August 9, brother Ali Bouzourène led our visitor to Oukhiti's, where El Kho, Hassiba, Ali, and I were awaiting her. The meeting started with an awkward, uncomfortable air that Oukhiti, ever the welcoming hostess, did her best to overcome. In welcoming Tillion, El Kho asked her with an exaggerated air, "I heard that you almost fell victim to one of our bombs?"

She replied icily: "If your bombs had claimed a single victim, I would not be here before you right now."

Her expression and intonation shocked me more than her response. I recognized a touch of the disdain to which we had grown accustomed when speaking with Europeans: a mixture of haughty certainty and arrogance. I wanted to throw right back in her face all the "judicial murder" committed and all the heads severed in the name of human rights, but a look from El Kho dissuaded me. Agitated, I left the room. Oukhiti followed me into the kitchen and offered me a coffee, reminding me of one of our old sayings: "Kiss the hand that you cannot bite." She was right.

When I finally returned to the room, the discussion was in full swing. There was talk of Tunis, Paris, brother Kamel (Deputy Judge Hadj Smaïn), and more. El Kho's eyes were shining, his pensive gaze fixed on Germaine Tillion. Next to him, Ali followed attentively, occasionally nodding in agreement. Hassiba sat beside our visitor, her face impassive, her legs crossed and blue eyes darting from El Kho to Madame Tillion. After following their discussion for a few minutes, I realized that the French government seemed to have "momentarily revisited" the idea of a moratorium on executions due to combined pressures from certain circles in France, in Algeria, and in the army. But they wanted to get into contact with our senior political and military leadership in Tunis for an exchange of views that could eventually lead to more specific discussions.

I saw in El Kho's eyes a great jubilation that I understood well. We urgently needed to restore contact with our elder brothers in Tunis, and our visitor was offering us an unexpected opportunity to do so. Under the pretext of informing them of our exchange with Tillion, we would be able to communicate to them the precise state of the AAZ in the aftermath of Si Mohamed's assassination and send them a comprehensive evaluation of our needs, especially our supplies for combat. They chose brother Kamel for the mission and decided that he would travel to Paris on a date to be communicated to Madame Tillion as soon as she had received her government's approval. Then they agreed that the Paris-Tunis roundtrip would be organized by Madame Tillion herself.

After her departure, we let our joy pour out. We were sure that once our brothers in Tunis knew of the AAZ's extremely precarious situation, they would do anything to get us the aid we needed. El Kho immediately ordered me to prepare the report, with Si Mourad's help. So we set about outlining a comprehensive and accurate inventory of the situation in greater Algiers, stressing the fact that the French army had virtually decimated our political-military organization and dealt fatal blows to the officer corps. We explained that the reorganization of the political and military networks was ongoing but was advancing slowly due to our limited resources.

We informed them that we had launched a campaign denouncing the Nazi methods used against our activists, our combatants, and our people, but that the campaign also suffered due to the rudimentary means at our disposal, limiting its scope. We concluded the report with a comprehensive inventory of all our military, communication, and financial needs. In fact, the fundraising networks had been among the first to fall, and the arrests of our contributors drastically decreased our financial resources at a time when our population needed aid.

Once the report was ready, El Kho decided to copy it himself so that the big brothers—who knew his handwriting—would have no doubt about the document's origin and authenticity. However, it wasn't just the elder brothers in Tunis who were very familiar with El Kho's writing: Colonels Trinquier and Godard and their teams were, too. That's why I have always felt that we made a grave mistake, in violation of our security regulations, by letting El Kho transcribe the report. Without this, if Kamel were later arrested, he could more easily have denied knowing the AAZ chief. But I will recount that episode in due time.

Mobilizing the Women

Starting in June 1957, I made a habit every afternoon of joining Si Mourad in his refuge at 14 Rue du Nil to review the huge volume of mail. Ever since the reorganization of the Algiers Autonomous Zone, Si Mourad had headed the political-administrative department. All the reports landed on his desk, including those from the various officials in charge of the intelligence, political, recruitment, training, mobilization, and orientation committees. We handled all the files together, responded to mail from all the various officials, discussing solutions to the problems raised in the letters, studying and considering actions to counter and defeat the colonial propaganda machine, and submitting reports to our big brother El Kho.

It was at this time that the idea of creating a women's organization took shape. It would be under the FLN's supervision but distinct from our existing political-administrative structure. Its purpose would be to denounce the mass arrests, disappearances, torture, and abuses. I suggested that the first activity should be a large street demonstration involving the largest possible number of women, all veiled in white *haïks* and marching in silence from the Place du Gouvernement toward the Préfecture. It would be a spectacular way to seize attention and sway international public opinion. What's more, it would galvanize our women and anchor the FLN even deeper in our society, while offering a new, dynamic base for our liberation struggle.

Ever calm and collected, Si Mourad was a rigorous man, but one with a deep human side that made him particularly sensitive to others' suffering. He supported the idea and asked the officers of the various sectors to test it out among their entourages. Gradually, as the answers flowed back in, it was decided to organize a sit-in of women in front of the Préfecture rather than a march (which would be easier for the French forces of repression to suppress and block). Once this was decided, the officials were mobilized. Each leader had to pass along the names and addresses of the families affected by French abuses; a list of those arrested, detained, or missing; and the name of one woman in each neighborhood who could mobilize others around her. Once the list of women was readied, it was decided to convene them by sector to inform them discreetly that an activity was being planned and collect their opinions and suggestions to convince and mobilize the women.

Brother Abderrahmane Benhamida, a student at the Algiers French-Muslim School who was still unknown to the French police, would set dates in collaboration with the sector officials, who were best placed to assess the possibilities. This work complemented the task that El Kho had charged me with: to prepare files on the victims of abuses, which Vergès would need to launch his trials and campaigns. And so a vast quantity of precise and precious information flowed through 14 Rue du Nil. Si Mourad and I worked with jubilation at the thought that we would soon be opposing Massu and his propaganda with the most beautiful and unexpected demonstration.

Si Mourad refused to rush and required the utmost rigor and caution. He repeated endlessly to us that the demonstration must only be unveiled at the last possible moment, which meant holding the meeting as close as possible to the day itself. I learned a tremendous amount by working with him. He taught me to better decode public statements, read between the lines of important articles, and flush out the hidden agendas behind political, economic, social, or cultural proposals. It was he who initiated me into all things organizational, from managing relationships with our activists to their recruitment, training, and mobilization.

But Si Mourad could also surprise with his fierce sense of humor, to the point that we sometimes fell into fits of irrepressible laughter, which seemed so out of place in this silent safe house run by two cantankerous old women, Mahfoudh's aunts, who had apparently ended up adopting Si Mourad. He must have softened them up with his discretion and a thousand little gestures. Back at Rue Cato, I told Hassiba of the Si Mourad I had discovered and whom she obviously knew well. She sometimes accompanied me to 14 Rue du Nil where, after our work, we would be joined by Mahfoudh and play cards or dominoes, working ourselves up about the radiant future that doubtlessly awaited us under the sun of independence. But often Hassiba and Si Mourad discussed their days at the bomb laboratory. The memory of our arrested and executed comrades was painful. Si Mourad would pull out his best, most optimistic arguments to lift our spirits. He reminded us that despite the total war waged by France and its army, despite the vast disproportion of means, "the FLN is everywhere—north, south, east, west, in all the towns, in all the villages, across the countryside, in the mountains, and not only here but also in mainland France. They will face war from Dunkirk to Tamanrasset until our national liberation. Colonialism's future lies in the cemetery!"

One day, when I was handling the incoming mail, one letter in particular raised immense anxiety in me. It was addressed to El Kho, from a colonel in Wilaya III. He solicited our help in alleviating the tragic state his troops were living in, with nothing to eat except grass. He asked for essential supplies, or money to buy them.

When I showed it to Si Mourad, he dictated to me a draft reply to submit to El Kho, then took it upon himself to explain to me once more the importance of the Algiers Autonomous Zone: "The AAZ is both the rear guard for our neighboring *wilayas* and the irreplaceable sounding board of our national liberation war. That's why it must always remain standing and functional. Here more than elsewhere, we need to make sure that whenever one of our own falls, two others rise to take his place. And for that, we need to work tirelessly to raise awareness, recruit, mobilize, and supervise."

To avoid bothering our hosts and to reassure Mahfoudh's aunts, we worked in the shelter that Ali la Pointe had built. It was spacious, covered with a large canopy of woven reeds. Mattresses piled atop one another served as our beds when the work obliged us to stay for a good part of the night. The shelter was lit by a lamp rigged up to the local electrical wires. One evening, so exhausted from hours of writing that our eyes and fingers ached, while we were getting ready for bed, each in a corner, Si Mourad told me—still in his serious tone, as if he were announcing some everyday fact—that he felt "feelings" for me and that, if they were mutual, we could notify Ali and El Kho and then marry.

My shock was so great that I struggled to make sense of the words reaching my ears. I had joined the struggle like one joins a religion, so his words rang in my ears like a profound blasphemy that caused my brain to short-circuit. Worse yet, it was an unpardonable sin given everything I'd been taught. I was mentally and physically incapable of emitting the slightest sound. My mind froze up. I turned my back, laid my mattress down in the corner opposite the one where my brother in arms stood, arranged my bedding with brusque gestures and fell asleep like a log, my face toward the wall and my pillow over my head until the next morning. When day broke, I left without sharing coffee or words. When I reached 4 Rue Cato, I buried myself in work. I asked El Kho to excuse me for some time from my collaboration with Si Mourad. Hassiba, to whom I hadn't said a word, replaced me.

Some days later, an urgent meeting was called in a house in some small dead-end alley. El Kho instructed me to inform Si Mourad and lead him to the rendezvous site. I went to Rue du Nil and delivered the message, acting as distant and icy as I could. Then I walked out. Si Mourad trailed a few steps behind me, following our usual protocol. When we reached the alley, he quickened his pace and called out to me to slow down and wait. When he reached me, he said, "Ya khtou! I'm incredibly sorry, and I deeply regret burdening you like that the other night. I sincerely beg you to excuse me, and hope with all my heart that you will not resent me any longer. I really hope that we can maintain our fraternal relationship."

Si Mourad was genuinely sorry and awaited my pardon. But I was young and not yet mature enough to know how to offer gestures or words to make amends. I didn't yet know that friendship and brotherhood are worth offering every forgiveness. The worst was that I didn't then know it would be our last meeting.

A Heroic Battle

On August 11, Ramel and Si Mourad informed El Kho that the day before, around two in the afternoon, they had miraculously escaped the paratroopers, who had again surrounded their neighborhood and started to close off all the streets and alleys. Knowing that the French army was conducting raids, extreme vigilance at every moment was our rule. Thanks to this endless lookout and to the help of the residents, they managed to reach another refuge. In their report, Ramel and Si Mourad specified that they had scrubbed the old safe house clean of all traces of their presence and had taken the last of the bombs with them. However, they stressed their difficulty finding shelter and asked El Kho to help them find a new safe house. He promised to resolve the problem soon.

The muggy heat was stifling, especially at night. Ever since our move to 4 Rue Cato, El Kho had decided that we had to spend the nights in the shelter, as a safety measure for our hosts, but it was cramped and extremely difficult to access. It overlooked one of the galleries of the patio, and we accessed it through a skylight built to ventilate the room. Every evening, El Kho, Ali, Hassiba, Petit Omar, and I wedged ourselves in, packed side by side like sardines, legs drawn up to our chest. We rested our heads on our knees and hoped to sleep a bit, but it was a lost cause, between the painful discomfort of the posture and the suffocating heat that left us sweating from head to toe. Each morning we returned like zombies to the room provided for us, bodies disjointed, faces haggard, each of us trying to put on a good face.

One morning in late August, while we were still trying to wake up after a cold shower and hot coffee, Si Mustapha entered the room looking concerned. El Kho urged him to have some coffee with us. He sat down, took a cup, and said in a voice that he was trying to keep steady, "It seems that the paratroopers are preparing to lock down the Casbah."

Mahmoud climbed up to the rooftop to have a look around. Helicopters flying low confirmed that something was happening, or soon would. As we prepared to return to the shelter, Mahmoud went out to get some news. He returned quickly to confirm that an army of paratroopers and elite Zouave units were blocking the lower Casbah, which was already under siege, forcing everyone coming from Rue de la Lyre, Rue du Divan, and Rue Boutin to surge back into the center of the *medina*. Suddenly the terrifying noise of rotors and steady bursts of machine-gun fire filled the sky and the house. We climbed up to the rooftop. All around, others were doing the same.

We all looked in the direction of the latest shots. Soon the rumors reached us: "Ramel and Si Mourad are surrounded! They're fighting it out!" For hours, an eternity, we watched helplessly. We would later learn that our brothers met their end while fighting droves of soldiers armed to the teeth, backed by helicopters and light tanks, and led by the bloodthirsty captains Léger, Chabannes, Lenoir, and Colonel Jeanpierre. We knew our brothers had very little ammunition, yet they held hundreds of fully equipped paratroopers and Zouaves in check for hours. Only Ramel had a Stein machine gun—recovered from old World War II stocks—and some clips. As for Si Mourad, according to El Kho he had nothing but a P45 pistol, two or three homemade bombs, and maybe some grenades.

As for us, helpless, with rage in our hearts and death in our souls, we watched our brothers' final sacrificial combat. We had neither men nor arms to rescue them. All paths were blocked off.

In the neighborhood around them, the population was ordered to remain locked inside their rooms. The door of each house was watched by soldiers ready to blow it all up, and all the rooftops in the area had been occupied by masses of paratroopers and Zouaves. However, despite the French army's frenzied and unprecedented deployment of force, our brothers would write with their blood a saga every bit as epic as those our mothers used to recount to us of Sidna Ali or Salah Eddine El Ayoubi.[1]

As we stood there in the hot sun, following our brothers' battle from a distance, I imagined I was beside them; they were calm, determined, collected, and exceptionally intelligent. It was an intelligence of mind and of movement. I could see them coordinating without even needing to talk, using their gestures and words sparingly, like their scarce ammunition, ready to share the same fate with dignity and in brotherhood, to face with honor the death that besieged them.

All of Algiers held its breath. Ali, pale, paced across the rooftop like a caged lion. He harassed El Kho: "Maybe we could create a diversion?" But he knew as well as any of us that we could do nothing—except perhaps to pray, like all the inhabitants of the Casbah, who implored heaven and all the saints for a miracle. For hours the people stood under the blazing sun, eyes

---

1. Sidna ("Our Lord") Ali was the Prophet Mohammed's nephew, renowned for his legendary courage. Salah Eddine El Ayoubi, also known as Saladin, led the Arab army that liberated Jerusalem from the Crusaders. Both are renowned figures across the Arab and Muslim worlds.

fixed on the block where the sound of gunfire originated, all holding their breath. Despite the roar of the helicopters, the sound of detonations reached us clearly. Ali couldn't bear it anymore. He cried out: "That spurt, that was Ramel's Sten. He must have taken out a few of those dogs!" "That's a grenade, *Kho*! Did they have grenades?"

I wished he would be quiet so that I wouldn't miss anything. But when he was silent for too long, I was gripped by anguish, because to me his silence signified the death of our two brothers. God, how it is hard to live through the death of one's brothers! The injustice of their departure is unbearable, an injustice that shreds the heart and leaves a wound that never heals.

The helicopters had left without us noticing, so concentrated were we on deciphering the sounds of the battle. Then a silence like death settled. Hassiba and I looked at each other and began to cry. The tanks that had sealed all the Casbah's exits for hours pulled back, the troops returned to their barracks and, little by little, people began spilling into the streets in search of news. El Kho sent Mahmoud to find out what had happened. Here is the version that our big brother considered definitive.

Ramel and Si Mourad's liaison officer was a member of the family that hosted them. He had left home that morning as usual but was apprehended by the "blues" and arrested. Ramel and Si Mourad didn't know that he had been arrested and, almost certainly, tortured. Soon after, the Casbah was locked down.

Ramel and Si Mourad were caught up by surprise in the lockdown as the paratroopers invaded the rooftops and alleyways, closing off all the exits. Our brothers tried to escape, without success. After assessing the situation and concluding that they had no chance of survival, they decided to try to take Colonel Bigeard down with them. From the second-floor window overlooking the Impasse Saint Vincent de Paul, which teemed with paratroopers, Si Mourad announced to our enemies that they would surrender, but only to an officer of the same rank as their own. They were both colonels in the ALN, and demanded to address Colonel Bigeard directly. Several other French officers presented their name and rank, assuring them that they could negotiate. But Si Mourad stubbornly called for Colonel Bigeard. When he finally arrived, Si Mourad told him he was going to present the conditions of their surrender, which, if accepted, had to be signed by the colonel personally. The French soldiers all stared up at the window, watching the slow descent of a small basket attached to a rope containing "the two outlaws' conditions of surrender."

At the last second, Colonel Jeanpierre realized the trap they were about to fall into. He had just enough time to shove Colonel Bigeard to the ground before the bomb hidden in the basket exploded. "The damage was considerable," according to French military sources

Oh, Si Mourad! I imagined him, calm and determined, calculating how much time would be necessary to lower the basket. In response to their scornful laughter, I imagined him grinning into his mustache as the basket descended. Our brothers' message was as simple, clear, and evident as their courage: "A soldier does not surrender. He fights to the death."

After the explosion, Ramel decided to go out and face the enemy army and its faithful companion, death. He wounded and killed several on his way down to the doorway, then continued forward, firing his last bullets as a deluge of fire fell upon him. Witnesses recounted that, riddled with bullets, he made another two or three steps, his gun pressed to his body, and then fell in one long arc, like a tree, without bending. Si Mourad, a faithful veteran of our explosives lab, had kept one final bomb, which he armed and strapped tight against his chest in order to blow himself up outside in the midst of the paratroopers. He ran out and was greeted with another deluge of fire that only ceased when the bomb exploded.

That night, I think that each of us felt somehow that Ramel and Si Mourad's deaths were the harbinger of terrible events to come. Ali was losing his talkative nature. He made no effort to hide his desire to resume attacks, including in the European city. Hassiba no longer concealed her tremendous sadness. Si Mourad had taken her under his wing in the bomb lab and she had spent long days working alongside him, building close ties. As for me, I was consumed by shame and regret and overcome with remorse. I bitterly regretted having ceased working with him after his proposal and not accepting his apology. Wherever he is, all I can do is hope for his forgiveness. Don't bother looking for the final resting place of Chérif Debbih, a.k.a. Si Mourad—he lies forever in our hearts.

As for our brother Hadji Athmane, a.k.a. Ramel, Ali's alter ego, he had always shown a dogged determination, unfailing commitment, and sublime courage. Whenever there was an attack to carry out, we teased him: "You always want to be the first to face the enemy so you can redeem your Turkish ancestors for what they did to our country, to wash away the shame of your *Dey* who abandoned it to the French." He gave his life heroically that August 27, 1957, so that our people could be free and our country independent.

El Kho suffered in silence. His rank and responsibilities prevented him from pouring his heart out or giving free rein to his pain. But we knew that with the deaths of Si Mourad and Ramel, El Kho lost more than just brother officers. He lost a part of himself—and two major pillars of the Algiers Autonomous Zone.

Hassiba's Prophetic Dream

When Ali awoke in the shelter screaming from a nightmare, El Kho authorized us to sleep on the rooftop. It must have been a little after midnight. The Casbah was silent, bathed in the gloom of death. Ali recounted his nightmare to us in a whisper, and Hassiba and I cried ourselves to sleep.

Early in the morning, Ali shook us awake. "Get up. Go inside the house. It's too humid, you'll get sick!" Hassiba, nestled by my side, looked at me, dazed. It must have been around four in the morning; I helped her get up and head for the room where we usually spent our days. We silently drank one cup of coffee after another to chase the numbness from our bodies and minds. With the cup nestled in her palms, her beautiful eyes full of sadness, Hassiba recounted to me the dream she had had that night on the rooftop.

"I was still in my dream when Ali shook me. It took me a few seconds to realize where I was. You know, all I know about your dormitory was what you've described to me. In my dream, I went to the campus and found my way to your room, knowing that it was unoccupied and that I could rest there. When I opened the door, I was surprised to discover that it was occupied. Si Mohamed was sitting at your desk, his head propped on the palm of his hand, his elbow resting on the table. He followed my gaze and smiled the same proud smile as the day he had decorated all four of us—Samia, Djamila, you, and me—with medals. As soon as I entered the room and was closing the door, I saw Ramel, Si Mourad, and Dahmane sitting side by side on your bed, facing Si Mohamed. My heart leapt with joy. They welcomed me and Si Mourad called out, 'Come sit here between Dahmane and me. This is your place; we kept it for you,' he said, patting the empty space between him and Dahmane. I sat down and Dahmane put his arm around my shoulders and laughed aloud: 'The situation will only get worse, my sister!' Just at that moment, Ali shook me awake. But I know this dream is a prophecy."

She wasn't crying, but I saw a gleam in her eyes that frightened me, like a quiet resignation to a macabre end. I found myself lecturing her, prodding her, accusing her of letting herself get knocked down, wanting her to pull herself together.

"Listen, Hassiba, for months now, we haven't only seen death up close, we've also lived through it as a group. What do you expect? It's just a dream! It's normal for you to dream about Si Mourad and Ramel just after they met their end." I fell silent as my tears choked me.

Hassiba remained calm and said, with a clarity that terrified me, "I am neither discouraged nor depressed. I just wanted to share something certain with you: I will die soon. You know well that in our interpretation of dreams, when the dead come to look for you or reserve you a place at their side, it means that you will die. That's all."

Without thinking, I replied, "But you said you were sitting between Dahmane and Si Mourad. Dahmane is in prison. He isn't dead."

Hassiba, the youngest among us but our great sage, put an end to this surreal exchange by taking me in her arms and speaking softly, almost in the ear, "Yes, Dahmane is in jail and sentenced to death. If you think they will forgive him for having created the lab, for being our chief bomb-maker, our great chemist without whom the war would never have been brought to their city, you are mistaken. I wish Dahmane a long life, but his importance makes me fear he'll get the worst. Besides, my dream says to me that our martyred brothers have come to get us, me and him."

I felt stupid responding to her with a traditional saying: *"Koulchi bel mektoub!* [Everything is a matter of destiny!] Time will tell!"

This last helpless saying reminded us of Samia, who often hummed the chorus of the popular 1956 song "Que Sera, Sera." We wondered what had become of our sister, from whom we hadn't heard since late that previous year. We knew she had married her cousin Anis and was supposed to follow him to France, where he was finishing his studies. Where had she ended up? How had she taken all the deaths? We imagined, of course, that she must have suffered cruelly at each of our losses. El Kho had informed us of the paratroopers' terrible raid on Samia's parents' home after they had identified her as the one who planted the bomb in the Cafétéria. Fortunately, she wasn't home, but the paratroopers sacked their beautiful home on Rue Salvandy, and Qadi Lakhdari and Mama Zhor were forced to take refuge in Tunisia. Hassiba would never know what I learned when I met Samia and her husband and parents again years later. She had spent just a few weeks in France with Anis before choosing to settle in Tunis. Then she spoke to me at length of Ramdane Abane, whom she had the honor and privilege of getting to know, as he often preferred to take refuge in Samia and her husband's very modest apartment there. Abane discussed politics at length with her and read and wrote a lot. He was a real visionary genius, she told me, recalling Si Mohamed with his insight, his brilliant and rigorous analyses, his fair, clear, and steadfast positions, but to her he had seemed dark and pessimistic the last time he visited. It was the eve of his departure to Morocco, where he was, alas, assassinated by his brothers in the midst of a vile power struggle.

But it was still 1957, and Hassiba and I, without thinking, began taking the macabre toll of our group's members. I realized that most of the brothers and sisters in our wonderful group had been either killed, arrested and sentenced to death or to long prison terms, or were missing. Only the four of us still had our "freedom": El Kho, Ali, Hassiba, and me.

"Alilou is free too, but his misfortune is worse than death. He is wandering the Casbah, half crazy, destroyed by the torture, despised for life when he was once idolized," I said to my young sister.

After a long silence, Hassiba said: "Before meeting you at Lalla's in the Belhaffafs' house, I had seen you and Samia one day as I was leaving and the grocer and you were entering. I immediately understood that we were working with the same officers, Boualem Oussedik and young Abdallah, known as Petit Mourad. Do you know that it was him who saved my life the day the El Biar lab blew, taking Rachid Kouache's life? Oh that little gentleman, how I miss him so. He and Boualem must be in the *maquis*. *Inchallah* they will survive the war. You never knew the Birkhadem and El Biar teams—amazing people, most of whom are now dead or arrested. I'm sure you would have gotten along well with the Timsit brothers; they were extraordinary activists, so very committed, so brotherly and unbelievably funny. They are in prison. Do you realize that Uncle Mustapha, Si Mourad, and Ramel have all been slaughtered, and Djamila, Dahmane, and Abdelghani are in prison and sentenced to death? It would be a miracle if they escaped execution—especially Dahmane, who was the soul and the genius behind the lab at Impasse de la Granada. I'm really afraid they won't make it. It's horrible to say, but that's what I feel. And then the dream confirmed my premonition. I am a believer, and I can already see myself joining my brothers in the hereafter. But don't worry, I will not give up. I am clearheaded and ready to face Massu in person, so long as Ali is with me to shoot and Petit Omar to guide me. And unshakable Oukhiti, with her smooth talking and her tricks that solve all problems, her delicious recipes and her letter from Captain Chabannes. I hope Oukhiti will always be nearby." Then she burst into a self-deprecating laugh that split my heart. I stayed silent because the only answer that came to mind—"As long as there is life, there is hope"—was patently useless. She continued, as if speaking to herself: "Deaths, arrests, ransacked homes, these beautiful brightly colored houses glistening in the sun, people and families devastated, disappearances, executions, the torture factory . . . who will be left someday to take stock of it all?"

My throat was in a knot because, back home on the high plains, we would consider this a kind of farewell speech. (*Kanet etouadaâ*—"she was saying *adieu*.") She was only nineteen and so fragile, so smart, so committed, so brave, and, my God, so beautiful—back home, again, we would say that she had "a beauty made for the hereafter." I recounted the great lesson that Si Mohamed had taught Djamila and me on the meaning, objectives, and means of our struggle: "We must always coax France to meet us on the political battlefield, for it is there that we will always defeat her." He insisted we were not the murderers Massu alleged we were. "We are ALN combatants, FLN activists, motivated by the most historically just and politically legitimate of causes: the liberation of our country and our people from foreign occupation," Ben M'hidi had concluded. A glow of life drove the resignation from Hassiba's beautiful fair eyes.

Discovered

The date of brother Kamel's departure for Paris was set for September 25, 1957, and El Kho decided they should have a final working session the evening before his departure, at Oukhiti's at 3 Rue Cato. Kamel was warned he would have to spend the night with us because of the curfew. Hassiba, Ali, and Petit Omar would remain at 4 Rue Cato. The decision to hold the meeting in our safe house and to host Kamel there the same night would prove to be our second mistake.

On September 23, Kamel arrived in early evening as agreed. It was our first meeting with him. I thought he was the right person for this mission and was feeling quite happy with Kamel's preparations. We had just adjourned for dinner when Oukhiti dashed down the stairs from the rooftop, where she had been keeping watch. Panting, she informed us that a column of paratroopers had secretly homed in on our part of the neighborhood.

At that very moment, she added, soldiers were jumping from rooftop to rooftop toward 3 Rue Cato, where we sat. We were convinced that our hiding space was safe. Besides Oukhiti and the adults living with her, only the four of us knew it: El Kho, Hassiba, Ali, and me. Even the family that hosted us across the street at 4 Rue Cato didn't know where we went when we left their house. What's more, our safe house at 3 Rue Cato had a shelter that was very difficult to detect. Ali had transformed a built-in alcove of the ground-floor room into a hiding space, with its opening perched above the stairwell and undetectable to the naked eye. The sole—but major—problem was the presence of Kamel, who was a stranger to this house and to our group, even if he was a fellow combatant. Our strict rules of discipline and security demanded that we not reveal our shelter to him. Not for lack of confidence, but out of certain knowledge of the torture methods that could make even a mute person talk. Also, Massu had decreed that anyone from outside a "native" quarter had to inform the local police station of their visit and the reasons behind it; Kamel had certainly not respected that formality, for obvious reasons. With the paratroopers about to reach us, I saw two options before us: either send Kamel into another room while Oukhiti helped me and El Kho into the shelter—that way, even though the paratroopers would certainly cart him off for an ID check, he would never know where the shelter was—or let Kamel join us in the shelter. The latter would be both a violation of our strict security rules and an enormous danger, for him but also for us all, if he were later arrested. I grew impatient at El Kho's hesitation: we needed a quick decision and I was sure that El Kho would never choose to violate the security rule. He looked at me, questioning. I went up to him and whispered: "*Kho*, the paratroopers will easily believe that Kamel is a gentleman friend of Oukhiti's. She is a beautiful young widow. To a Westerner it will seem normal." But El Kho chilled me to the bone when, without looking at me, he spat out: "It is out of the question to tarnish Oukhiti's reputation and undermine the honor of Si Mustapha, may God rest his soul!"

He turned to Oukhiti and asked her to bring him the family's copy of the Quran. She complied, like lightning. El Kho instructed Kamel to lay his hand on the Quran and swear to forget this house and our hostess and never reveal the place whatever the circumstances, however painful. I was speechless! But Kamel—who I'm sure did not really understand the reason for this oath, since he knew nothing of the daily stresses of this clandestine lifestyle nor the dangers of knowing where the AAZ's leader was hiding—calmly did as instructed.

Oukhiti urged us to make for the shelter as the paratroopers prepared to break down the door. Accompanied by Kamel, we slipped back into our shelter, the rim of the opening serving to hold the long ladder that Oukhiti kept resting on the narrow stairs below the opening. Once inside, El Kho and I resettled the thick, heavy slab that fit down to the very last millimeter into the shelter's opening. Then we dragged an iron bar horizontally until it was wedged firmly between the slab and the far wall.

Like that, the slab was so perfectly set that an unsuspecting eye could never imagine a possible opening in the wall. In the same way, this system also provided complete soundproofing; it was completely sealed. El Kho, Kamel, and I felt doubly safe in our cache. For one, our shelter was undetectable by anyone who didn't know of its existence, and second, Oukhiti and her house were "protected" by the document with the stamp and signature of Captain Chabannes, unit commander of the paratroopers stationed at Bab Jdid, attesting that Oukhiti was an informant who should be given help and protection.

With the paratroopers in the house and throughout the neighborhood, we waited quietly for the operation to end. We were plunged into a deep, suffocating darkness. El Kho whispered in Kamel's ear, no doubt explaining to him the reasons for the oath he had asked of him before revealing the shelter. I had trouble breathing once the slab was put in place, hermetically enclosing us in what, to me, had seemed from the very first time like a tomb. Not a ray of light, not a sound, just an increasingly depleted supply of oxygen.

I struggled to control the panic that took hold of me each time. I tried to control the beating of my heart, which I felt and heard up in my throat. I felt apart from the world of the living. Even El Kho and Kamel seemed absolutely unreal to me that night in the shelter. El Kho's whispers gradually dissipated my claustrophobic panic, and I plunged into an attitude of resignation I had never known before and would only understand later.

In my core, I was convinced that our brother Kamel did not really understand El Kho's explanations, because they related to a reality that you could only understand by living it firsthand. How could our brother the deputy judge—who had never witnessed death, torture, weapons, explosives, or arrests—ever understand? How could our brother who had never lived as hunted prey, on alert at every moment, how could he grasp what El Kho was trying to explain to him? How could Kamel, who had not lived through the shared misery and agony of the night of February 2, have the slightest idea what torture was and what consequences it rendered on bodies, spirits, and wills? No, he did not know and could not understand in any way. That was why, adopting Hassiba's favorite position, seated and hugging my legs to my chest, I laid my head on my knees, slowed my breathing, and began to wait for our deliverance. I had the ominous feeling that my life as a combatant would end here.

Oukhiti finally came to rescue us. The day was already rising. I had an uncontrollable urge to return to "normal life," to reconnect with the simple gestures of the everyday life of ordinary people whose lives were not forfeit by decree of General Massu. Oh, how far away they seemed, those warm, monotonous, long summer days during summer vacation in my little highland village of Vialar! The cave of our shelter had embellished the memories, wrapping them in the delightful nonchalance of those lucky enough to live normally, to the rhythm of the seasons. But nostalgia was dangerous. So I sent it to the devil, shook myself, and decided to "live fully" that day—September 24. The dawn was already so sweet, scented with fragrant jasmine and sea breeze sent like a mother's caress by the sumptuous Bay of Algiers to the Casbah, her favorite daughter, violated and chained daily by the godless soldiers. The breeze arrived to breathe into her, all at once, the desire, the will, and the courage to stand upright, to resist her assailants and throw them back to the other shore. I climbed up to the rooftop to breathe and come back to life. Our neighborhood was cleaning out the offensive traces of the paratroopers while the rest of the *medina* still dozed. Echoing the sounds of buckets of water thrown by women, I thought I could hear the breeze saying to us, "Get up! Fight! At the end of the combat and sacrifices, honor and freedom await you!"

I ran back downstairs and asked Oukhiti to let me prepare breakfast. With incredible joy, I rediscovered the simple acts of getting out the coffee cups, preparing the tray, filling the sugar bowl, tossing coffee grounds in boiling water, watching it bubble to keep it from overflowing, monitoring the milk on the stove. . . After the nightmare of being confined in that cave, these simple actions were a delight, a rebirth. I wanted to hum, but recalling Lalla's lessons on the behavior expected of a *moudjahida* stopped me. Memories of dearest Lalla, the beautiful and gentle Zineb, their wonderful family, our brothers in arms Abderrezak, Nafaâ, Amokrane, Abdallah, the whole Belhaffaf family came flooding back to me, warming my heart and making me smile with gratitude. Oukhiti asked me why I was wearing such a blissful smile, and I recounted the episode of the prayer sessions behind Lalla, my wonderful *imam*. We laughed together, forgetting that a stranger in the home, Kamel, might hear us. So much for dear Lalla's lessons—we were so happy to have escaped the paratroopers once again, even if we didn't say so. The smell of coffee filled the whole house. El Kho and Kamel enjoyed their breakfast in silence, while Oukhiti and I never stopped chattering and laughing, as if we were catching up after a long time apart. No doubt we needed to create an illusion of normalcy in our lives, even just for a few hours, a few minutes. In any case, after my near death in the shelter and Oukhiti's intense stress when dealing with the paratroopers, we were so happy to feel alive. We wanted to stop time to make this moment of gaiety and fulfillment last for all eternity.

Thinking back on those moments later, I became convinced of just how right one of our common adages from back home was: *Hata el mout taâti erraha.* (Even death gives a kind of rest.) I never stopped blaming myself for not having realized that this unprecedented moment was a harbinger of tragic events to come. Neither El Kho nor Oukhiti nor I had recognized that this moment, when we gathered at dawn with an unknown brother, was unthinkable, against all the rules. Our code of clandestine living instructed us in that moment to leave the house and the neighborhood immediately.

But we did the exact opposite.

As we savored our breakfast, at first I didn't realize El Kho's severely depleted state, but his high fever and splitting headache soon showed. Oukhiti urged him to go rest. He refused to go until he had finished copying the precious report to be sent to Tunis. Kamel was to fly the next day to Paris, where Germaine Tillion would await him as arranged. El Kho reminded him of his instructions: he must not forget to confirm in a letter by five o'clock that very afternoon that all the conditions for the trip were in order. Kamel left after tucking the precious document in among his work files. El Kho returned to bed in the room facing 4 Rue Cato, where Ali and Hassiba were. As Oukhiti came to give him some painkillers, she realized just how serious his condition was. He had a fever of almost 104°F, had been fatigued for several days, and had severe headaches and a hard time swallowing. Oukhiti quickly transformed into a nurse, examining his mouth and throat and deciding to treat him with traditional remedies in hopes of overcoming the evident infection. I let her soak his head, hands, forearms, and feet in vinegar, make him swallow concoctions for which only she knew the recipe, and go warn Hassiba that El Kho was very ill. Ali sent medicines and informed us that he was doing everything to find a trustworthy doctor. He ordered El Kho to stay in bed and said that he and Hassiba would join us around three or four in the morning, when the patrols were scarcer.

Throughout that day, Hassiba and I spoke several times across the gap of Rue Cato. Only our voices passed across, as Hassiba was concealed by the wooden *moucharabieh* screens that covered her window, and me behind the Persian blinds of the room where El Kho, nearly unconscious, was bedridden. Full of energy, I helped Oukhiti with the housework, took care of the children, and spent a while in Yemma's company on the second floor. She had great difficulty moving around and spent her days sitting cross-legged, aloof, fingering her prayer beads, defying time though it had not spared her. I found her surrounded by her grandchildren: consoling a crying one here, responding to another's questions there. I sat with her on her thick white sheepskin and listened with delight as she discussed her home region of Jijel, with the unparalleled beauty of its sea and mountains. She spoke of past celebrations in Jijel, in the Casbah, in Belcourt, and inevitably of her son the *chahid* (Uncle Mustapha) and her granddaughter Djamila, sentenced to death. It was as if she were completing a ritual to defy forgetting, ward off misfortune, and tame the pain.

From time to time, I came back to ask about El Kho's status. His fever was refusing to fall. In the kitchen, Oukhiti was preparing a feast instead of a dinner. Around five o'clock, Petit Omar brought the mail. I immediately noticed the alarming absence of a letter from Kamel. This was serious, very serious. I woke El Kho, alerted him, and asked him what steps to take. He replied: "Inform Ali. Tell him to stay on alert," and fell back into his torpor.

Convinced that his fever had dulled his senses and that he hadn't grasped all the information and its serious implications, I shook him again, repeating that Kamel had not confirmed his departure for Paris by letter as agreed. But El Kho managed to choke out: "Don't worry. Kamel isn't used to living in hiding. He can't understand." Then he plunged back into his semi-comatose state. I was not so reassured: I knew perfectly well what the absence of an expected letter meant, and I couldn't help thinking that if our brother weren't so seriously ill, he would have ordered us to immediately leave the home and its surroundings. Once informed, Ali and Hassiba confirmed that they would join us at dawn. Why didn't I dare to insist, to share with them the stifled anguish that was eating away at me? Why didn't I tell them of the pangs in my heart that were compressing my chest? Instead, I suppressed my inner trembling and returned to Oukhiti, Yemma, and the children around the *meïda*.

I decided to plunge back into my work, preparing the upcoming wom-en's demonstration. The lists of group organizers proposed by our sector leaders had to be sorted by neighborhood, a calendar of meetings estab-lished, and all of it discussed with brother Benhamida before submitting to El Kho for approval. I was working in the room where El Kho slept. After dinner, Oukhiti put her children to bed and came to join me. We were sit-ting on the mattress where I was to sleep, talking in a low voice so as not to disturb our patient, when a man's voice reached us from right nearby, out in the night. The voice was addressing the *moudjahidine*, to pay them hom-age while cursing those who, among the *oumma* of the Prophet Mohamed (peace be upon him), had betrayed their own people. We listened to the voice, which seemed to be addressing us. Oukhiti sprang to the window and, through the blinds, peered long into the night. She came back to me, grumbling, "He's against the wall of the *hammam*, not far from the house. You'd think he knew you were here and was speaking to you two . . ." The night's silence was broken only by the voice, which after a long pause picked up its invocations of the spirits of all the saints to protect the *moudjahidine*. We decided to ignore it, convinced that it was a provocation from a "blue." Was this yet another alarm bell that, unconsciously or not, I decided to ignore? I'll never know, even if years later, in prison, thinking back to that night that would continue to haunt me, I thought I could make out Alilou's voice. Poor Alilou, transformed by his torturers into a "blue," had he tried to alert us? It wouldn't have surprised me. But we decided to ignore the voice and continue our whispered conversation.

Around eleven-thirty that night, Oukhiti returned to her room on the second floor. I turned off the light and lay down with delight on the mat-tress, burying myself in the freshly washed sheets that smelled of lavender. It had been ages since I had slept in sheets, lying on a mattress. My thoughts went to my dear Hassiba, who must have been curled up in the tiny shelter at 4 Rue Cato. I sank into a deep sleep, so deep that when I opened my eyes a few hours later, I was gripped with panic. Oukhiti squatted in front of me, shaking me, but I couldn't recognize her. I saw a brunette woman opening and closing her mouth, but heard no sound. I looked around me, dazed, not knowing where I was. I was still in my dream, on my grandfather Hadj Abdessalem's farm. I stood in the middle of a vast brick-red plain, facing a hill that rose in the distance.

Atop the hill, my old uncle Cheikh Sid Ahmed walked slowly, his arm outstretched toward me in a sweeping gesture, while he spoke to me in a low voice: "Leave and fear nothing. Salvation and protection are with you!" Oukhiti's violent shaking finally overcame my dream and brought me back to reality. She begged me to get up and hurry to the shelter because the paratroopers were on the roof and might break down the door at any moment. She shook me with one hand while sprinkling black pepper on the carpet where my bed lay. A pile of wet laundry waited at her side, ready to be dumped on the mattress to absorb my body heat as soon as I rose. I jumped up, exclaiming "And El Kho?" She replied: "He's already in the shelter. Run, run, the door won't hold!" I grabbed a few documents around me and ran. As soon as I climbed the last rungs of the ladder, Oukhiti dragged it away to the *hammam* and went to open the door, clutching Captain Chabannes's attestation that was supposed to protect her from the repeated incursions of the French. As soon as I was in the shelter, I pushed back the thick, heavy slab, locked it in place with the iron bar, and sat down below the opening. El Kho was lying down, apparently still in bad shape and unconscious. I curled up against the wall and began to wait for Oukhiti to come and rescue us. The long silence that followed led me to believe that the attestation had had the desired effect.

Suddenly a loud voice penetrated the walls of our fully sealed shelter, repeating in French, "Yacef! Yacef! We know you're in there!" It shook me from head to toe, and to make sure I hadn't just hallucinated all these sounds, I put my ear to the groove of the opening. The voice continued, even stronger, "Yacef! Yacef! We know you're there! Give yourself up! You have no chance!"

No doubt: a paratrooper was addressing my big brother, who still lay there as if in a coma. I decided to cling to the crazy hope that if the paratroopers were in the house and addressing El Kho, maybe they still didn't know the shelter's exact location. They must have received some vague information that they were hoping to verify. I worried about my dear Oukhiti, convinced that she was going to be taken away and tortured again—and they would make it terrible for her this time because of the ruse she had played on them. I concluded my reasoning by deciding that El Kho and I must continue to play dead. But the voice started up again: "Yacef! Yacef! We know you're here. Give yourself up! You have no chance!" The difference between this and all the times the paratroopers had visited and walked away empty-handed was glaring. I approached our brother and shook him awake: "Kho! Kho! Wake up! The paratroopers are calling you. They know you're here!" El Kho, burning with fever, sat up, leaned against the wall, loaded a clip into his gun, and remained motionless.

In the shelter, it was pitch black. Silence fell again. Perhaps they had left, taking poor unfortunate Oukhiti with them? The silence was thick and palpable and the darkness more threatening than ever. Suddenly violent blows fell upon the wall. From the noise and shaking, it was clear the paratroopers were attacking the thick, heavy slab that sealed our shelter. They knew not only our safe house but the exact location of our shelter. But how?

We were going to die like rats in a hole. We would have no chance to wage a final battle since our shelter was suspended above the house's stairwell. I was sure that we would have to just sit and wait for death in whatever form it came. But I had an urgent, critical task to complete: destroying all the documents, especially the lists of women that we had been collecting since July to prepare the famous march. Letting that information fall into the paratroopers' hands was out of the question. The blows continued to fall on the slab while in the shelter, the darkness was blinding. Groping around, I swept the ground with my hands, gathering all the papers into a pile in what seemed to be the center of the shelter. God, it was dark! As I fumbled, I felt a hard, oblong object roll under my hand, and grabbed it: a grenade. I groped my way over to the wall to find El Kho. My hand met his burning cheek, and whispered to him: "Give me your hand, I found a grenade!"

I placed it in the palm of his hand and finished pulling together all the papers I could find. The blows, strong and regular, continued. El Kho and I leaned on either side of the slab, which had so far resisted and not budged. I had a tender thought for my brother Ali and his extraordinary skills. Maybe he was going to save us once again. Hope, as unreasonable as it was impossible, overcame me, sweeping away the terror. Suddenly calm, I repeated Auntie Baya's phrase to myself: *"Rana fi âanayat Allah."* (We are under God's protection.) When the point of the spike finally poked through the slab, El Kho and I, without even speaking, slid back the iron bar and jerked the slab sharply back toward us. Without hesitating, El Kho threw the armed grenade. It exploded amid the soldiers filling the stairwell. Screams mingled with the crackling bursts of El Kho's machine gun. Below, it was total panic.

Voices cried out, shouting over each other among groans, screams of pain, running footsteps, men scrambling all around. I crouched low and set fire to the documents. The flames rose. In their glow I could make out El Kho sitting with his back against the wall beside the opening, machine gun held tight between his legs, which were tucked up against his body. He already looked detached from the living world.

I took the gun and extended the barrel visibly past the edge of the opening to deter any paratroopers from approaching to throw a grenade into our shelter. I placed myself in front of the opening, gun in hand, trying to guess what was going on downstairs in the patio. After the screams, a silence had fallen. I heard El Kho asking me to extinguish the fire. The smoke was choking. But I decided to disobey and let the fire do its precious work, destroying the documents. In any case, we were about to die.

My thoughts went to Ali and Hassiba. What would become of them if the paratroopers forcibly evacuated the entire quarter in order to blow it up? Would they stay in their shelter and go down with the house? Would they be able to hide and escape? Hassiba might conceivably sneak out amid the women. But Ali? I was sure he would not hesitate to fight, thinking not only of defending himself but also of helping us. Perhaps all four of us would die. I was praying to God to help Ali and Hassiba to leave the area and change shelters when I noticed that the fire had flickered out.

The Traitor

I was about to ask El Kho to take my place so I could rekindle the fire when a loud voice startled me: "Yacef! Turn yourself in! Turn yourself in! It's all over for you! You're alone! Your brothers have all abandoned you! Safi is with us, Safi is one of us!"

I leaned out to try to see the doorway to the patio, and shouted at them: "Liars! You're nothing but liars! We know your methods! We know your tricks! Bloodthirsty assassins!"

But the voice continued, still addressing El Kho: "Yacef! Safi is one of us! He is here beside us, with us!"

I leaned over to El Kho, shouted to him: "Kho! Kho! Did you hear? Safi was arrested. He's here."

At the same time, I thought: *But Safi doesn't know this home!*

I leaned over to try to see the bottom of the stairs and figure out where the voice was coming from, shouting, "Safi! Safi! Is it true what he's saying? Are you there? Were you arrested?"

I had never met Safi. But I knew that Hacène Gandriche, also called Zerrouk or Safi, had replaced Ramel as the AAZ military commander while Benhamida took Si Mourad's place as the political chief.

A hesitant voice responded, "Yes, I'm here."

And I continued, refusing to believe the obvious, unbearable truth: "They tortured you, the bastards, the Nazis! They tortured you, right?"

The first voice replied calmly: "He is here with us voluntarily. Yacef, Safi is with us. He saw that you had tricked him!"

I was mad with rage. They dared to tell us that our own brothers had willingly gone to their side! I resumed my screams: "Torturers! Nazis! Assassins! Safi, come up here so I can see you!"

Safi's hesitant voice hit me like a bullet in the heart. "I can't, I can't. I'm afraid of our brother."

Crushed, no longer able to hide from the terrible truth before me, I spat back with a sardonic laugh, "If only you had been afraid of him when you were denouncing him! Dirty traitor!"

I was facing a cruel, unbearable fact: our military leader was a traitor! He was delivering us, bound hand and foot, right to Massu. But what did he know? Did he know where Ali and Hassiba were? I was going mad with anxiety. Suddenly I recalled the image, one day when we were in our shelter at 4 Rue Cato, of El Kho bounding down the stairs to the front door to grab Mahmoud, our liaison officer with Safi, to order him back out into the street to retrace his steps because two young men, one wearing a dress shirt, were following him. El Kho was sure, since at that time he spent his afternoons sitting in front of the *moucharabieh* screen overlooking the Djamaâ Lihoud synagogue and Rue Randon, watching the passersby and comings and goings. Mahmoud was returning from one of our mailboxes and El Kho had noticed that two young men were walking behind him at the same pace, tailing him, and had stopped when our messenger turned toward our safe house. Unfortunately, when Mahmoud doubled back, the two young men had vanished down the stairs that led from Djamaâ Lihoud to Rue Boutin. At nineteen, Mahmoud was a sincere and committed activist but a novice nonetheless; he knew nothing of the art of tailing. I remember El Kho's sole preoccupation after this incident: leave the area as soon as possible.

I recall whispering to Hassiba: "There he is, all antsy again! We'll never find a better safe house than this one! Here we can see the paratroopers' every move." But El Kho was right, of course. That had been just a few days earlier—an eternity.

But at dawn we found ourselves trapped in the shelter. I tried to gauge the extent of the disaster: the traitor had been feeding the French army's intelligence services everything for a long time now! El Kho was silent. Had he heard my back-and-forth?

The calm, confident voice reached us again: "Yacef! Yacef! Everyone has given you up! Kamel! Kamel is here. He's on our side!"

I bent down and shouted, "Liars! We know how you work. Kamel! Kamel! Answer me! Is it true what he says? Answer!" I did hear a voice respond, but so weak that I shouted again, "Kamel! If you're there, I want to see you! Come up!"

My head was ready to explode. Kamel had still been with us the evening of September 23. He had left us the next morning at eight o'clock. How had he been arrested? Where? When? A few seconds later, Kamel appeared on the stairs, moving with difficulty, leaning against the wall. It was him, but my God, what a state he was in! His face had been beaten to a pulp and one of his eyeballs protruded from its socket; he held it in place with one hand. What a nightmare.

I couldn't help but scream out my hatred at the paratroopers and their barbarism, cruelty, and especially hypocrisy: "Of course! The French don't torture, these fathers of human rights who call themselves humanists and denounce the Nazis' brutality at great length. Let's have a laugh at that!" Kamel turned his face—or what was left of it—up toward me. His whole body exuded horror and fear. I shouted at him, "Well, talk! Tell us what they did to you, these criminals!" Nothing could stop me. The rage and powerlessness to which I was reduced had removed any sense of fear, and I really wanted to have at them. But how? I searched deep inside for something that could hit them harder even than bullets, and let fly with all the rage I could muster: "Yes, we will be free, whether you like it or not! We'll boot you all out of our country! Yes, Algeria will be free of you and from you!" My words and my voice were all I had left. So I didn't stop talking and screaming, reasoning that this way at least my voice would continue to resonate in their heads, offering them no respite. "Yes, Algeria will be free!"

Then Kamel disappeared from my sight and a silence fell again, heavy and menacing. I remained standing in front of the opening, still pointing the gun out. The fire had completely gone out and the smell of charred paper filled the shelter. El Kho got up, moved beside me, and nudged me aside to take my place and his machine gun. I decided to sit down. With my back against the wall beside the opening, I drew my legs to my chest and rested my head on my knees. This seemed like the only way to ensure that my body might be found in a dignified posture, were the house blown up. Finding some strength in this absurd idea, I wedged myself in as best I could, pulling the folds of my *seroual* around to better cover myself, and set about waiting for death. I recited the profession of faith, prayed for God's grace, and appealed to the spirits of all the saints and my ancestors.

My last dream came back to me, interrupting me in my wait for the cold hand of Death. So I began to chant what Samia and I had always repeated back when we first joined the cause: "Our lives are not worth more than Zabana's." And I added, "My life is no better than Si Mohamed's, Uncle Mustapha's, Si Mourad's, Ramel's . . ." I repeated my profession of faith. I thought of my parents and all the suffering I had inflicted on them, and asked their forgiveness.

Then the sound of Oukhiti's voice and a wailing baby right nearby made me shudder. I opened my eyes and sat upright, once again on alert. What was Oukhiti doing on the steps with her baby in her arms? Her voice was clearly right outside the shelter. She was addressing our brother, repeating over and over a phrase about how "they" were determined to blow up the house and the neighborhood if we refused to surrender, since "they" were keen to preserve their officers and soldiers after some of them, including a colonel, had been injured by El Kho's grenade and machine-gun bursts.

It was indeed Oukhiti, and her voice, but the words that reached me didn't sound like hers. I knew by heart the unwavering courage, determination, and composure she had shown again and again. In a split second, I realized that the real message she was sending to our brother was the one she was communicating with her eyes and facial expressions. I raised my head to read her face, her gestures, and her glances. And I understood. Her eyes insisted to me to remind El Kho firmly that Ali and Hassiba were in the house across the street, and they were doomed to certain death if we refused to surrender. Oukhiti was pleading for us to give ourselves up, telling El Kho forcefully that he had a duty to stay alive to keep fighting and an obligation to preserve the lives of his fighters. With her eyes and expressions, she was pointing to the house where Ali, Hassiba, and Petit Omar were hiding.

At one point she called to him, "What did Mustapha and Si Mohamed die for? I'm sure that if they were alive, things would have turned out differently." She didn't let up. El Kho was silent. She called to me. But I refused to look her in the eyes. I didn't want to meet her gaze because I didn't want her to tear me from my death vigil; I would have just disappointed her, since my mind was already made up. I chose death for fear of torture, fear of its humiliation, fear of not being able to withstand the torment, fear of having to live with the shame of knowing I had cracked. I stayed silent, resigned to my death, but El Kho's extreme solitude and sense of honor leapt to my mind and pierced my heart. As our leader, El Kho had refused to surrender, and backed up that decision with a grenade and bursts of gunfire launched at the enemy. But as political and military leader in the AAZ, he had the sacred duty to preserve the lives of his fighters and of his people. Ali was a colonel in the ALN: preserving his life was an obligation. And I knew El Kho held dear young Hassiba and Petit Omar's lives above his own. But I couldn't bring myself to intervene in the surreal exchange.

I wanted to get it over with, but death wouldn't come. Instead, a heavy silence fell, enveloping the shelter and the whole house, beating back Oukhiti's voice. I couldn't say how many times our sister in arms and protective host climbed up to us and went back down. Finally, El Kho's voice made me raise my head and sit up. He told me we had to go downstairs, that I had to go down there right away. He repeated that I needed to understand. I knew he was referring to saving Ali and Hassiba, but how could I explain to him that my fear of torture was stronger and more terrifying than my fear of death? He shook me, repeating, "We have to do it. Get down, right away!"

So I stepped over the edge of the shelter's opening and placed a foot on the ladder, mortified to surrender to the enemy. From the last rung of the ladder, I had to jump down to the stair. As I landed, the little 6.35 revolver fell from my waistband and clattered to the ground. In the silence that accompanied my descent, the gun's impact on the slate pavers echoed loudly. I stared with amazement at the desperate stampede of paratroopers who, seconds before, had also been in the stairwell. Terrified by the noise of the gun on the slate, they fled for safety! I regretted not having had a grenade and burst out laughing: "That's the bravery and courage of the great French army? Deserting at the sound of a little revolver hitting the ground? In the face of an unarmed woman?"

But I was already being jostled and pushed down to the courtyard, which was harshly lit and packed with paratroopers. Blinded by their floodlights, I couldn't make out any faces but was impressed by the numbers they had mobilized to subdue us. It's true that the catch was a big one—the AAZ leader himself—but the disproportion shocked me and left me feeling like a grain of sand facing a tornado. I perked up again immediately, told myself not to flinch, and coolly asked to go change clothes. I wanted to swap my Algiers housewife outfit for more businesslike attire to represent my position as an ALN fighter—and proud of it, come what may. To my great surprise, they accepted. A swarm of soldiers surrounded me (as if I could have escaped) and pushed me up to the second floor. Oukhiti had already prepared a change of clothes: a skirt and a sleeveless top. I barked at the paratroopers to leave the room so I could change. They obeyed and I closed the door to get dressed. Yemma, as usual, was sitting on her sheepskin, fingering her prayer beads. The crimson shade of her face was the only sign of her emotion. I went to her, kissed her several times, and asked her forgiveness for the uproar. She ran her fingers through my thick, short hair, whispering verses from the Quran, then told me, "You are a *moudjahida* blessed by God, and you must fear no one but God Himself, the Almighty."

I hugged her one last time in my arms, then slipped on my clothes and ballet flats. I turned back to the five little ones, hugged them tight in my arms, kissed them, and asked them to be brave, knowing that their mother would be arrested.

Then I headed for the door and stepped out. I was handcuffed and pushed toward the courtyard.

Arrest of Zohra Drif (picture from which cover is derived)

In Godard's Office

Outside, I found myself in the middle of a pack of paratroopers, who shoved me into the back of a military Jeep. El Kho was already sitting inside, also handcuffed. I sat beside him, my back to the front cab. The sun was just beginning to break as the Jeep drove off. I watched Rue Cato disappear, including number 4, where Ali and Hassiba remained. I knew they would keep fighting, keep the AAZ alive, put it back on its feet, and strengthen it.

As soon as they learned of our arrest, they would leave their safe house and the area, in line with our rules. But how could we get them the two critical pieces of information, Kamel's arrest and Safi's betrayal? I prayed that Ali would change everything, including his military officer, Safi the traitor! It was then that the idea hit me. I slid as close as possible to El Kho, rubbing my face with my bound hands and whispered, "Ali and Hassiba are in the *maquis*." El Kho coughed to signal his understanding. The Jeep sped swiftly, swerving onto Rue de la Lyre, as I continued, still whispering, "I am not from the Casbah. Whenever I moved I was always guided by a scout that I didn't know. I served as a liaison officer and secretary. I executed all the orders that were given to me under the strict rules of secrecy." My brother in arms agreed with another cough. I watched Rue de la Lyre speed past and bid farewell to the Place du Gouvernement and the twin minarets of Ketchaoua Mosque, remembering the heroic suffering of Dahmane, of whom I had no news. I stared with moist eyes at the Casbah, my beloved adoptive city. She who had welcomed me with open arms, offered me not just her heritage and marvels, but also her beauty and that of her children, her hospitality, and her inhabitants. I had arrived there almost a year before and even when arrested, handcuffed, and hustled off by the sinister paratroopers, I left it more enriched than I could ever be again. I already knew our people's hospitality, generosity of spirit, and sense of dignity. But the Casbah introduced me to the generosity of the humblest of the humble, their unfailing courage, and the richness of their hearts—ever vaster than their deprivation.

We didn't go much further before the Jeep rolled to a stop. Paratroopers jumped into a line, forming a human noose around us. They led us into a Moorish-style building, pushing us toward a staircase at a run. We crossed a series of courtyards and galleries, ending our march in a large office where a man in military dress was seated stiffly behind a desk. I learned later that it was Colonel Godard. My eyes didn't linger on him; I was attracted—almost

Arrest of Yacef Saâdi

magnetically—by a huge board on a tripod over the colonel's right shoulder. Here before my eyes, reconstituted in its entirety, was the complete organogram of the AAZ. Atop the chart was a title in bold capital letters: ALGIERS AUTONOMOUS ZONE.

Below were four names in boxes: YACEF SAADI, ALI AMAR (that was Ali la Pointe), ZOHRA DRIF, HASSIBA BEN BOUALI. I scanned the panel and realized that the boxes with thumbtacks stuck in them indicated those who had been killed or arrested. So few boxes without tacks! The extent of the disaster was clear to see.

Godard spoke to El Kho but, too absorbed with the board, I couldn't hear his words. I was waiting for him to rise and pin our names, expelling us from the AAZ and signing our death warrants. Strangely, I was no longer afraid. A more degrading and destructive feeling had crushed me. Even today, I look back on that instant as the most bitter humiliation in my life. It was not that I was arrested, but that I was arrested because of the betrayal of one of our own. Indeed, Godard savored his victory and recounted to us—and his officers and soldiers—how he himself had dictated to Hacène Gandriche (Safi, known as Zerrouk at the time) the response to the first letter El Kho had addressed to him after Ramel and Si Mourad's death. I also learned from Godard himself that it was Gandriche who had helped locate and kill Ramel and Si Mourad.

Godard exulted, going so far as to explain that the arrest and beating of the liaison officer linking Ramel and Zerrouk had been staged in order to protect their mole, knowing that El Kho would conduct an investigation to determine how the paratroopers had located their refuge. Laughing, Godard merrily recounted how he came up with the idea to change Gandriche's pseudonym, Zerrouk. After Ramel and Si Mourad's deaths, he had dictated to Zerrouk a passage of his response letter to El Kho expressing his "immense pain of losing two courageous brothers," volunteering to continue their fight, and announcing that henceforth he would adopt the new alias Safi, "pure" in Arabic, to confuse the enemy. If I'd had hemlock then, I would have drunk every last drop!

Then Godard sarcastically asked El Kho where he had "lost his devoted bodyguard Ali la Pointe."

El Kho, with detachment, said, "Ali and Hassiba fled to the *maquis* long ago."

I was tormented by the idea that Ali and Hassiba would inevitably reestablish contact with Safi. The only one who could warn them of his treason, Oukhiti, was probably already in the hands of the torturers. My eyes wandered around the room. I was taken aback by the number of officers, all armed to the teeth. This obscene deployment of brute force against two activists—who the enemy must have known were in bad shape thanks to Safi the traitor—restored my pride.

Then they asked us to get up so they could escort us out, and the huge assembly of troops leapt into motion as if preparing for the battlefield. As El Kho and I were advancing between two rows of soldiers, I met a gaze staring back at me. Instead of glancing aside, I looked him right back in the eyes: it was the husband of Marguerite, the close friend of Madame Caux, in whose home I had taken refuge just moments after planting the bomb at the Milk Bar. We looked each other straight in the eye, neither of us trying to look away. I think the colonel and I shared the same conviction: the relationship of dominator to dominated doesn't allow for real friendship. He did his duty and I did mine.

Suddenly, from amid the human gauntlet the soldiers formed around us, a bright light blinded me and left me blinking. After a few seconds, I realized that these were flashes from photographers and journalists. The photo of Si Mohamed handcuffed leapt directly to my mind: I had to face them with dignity. I stood straight upright and looked them up and down, trying to send a message: "We are fighters from the ALN and proud of it. We are the enemies of your arrogant world. Your brute force will not diminish us. Free and independent Algeria will live, despite everything!"

Isolated at Villa Nador

We were stuffed into a prisoner transport van. It was daylight now, but the only light inside filtered in between the bars on the van's two rear windows. We were still handcuffed and surrounded by heavily armed paratroopers. I told myself that Godard enjoyed sowing fear. The van sped rapidly along the still-deserted streets. I recognized the route. The van stopped with a squeal in front of a building across the street from the Lycée Fromentin, where I had spent seven years of my young life. I recognized the place: Villa Nador. I hadn't known it belonged to the military. Right away, I decided that this location was an auspicious sign.

I remember it as a black hole. I still don't know how I landed in such a dingy room, lit only by a single dim bulb dangling from the ceiling. The door closed behind me. When my eyes adapted, I saw a straw mattress on the floor in the corner. After more than thirty-six hours without sleep, I was exhausted, disoriented, and overwhelmed by the avalanche of sudden, violent events. I slumped down onto the suspicious mattress, assailed by conflicting emotions, fatigue, and a host of questions. First, the enigma of Kamel's arrest. Outside our tiny group, only Ali Bouzourène was aware of our meeting. Maybe he had been picked up and tortured? But that didn't add up because the army had raided our safe house the evening of September 23 and left empty-handed, since El Kho, Kamel, and I were in the shelter.

Safi's obvious, devastating betrayal stood out for its violent clarity, like the flash of a bomb. I shuddered. A new pain that I had never experienced until then wracked my insides: the very unique pain of betrayal. Not only is its intensity particular, but also its extent and the way it destabilizes you and your whole world. Suffering a betrayal destroys your points of references, the certainties necessary for life and for trust in the human race, including in yourself.

I suddenly understood why Godard had exulted before El Kho and me while divulging how Safi the traitor gave up Ramel and Si Mourad. He wanted to annihilate our humanity. I surprised myself by duplicating Si Mohamed's gesture the day he heard Ben Alla El Hadj on the radio: I pinched my forearm, thinking about my capacity for resistance, the cyanide capsule that I didn't have, and the brutal interrogation that awaited me.

What would they ask me about? They already knew the entire AAZ organo-gram, thanks to Safi. Would they ask about Ali and Hassiba's whereabouts? But Safi the traitor must already have explained our rules: Ali and Hassiba would have already changed safe houses. And El Kho had said they were in the *maquis*. As long as they didn't get back in contact with Safi immediately, the paratroopers would end up believing El Kho. So it was up to us to hold fast to our version, come what may. I began to recite it like an incantation, as if I were chanting Koranic verses: "Ali and Hassiba are in the *maquis*. The proof? When El Kho was arrested, he was without his inseparable brother Ali la Pointe." My secular incantations came from an irrepressible desire to condition myself, but the fear of speaking under torture haunted me. I decided to fight against it with all my strength by forcibly summoning all my will, my reason, and the certainties that Godard had failed to destroy.

The strongest certainty was that Hassiba and Ali, as surely as El Kho and I had been arrested, had already changed safe houses. But the memory of our difficulties finding alternative safe houses assailed me. At this point in my attempted exercise in rational reasoning, I began to cast about like a shipwrecked sailor for any hope to cling to that, for lack of another refuge in the Casbah, Hassiba and Ali would abandon the old city and leave Algiers. But to leave Algiers, they would absolutely need to contact the traitor Safi. The noose tightened around me, choking me, throwing out my reason, and plunging me back into the glowing torments of the hell that is betrayal.

Thinking hard about Yemma and Auntie Baya, and their saying "*Rahoum fi âanayet Allah*" (They're under God's protection), I calmed myself but without appeasing my questioning mind.

I resumed my chanting, "Hassiba and Ali are in the *maquis*," trying to imagine myself facing my torturers. Exhausted, curled up on the mattress, my numbed limbs ached. I tried not to abandon myself to sleep for fear of being caught by surprise when they came to get me for the interrogation. So I decided to sit up and explore my cell. My eyes had adjusted to the dark-ness. I saw a window with its wooden shutter drawn. Then, in front of the window I noticed a figure. Scrutinizing it for some time, I eventually real-ized that it was a person sitting in a chair. No doubt a man, a soldier.

My reaction was to shove myself into the corner and observe him warily. I don't know how long I remained there, watching him. It was long, because I fell asleep. When I awoke with a start, he was pacing from one wall to the other like a caged animal. I caught his hateful gaze and decided to escape from him by shutting myself in the corner in Hassiba's favorite position, with my head turned to the wall and my chin on my knees. I had lost all notion of time. I didn't know how long I had been there or whether it was day or night. Even today I can't remember eating, drinking, or using the toilet there. I only have a vague memory of long cries and moans. Perhaps I imagined them. I remember that the door was ajar at times and that a man stood there in the doorway. I knew he was staring at me, but I didn't look at him. In any case, I had decided to no longer open my eyes, to prevent them from reading me. From where I sat I couldn't make anything out anyway.

The door opened all the way, admitting a new soldier. I opened my eyes. He stood looking at me for what seemed like a long time, then stepped forward and introduced himself as Captain de la Bourdonnaye. The guard in the cell stood at attention. He continued: "Could we chat, perhaps?" Captain de la Bourdonnaye launched into a monologue on France, its grandeur, and the need to put an end to this "fratricidal" war. In short, it was all the same messages that the loudspeaker trucks crisscrossing the Casbah serenaded us with, just in the style of a captain with a fancy name. I did nothing and said nothing, but made a silent wish: *Get out!* Instead, he spoke endlessly. I stared sternly at him with cold, distant eyes until he stopped his pointless soliloquy and left. A swarm of paratroopers invaded my cell and ordered me to get up and follow them. I stood, smoothed my skirt with my hands, and ran my fingers through my hair. They slipped handcuffs on me. As I crossed the threshold, I tried in vain to situate myself in the villa. Beefy paratroopers surrounded me and pushed me forward so I couldn't see anything. They shoved me into a van whose wide-open back doors waited at the exit to the villa.

Facing Trinquier

I didn't know what day it was. Based on the light, the angle of the sun, and the heat, I concluded that it was well into the afternoon. I held my head up to follow our route through the two barred windows. The number of paratroopers around me and the amount of their equipment didn't bode well, but I was so tired, so exhausted, so sapped by the waiting that I felt relieved at the prospect of finally meeting my torturers and being done with it. I decided to fill my eyes, my head, and my heart with every bit of Algiers that passed by. I silently repeated my incantations as I snatched a glimpse of some greenery and a patch of blue sky, watching closely for a glimpse of the sea. I recognized the white walls of the Summer Palace, the Saint George Hotel, the Bardo, the university, the Grande Poste, Bresson Square, and the sea. The van stopped in front of a building. (I would learn much later that it was the Palais Bruce. At independence, it would become the FLN headquarters, led by my future husband, Rabah Bitat.)

The paratroopers marched me hastily to a room, dumped me, and shut the door behind me. Bright sunlight entered through a large window. I was happy to feel the sun's warmth on my face and to be freed from the handcuffs. I felt a presence. I turned my head to the right and, oh, a miracle! Brother Yacef was there, seated on a bench, his face lit by that inimitable smile. We both spoke at the same time, each asking about the treatment the other had received, confirming that neither of us had suffered abuse. With my eyes, I asked him why we found ourselves together in this room. And with his eyes he replied that he didn't know. We sat for a long moment, side by side, silent. We were certainly being watched.

Thinking back to my spy novels, I slid my hand under the bench, along the wall, searching for the inevitable switch or mirror . . . nothing. I got up to explore the room, to go to the window that attracted me like a magnet, sure that it would give me a view of the lower Casbah. I walked on tiptoe, looking around, expecting to hear a voice ordering me to sit back down, when I caught sight of a newspaper spread out on the table. Was it for this that they had dragged us across Algiers? I thought immediately of Hassiba and Ali, and my heart began to beat furiously. I approached the newspaper, which was laid open to the two central pages. A headline in bold capital letters read: "HOW THEY TORTURE IN ALGERIA." It was followed by a detailed exposé. I read quickly, afraid I would soon be interrupted. I immediately recognized the report we had prepared and sent to our brothers in Tunis on the various torture methods used by the French army. We had sent it to our senior leaders without much real hope that it would reach them. My eyes riveted on the paper, I called El Kho to come share the immeasurable joy that overwhelmed me upon seeing this miracle.

For several months I had thought that we were leading the fight alone, cut off from everyone else, but here was the rejuvenating, intoxicating evidence that we had never been alone or cut off from our leaders. My quick skim was enough to recognize my own style and flourishes and Si Mourad's shocking phrases: everything was there, down to the tiniest details. I checked the front page, curious to see what newspaper had had the courage to publish an exposé so thoroughly documented and damaging to our enemy. I was sure I was hallucinating: *El Moudjahid!* I started shaking El Kho.

"Kho! Kho! Do you see what I see? We have a *real* newspaper, just like them!" I think I was in a trance. The last publications from our information service that I remembered having in hand had been simple mimeographed sheets. We stood side by side, El Kho's eyes—like mine—racing feverishly from one headline to the next, from one page to the next. I couldn't stop talking and commenting on everything as I quickly scanned the paper: "Kho! Do you see? Are you reading this? There's lots of info on the international front, and look, there's even info on the attacks here on the home front!" He read calmly, leaving me to my delirium. I think at that moment I experienced what my people would experience on July 5, 1962: *El Moudjahid,* in the form of a true modern newspaper, confirmed the truth that my country would inevitably be free.

More than that, for me *El Moudjahid* made the Algerian state real. Godard and his sarcasm were swept aside, along with my fear. The existence of *El Moudjahid* rendered any apprehension pointless. At that instant—as unreasonable as it may seem today—there in that prison I experienced a moment of absolute freedom.

A dry, shrill, unpleasant voice assaulted my eardrums. I turned toward it. A short man in an immaculate uniform, his chest covered in medals and tricolored distinctions, advanced toward us stiffly. *All he needs is a riding crop in his hand and the Nazi package would be complete,* I thought. He stopped beside us. Pointing his finger at me, he exclaimed "You! It's you, isn't it, who wrote this web of lies?" I understood immediately that he was referring to the torture exposé.

Shocked, I replied, "You mean the article on the torture methods you use against us? To me, to us, you dare to claim that the contents of this article are false?" I was sincerely flabbergasted. I turned to El Kho, taking him as a witness: "You heard that? Did you hear what he said? He's daring to claim that what the article says is false!"

The officer's finger pointed at me again, violently, and he exclaimed: "It is you! You're the dangerous one here! The black angel! It is you who have perverted everything!" I stared, dumbfounded, absolutely astounded to hear a senior officer of the French army speaking in this way, articulating judgments worthy of the most backward men. I didn't know what else to do besides repeat to El Kho, "Do you hear this? Did you hear what he said?"

He continued in his high-pitched, nasty voice with a hatred that froze my blood: "In my country we have a saying: 'One day everyone finds a shoe for his foot.'"

I didn't know this saying but I understood what he was suggesting: that I was standing before "my master," the one who would reduce me to dust. I shuddered, seeing that he had the physique for the job. I had no doubt about his cruelty or sophisticated sadism. I wasn't mistaken: before me was Colonel Trinquier, known to his colleagues as "the Asian" for how many he had killed in Indochina. But I would only learn that much later. Stunned, I continued to stare. He attacked me with a frightening aggression.

"You have deceived a whole nation! You are responsible! The one truly responsible!"

"Me, deceive my people? Well, come with me to the Casbah. Let's present ourselves, you and me, alone, without your minions. And we'll see how each of us is welcomed." My remark just managed to incense him further.

He said in a hiss that oozed with the full force of his cruelty, "If I were the Supreme Judge, it is you and you alone that I would condemn to death." Then he turned his back in an impeccable spin, marched toward a low door we hadn't noticed embedded in the wall, and disappeared.

Colonel Trinquier's violence left me speechless. I had never imagined that I could arouse such crippling hatred. Even though we were at war, none of my brothers and sisters—not one—was capable of such hatred. El Kho and I remained silent, still standing beside the table where *El Moudjahid* was spread flat. To purify myself, I plunged back into it, seeking the warm brotherhood of my people. The reports on the attacks led by our National Liberation Army restored my calm, warmed me, and stimulated me. Damn all the Trinquiers of the world! Long live the ALN!

That was my mindset moments later, as I followed the soldier who had come to fetch me. I hugged my brother before leaving him, whispering to him, "*Inchallah*, God will protect our brothers." I was thinking of Hassiba and Ali. He understood.

The sentry took me into an office where I saw, seated behind a desk, the colonel who had just promised me death. He was as stiff sitting as he was standing. He motioned for me to sit in the chair across from him, then handed me a sheet of paper and a pen and ordered me to write what my activities had been in the FLN/ALN. Not understanding where he was going with this, I didn't move. He repeated his order, barking now. I could feel how tense he was, gripped with a dull anger, his disappointment contrasting with the hatred and cruelty in his eyes. Even today I shudder just thinking about him. His whole body radiated a violence he struggled to contain. He barked again. I complied.

First I explained in detail the reasons I had joined the ALN's ranks. Then I explained the tasks entrusted to me: secretarial work, transportation, liaising, distribution of leaflets, supporting the people. Finally, I stated that my activity had taken place in the Casbah, stressing that since I was not from the old *medina*, I was always guided by an activist but didn't know their names due to our rules of secrecy. As for the team with whom I worked, I gave the names of all those who were already dead or arrested and sentenced to death: Djamila, Dahmane, Ghani, Si Mourad, Ramel, and of course Yacef, with whom I had been arrested. He took the paper I had signed, handed it to the soldier serving as clerk and dismissed me. That was all.

In the van that brought me back alone to my cell in the Villa Nador, I remained concerned. What was I to make of his attitude? He hadn't submitted me to interrogation, leaving me to decide what to declare, and then made a show of not bothering to read what I had written. Obviously he didn't need me for information. The only thing I was sure of was that the French army wanted to hold me in solitary confinement, without any possibility of contact with the outside world. A sentry was always at my side. Two or three of them took shifts throughout the entire day—as if I could have escaped. The reason was clear: they wanted to make absolutely sure that Hassiba and Ali would not be informed of Safi's betrayal.

I wondered if Godard and the others, in their euphoria at having arrested one of the French police's most wanted men, hadn't committed a tactical error by parading us before the press. Would they repeat the Ben M'hidi episode with El Kho? But they had no interest in doing so, given the objectives they were pursuing and just how much the realities on the ground had shifted against us. Especially since El Kho had nothing they didn't already know. Safi's treachery and Kamel's arrest and torture had given them everything. What's more, they now possessed the detailed report we had prepared. Only Ali and Hassiba were missing from their trophy case. El Kho had declared that "Ali and Hassiba fled to the *maquis* long ago." I suddenly understood that Godard hadn't believed him. If he had, then why keep us isolated? I was sure that El Kho was also cut off from the outside world. They had no need to question us, since Safi's betrayal had given them the whole AAZ. They knew that our sister and brother had moved. They just had to wait until Hassiba and Ali resumed contact with Safi—which is to say with Captain Allaire, Colonel Trinquier, and Colonel Godard. So why show us off to the press? For at least three purposes: First, to affirm the merits of Massu's "Battle of Algiers" and the alleged invincibility of the French army, which had managed to "arrest and neutralize Yacef Saâdi, the great terrorist leader." Second, to reassure the settlers. Third, to destroy in the eyes of the "natives" the legend that was Yacef Saâdi.

I knew all these efforts were doomed to failure. They were the enemy: political, military, cultural, and religious. The existential enemy. The enemy of our people, our land, and our Prophet. Their word was blasphemy, their presence a sacrilege, their actions a desecration. But their blindness didn't allow them to grasp these fundamental subtleties. I decided to cling to the only certainty that remained: detaining me in isolation and guarding me personally at all hours of the day and night were attempts to keep Safi's betrayal a secret until Ali and Hassiba contacted him.

Their fate tormented me. I was convinced that Godard, Trinquier, Allaire, and their soldiers were well aware of Ali's psychological profile, fearlessness, and intelligence. If they managed to locate his new safe house, they wouldn't come up with any other strategy than to blow up the house. The army would refuse, I was sure, to risk repeating their battle with Ramel and Si Mourad. They would not want to face the formidable Ali la Pointe. I began to pray with all my soul that Hassiba would prevail upon our brother to accept a pause and break off all external contact, including with Safi.

A Catastrophic Blow

Prostrate in the gloom of my cell, beyond all reality, detached from all the groans and piercing cries I heard, I waited. It might have been day or night, I'll never know, when two long legs came to a stop beside my head as I lay on the straw mattress. A sheet torn from a notebook was laid by my head. I understood immediately, even before picking it up. Captain de la Bourdonnaye had left the door wide open to let the light in. On the sheet, I recognized Hassiba's writing. It was a letter, addressed to "Brother Safi." Ali had resumed contact with Safi, and so with the French army's intelligence services, and thus with certain death!

"We will wait until our sister and brother are taken to prison, and then we will make a bonfire for them in Algiers," they had written, sealing closed the trap. I wanted to scream but no sound came out of my throat. In the custom of funerals in my home on the high plains, I wanted to cry the ancient way, by proclaiming in the vile captain's face Ali's courage, bravery, great feats of arms, generosity, and huge heart. I wanted so much to scream in that cell how Ali was right and good, how he loved life and Algeria. I wanted to cry the way we did back home, loudly, for the certain death of our brave knight, to cry for the final battle that these cowards would refuse to give him, to cry at the type of death that they would impose upon him, this death—the only one he feared—buried under the rubble of a house before his weapon had even spoken. And Hassiba, oh! My God! Hassiba our youngest, Hassiba our little sister. I wanted to scream her name so that she would haunt them forever, to profess her beauty, her complete devotion to our people and to the liberation of our bound and raped homeland. I wanted to sing, yes, to belt out at the top of my lungs our funeral songs in honor of her ingenuity, her intelligence, her selflessness, and her courage that were matched only by the tenderness of her personality and her age: she was only nineteen.

But the sounds wouldn't come out of my throat, which was knotted up by the terrifying realization that my sister and my brother would be finished off. I curled back up in the oppressive darkness, adopting Hassiba's position. I don't know how long I sat there as incessant, burning tears fell onto my knees.

A bright light made me raise my head. The angel of death, Captain de la Bourdonnaye, handed me a newspaper. I understood and refused to take it. I couldn't bear to see it materialize in bold black letters: Hassiba's death, Ali's death, the death of two parts of myself. I wanted to keep them alive inside me, just the way I had left them. The messenger of death still held out his newspaper, but I refused to take it. I put my head in my hands and flung myself backward, hitting my head against the wall in an endless litany made painful only by the certainty of my brother and sister's death. The way they were killed by the foreign occupying army was as clear to me as if I had been right there. Knowing the cowardice of the French officers, I was certain that the paratroopers had blown up Hassiba and Ali's safe house, after evacuating the other residents in complete silence in order to take them by surprise. I was also convinced that if Ali had suspected that the paratroopers were occupying the house, he would have sprung from the shelter with his machine gun spitting fire. Ali wasn't a man to sit waiting for death to come to him.

Later, when I was committed to Barberousse Prison, I learned that Mahmoud Bouhamidi, the liaison officer between El Kho and Safi and the

A French bombing kills Ali la Pointe, Hassiba Ben Bouali, Petit Omar, and Mahmoud Bouhamidi

nephew of the owner who hosted us at 4 Rue Cato, had been alongside Hassiba and Ali, as well as El Kho's nephew Petit Omar. They, too, would die shredded by the bombs. I never brought up their deaths, except when I met Djamila in prison. From her I learned that an entire part of the Casbah was blown up along with our sister and brothers, taking the lives of a score of innocent civilians—women, men, children, and elderly, all fast asleep— along with innumerable injuries. Today I hope it is understandable that a black rage grips me every time I hear someone talk about the Casbah while ignoring the crimes committed by the French army against its children and its heritage—and not just during Massu's cruel "Battle of Algiers." It started in 1830, when General de Bourmont razed our symbolic seats of power and religion: the El Djenina Palace and the Essayida Mosque. They were buried under the Place du Gouvernement, at the center of which pranced a statue of that same sinister general, victorious on his horse.

I hope with all my heart that our universities and architecture schools will one day teach the truth, the whole truth, about the systematic, willful erasure or perversion of our cultural and historical heritage. Only a perfect knowledge of those 132 long years of cultural genocide can prevent its recurrence. The archives exist, though today they are still in France. This is another battle to wage: reclaiming our archives to fill the gaps in our collective memory, which was so severely pillaged, so that we can finally rebuild ourselves. As the famous Kabyle poet and linguist Mouloud Mammeri has written: "By recovering their independence, the countries of Africa and Asia had broken the barrier that separated them from themselves. They finally had an identity, but not yet a face, since they had been trained long and methodically to forget, and sometimes to despise, themselves."[2]

I confess today that I refused to take the newspaper. Even when he threw it down beside my head, I refused to look, to read of Hassiba and Ali's death. This refusal to read what their killers and their newspapers had said and written would last fifty-six years. It was only when I decided several years ago to go back in time to revisit this period of our revolution—to recount how our people in the Casbah, our activists, our *fidayate* and *fidayine*, had faced the French so that Algeria might be free and independent—that I resolved to read the colonial press in the depths of our National Library.

Even then, it was torture for me to read of the deaths of Hassiba, Ali, Mahmoud, and Petit Omar, as reported by the *Echo d'Alger*, *Dépêche Quotidienne*, and *Journal d'Alger*. The first thing that struck me was the hatred with which the French military—but also the journalists of the colonial press—pursued my sister and brothers, even after they were dead. The relentlessness that drove them to profane Ali's shredded body for the length of a full page, complete with photos, shocks and disgusts me to no end. Such a sad and sickening image of those people, who were supposedly sent to civilize us. Still today Ali's body is desecrated by their newspapers, showing his bare legs in the filthy and vain hope of destroying his aura among his own

2. Mouloud Mammeri, *Dawn of the Damned.*

people, even after his death. It revolts me and hurts me deeply. Only the conviction that Ali lives on—like Hassiba, Mahmoud, and Petit Omar—in the pantheon of our hearts as an immense and eternally invincible hero soothes me.

Nonetheless, these newspapers allow me to fill in some of the gaps about my friends' assassinations. I would learn that Ali and Hassiba had left the safe house at 4 Rue Cato where we had left them the day of our arrest, September 26, 1957. Within a day they had applied one of the sacred rules of clandestine survival: immediately cut all ties with what the arrested person knew of "the organization." They found refuge at 5 Rue des Abderames, a safe house whose existence I didn't know of at the time of my arrest. The newspapers gave extensive coverage to the press conference Colonel Godard held to announce "the discovery of the mutilated bodies of Ali and Hassiba": Friday, October 11, 1957, four days after their violent explosion shook the Casbah. The papers reported that the explosion was heard in areas as distant as Hussein Dey and Kouba, on the other side of the city.

Colonel Godard began the press conference by emphasizing the crucial role of the intelligence services in locating the shelter where Ali and Hassiba were hiding:

> Since the end of September, an intelligence officer had been close on his trail, managing to locate the approximate site of Ali la Pointe's cache on a map of the Casbah. He was so close that few details remained to confirm. So much so that a part of the regiment was on permanent alert. The evening of October 7, Captain Allaire got the final detail he needed: Ali la Pointe was at 5 Rue des Abderames in a shelter on the second floor. . . . It is we who have attacked Ali la Pointe, who was holed up in an airtight spot whose two exits have been locked from the inside. To neutralize him, it was necessary to use a reduced load of plastic explosive against one wall. It turned out that a stockpile of explosives was stored inside and, when lit, it caused serious damage to neighboring buildings.[3]

In this statement Colonel Godard provides proof, if any were needed, that the paratroopers had rigged and blown up Ali and Hassiba's safe house while they were there alongside Mahmoud and Petit Omar. The sinister colonel also asserted that the paratroopers had emptied the house of its other

---

3. *Journal d'Alger*, October 11, 1957.

occupants in advance.[4] In fact, just as we had done every evening after dinner, Ali, Hassiba, Mahmoud, and Petit Omar certainly climbed into the shelter—hermetically sealed, according to Godard's testimony—so as not to endanger their hosts' lives in the case of a paratrooper raid.

These criminals did indeed raid the house that night, not to search for and arrest Ali and Hassiba but to massacre. They must have raided the house and the surrounding ones in the night in complete silence, by the hundreds, forcing the other occupants to leave silently under the threat of their bayonets. This cowardly army was so afraid of Ali that they took no chances, knowing perfectly well that if my brother were alerted, he would have fought alone against all of them and that, even if they fired the fatal bullet, just before he fell he would take a few more cowards with him. The army, that heir to the Vichy regime, must have rigged all the walls heavily, knowing full well that the explosion would take out the entire neighborhood. Which was exactly what happened. A "reduced load of plastic explosive against one wall," as Godard claimed, does not kill twenty people and does not destroy a whole neighborhood. Take it from a *bombiste* herself.

Besides, we were sorely lacking arms, ammunition, and especially explosives. That was precisely why El Kho had taken the risk of meeting Germaine Tillion a second time and divulging the address of our shelter at 3 Rue Cato to Kamel. On the other hand, Godard and his newspapers described the shelter where Ali, Hassiba, Mahmoud, and Petit Omar were hiding as "an airtight cage three feet high and six feet wide." How, then, could it contain an "explosives stockpile" when four people—including tall and athletic Ali—must already have had great difficulty fitting inside?

In truth, only Ali had on him, as always, his Mat 49 and some clips. Maybe one or two grenades, but that is far from certain. When it came to arms, we were really down to nothing. Godard was lying. And like all liars, he forgot that he himself had read aloud at his press conference from the letters sent by Ali to a correspondent whose identity Godard refrained from revealing (of course, this was none other than Safi, of whose treason Ali had been ignorant). Some days after our arrest and our isolation, Ali had resumed contact with Safi and given him instructions. (The newspapers had published the extracts, which Godard read aloud.) Our brother acknowledged that

---

4. *La Dépêche Quotidienne*, October 9, 1957.

"The political organization, like the military one, is destroyed." He ended his letter with the words, "Do not worry, we will soon receive arms."[5]

Today, reading the newspapers brings me to the same conclusion I reached then in my cell at Villa Nador, even if I was cut off from the outside world then. To kill Ali, whom they feared more than anyone and knew they could never take down without significant losses in their ranks, Massu, Godard, Trinquier, Allaire, and their paratroopers didn't hesitate to blow up not only a house but an entire neighborhood.

But Ali's death didn't quench Godard's thirst. At the same press conference, he said, "Now we must destroy the legend of Ali la Pointe." His racism, his profound contempt for our people, and his blind hatred prevented him from realizing that his statement was a measure of the fighter and the leader that was Ali la Pointe—not just in our eyes, but in the enemy's too. Throughout the poor Casbah and the "native" quarters, they dumped thousands of leaflets whose inanity would have made us smile were it not for the total war they were leading against us: "Crime doesn't pay. . . . Ali la Pointe is dead! Crime is always punished. The FLN has lost the game. . . . Inform yourselves, and put an end to the terror he imposes on you."[6]

The Algerian people they so despised and the FLN they hated just as much responded less than a year later by bringing the war of national liberation to their home front back in France, thus fulfilling Ben M'hidi's prophecy to his assassins: "France will see war, from Dunkirk to Tamanrasset." In fact, from August 1958 onward, the FLN launched—thanks to the men and women fighters of the FLN's Federation of France—a series of spectacular attacks on military and economic targets such as weapons factories, airfields, fuel depots, and refineries, but also police, soldiers, *ultras,* and Muslim elected leaders who had betrayed our country. For the first time in the history of decolonization, a colonized people, the Algerian people, brought their war of liberation back to the colonizers' homeland. This people, long despised, humiliated, deprived, and massacred, would give their ultimate response, the fatal blow to "French Algeria," on December 11, 1960, in Algiers, when demonstrators flooded the city streets. As if to say that Ben M'hidi, Ramel, Si Mourad, Dahmane, Ali, Hassiba, and all the others were not dead, it swept over Algiers like a torrent that nothing could hold back. From all the "native" quarters—so often ransacked, bruised, and outraged—a powerful

---

5. *Journal d'Alger,* October 11, 1957; *Dépêche Quotidienne,* October 11, 1957.
6. *Echo d'Alger,* October 11, 1957.

human wave of children, youths, and women struck the European town, unarmed, throats unprotected, faces uncovered, shouting in the face of the French army and government their commitment to the FLN—their one and only representative—and their unwavering determination to live freely and independently. They were already waving the national flag.

In October 1957, only the belief that the tragic death of Ali and Hassiba did not at all signify the end of our liberation struggle, only the certainty that other Alis and Hassibas were already preparing to reconstitute the Algiers Autonomous Zone (surely with new methods, now that they knew how the French army had destroyed our organization) allowed me not to succumb, and to pull myself together and keep all my hopes alive.

Seeking Answers

I was committed to Barberousse prison on the sunny afternoon of October 14, 1957, and passed, along with many other sisters, almost five years in prison in France. During all those years, a question nagged at me: Why weren't El Kho and I ever subjected to the paratroopers' infamous interrogation?

The explanation that Godard and Trinquier had nothing left to extract from us didn't satisfy me. I knew the blind hatred and mad fury with which all the military corps had sought El Kho. I knew that if they could have given him the same fate as Hassiba and Ali, they would have. Another explanation, which I find more plausible, was given to me in prison: that El Kho and I got the unusual treatment we did thanks to the strong and rapid intervention of Germaine Tillion, who acted as soon as she learned of our arrest. Oukhiti's family suspected her of having disclosed the address of our refuge. I sincerely believe that these suspicions must have been unbearable for a genuine resistance fighter who knew in her flesh and bone the disgrace of a denunciation. El Kho and I owe her for having spared our lives. May she and her family accept my eternal gratitude.

Alas, one last explanation—a serious, slanderous, despicable charge— was peddled at Barberousse. Its ignominy, so unbearable, was intended not only to drive us to suicide or madness, but to destroy us, to annihilate us even beyond death. It was peddled and organized, of course, by the psychological services of the French army, which riddled the prisons with agents, including among the women in Barberousse. They said El Kho and I had denounced Ali and Hassiba! Only Trinquier, Godard, and Allaire could imagine such a horror! It was their way of killing living legends like El Kho and even dead ones like Ali. But what could the paratroopers have learned from El Kho and me that they hadn't already gotten from Safi the traitor? The only thing they didn't yet have was the address of Hassiba and Ali la Pointe's safe house. El Kho and I had left them on September 25 at 4 Rue Cato, knowing that they would move. But they were killed at 5 Rue des Abderames, an address unknown to us. The shelter at 4 Rue Cato was never visited by the paratroopers, because neither El Kho nor Oukhiti nor I ever talked about it. The great Mammeri wrote it well: "But search also with the enemy, . . . in all the documents where so often he has tried to distort us, but where it is easy to penetrate the masks to finally reach the truth, *our truth*."[7] The French intelligence services published letters I am alleged to have sent to Hassiba asking her to "surrender."[8] I never wrote these letters. I was living with Hassiba on the dates of the letters. Why would I write to her? What's more, to give credit to this criminal montage is truly not to know Hassiba and me. We were two soldiers of the AAZ. We had made the choice, like other sisters, to be volunteers for death—not for surrender.

Another question haunted me during my years of detention, concerning the circumstances of brother Kamel's arrest after he left 3 Rue Cato. Brother Ali Bouzourène, whom I found after my release from prison and my transfer to Tunis in May 1962, enlightened me. Upon returning home, Kamel had set down the detailed report we had prepared, which he was to deliver to the brothers in Tunis. But one of the AAZ activists sought by the security services had stayed in his home before departing for the *maquis*. The latter was arrested there during a clash and brought to Massu's services in Algiers. While being tortured to death, he would lead them the morning of September 24, 1957, to Kamel's home. The paratroopers didn't even have to search. Perfectly visible on a shelf beside the door was the report, written in El Kho's hand. Kamel was immediately arrested and subjected to the worst torture. The rest we know.

In the aftermath, it was neither my arrest nor my detention for five years that have tormented me. Those were the risks of my commitment, of choices that I made in good conscience. What has always tormented me is the fear that the living, especially our youth, might forget the sacrifices made by our people—that they might forget the price paid for Algeria to be free and independent, and therefore forget how it must always be defended.

---

7. Mammeri, *Dawn of the Damned.*
8. From *Le FLN, Documents et Histoire.*

My hope now is to have the energy and strength to deliver my testimonial—to our youth—about my years in detention alongside dozens of sisters, about the euphoria of independence and then the difficult work of building our country. *Inchallah*, if God grants me life.

Long live Algeria, free and independent,
All honor and glory to our martyrs,
Zohra Drif

GLOSSARY

âabaya: a traditional robe

âadjar: a triangular face veil made of embroidered lace and silk, traditionally worn by Algerian women in combination with the *haïk*

aârouch: tribes

adel: clerk, in an Islamic court

AEMAN: Association of North African Muslim Students, a Muslim student union in the early 1950s

ALN: Armée de Libération Nationale, the armed wing of the national liberation movement beginning in 1954; also the name of Algeria's post-independence army

AML: Amis du Manifeste et de la Liberté (Friends of the Manifesto and Liberty), a liberal nationalist group led by Ferhat Abbas in the pre-1954 period.

aoun: assistant clerk, in an Islamic court

baccalauréat: the standardized test that students take before graduation from high school, in the French education system; results determine options for university education or other training

bach adel: a deputy judge in an Islamic court

bchaker: towels

bouqala, pl. bouqalate: short poems recited in private gatherings among Algerian women, serving to reinforce bonds, predict fortunes, and transmit traditional stories.

burnous: cloak worn by men

caïd: an Algerian appointed by the French as a colonial administrator, and thus viewed by many fellow Algerians as a traitor to his people

cassacate: women's tops

341

CCE: Comité de Coordination et d'Exécution (Coordination and Execution Committee), the leadership of the national movement established in 1956 at the Soummam Congress

chèche: a long strip of cloth worn by Algerian men as a scarf or turban

chéchia: small traditional caps known in other parts of the Arab world as *fez* or *tarbouche*

cheikh: a term of respect for a man, especially a leader

chouhada: martyrs; the singular is *chahid*

derssa: a spicy sauce made of garlic and hot peppers

elham beldolma: vegetables stuffed with meat

Évian Accords: the negotiated agreement that resulted in Algeria's independence from France in March 1962

fidaï, pl. *fidayine:* a male freedom fighter; literally, one who sacrifices himself

fidayate: female freedom fighters

fiqh: jurisprudence, in Islamic legal systems

FLN: Front de Libération Nationale, the liberation movement that started the Algerian war for independence on November 1, 1954

fouta: towel

gandoura: robe

gaouri: a European, in Algerian dialect

haïk: a white silk sheet worn by women to cover the head and upper body, often worn along with an *âadjar* face veil in pre- and early post-independence Algeria

hammam: a communal bath, known today in some regions as a Turkish bath

harki: Algerian collaborators with the French during the war for independence, despised today by many Algerians as traitors to their people

horma: strict separation of the sexes

koffar: the unbelievers

lycée: high school

m'dhal: a straw hat worn especially for shade

maharmates el ftoul: satin scarves with long fringes

maqrouta: a snack (also *maqrouts* when not in an Arabic sentence) *maquis*: mountains/wilderness, often used to refer to remote areas where FLN fighters held out against the French

matloue: bread

mbardja: a snack made of semolina and date paste

medersa: a school, particularly one that taught reading, mathematics, and other Islamic sciences in Algeria's traditional education system

meïda: a low table used for serving food, with diners sitting directly on the floor, on cushions, or on low couches

mektoub: destiny, "it is written"

menzah: a rooftop terrace

mesk ellil: night-blooming jasmine

MLTD: Mouvement pour le Triomphe des Libertés Démocratiques (Movement for the Triumph of Democratic Freedoms), the nationalist movement formed by Messali Hadj after World War II from which much of the FLN leadership emerged

MNA: Mouvement National Algérien (Algerian National Movement), a rival to the FLN led by Messali Hadj in the late 1950s and tacitly encouraged by the French as part of a divide-and-rule strategy

moqqadem: the caretaker of a *zawiya*

moucharabieh: wooden screens, often intricately lathe-turned

moudjahid (m), moudjahida (f) moudjahidine (pl): fighters, combatants, literally those who carry out jihad

mqatfa: soup

msemna, pl. *msemen*: a snack

ouléma: a body of Muslim scholars

OS: Organisation Spéciale, a clandestine branch of the MTLD in 1948 from which several FLN militants emerged after serving several years in French prisons

PCA: Parti Communiste Algérien (the Algerian Communist Party), mostly made up of European colonists; the PCA initially opposed independence, but later supported it

pied-noir; pieds-noirs (pl): persons of European (often, but not exclusively, French) descent living in colonial Algeria, literally "black feet"

PPA: Parti du Peuple Algérien, a nationalist movement in the 1930s led by Messali Hadj; a precursor to the MTLD

qachabia: a thick woolen cloak

qadi: a judge in the Islamic courts

qamroun: calamari

qazdira: a milk jug

qouiyet: a lady's outfit consisting of traditional pants and a fine matching vest

Quran: the holy book of Islam

ro'ya: a vision

ronda: a card game

roumi: a foreigner, literally a Roman

sappa: a wicker basket

seroual: pants

seroual el messelmine: traditional trousers for women

sfiria: a dish of lamb and bread meatballs

souhaba: the companions of the Prophet Muhammad

Soummam Congress: a policymaking gathering held in August 1956 by the internal FLN leadership; it decided to prioritize the internal part of the FLN over the external parts, and political activities over military ones

sqifa: a foyer

tabani: a headdress

taminet ellouz: almond paste

ultras: violent *pied-noir* gangs dedicated to repressing indigenous Algerians and maintaining "French Algeria"

umma: the community of Muslim believers

UDMA: Union Démocratique du Manifeste Algérien (Democratic Union of the Algerian Manifesto), a liberal branch of the national movement led by Ferhat Abbas after World War II.

UGEMA: Union Générale des Étudiants Musulmans Algériens (General Union of Algerian Muslim Students), the student wing of the FLN formed after 1954

wali salah: a local patron saint

wast eddar: a home's central courtyard

wilaya: a military region during the war of independence; there were six altogether

zawiya: a center of prayer and education built around a mausoleum; often associated with Sufi Islam

ABOUT THE AUTHOR

 Zohra Drif is a hero of Algeria's war of national liberation. Born in 1934 in Tiaret, in western Algeria, she studied law at the University of Algiers before joining the National Liberation Front. As a core member of the movement's armed wing in Algiers, she conducted or supported several high-profile operations that advanced the revolutionaries' struggle to draw international attention to France's abuses against the local population and the Algerians' need for freedom. Ultimately captured by the French and condemned to twenty years of forced labor for "terrorism", she spent five years in prison in Algeria and France, during which she continued her legal studies and her activism.

In 1962, upon her country's independence, she was elected to Algeria's first National Constituent Assembly. She co-founded an organization to support youth orphaned in the liberation struggle and later practiced as a criminal lawyer in Algiers. A senator in Algeria's Council of the Nation from 2001 to 2016, she served as a senate vice president from 2003 on. In 1962 she married Rabah Bitat, one of the founding architects of Algeria's liberation movement, with whom she had three children. Today, she lives in Algiers and has five grandchildren.

AUTHOR'S ACKNOWLEDGMENTS

My heartfelt thanks go out to Khalida Toumi, who offered me the encouragement that proved decisive in seeing this memoir published. For many long years prior, I held within myself the memoir I deliver today to the youth of my country and the world. I had kept it inside out of reticence or simply because I was too busy, and convinced that silence was all that was needed to turn suffering into happiness. Each time I recounted an episode of my life as a *moudjahida*, Khalida would urge me—with kindness,

345

skill, and persistence—to recount these events that had determined much of what followed in my life and my country's. Finally, I set about plumbing the depths of my memory—and those of many other fellow participants and witnesses—to produce this account. It is an account borne in pain, suffering, and the death of so many dear departed heroines and heroes, who perished so that those who survived them could do so in liberty and dignity. Oh, how right you were, Khalida, when you urged me to give these memories life anew so that none might forget, and so that all of Algeria's children might carry them in their hearts to build a prosperous and peaceful future.

Thank you also to all the others who helped me to prepare the first publication, including Salima Hadjerès, Zehira Yahi, Slimane Hachi, Rachid Hadj Naceur, Naget Khadda, Habib Ayyoub, and the team at Chihab Editions.

For this English translation, I would like to thank Bill Quandt, whom I first met when he was just a young researcher visiting Algeria soon after our independence, and his wife, Helena Cobban, of Just World Books. Their desire to share this story of Algeria's liberation struggle with wider audiences has been instrumental in bringing this English edition to fruition. I would also like to thank Andrew Farrand for his meticulous translation of the original French text's word and spirit. Andrew's mastery not only of French, but also of classical and Algerian colloquial Arabic, was the right blend of skills to bring an Algerian story to life for English speakers around the world. Thank you also to Lakhdar Brahimi, whom I first met during our days as law students, before he began his illustrious diplomatic career, and who has helped me here to introduce our country and its struggle to new readers.

Finally, on behalf of all the martyrs and all the survivors of our liberation struggle, thank you to all those around the world who seek to understand why we fought and sacrificed so much.

TRANSLATOR'S ACKNOWLEDGMENTS

Thank you to Madame Drif and the entire Drif-Bitat family for trusting me to bring her story to new readers;

To the dear friends, family, and teachers who made it possible for me to do so;

And to the people of Algeria, who have taught me much in just a few short years—and who still have many stories to share with the world.